Knowledge, Renewal and Religion

Repositioning and changing ideological and material circumstances among the Swahili on the East African Coast

Edited by

Kjersti Larsen

NORDISKA AFRIKAINSTITUTET, UPPSALA 2009

Indexing terms:
  Indigenous knowledge
  Traditional culture
  Social anthropology
  Cultural anthropology
  Cultural identity
  Islam
  Social change
  Modernization
  Social History

Cover photo: Kjersti Larsen
Two 'walimu' in Vikotoni area, Zanzibar Town, on their way to read the Qur'an to someone who is ill.
Language checking: Elaine Almén
Index: Rohan Bolton
ISBN 978-91-7106-635-0

Contents

Glossary

Below follows a limited glossary of Swahili terms. The glossary does not include all the words used in the volume, only terms that appear more than once or hold ethnographic or theoretical significance. Swahili words used in the notes are not included. In Swahili nouns have no gender; they are classified according to meaning. There are in all eight different classes. Prefixes are used to indicate noun classes in singular and plural form such as: m-/wa (human beings and animals); m-/mi (objects and plants); ki-/vi (objects); ji-/ma (objects and organic material); u-/u (objects and abstract nouns); mahali denotes places. *Ku-* is a prefix for verbal nouns. Hence, most Swahili words consist of a root to which prefixes and suffixes are appended, for instance, *Wa-*, denoting people; *M-*, a person; *U-*, a place; and *Ki-*, a language or also cultural manner, more generally. *Ya-*, is the genitive form such as in *ngoma ya sheitani*. Although Swahili is a Bantu language, many Swahili words are also related to Arabic, Hindi and Farsi and some to Portuguese or English.

a – she or he
adabu – manners
ari – honour

baraka – blessing, grace, prosperity
baraza – a stone bench against the outer wall of the house
binadamu (pl. *wanadamu*) – human being

Chama Cha Mapinduzi – The Revolutionary Party
chinja – slaughter
chuo (pl. *vyuo)* – Qur'anic school

daima – permanently, continually, always
dawa (pl. *madawa*) – medicine, medicament, remedy
dawa ya kichina – Chinese medicine

desturi – custom, habit, practice
dhikiri – sufi ritual, dikhir
dini – religion
dunia – the world (as it is experienced)

fitina – chaos, discord, antagonism

ghururi – arrogance, vanity, folly

habeshia – spirit from Ethiopia
hadharani – in public
hatari – danger
heshima – respect
hitima – a Muslim service in conclusion of some event, i.e. a reading of certain parts of the Qur'an

Ibilisi – Satan
Idd-al-hajj – festival in commemoration of the pilgrimage to Mecca

jahiliyya – ignorance
jamaa – family, community member with whom you have family-like relations
jini (pl. *majini*) – spirit, jinn

khanga – colourful, rectangular cloth worn by women, shawl
kibuki – spirit from Madagascar
kikao – place to sit
kikunde (pl. *vikunde*) – group, guild
kilinge (pl. *vilinge*) – ritual group, a place for performance, secret meeting
kimondo – satirical dialogue poetry
kinyipesi – light (in weight)
kitabu – book
kizito – heavy (in weight)
kufutana na wakati – going with the times
kupindua – to overturn

madrasa – Qur'anic school
maendeleo – development, modernization
maisha magumu – life is difficult, hard life
mambo ya kisasa – modern ways, new developments
mapinduzi – revolution
mashindano – competition
mateso – persecution, affliction
maulidi – reading of Prophet Mohammad's life
mazungumzo – discussion, conversation
mchawi (pl. *wachawi*) – witch
mganga (pl. *waganga*) – specialist in matters of illness and health / traditional healer
mila – traditions (often referring to traditional aspects of religion)
mjomba – maternal uncle, mother's brother
msahafu – the Qur'an

mstaraabu (pl. *wastaraabu*) – learned person
mtalaamu (pl. *watalaamu*) – intelligent or knowledgeable person
mungu – god
mwalimu (pl. *walimu*) – teacher, a person learned in the Qur'an
mwanadamu (pl. *wanadamu*) – human being
mwele (pl. *wele*) – person to be healed during a ritual, patient
mwenye elimu – a person with education
mwenye maarifa – a person with knowledge or insight
mzee (pl. *wazee*) – elder/old man
mzungu (pl. *wazungu*) – European, foreigner, stranger

pepo – spirit
punga – to summon spirits; sway, move to and fro
pungwa – summon spirits

shamba – agricultural land, rural area
shehe (pl. *mashehe*) – a person learned in Islam, religious leader of a mosque
sheitani (pl. *masheitani*) – spirit
shoga – female friend
siku ya arafa – the day of Arafa
simama – stand
soko huru – the free market
uadilifu – ethics
uaminifu – honesty
uchawi – witchcraft
uganga – sorcery
ujamaa – relationship, 'community'
ustaraabu – civilized

vikunde (sing. *kikunde*) – groups, parties, guilds
vyama vingi – multipartyism

wachochezi – agitators, troublemakers
wafadhili – donors
waganga (sing. *mganga*) – specialists in matters of illness and health / traditional healers
walimu (sing. *mwalimu*) – teachers, persons knowledgeable in the Qur'an
wastaraabu (sing. *mstaarabu*) – learned persons
wawekezaji – outside investors
wazee (sing. *mzee*) – elders
wazungu (sing. *mzungu*) – Europeans, foreigners, strangers

Preface

This volume arises out of the sixth conference in an on-going series of inter-disciplinary workshops. It started out as an Anglo-French workshop held alternatively in London and Paris. The first of these took place in 1987 and its theme was "Social Stratification in Swahili Society" (Parkin and Constantin 1989). The following years the themes for the various workshops were "Networks and Exchanges in the Coastal Societies of East Africa" (le Guennec-Coppens and Caplan 1991), "Continuity and Autonomy in Swahili Communities: Inland influences and strategies of self-determination" (Parkin 1994), "Authority and Power in the Coastal Societies of East-Africa" (Le Guennec-Coppens and Parkin 1998).

Then, when the fifth workshop was to be organized, it was decided that it was time to invite scholars from a wider spectrum of countries. Hence, those who participated came from different European countries, America, Kenya, Tanzania, as well as colleagues from Mexico, Canada, Zanzibar, Ghana and Kenya working in Europe. The publication resulting from this workshop is called *Swahili Modernities: Culture, politics, and identity on the East Coast of Africa* (Caplan and Topan 2005).

The sixth workshop was held at the University of Oslo in the spring of 2005 and participants came from Tanzania, Zanzibar, England, France, America, Italy, The Netherlands, Finland, Sweden and Germany as well as colleagues from Zanzibar and Ghana working in Europe. The theme of the workshop was "Knowledge, Renewal and Religion."

The theme "Knowledge, Renewal and Religion" is meant to inspire us to consider the concepts of knowledge, experience and cosmology in relation to recent ideological and political changes in Swahili culture and society. How and to what extent have recent political, ideological and economic changes, including increased mobility and migration, affected local forms of social organization and thus, the production of knowledge? How should the perceptions Swahili-speakers of the coast and inlands of East-Africa hold of their institutions and values be understood and how do they relate to those of others?

During the three day workshop 17 papers were presented and discussed eagerly by all the participants present some of whom had agreed to contribute as discussants only. Sincere thanks to José Kagabo and Abdulaziz Lodhi for their significant contribution as discussants as well as to Hege Wallevik and Pernille Schulerud Søland for their invaluable participation. Gratitude also goes to our colleagues Adam Shafi Adam, Jean-Claude Penrad and Justo Lacunza Balda for their participation with papers in the workshop. Unfortunately their excellent papers are not included in this volume.

The authors who have contributed to this book, all have extensive field-work from the Swahili Coast and the Indian Ocean Region. The authors represent different disciplines such as anthropology, archaeology, political science, history and linguistics and to a certain extent different perspectives on how to understand society, culture and history on the East African Coast. Given the authors' longstanding experiences from research in Swahili societies, the various papers reflect upon ongoing processes of change and document not only the changing political, ideological and economic circumstances, but also, people's own perceptions of and experiences in the wake of the very same changes as well as their reactions and repositioning as evoked by the ongoing changes. Some of the authors have conducted research in the same societies and communities since the early 1960s until the present, others since the 1980s, while younger scholars have only started their research during the 1990s. The fact that the authors have entered into the world of the Swahili at different points in time, implies that they have been positioned differently within the society, but also that they see the society differently. This is due both to the 'nature' of Swahili society at the time when they entered the field, but also due to the fact that they have been influenced by different theoretical perspectives and ideological waves at the time when they started their research. All this affects their discussions, perspectives and analyses and thus brings, perhaps, an unintended richness to the book as such – both regarding approach, ethnographic material and focus as well as line of analysis.

Kjersti Larsen
December 2008

CHAPTER I

Introduction

Kjersti Larsen

It is as though men were stricken suddenly blind to fundamental distinctions such as the distinction between meaning and end, between the general and the particular or, grammatically speaking between '…for the sake of…' and '…in order to…' (…) And the moment such distinctions are forgotten and meanings are degraded into ends, it follows that the ends themselves are no longer safe because the distinction between means and ends is no longer understood, so that finally all ends turn and are degraded into means. (Arendt 1993/1961: 78)

Currently, religion has entered political debate and is evoked in relation to a variety of events taking place all around the world. Religion and religious differences, not political, economic or social, are claimed to be the cause rather than an expression of – or even a reaction to – ongoing problems. Islam and Christianity (or also Islam and Hinduism) are, in most cases, represented not only as opposed, but also as incommensurable worldviews, value systems and identities, where the one is threatening the existence of the other. Yet to understand the meaning and implications of the interconnectedness between religion, politics and identity, the analysis would have to be grounded in a particular place and cultural area. It concerns issues related to knowledge, morality and experience, and to the interrelatedness of these themes – themes that cannot be understood without clear references to the historical processes and societies constituted by the very same processes. With respect to the Swahili on the East-African Coast, the above mentioned trend provokes questions related to whether we should approach what appear to be expressions of religious positioning in terms of renewal of previous understandings and relationships, or as a rephrasing of complex and conflictual matters that were always part of Swahili society. The various papers in this book reveal that the Swahili are experiencing worsening economic, political and social conditions. Within these circumstances, Islam is re-invoked as a source of knowledge that not only explains the current state of life and living, but also gives directions on how to cope with and to change the situation for the better. Islam is both what reinforces Swahili identity and a particular way of life, and at the same time, given the current international climate, further marginalizes Swahili society and culture in the eyes of the "other". Yet, Swahili culture, according to Pat Caplan (1996), which has been variously termed syncretic, hybrid or creolized, resists simplistic definitions as well as the imposition of clear boundaries. Hence Swahili society and culture have a common mooring, and this book studies specificity in space and time within a broader comparative framework.

As the various articles in the book confirm, among Muslims on the coast of Eastern Africa there are continuous discussions concerning what it means to be a good Muslim, the authority of different interpretations of significant texts, theological principles and ritual practices. Is there, as Farouk Topan (this volume) asks, a recycling of knowledge, or are new forms of knowledge and meaning generated? And, moreover, to what extent and how are relationships, values and practices of the past re-invoked in present society? Repositioning and adaptation to changing material, political, ideological and social circumstances are basic dynamics of society itself. David Parkin (1994) has argued that what constitutes the Swahili cultural and linguistic complex is always being in a state of development and flux. Yet, there is variation in how adaptations to ongoing changes are expressed and managed. Recently, certain rituals like the *Siku ya Arafa* in Tanga in Tanzania, explored by Gerard van de Bruinhorst (this volume), have been the target of such discourse and positioning related to socio-political changes, both within Tanzania and in the wider region. Ongoing disputes on how and why to perform the *Arafa* ritual reinstall, as Bruinhorst shows, new hierarchies and practices. His paper discusses how the Muslim rituals *Siku ya Arfa* and *Idd el-Hajj* have become the focus of political issues revealing a deeply felt political and social unease among Muslim populations in Tanga. Francesca Declich's (this volume) work from Southern Somalia examines tensions between female and male milieus regarding claims to Islamic learning. Declich shows in her paper how women's knowledge practices, their interpretations of and knowledge about Islam, have recently been challenged and restricted by so-called theologically correct versions, represented by men claiming authority with regard to Islamic texts. A question to be addressed is, in what sense can ongoing changes in material matters be said to make a difference regarding knowledge systems and political and religious repositioning?

Generally speaking, religious identities and ideologies seem to have turned into major moral and political concerns. These concerns seem to have dramatic consequences, not only with regard to knowledge systems and social relationships as such, but also for interregional and international relations. Indeed, religion has re-entered the political sphere and has become a legitimate theme for policy formulations and political action, even within the context of secularised nation states. Interestingly, this re-evocation of religion, and thus religious knowledge, takes place within a historical period denoted as modern. In this connection it is interesting to note that Hannah Arendt, already several decades ago, was concerned with our understanding of the term 'secularization' and the possible misinterpretations of it. In accordance with the principles of modernity – usually defined with reference to the split between the political and the religious, and removal of religion from public life – all religious sanctions should, according to Hannah Arendt (1993/1961), be removed from politics.

If, as Arendt argued (1993/1961), secularization means simply the separation of religion and politics, and not a transformation of religious categories into secular concepts, this means that what, at any time, is defined as secular, would be the worldview of those in power. In our notion of history, secularization forms part of the modern, of modernity, that is; a period starting with the end of the Middle Ages and continuing until the present. In the social sciences, modernization has, as Pat Caplan (2004a) explains in the previous book in this series,

> ...been defined as all those developments which have followed in the wake of industrialization and mechanization. It thus serves broadly as a synonym for capitalism, globalization and those aspects of society which are held to differentiate the modern West from other 'traditional' or 'developing' societies. (2004a:1–2).

And, as a part of this process of differentiation, we find the tension between cultural homogenization and cultural heterogenization – a process also affecting Swahili societies on the coast. As modernity in its current form seems to reinforce and revitalize religion, and in its wake moralization into public life and discourse, it is particularly interesting to discuss knowledge, religion and renewal on the Swahili coast – a region composed of secular nation states inhabited by people who explicitly acknowledge and celebrate religion as part of their knowledge base. Islam, on the east coast of Africa as elsewhere, concerns both theology and practice, and what is explored by the authors contributing to this book is mainly Islam as knowledge practices. The constant debates concerning interpretations of Islam and what it means to be a good Muslim, all claim authority with reference to the text itself – the Qur'an and Hadith – but also by reference to various local understandings and practices (Topan 1992, Lacunza-Balda 1997, Bang 2003).

Worldview and knowledge are related to power. Yet, knowledge is about meaning and has to be recognized as meaningful in the sense that it forms part of the means and ends of life in any society. A worldview or a knowledge system should, following Clifford Geertz (1973), provide reasonable models of the world – perceptions that make sense of events and experiences – and sensible models for acting in the world. Knowledge seen as a social phenomenon relates to cosmology, practice, experience and social organization; it is continuously generated; it may change, be reorganized and renewed. It is collectively defined and constituted as well as challenged and redefined (Lambek 1993, Larsen 2001, 2007). It is, as discussed in this book, made manifest in written texts, recitations, oral exchange, ritual, performative acts, organization of time and space, statements, and political interventions. These are all practices referring to knowledge and activated by people in order to produce and make sense of their worlds: to re-produce meaning. Knowledge is always, as Fredrik Barth writes, 'involved when people engage the world, whether by magic, worship, or whatever' (1993: 306). This also means that knowledge, not truth, is involved in the formulation of politics, policy making and development initiatives. What is referred to above is, precisely, knowledge in the sense of morality and perceptions of change, including notions of what ought to constitute a good life for oneself as well as for others.

Knowledge is not only a major concern for people; it also affects the world and people's life-worlds (Lambek 1993). How are concepts of religion and knowledge about life and society interconnected in Swahili society? How, and in which contexts, are these interconnections experienced, expressed, and negotiated, by whom and in what ways? This book considers the above mentioned dynamics by focusing on the currently changing ideological and material circumstances characterizing the life of people on the East African Coast. How do they perceive these changes; how do they explain them, and to what extent is religion involved?

Swahili Society and the Western Indian Ocean

The Swahili tend to be perceived by others, and to see themselves, as distinct from other East Africans. Common for the Swahili is that they share the same language, and that the majority of the population is Muslim. This does not, however, imply that the Swahili can be seen to share a political or social identity. Nevertheless, there is a prevalent imagining of a common Swahili identity and way of life. Within the Indian Ocean Region, trade has been a major activity since the earliest times, as has migration. Hadhramis, Indians, and Omani, as well as East Africans, have moved on a more or less permanent and voluntary basis, though often, with regard to East Africans, through enslavement. As shown by several scholars, a better understanding of the so-called Swahili Coast would be achieved if the common Africa/Arabia, Africa/Asia and Christian/Muslim dualisms are avoided, and the coast of Eastern Africa and the islands were approached as a Western Indian Ocean Region (Swartz 1991, Myers 1995, Larsen 1998, Gilbert 2002). Focusing on the Swahili within the larger Indian Ocean Region would imply an approach from the sea rather than from the land.

The sea is, as argued A.H.J. Prins, an integrated part of the Swahili environment and culture (1965). According to Erik Gilbert (2002), this is, at least, true for the period 1750 to 1960. In the above mentioned period the peoples of the Western Indian Ocean shared a history, and its inhabitants were involved in a common social, economic and cultural project. Saying this does not imply that indigenous roots are ignored, or that the region is presented as only a recipient of other cultures, or as a passive economic and political entity (Middleton 1992, Gilbert 2002). Rather, this approach implies, as clearly pointed out by Abdul Sheriff in his works (1987, 1991, 1995), that the sea gives unity and coherence to the region. It is exactly this unity and common history that provide Swahili society references, beyond their immediate society and life-style, and the structural flexibility necessary to accommodate what could be seen as otherness (Larsen 1998). Yet, despite a notion of regional unity, it is a sociological fact that people are positioned differently within society and hold different recollections of the historical processes that have taken place. The Swahili are thus also confronted by history and cannot, as already mentioned, be seen to share a single political identity (Horton and Middleton 2000, Caplan 2004b).

On the basis of extensive archaeological research in Kilwa, Felix Chami contends in the prelude to this book that most Swahili societies were agriculture- and fishing-based societies. The importance placed on fishing and the sea also supports the understanding of the Swahili as a maritime people engaged in trading. Chami, in line with Michael Horton (1996), shows that the people who created the Swahili towns were of the same culture as the people of the coastal hinterlands. The roots of the Swahili civilization have been convincingly shown to be local.[1] This perspective does not imply an

---

1. Previously, there have, however, been some claims that Arab invaders and migrants played a central role in the creation of Swahili civilization. According to, for instance, James Kirkman (1954), it was Arabs who brought urbanism and Islam and this civilization to the coast.

argument based on origins, or one which sees culture as essential and static. Rather, the point emphasized by Chami is that the Swahili Coast, which to a large extent used to be seen as non-African in culture (Kirkman 1954, Chittich 1974), has actually continuously interrelated with other African cultures. Archaeological excavations of material objects, such as pottery and burial sites, support this understanding.[1] The cultural aspects of the early Swahili communities are very much African rooted, Chami argues, although there are traces of religious and social customs related to Islam and the Arab world. It is important, he holds, to keep in mind that Islamic rather than Arabic traits are predominant. And although, as Farouk Topan (this volume) reminds us, Islam's core theology was already formulated by the time it reached Africa, the meaning conveyed was also coloured by the customs and values of the preachers of Islam on the East African Coast, whether these originated from Arabia or from the coast itself.

The Swahili in a Changing Environment

The sea is no longer a major source of interaction in the sense of steam and dhow trade, even though seaborne trade has grown dramatically. By the 1960s the unity of the Western Indian Ocean was collapsing due to both economic and political changes. This was the period of decolonialization; the Gulf oil boom, and what can be called a transportation revolution (Gilbert 2002). Today tourism, based mainly on nostalgia for the pre-1960 trading world (Beckerleg 1995, Larsen 2000), has largely replaced the trading world.

After Independence the new states Kenya and Tanzania were ruled by governments that saw nothing positive in the Western Indian Ocean Region; instead they sought to identify themselves with continental Africa (Lofchie 1965, Bennett 1978, Gilbert 2002). The coast, with its history of regionalism and cosmopolitanism, was either ignored or seen as a threat to the proclaimed African identity of the new states. Within this context, being of Arab or Indian origin became a political liability. Moreover, the newly independent states sought to limit migration, which had characterized previous periods. In the wake of the socio-political project of reshaping the identity of the new states, the maritime regional perspective was lost. Furthermore, prejudices against certain identities such as Arab and Indian/Asian were, as mentioned above, reinforced, and their presence in coastal

---

1. Furthermore, that the Swahili language belongs to the north coast branch of thel-larger Bantu family of languages is well documented (Nurse and Spear 1985).

societies was associated with colonialism and oppression of everything that, in this period, became defined as African or indigenous identities and cultural traits (Lofchie 1965 and 1970, Bennett 1978, Cooper 1977 and 1980, Babu 1991). In today's political environment, Greg Cameron (this volume) brings our attention to a present problem of counter-production of knowledge and shows that there is, in Zanzibar in particular and on the East African Coast in general, an evocation of political rhetoric that again aims at essentializing origins and labelling 'others' in particular ways, playing on dominant interpretations of significant historical events such as slavery, colonialism, and the 1964 Revolution in Zanzibar. Discussing the Tanzanian situation Cameron shows that both the Dodoma and Zanzibar states have become increasingly nationalistic in the way that they frame the opposition within a particular moral universe that serves to justify repression whenever challenged. Within this framework, identities are represented as essential in ways that challenge the multicultural dimensions that historically form part of Swahili society. In the context of Zanzibar, the political opposition to the ruling party CCM (*Chama cha Mapinduzi)* is, as Cameron says, "othered" with reference to historical/ethnic categories. Cameron writes that the CCM elite, in the context of multi-party elections, conveyed that the spectre of violence would do a "replay" against those seeking to overturn the revolutionary verdict of 1964. Within the current political atmosphere, religious and cultural diversities also represent a social and a political problem.[1]

During recent years, communities along the East African coast have increasingly been confronted with scepticism, both from within East Africa as well as internationally. Prejudices have, for instance, been voiced regarding their Muslim faith, and rumours are today heard claiming that Swahili society is fostering positive views on political Islam and so-called terrorist sympathies. Moreover, a rather common opinion is that Swahili society resists modernity in life-style, attitudes and worldview. The opinion builds on an assumption that when society modernizes it will become less religious (van Ufford and Schoffeleers 1988). This, however, is not, as Susan Beckerleg (1995 and 2004) has shown, valid for societies on the Kenyan coast, where

1. In this context it is interesting to pay attention to the Zanzibari Parliament's bill (2007) that outlaws homosexuality and lesbianism. The bill imposes penalties which include up to 25 years imprisonment for those in gay relationships. For those in lesbian relationships a seven year jail term is imposed. This is, according to the attorney-general, to prevent Zanzibari culture from being corrupted. The president is expected to approve the bill into law (BBC News: http://news.bbc.co.uk/go/pr/fr/-2/hi/Africa/3625269.stm).

Islamic revival is occurring in the wake of rapid modernization, including a tourist boom. Yet the above mentioned critical voices, although not necessarily representing a majority, have led to a general questioning of identities formed with reference to Islam as well as linkages to the Arab peninsula and notions of Arabness. Such questions should, however, be seen as resulting from essentializing and static understandings of both culture and identity. The above mentioned statements and strategies appear particularly awkward when considering the historically grounded multicultural and cosmopolitan character of Swahili society, including, at least to a certain extent, rural communities. The fact that ethnic and cultural identities are less the product of origins – historical or continental – than they are the product of shifting and contingent historical forces, would also have to be considered.

The East African Swahili population – if we accept that such a term may be applied – celebrate political and economic developments associated with both Western Nation States and the life-world and knowledge of Arabian and Asian societies. Entangled in this dynamic relationship and the political rhetoric constituted by either side, the Swahili manage in their own way to reproduce their life-worlds. Simultaneously, the Swahili seem to adapt to a changing environment – although in different ways, according to their socio-economic standards and different social and political positions. As Horton and Middleton (2000) have argued, the term 'Swahili' refers today to a rather marginalized and internally divided category of people. This implies that this term cannot be claimed to refer, in any obvious sense, to a single political identity (Caplan 2004a), as the population is politically and socially divided. Given the current political and economic trends within East Africa and beyond, contemporary discourses affecting identity issues, as well as political and economic relations, are focusing on Islam vs. Christianity, Arab vs. African, and modernity and globalization vs. traditionalization and localization. A compelling question to be asked is thus: how and to what extent have recent political, ideological and economic changes, including increased mobility and migration, affected local forms of social organization, and thus the production and distribution of knowledge?

Currently, inhabitants of communities on the coast of Eastern Africa, of which the majority form part of the modern nation-states Kenya and Tanzania, are as other citizens confronted with the effects of the recent Structural Adjustment Programmes, the introduction of multiparty political systems, the growth of tourism, and the misfortunes caused by ill-health and death due to the devastating presence of malaria and HIV and Aids infection. As discussed by Caplan (this volume), the more official reporting on the above mentioned problems and how these are experienced, remembered, and recollected by people in order to explain and foresee the future, do vary. Facing and coping with present day living conditions, what is seen as a growing criticism and apprehension towards Islam and Muslim ways of life in the wider region of East Africa, seems rather puzzling to those it concerns. For them, the main problems are linked to governmental policies which, in their view, further restrict their access to natural resources as well as to education, health services and employment (see Caplan, Assibi, Camron, Bruinhorst this volume).

Women and men in coastal communities feel a dramatic loss of agency within existing political structures. This loss of agency (Caplan and Assibi this volume) motivates Islamic revival. And in times of misfortune, people turn towards extra-human agencies, such as witchcraft or other forms of extra-human agency, in order to secure some capacity to cope with life and to renew the moral community (Caplan this volume). Elisabeth Hsu's paper on perceptions of Chinese formula medicines, used in particular in relation to the conservation of male potency, also verifies the latter point. *Dawa ya kichina* are by some seen to be imbued with magical powers, while others emphasize that these are traditional, advanced medicines. East Africans claim to know that the Chinese understand how to do magic, and thus make potent medicines. They support their view by referring to narratives about their building of the Tazara railway from Dar es Salaam to Lusaka. Chinese doctors are much appreciated, Hsu argues, because they do not moralise or interfere, and do not engage in discussion and questioning of morality and life-style when examining and healing patients. Learning this one may ask: how should the perceptions Swahili-speakers of the coast and islands of East-Africa of their institutions and values be understood, and how do these perceptions relate to those of others?

Focusing on policy and identity-related issues in the light of multipartyism and the political rhetoric in its wake, Greg Cameron (this volume) shows that essentialization of identities, rights and questions of belonging, are revitalized much in line with the political rhetoric of what he denotes as the pre-decolonization period. Michael Lofchie's work (1965) has already shown how both internal dynamics of coastal society and the policies and regulations of the colonial state produced conditions under which the population, during the period of decolonization, defined itself in opposition to each other as either local and African or of Arab or Asian background. In today's situation it is thus particularly interesting to note Cameron's present analysis concerning the role of unfulfilled expectations about democracy when it comes to political activism and political claims grounded in identity politics. He argues that "where Islamic coastal society drifts may depend upon two sets of processes: electoral prospects for substantive democracy and an ever enlarging religious piety where cultural critiques against secular nationalism and capitalism deepen". Unfulfilled expectations with respect to modernity take different forms. Francesca Declich (this volume) examines critique raised against Muslim women's rituals and their interpretations in Somalia, where certain notions of modernity seem to link up with claims to male authority.

Several definitions of modernity and what it takes to be modern exist. Access to, and appropriation of, the same ideological and technological innovations do not necessarily mean that people and societies become alike. Ulla Vuorela (this volume) holds that although people both in Bagamoyo and in Europe use the mobile phone, this does not mean that they are sharing the same kind of life or living standard. A major concern for people in Bagamoyo, as well as elsewhere along the coastal area, is still the problems of how to sustain a viable livelihood and to find a footing within the Tanzanian Nation State.

In general, the Swahili seem to remember happier times. The present seems to provide only deteriorating life conditions. The future is not conceived as being particularly bright according to the views of many women and men on the East African coast. Most people blame what they call "development" (*maendeleo*), or modernization (*kwenda na wakati*; *mambo ya kisasa*). People struggle to make sense of the promises of modernity and their disappointments. Seen from this position, religion, that is Islam, and the fact of being Muslim and living a Muslim way of life become a concern.

Knowledge, Ritual and Politics

The importance of Islam as a knowledge base – whether oral or textual – is well documented. Yet tensions between scriptural and oral or practical interpretations of Islam and what it means to be a good Muslim also exist in coastal East Africa. Moreover, the meaning and status ascribed to ritual and performative acts are disputed. To what extent are appropriations and reinterpretations related to presently perceived crises (Schneider 2006)? As already mentioned, knowledge relates to cosmology, practice, experience and social organization, and is rendered manifest in written texts, recitations, oral exchange, ritual, performative acts, statements, and political interventions. Knowledge affects the world (Lambek 1993) and people apply knowledge, including new and renewed interpretations of previously celebrated sources, to influence the world and to position themselves and their communities within the wider setting. Rituals, in the wide sense of the term, are significant for expressing concerns as well as accommodating new knowledge. As shown by several scholars it is, in any Swahili society, precisely through ritual and other performative contexts that politics – both of everyday life, party and national politics – is confronted and thus, gradually, society shaped (Ranger 1975; Strobel 1979; Geiger 1987; Larsen 1990, 1998; Fair 2001; Caplan 1995; Ashew 2002, 2004).

Rituals are closely linked to events and worries emerging from everyday life. It is people's daily experiences, as well as their common livelihood-related concerns, that are dealt with through rituals, although the rituals as such are defined with reference to phenomena of a more cosmological order. Marie Pierre Ballarin's (this volume) research among the Sakalava on Madagascar, shows how current political actors within Sakalava communities appropriate the royal ancestors' cults, in order to reposition themselves in the larger society. Ritual practices are transformed and adapted according to ongoing political and social changes. Ballarin discusses how the new social position of people from migrant and slave lineages, from the period of maritime trade, have challenged the Sakalava dynasties and their claims to land rights and local territory. In this context, and as part of the challenge, they have created new religious practices based on reinterpretations of previous rituals, but still in opposition to royal values involving a particular form of hierarchy. Ballarin's paper shows how new forms of social relations and reinterpretations of Sakalava symbolism relate to changes in political and economic structures. It illustrates, as also Maurice Bloch has shown in his work from the Merina society in Madagascar (1986), how ritual practices legitimate power and authority to conquer land and power over people.

The question of how, and to what extent, knowledge and ritual practice are transformed and adapted in different contexts and historical periods, is also explored by Linda Giles in her extensive study of spirit possession on the Swahili coast (Giles 1987, 1992, 1995). The phenomenon of spirit possession does not challenge Islam, but forms part of an Islamic cosmology and is perceived to be in accordance with a Muslim mode of life. Farouk Topan (this volume) writes that spirit possession has not been discarded as non-Muslim in Swahili society, but has certainly been influenced as a result of the phenomenon's dynamic relationship with Islam. Based on ethnographic material from the coastal region, Giles (this volume) argues that the practice of spirit possession continues to show vitality and is continuously adapted so that it relates to people's current concerns. The phenomenon of spirit possession, as it is conceptualized within the wider knowledge system, is such that it incorporates continuity and change as well as acceptance and critique of changing circumstances and lifestyles. As such, it remains a context for social discourse and production of meaningful interpretations of lived experience. It provides perceptions that make sense of events and experiences (Giles this volume). This understanding is also confirmed by my own work on spirit possession in Zanzibar town (Larsen 1998, 2001, 2007). In this society, the space created through the plausible presence of spirits makes possible negotiations of social relationships and realities where all parties involved – humans and spirits alike – are allocated responsibility for the outcome. Ritual practices related to spirit possession provide people with a capacity to act. This capacity is created by people engaging in and using certain modes of negotiations in order to manipulate and transform social relations and to re-establish and in some situations renew, at least aspects of, the moral order. The ritual practices provide agency irrespective of the social position and gender of those involved.

Knowledge, morality and change are themes evoking reflections about gender and gender differences within any society, whether these are discussed with reference to ideology or practice. Sex-segregation is a significant organizational dimension in Swahili society (Caplan 1975, Strobel 1979, Larsen 1990). It is based on the idea that women in daily and ritual life should perform activities and occupy arenas different from those of men. This means that in addition to the classic divide in social theory between public and private spheres (Habermas 1962/1990; Loimeier this volume), women and men also partake in different public spheres.[1] The public spheres of both women and men are characterized by ongoing political discourse. However, the fact that women and men to a large extent operate in separate arenas also influences their knowledge traditions and ritual practices. Given the fact that women and men are positioned differently in society – engage in different activities and in separate arenas – they also have partly different experiences in society as well as understandings of society and in society. Their degree of involvement in, and access to, institutions, events and practices also differs. A principle of sex-segregation generates an organizational divide based on gender, but it also ensures social spaces, where women as women and men as men form their particular understandings, ways of

---

1. Public sphere, that is, in the meaning of social space that allows for the free circulation of information and ideas, outside the control of the state.

communication and relationships; this is not possible to the same extent when a common public space is to be equally shared. In many cases, as in the Somali case discussed by Declich (this volume), public space shared by women and men leads to a situation whereby only male authority is recognized, and women's religious knowledge and ritual practice are devalued.

In her discussion of spirit possession, Linda Giles argues that the prevalence of this ritual practice has to be seen in relation to women's position in society and their limited access to extra-domestic spheres. She argues that Swahili urban communities have historically put more emphasis on Islamic constraints on female roles and behaviour, than is the case in rural communities. This should, she holds, be seen in connection with the vitality of Swahili possession rituals in urban settings, where, generally speaking, the majority – but far from all – of the participants are women. Seen from a gender perspective, the possession ritual takes on added importance, Giles argues, because it provides women with opportunities for social interaction, support, status and power beyond their domestic setting. In addition to providing agency, it becomes, as it were, women's public sphere. The argument provokes, however, questions about what this ritual practice provides for male participants.

In the Somali society studied by Declich, women are not formally accepted as authorities in questions of Islam and Islamic theology. However, focusing on the *nabi-ammaan* of Abbay Sittidey, a Muslim celebration performed by Somali women every week and on other prescribed occasions to praise female personalities such as Eve, Fatima, Zeynab and Mariam, Declich gets access to women's knowledge and their negotiations of moral practices and meanings. Declich (this volume) emphasizes the necessity to study knowledge production and moral interpretations from women's perspective, especially in societies where women are, more or less, excluded from formal positions associated with knowledge.

Religion and the World – Religion in the World

Exploring Swahili knowledge, perceptions and belief, the dual concepts *dini* and *mila* are significant. Farouk Topan (this volume) confirms that *mila* refers to customs that are largely indigenous to the Swahili, while *dini* refers to beliefs and practices which are understood as Islamic and were brought to the coast by the Arabs as messengers of Islam. *Dini* and *mila* share a common goal for the individual, in that both aim to preserve his or her well-being and that of the community to which he or she belongs. Values and practices, whether denoted as *mila* or *dini,* are equally important in order to live what is perceived as a Muslim way of life (Topan this volume). A morally acceptable way of life is not associated with stagnation or reproduction of the past. On the contrary, it is considered important to be "going with the time" – *kufuatana na wakati* (Topan this volume; Saleh 2004). What is expressed is exactly an awareness of the need to change according to circumstances, to appropriate new learning. The notion *kufuatana na wakati* should be seen in relation to the constant debates concerning continuity and renewal of knowledge and understandings of what it takes to be a good Muslim. Involved in these negotiations are precisely the concepts *dini* and *mila* and questionings of what kind of practices and teachings they refer to. Justo Lacunza-Balda has extensively examined how the translation of the Qur'an into Swahili has formed a departure point of Islamic revival, and also constitutes what he describes as an "Islamic process of self-identification, whose constant dynamism influences political, religious, and social culture in East Africa" (1997:123). Generally speaking, Muslims argue that the Qur'an cannot be translated since Arabic is the language of Allah's revelation. Yet, translation into Swahili has, according to Lacunza-Balda (1997), contributed significantly to the Islamist movement in East Africa. Moreover, the fact that Muslims can have access to the text without having knowledge of Arabic, or without using arabophone scholars as intermediaries, has also played an important part in the process in which established Muslim scholars are losing their monopoly of interpreting the sacred text (Lacunza-Balda 1993, 1997). Having access to these texts, in one way or the other, men and women of the Indian Ocean Region engage in discussions of cosmological issues and morality: their meanings and consequences for daily life and ritual practices.

Mohamed Ahmed Saleh (this volume) brings in the expression *dini wal duniya,* that is, "religion and the world". The expression, he argues, is much used especially by Zanzibari urban dwellers in order to state the flexibility of Islam and the importance of balancing between their temporal and spiritual life. Saleh reminds us that what is emphasized, particularly by men, is the understanding that being a good Muslim may have different meanings in different periods of one's life and in different life situations – according to them there are no absolutes. This point is also illuminated in Gerard Van de Bruinhost's article discussing the Arafa meeting in Tanga. He shows that for participating men and women, the meeting concerns not theological issues as such, but rather how to be and live as Muslims and Swahilis in the present political and ideological climate. This issue has become crucial to them, as they feel their position is questioned by other Muslims, theological authorities as well as non-Muslims, while, at the same time, they strive to construct their own authenticity. Declich's (this volume) discussion of how men with formal religious education in Somalia challenge and dispute religious rituals performed by women, together with the knowledge they convey during these rituals, indicates similar circumstances. Men argue that women's demands for knowledge, as well as their performances, are immoral, and thus not legitimate according to scriptural or scholarly Islam.

Changing Material Circumstances

On the coast of Eastern Africa, people in general seem to experience a worsening of their life-conditions – expressing concerns about cultural and economic marginalization. Both Pat Caplan's and Assibi Amidu's articles (this volume), respectively focusing on Mafia Island, Tanzania, and Lamu, Kenya, illustrate how development (*maendeleo*) is seen as a process which makes Swahili society and culture deteriorate, and which leaves people marginalized in their "own" societies and in the wider nation states. The Structural Adjustment Programmes, the problem of multipartyism, foreign investment and the expanding tourist industry, and for Mafia Island, extensive prawn farming, have severe consequences regarding access to, and control over, land and sea rights as well as other resources securing their livelihoods. These are all emphasized as elements which worsen life conditions for the affected communities. This context produces a situation where many see themselves as left not only without property or resources, but also as politically voiceless, without authority within their own societies. In line with these observations, Elisabeth Hsu's paper on Chinese formula medicine conveys that the relationship between China and Africa is currently heavily flavoured by an anti-Western bias that causes Africa to see China – and China to present itself to Africa – as an alternative to the prescriptive, or neo-colonial, forces of the West. Referring to a history of political relations, the preference for Chinese medicine may be linked to the fact that, in the 19th century and early 20th century, European powers such as Britain, France, and Germany were highly present in Africa. In the 21st century, China is emerging as a major power on the African continent, challenging Europe's traditional dominance. China's state media time and again affirm China's commitment to mutual respect and 'non-interference in each other's internal affairs' (van der Wath and Kotze 2006). It seems to be a general notion that China, in contrast to Western nation states, engages in economic activities in Africa without interfering in political, ideological or moral issues.[1] Whether structural exploitation will still take place, remains to be seen.

The expressions *dunia mbaya* and *maisha magumu* (life is difficult) are often heard. However, one may ask whether life was ever easy on the East African coast. In socially stratified Swahili communities there were always those who were poor – a point that Ulla Vuorela (this volume) discusses in her paper, exploring how slave relations disclose themselves in contemporary society, and how these relationships are still involved in social differentiation in a small village in Bagamoyo District in Tanzania. The social stratification of Swahili society is historically linked with the existence of slavery and various forms of slave relations. People's memories, remembrances and practices often reactivate slave-master relationships, she argues, and concern the question of whose families were slaves and whose were free.

Problems of social differentiation and stratification are also brought up by Amidu in his paper. He examines the divide between Lamuans and those considered non-Lamuans in Lamu – a town considered by the Lamuans themselves as a holy town, as a Mecca of Islam. Citizens, as well as religious and political leaders of the town, are expected to exhibit a high standard of social and political morality. The claimed morally superior position of the town, as well as that of its (real) citizens, is, according to Amidu, challenged both by the tourists and their sites, as well as by the recent planners and investors from the mainland. These, argue the Lamuans, leave them dispossessed in their own town. In this situation, change for the better can, from many Lamuans' point of view, only take place within the context of an Islamic religious purity, where the people of Lamu will once again gain their rightful position within what they consider to be their territory.

While Amidu shows how Lamuans feel marginalized within their 'own' town, Roman Loimeier (this volume) discusses how Zanzibari men inhabit 'their town' in ways which simultaneously express perceptions of differences between categories of men. Loimeier defines the *baraza*[2] as part of the public sphere and explores this arena as male social space that allows for free circulation of information and ideas and is outside the control of the state. The *baraza*, he argues, is also a marker of time. At what time its members meet varies between the different *baraza*, and the timing becomes an in-

---

1. In the 15th century the Ming Dynasty admiral, Zheng He arrived at the East African continent during one of his e
2. The term *baraza* has many meanings, such as a stone bench against the wall outside a house, a stone seat in the entrance hall, a place of public audience or reception, a veranda.

dication of the identity and status of the various groups of men. Time becomes a marker of difference. Loimeier shows that in the Zanzibari context the *baraza* represents a continuum between the public and the private, the formal and informal. However, analysed in terms of social and temporal space, the *baraza* is also part of what constitutes differences between men. The formation of male identity is linked to questions of social position and political sympathies and marked through participation in different public arenas such as the *baraza*. The formation of male identity with reference to politics and religion is also Mohamed Ahmed Saleh's (this volume) main concern. While Loimeier explores men's participation in the public sphere according to the dimensions of space and time, and how men's social and political identity become marked by these dimensions, Saleh examines how male notions of what it means to be a respectable Zanzibari man change with time, that is, through different periods of life; from being a young man to becoming adult and elderly. It concerns public appearance and reputation, but also personal reflections. Saleh focuses in particular on the impact of religious knowledge, and different interpretations of certain religious texts, on the conceptualization of male urban Zanzibari life-style of which the *baraza* plays an important role. However, while Saleh is more concerned with the fact that many men change their interpretations of what it means to live as a good Muslim as years go by and as they reach their late forties, Loimeier discusses how political discourse is part of male public life; moreover, he notes how life-style, political orientation, religiosity and neighbourhood decide which *baraza* a man belongs to or, also, which *baraza* a man belongs to at what time of the day. Hence, both papers indicate the potential complexity of male identity, in and across time and space. Loimeier and Saleh do not discuss public life in relation to sex-segregation and the meaning of gendered worlds, although they do emphasize the fact that they examine men's life-worlds. Gender is, however, as already mentioned, explicitly dealt with in Declich's paper about women's religious rituals and participation in public space in a society stratified with reference both to social rank and gender identity.

A Muslim identity is usually taken as a marker of difference between the coast and the mainland/inland. Simultaneously, Islamic and Muslim ways of life are used as explanations of why coastal societies within East Africa are left behind in the modernization process (Caplan 1997, 2004b). Life-style, value system and ideology are, both by the Swahili themselves and main- or inlanders, used as an explanation of progress or the absence of it, in addition to the political and economic realities. Pat Caplan (this volume) adopts the concept of risk and draws our attention to Mafia Island and people's experience of decreasing food security, unemployment, lack of medical care and education, as well as corruption and misuse of public resources by government employees. On the one hand, people blame the government for mismanagement, and on the other they explain the present situation by referring to the deterioration of kin networks and as *kazi ya Mungu* (God's work), or as a result of *wakati* (state of the times).

Interesting in this context is the extent to which Swahili society celebrates what is seen as typically Swahili and, at the same time, engages in political, economic and ideological processes of change. The problem of socio-cultural and economic change – both those experienced and the wished-for changes for the future – are usually expressed both in the form of political analysis and with reference to religious values and practices. Main questions address to what extent democracy and multipartyism according to a Western model are compatible with the aim of securing a viable and morally acceptable society. What does it mean to be a good Muslim? How can one create or even, recreate a good Muslim society? What represents true knowledge? Following Caplan (this volume), the only way to gain further learning is to include local understandings of the present crisis as part of the analysis. How are these significant issues experienced and discussed in everyday life and among so-called ordinary people in various communities along the East Coast of Africa?

The authors are all concerned with local understandings: how do people see their society and their position within it, and how do they perceive and explain ongoing changes? How do people cope, and how do they make sense of it all? This means that the focus of the various arguments presented in this book is grounded in what Maria Mies (1978) in her feminist research methodology defined as "a view from below", and which has to a large degree inspired a concern about how to grasp local understandings and perspectives. Engaging in this effort, it should be kept in mind that what are referred to as local understandings will always be informed and influenced by a multitude of experiences, rumours, impressions and knowledge about what goes on and why, elsewhere. Local understandings are not equal to narrow, or even uninformed, understandings. Rather, local understandings are about how international issues, events and debates are interrelated and experienced in particular places as well as perceived and coped with by particular people. Hence, the aim of this book is to explore the internal pluralism and multiple discourses in contemporary Swahili society.

By Way of Conclusion

The theme of this book, knowledge, renewal and religion, is meant to capture the various ways in which people perceive and shape their lives, as well as how they see themselves in relation to others. The various papers address the problem of knowledge; how it is produced and challenged within the current climate, and where claims to secularization seem both to undermine and renew forms of learning already generated within Muslim life-worlds. Between Islamic revival and perceived need for change, knowledge practices are politicized, but to what extent is new and more adaptable meaning generated? How is knowledge used in order to establish a common destiny or, rather, the notion of a common history and identity? What characterizes today's knowledge practices, and can these practices accommodate changing concerns and circumstances in Swahili society?

Changing ideological and material circumstances on the East African coast provoke repositioning of persons and communities in relation to each other, the 'other' and the outer world; in many cases, Islam is evoked in order to question and oppose what is, from the coast, seen as African authority.[1] The contributors to this book – their papers summarized below – all approach these problems, but in different ways and by highlighting different aspects of social relations and society on the East African coast. Main concerns relate to material and ideological transformations in Swahili society, and how changing circumstances are affected by and interlinked with ongoing political and economic processes, in East Africa as well as in the wider global context. A common interest is to examine how ongoing processes – ideological and material – affect relations within and between societies. What is changing and what remains the same? How do various communities perceive change and how do they react? How do different reactions affect our understanding of the 'other' and our conceptualization of otherness? To what extent is knowledge evoked in order to advocate the need for change and the significance of continuity, and why has religion suddenly become the heart of the matter in politics on the level of the community as well as nationally and internationally? These are all questions explored in this volume.

---

1. W. Montgomery Watt (1966:44) writes as follows: '(...) there are grounds for thinking that in 20 or 30 years time Islam may well be a dominant factor in East African politics. It would be rash to forecast the future, but Islam is already potentially a political force of the first magnitude, and it is urgent that it should receive more attention from students of politics'.

The Book

As a prelude to the following papers, **Felix Chami** explores the history and culture of the town of Kilwa in relation to the other Swahili settlements that spread from the southern coast of Somalia down to Mozambique and the islands of East Africa, the Comoro Islands and Madagascar. Based on archaeological findings he re-examines the antiquity of the town of Kilwa on the southern coast of Tanzania – probably the largest town of the Swahili coast between 1000 and 1500 AD. Chami confirms that most Swahili societies were agricultural and fishing-based societies, oriented towards the sea and engaging in trade. Chami argues further that the Swahili coast, which used to be seen as non-African in culture, has continuously interrelated with other African cultures. This means, among other things, that the cultural aspects of the early Swahili communities are African rooted. There are, however, traces of religious and social customs and practices related to Islam and the Arab-world. Yet Islamic rather than Arabic traits are found to be predominant.

Farouk Topan focuses on the Swahili concepts *dini* and *mila*, where the first represents Islam and the latter connotes indigenous beliefs and practices, in order to explore the legitimacy of distinctions between popular and scriptural Islam. It is only the boundaries and means that differentiate *dini* and *mila,* he argues. This conceptual dualism produces fields where Swahili women and men in their daily lives partake in negotiations of practices, morality and knowledge. Topan examines the above mentioned concepts in the practices of spirit possession – often seen as non-Islamic – in order to permit a better understanding of Swahili religiosity, past and present, and asks: what is Swahili knowledge, what are its premises and principles, and does it change?

Marie Pierre Ballarin examines how religious traditions are understood and interpreted by local communities among the Sakalava on Madagascar. She focuses on how political actors within Sakalava communities appropriate the royal ancestors' cults in order to reposition themselves in the larger society. In this context, Sakalava traditions are reinterpreted by local communities in relation to ongoing social and political changes. In the case of the Sakalava royal cult, Ballarin illustrates how ritual practice actually may legitimate power and authority to conquer land and aquire power over people. The paper demonstrates the extent to which ritual can be transformed and adapted in different contexts, and it demonstrates the part played by religious practices and ritual in the creation of social practices and identities.

Linda Giles focuses on spirit possession rituals on the Swahili coast. She examines the effects of the changing political economy, urbanism, Islamic attitudes, government attitudes and policies, socioeconomic factors, geographical mobility, Westernized education, and the impact of Westernized biomedicine on this practice. Giles shows not only that the phenomenon of spirit possession continues despite modernization processes but also that in some areas there is an increase in spirit activities. The practice of spirit possession is an integrated part of Swahili cosmology, and it produces fields that incorporate continuity and change as well as acceptance and critique of changing circumstances and lifestyles. Spirit possession, she argues, continues to show vitality exactly because it relates to people's current concerns.

Francesca Declich explores the current questioning of women's religious knowledge by Islamic authorities in Somalia. The paper discusses the *nabi-ammaan* of Abbay Sittidey, a Muslim celebration performed by Somali women every week and on other prescribed occasions to praise female personalities such as Eve, Fatima, Zeynab and Mariam. Declich argues that the dynamics of interpretation, negotiation of meaning and recognized authority on moral issues ascribed to the *nabi-ammaan* Muslim celebrations and litanies by participants in a Somali context are gendered. Recent changes in attitudes towards knowledge and religion have resulted in the propagation of more restrictive moral behaviours, especially for women. As a result, more restrictions are placed today on the negotiation of meanings than used to be the case in the 1980s. The boundaries of what is negotiable have become more restricted, the importance of insisting on the existence of only one correct version of religious teachings and, moreover, accepting only particular rituals as theologically correct, have become increasingly significant. Within the framework of the assertion of this kind of authority and power, new restrictive moral behaviours, especially for women, can be propagated. This, of course, has important political implications and carries gender power imbalance.

Gerard van de Bruinhost discusses why the meaning and content of the Muslim rituals *Siku ya Arafa* and *Idd el-Hajj* turned into political issues in Tanga, Tanzania. The *Arafa* meeting, he argues, became a powerful ritual in order to express and to deal with a deeply felt social and political unease. For people involved in the *Arafa* meeting, the ongoing discourse concerns how to be and live as a Muslim and a Swahili in the present political and ideological climate. The trust in the ruling party CCM seems to be diminishing, and the previous organization of civil society that secured Muslims access to an equal share of development is gradually being destroyed. The paper examines how people on the East African coast feel their position questioned by other Muslims, theological authorities as well as non-Muslims, while they themselves strive to construct an authenticity.

Greg Cameron focuses on how recent political, ideological and economic changes in the wider global sphere are playing themselves out along the Swahili coast of Tanzania. He raises the issue of the counter-production of knowledge and the production of cultural hegemony, and examines the means by which global actors and the national regime seek to reach a consensus and to resolve conflict around the new forms of neo-liberal governance in Tanzania. Cameron discusses the diminishing prospects for parliamentary democracy on Zanzibar in a context where social tensions are deepening. The bifurcation of the ruling party CCM *(Chama cha Mapinduzi)* and the state is explored. Each wing has a narrative on the opposition that aims at essentializing origins and labelling "the other" in particular ways, while playing on historical events and the politically authorised interpretations of these. Where Islamic coastal society drifts may, Cameron holds, depend upon two sets of processes: electoral prospects for substantive democracy, and ever enlarging piety where cultural critiques against secular nationalism and capitalism are deepening.

Roman Loimeier explores how the public sphere in Zanzibar is connected with the *baraza*. He argues that an important feature of the *baraza* in the public sphere is that it actually represents a continuum between the public and the private, the formal and informal, that escapes clear-cut sociological definitions – in the same way as the distinction between the so-called popular and scriptural Islam does in the Swahili world. The *baraza* is approached as both space and place, but also as a marker of time. Different forms of knowledge are revealed, shared, challenged and generated at the different *baraza* and, moreover, at different times. Loimeier explores the well known *baraza* in Swahili architecture emphasizing its sociological rather than aesthetical importance.

Mohamed Ahmed Saleh explores the impact of religious knowledge in the conceptualization of the male urban Zanzibari life-style. His point of departure is the expression *dini wal duniya,* commonly used by urban dwellers in defining the meaning of life and morally acceptable ways of life. *Dini wal duniya,* which is referring to one of the traditions of the Prophet, is generally interpreted as "enjoy your temporal life while at the same time preparing for your life-hereafter – *akhera*". The commonly accepted interpretation indicates, according to Saleh, that a certain form of flexibility characterizes Islam as a religion in general. In the Zanzibari context Muslims are, he argues, encouraged to strike a balance between their temporal and spiritual life. The paper explores how the notion of *dini wal duniya* interrelates with political and moral discourses in different periods of, especially, men's lifecycle and, moreover, the notions of potency within recent political climates.

Pat Caplan applies the concepts risk and danger, trust and blame in order to investigate the Mafians' own understanding of ongoing changes in their society and their relations to each other and the wider world. She examines their changing understandings, both with respect to economic and political circumstances as well as to changes in values, that is, the field of knowledge and morality. She asks where people place responsibility; how they interpret their worsening living conditions, which they describe in terms of having "lost their culture" and what they see as "a lot of backbiting". Discussing the Mafians' perceptions, actions and reactions to development, modernization, and thus present political and economic affairs, Caplan examines whether and to what extent they connect with already existing notions and understandings of the world and its good and evil forces.

Assibi Amidu explores the influence of Islam on political and social perceptions in Lamu – a Mecca of East Africa – which today is seen as being in the grip of tourism and foreign investors. In order to grasp relations between the Lamuans and the increasing number of migrants settling in Lamu buying land and establishing various business enterprises, Amidu pays attention to the content of *Kimondo* verses. According to Lamuans, the standard of living has gone down, and they feel increasingly marginalized in their own town. In this situation the Lamuans appear, he argues, to the outer world, as lazy and unable to become modern and participate in what is seen as the modern life-style and value-systems. This reluctance is perceived as tied to Islam and the fact that Lamuans are Muslims. The paper clearly points to a recent delineation between value systems – one based in Islam, the other in Christianity.

Ulla Vuorela explores the ways in which history is preserved in story telling in a village in Bagamoyo District in Tanzania, where Nyamwezi influences are strong and remembrance of slavery still prevails. Vuorela is concerned with knowledge and how different layers of memory and history, articulated in the minds of people and preserved in story telling and material artefacts, inform their present practices and understandings of society and social relationships. She asks what the term "uncle", *mjomba*, implies when used today. To what extent does the term activate past meanings, and how may these meanings apply, or even redefine, relations in the present as well as for the future? In her analysis, Vuorela emphasizes the importance of addressing the distinction between "things old and new", and not to label the presence of, for instance, new technological innovations immediately as signs of consumerism. The paper conveys the complexity of cultural change and the challenges that confront us when studying knowledge, cultural change and social relations.

Elisabeth Hsu's paper is about Chinese formula medicines on the East African Coast, where these medicines are perceived as scientific and modern in contrast to so-called local traditional medicine and in competition with Western biomedicine. Chinese medicine is considered non-western yet as biomedicine; it becomes so-called alternative and complementary medicine. Drugs that come from China can be Western medical drugs, Chinese medical drugs, Chinese formula drugs or hybrids from among all these. Hsu demonstrates that *dawa ya Kichina* gains its fame partly because the Chinese are known for their magic powers, especially potency-enhancing medicines *(zhongchengyao)*. Some people think the medicines are imbued with magical powers, others value them as traditional 'advanced' medicines. Moreover, *dawa ya Kichina* are appreciated, Hsu argues, because they represent an anti-imperialist tenor against anything Western. The Chinese doctors do not interfere with local ideals and values; they make no particular effort to interfere in the life-style and morality of the society in which they work. It seems that an attitude characterized by non-interference in questions relating to morality and cosmology is currently highly appreciated on the East African coast.

References

Arendt, Hannah, 1993 (1961), *Between Past and Future: Eight Exercises in Political Thought*, New York: Penguin Books

Ashew, Kelly M., 2002, *Performing the Nation: Swahili Music and Cultural Politics in Tanzania*, Chicago: University of Chicago Press

Ashew, Kelly M., 2004, "As Plato Duly Warned: Music, Politics, and Social Change in Coastal East Africa," *Anthropology Quarterly* vol. 76, no., 4, pp.609–637.

Barth, Fredrik, 1993, *Balinese Worlds*. Chicago: Chicago University Press

Babu, Abdulrahman M., 1991, "The 1964 Revolution: Lumpen or Vanguard," in A. Sheriff & E. Ferguson (eds), *Zanzibar under Colonial Rule*, pp, 220–249, London: James Currey Ltd.

Bang, Anne, 2003, *Sufis and Scholars of the Sea: Family Networks in East Africa c. 1860–1925*, London: RoutledgeCurzon.

Beckerleg, Susan, 1995, "'Brown Sugar' or Friday Prayers: Youth Choices and Community Building in Coastal Kenya," *African Affairs*, Vol. 94, No. 374, pp. 23–38.

Beckerleg, Susan, 2004, "Modernity has been Swahili-ised: The Case of Malindi," in P. Caplan and F. Topan (eds), *The Swahili and Modernity*, pp. 121–144, Trenton: Africa World Press.

Bennett, Norman R., 1978, *A History of the Arab State of Zanzibar*, London: Methuen & Co.

Bloch, Maurice, 1986, *From Blessing to Violence: History and Ideology in the Circumcision Ritual of the Merina of Madagascar*, Cambridge: Cambridge University Press

Caplan, Pat, 1975, *Choice and Constraint in a Swahili Community*, London: Oxford University Press.

Caplan, Pat, 1995, "Law and Custom: Marital Disputes on Northern Mafia Island, Tanzania," in P. Caplan (ed.), *Understanding Disputes: The Politics of Argument*, pp. 203–22, Oxford: Berg

Caplan, Pat, 1996, "Reviewed Work(s): Continuity and Autonomy in Swahili Communities: Inland Influences and Strategies of Self-Determination, D. Parkin (ed.)" *The Journal of the Royal Anthropological Institute*, Vol. 2, No. 4, pp. 764–765

Caplan, Pat, 1997, *African Voices, African Lives: Personal Narratives from a Swahili Village*. London: Routledge

Caplan, Pat, 2004a, "Introduction," in P. Caplan and F. Topan (eds), *The Swahili and Modernity*. Trenton: Africa World Press, pp. 121–144.

Caplan, Pat, 2004b, "Struggling to Be Modern: Recent Letters from Mafia Island," in P. Caplan and F. Topan (eds), *The Swahili and Modernity*. Trenton: Africa World Press, pp. 121–144.

Caplan, Pat & Farouk Topan (eds), 2004, *The Swahili and Modernity*. Trenton: Africa World Press.

Chittich, Neville, 1974, *Kilwa, 2. Vol*. Nairobi: British Institute in Eastern Africa

Cooper, Fredrick, 1977, *Plantation Slavery on the East Coast of Africa,* New Haven: Yale University Press.

Cooper, Fredrick, 1980, *From Slaves to Squatters: Plantation Labour and Agriculture in Zanzibar and Coastal Kenya 1890–1925*, New Haven: Yale University Press.

Fair, Laura, 2001, *Pastimes and Politics: Culture, Community, and Identity in Post-Revolutionary Urban Zanzibar, 1890–1945*, Athens: Ohio University Press.

Geertz, Clifford, 1973, *The Interpretation of Culture*, New York: Basic Books.

Geiger, Susan, 1987, "Women in Nationalist Struggle: TANU Activists in Dar es Salaam," *International Journal of African Historical Studies*, 20(1):1–26: Vol.20, No. 1, pp.1–26.

Gilbert, Erik, 2002, "Coastal East Africa and the Western Indian Ocean: Long-Distance Trade, Empire, Migration, and Regional Unity, 1750–1970," *The History Teacher*, Vol. 36, No. 1, pp. 7–34.

Giles, Linda, 1987, "Possession Cults on the Swahili Coast: A Re-Examination of Theories of Marginality", *Africa* 57 (2): 234–257.

Giles, Linda, 1992, "The Role of Zanzibar and Pemba within the Swahili Spirit Cult Complex", *The International Conference on the History and Culture of Zanzibar*, Zanzibar 14–16 December 1992.

Giles, Linda, 1995, "Sociocultural Change and Spirit Possession on the Swahili Coast of East Africa", *Anthropological Quarterly* 68 (2): 89–106.

Habermas, Jürgen, 1990 (1962), *Strukturwandel in der Öffentlichkeit*. Frankfurt: Campus.

Horton, Mark, 1996, *Shanga: The Archaeology of a Muslim Trading Community on the Coast of East Africa*, London: British Institute in Eastern Africa.

Horton, Mark & John Middleton, 2000, *The Swahili: The Social Landscape of a Mercantile Society*. Oxford: Blackwell.

Kirkman, James, S., 1954, *The Arab City of Gedi: Excavations at the Great Mosque. Architecture and Finds*, Oxford: Royal National Parks of Kenya.

Lacunza-Balda, Justo, 1993, "Swahili Islam: Continuity and Revival," *Encounter*, 193/194, p. 29. Rome: Pontificio Institutu di Studi Arabi e d'Islamistica.

Lacunza-Balda, Justo, 1997, "Translation of the Qur'an into Suaheli," in D. Westerlund and Eva E. Rosander (eds), *African Islam and Islam in Africa*. London: Hurst, pp. 95–126.

Lambek, Michael, 1993, *Knowledge and Practice in Mayotte*. Toronto: University of Toronto Press.

Larsen, Kjersti, 1990, *Unyago – Fra jente til kvinne*. Oslo: Oslo Occasional Papers, no. 22.

Larsen, Kjersti, 1998, "Spirit Possession as Historical Narrative: The Production of Identity and Locality in Zanzibar Town," in, N. Lovell (ed.), *Locality and Belonging*. London: Routledge, pp. 125–146.

Larsen, Kjersti, 2000, "The Other Side of Nature: Expanding Tourism, Changing Landscapes and Problems of Privacy in Urban Zanzibar," in, V. Broch-Due and R. Scroeder (eds), *Producing Nature and Poverty in Africa*. Uppsala: Nordiska Afrikainstitutet, pp. 198–220.

Larsen, Kjersti, 2001, "Spirit Possession as Oral History: Negotiating Islam and Social Status," in B. S. Amoretti (ed.), *Islam in East Africa: New Sources*. Roma: Herder, pp. 275–296.

Larsen, Kjersti, 2007, *Custom, Adaptability and Conflict Mediation on Arid Land: Returnees and Stayees in Wadi al Mugaddam*. James Currey.

Larsen, Kjersti, 2007, "Dialogues between Humans and Spirits: Ways of Negotiating Relationships and Moral Order in Zanzibar Town, Zanzibar," in U. Demmer & M. Gaenszle (eds), *The Power of Discourse in Ritual Performance: Rhetoric and Poetics*. Münster: LIT Verlag, pp. 54–74.

Lofchie, Michael Y., 1965, *Background to Revolution*, Princeton: Princeton University Press.

Lofchie, Michael Y., 1970, "African Protest in a Racially Plural Society," in R. I. Rotberg and A. A. Mazrui (eds), *Protest and Power in Black Africa*, New York: Oxford University Press, pp. 924–927.

Middleton, John, 1992, *The World of the Swahili: An African Mercantile Civilization.* New Haven: Yale University Press.

Mies, Maria, 1983, "Towards a Methodology for Feminist Research," in Gloria Bowles and Renate Duelli-Klein (eds), *Theories of Women's Studies.* London: Routledge & Kegan Paul, pp. 117–39.

Myers, Garth A., 1995, "The Early History of the Other Side of Zanzibar Town," in A. Sheriff (ed.), *The History and Conservation of Zanzibar Stone Town.* London: James Currey Ltd, pp. 30–45.

Nurse, David & Thomas Spear, 1985, *The Swahili: Reconstructing the History and Language of an African Society, 800–1500.* Philadelphia: University of Pennsylvania Press.

Parkin, David, 1994, "Blank Banners and Islamic Consciousness in Zanzibar," in A. P. Cohen and N. Rapport (eds), *Questions of Consciousness.* London: Routledge, pp. 198–216.

Prins, A. H. J., 1965, *Sailing from Lamu: A Study of Maritime Culture in Islamic East Africa.* Assen: Van Gorcum.

Ranger, Terrence, 1975, *Dance and Society in Eastern Africa, 1890–1970: The Beni Ngoma.* London: Heinemann.

Saleh, Mohamed Ahmed, 2004, "Going With the Times: Conflicting Swahili Norms and Values Today," in Pat Caplan, and Farouk Topan, (eds), *Swahili Modernities.* Trenton: Africa World Press, pp.145–155.

Schneider, Arnd, 2006, *Appropriation as Practice: Art and Identity in Argentina,* New York: Palgrave MacMillan.

Sheriff, Abdul, 1987, *Slaves, Spices and Ivory in Zanzibar,* London: James Currey Ltd.

Sheriff, Abdul, 1995, "Introduction," in A. Sheriff (ed.) *The History & Conservation of Zanzibar Stone Town.* London: James Currey Ltd, pp. 1–8.

Sheriff, Abdul and Ed Ferguson, 1991, *Zanzibar under Colonial Rule.* London: James Currey Ltd.

Strobel, Margareth, 1979, *Muslim Women in Mombasa: 1890–1975.* London: Yale University Press.

Swartz, Marc J., 1991, *The Way the World Is: Cultural Process and Social Relations Among the Mombasa Swahili.* Berkeley: University of California Press.

Topan, Farouk, 1992, "Swahili as a Religious Language," *Journal of Religion in Africa,* Vol. 22, Fasc. 4, pp. 331–349.

Van Ufford, Philip Q. & Matthew Schoffeleers, 1988, *Religion and Development: Towards an Integrated Approach.* Amsterdam: Free University Press.

Wath, Kobus van der & Dirk Kotze, 2006, "Africa and China: A Neglected Opportunity," in African Analyst, issue 1, third quarter, pp. 43–59.

Watt, Montgomery W., 1966, "The Political Relevance of Islam in East Africa," International Affairs, Vol. 42, No. 1, pp. 35–44.

CHAPTER 2

Kilwa and the Swahili Towns
Reflections from an Archaeological Perspective

Felix Chami[1]

Introduction

The towns of East Africa can be divided into two periods: pre-colonial and colonial towns. The former grew up along the coast facilitating trade and communication between the rim of the Indian Ocean seaboard and the interior of Africa. Hence, the coastal cities were never only oriented to the ocean, but also to the African mainland. The towns, better known in history as Swahili city states, survived from about the beginning of the second millennium AD to about the 1890s. The towns which grew up after this period were mostly new administrative centres established with the launch of German and British rule in East Africa from about the 1890s. Only a few settlements from the colonial period have their history pre-dating the colonial era. Such towns include Mombasa which is a Swahili town and Kampala which was the seat of the Buganda kingdom.

The Growth of the Swahili Town

The Swahili settlements spread all along the coast and islands of East Africa (Fig. 1). The first settlements, ancestors to the Swahili towns of the 13th century seem to have been few and mostly built with mud and wattle. The concentration of these towns appears to have first occurred in the Mafia-Kilwa region on the coast of southern Tanzania and in the Lamu archipelago on the northern coast of Kenya. Yet, individual settlements seem also to have flourished elsewhere on the coastal littoral and virtually on every island large enough to accommodate settlements from the Lamu archipelago to the Comoro islands north of Madagascar. Madagascar itself has early Swahili towns such as Mahilaka (Radimilahy 1998). Archaeologists have found remains from early settlements and horizons such as early Islamic

---

1. I wish to thank Kjersti Larsen for having assisted me in the editing of this chapter.

goods including Sassanian Islamic ware, Islamic copies of Chinese pottery and early Sgraffiato.

Most likely, the largest and earliest settlement of the above mentioned period is that of Kilwa in southern Tanzania (Fig. 1). The settlement seems to have become a larger centre by about AD 1000 when the earliest stone structures were most probably built (see Chittick 1974). However, only a few stone structures would have been built at this point in time. It should be noted that it was the spectacular image of Kilwa centre in the first part of the second millennium AD that first attracted European archaeologists. The German colonial government became involved at the beginning of 19th century and, moreover, in the 1950s Kilwa caught the attention of British archaeologists. The renowned Mortimer Wheeler led a team of researchers in 1955, including Gervace Mathew, Freeman-Grenville, James Kirkman and Neville Chittick, to conduct a test excavation (Sutton 1998). This research paved the way to even more intensive archaeological research by Neville Chittick, not only in Kilwa, but also in other Swahili towns within the region (Chittick 1974, 1984).

Kilwa must have been a large settlement and its stone town itself is estimated to have been about 50 hectares in the early period. This settlement must have controlled other larger settlements within the region, even more so economically, as settlements of a similar nature exist on the islands of Mafia, off the Rufiji Delta, and on the nearby island of Songo Mnara. It is also probable that other settlements of the same period such as those found in Zanzibar and Pemba, the central coast of Tanzania, the Comoro islands and northern Madagascar as well as those on the northern coast of Mozambique and the related Zimbabwe monuments, should be related to the development of Kilwa. Archaeological work conducted on sites located in the above mentioned regions have revealed objects and goods, including coins, pottery and stone vessels, that indicate rather extensive exchange between the various settlements. These findings suggest that Kilwa was a centre with economic influence if not in direct control of the peer settlements both to the north and the south.

The early towns of the Lamu archipelago were excavated by Chittick (1984) and Mark Horton (1996). Settlements like Gedi, Malindi, and Mombasa grew to compete with those to the north and even with Kilwa at the time when the Portuguese had entered the region. What is clear in the archaeology of the coast of Eastern Africa is that there was interaction between the Swahili towns. Whether or not Kilwa controlled affairs in the whole region between AD 1000 and about AD 1400, needs further exploration.

In the later phase, from about AD 1300, larger Swahili towns were built of coral stones and lime mortar and roofed with mangrove poles, lime mortar and palm leaves. Archaeological research has also found a profusion of many smaller settlements, which were built of mud and wattle. The majority of the population of larger settlements may also have been living in simpler houses, that is, houses built from mud and wattle (see Horton 1996, Chami 2002, Pradines 2003). When Ibn Battuta visited the coast of East Africa in the 1330s, he did not see many stone houses even in larger towns such as Kilwa and Mombasa (Gibb 1939). His observations contrast with the current claims of archaeology. Whether Ibn Battuta's observation was due to a personal bias and surprise at finding only a few stone houses or whether he was only shown simpler town places is not yet properly explained (see discussion by Sutton 1998).

Another point of uncertainty is whether each larger Swahili town had its own trade and cultural link with foreign traders or whether trade was only controlled by one or two larger towns which collected foreign trade and organized the redistribution of goods to other towns of lesser political and economic importance. Ibn Battuta seems to have visited only two towns along the Swahili coast, Kilwa and Mombasa – a choice suggesting that those were the larger ones. However, in the same period a Chinese trip to East Africa led by Zeng He entered a town called *Malin*. Whereas some scholars think this place was Malindi on the Kenya coast (Chittick 1975: 21, Wheatley 1975:90–91), Fuwei (1996:190) suggests that *Malin* was Kilwa. Kilwa, in comparison with other Swahili towns, has probably the largest number of Chinese goods including a profusion of Chinese coins. These have been excavated by Chittick (Chittick 1974) and recently by myself (Chami 2006b). Another point in support of Fuwei's position is that Kilwa also had a resident community identifying itself as Malindi. Their mosque and tombs in front of the stone town near the old port suggest that the Malindi people or clan could probably have controlled most of the economic affairs of the town.

It is plausible that each large Swahili town engaged in trade abroad or, perhaps, engaged a set of traders who visited particular ports in the Middle East and India. Archaeologists have started identifying artefacts in northern Swahili towns similar to those found in India dating back to the same period (Horton 2006) – findings that indicate some degree of cultural and

Swahili Towns and settlements on the east coast of Africa

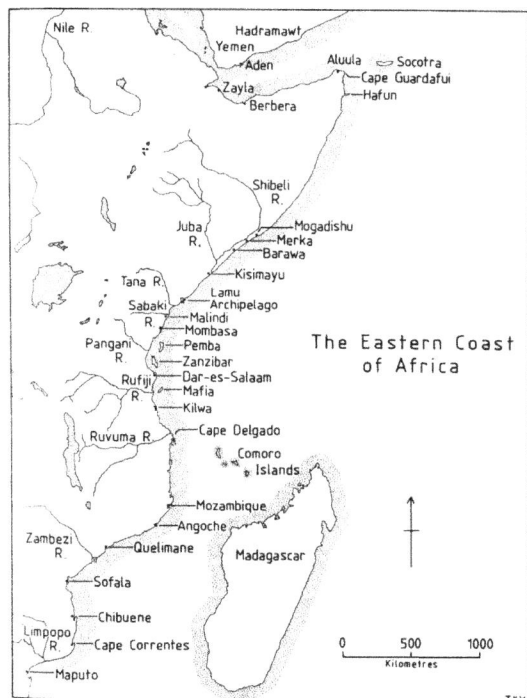

Map labels: Nile R., Hadramawt, Yemen, Aden, Aluula, Socotra, Cape Guardafui, Zayla, Berbera, Hafun, Shibeli R., Juba R., Mogadishu, Merka, Barawa, Kisimayu, Tana R., Lamu Archipelago, Sabaki R., Malindi, Mombasa, Pangani R., Pemba, Zanzibar, Dar-es-Salaam, Rufiji R., Mafia, Kilwa, Cape Delgado, Ruvuma R., Comoro Islands, Mozambique, Angoche, Zambezi R., Quelimane, Madagascar, Sofala, Chibuene, Limpopo R., Cape Correntes, Maputo, The Eastern Coast of Africa, 0 500 1000 Kilometres

aesthetical interaction. Archaeologists are also discovering many Swahili cultural artefacts, materials and sites in Yemen and other parts of South Arabia suggesting that people from the various Swahili towns were sailing to these, for them, distant lands where they possibly established settlements (see Sutton 1998, Horton 2006). It is likely that the profusion of foreign trade goods in all Swahili settlements could also suggest that particular towns engaged in long distance trade at least within the western Indian Ocean seaboard if not even beyond. This is testified to by the fact that several towns are now known to have produced their own coins. Furthermore, when Vasco da Gama reached northern Mozambique he had to get a person from Malindi, on the Kenya coast, to guide him to India, suggesting that the Swahilis were already in contact with India. Seemingly the southern towns were not co-operating with the Portuguese and this is, probably, why a guide had to be obtained from further north.

The Origin of the Swahili Towns

Up till the end of the 20th century scholars debated the origin of the Swahili people and their stone town culture. Such debates revolved around the question of who the Swahili people were (see Pouwels 1974, Allen 1974, 1983, Nurse and Spear 1985, Horton 1987, Chami 1994, 1998). The initial popular conception was that the Swahili people and their culture originated from the Middle East. The Swahili people were alleged to have arrived in waves of immigration. Individuals in these waves of immigration were alleged to have founded settlements from about the 10th century. Although Chittick (1974) thought that Kilwa had had a small local population at the time of the establishment of the first immigrant settlements, the dominant trend among scholars supported an interpretation claiming that the earliest Swahili towns were constituted by people from abroad and, moreover, that the Swahili coast had not been settled before their arrival.

It should be noted here that the above mentioned scholarly position was not universally supported. Rather, several scholars of the Roman documents of the first three centuries AD had already clearly suggested the existence of settlements on the Swahili coast which traded with Romans and Arabs. Scholars of the 1980s and afterwards have through their research explored further the above mentioned interpretation and argued that the very early documented settlements were located on the coast of Somalia and northern Kenya or their interior, near a town named Shungwaya (see Allen 1983, Horton 1990).

Several archaeologists, for instance, Horton (1987), influenced by James de V. Allen (1983), following the Shungwaya theory, suggested that the Swahili were people of Cushitic origin, from the north-east of Africa, who were originally pastoralists. It is suggested that the pastoralists, who are said to have ruled the Bantu speakers in a 'mythical land' called Shunguaya, mixed with Bantu speakers, adopted Islam and spread to the rest of the coast and islands of East Africa. According to this theory the Swahili people are seen as people from Africa who engaged and intermarried with people from the Middle East and who, in the process, converted to Islam and became involved in trade. This theoretical position was made more prominent in the 1990s (see Horton 1990, Abungu 1994–5, Sutton 1998) in the attempt, I hold, to quash the new discoveries that clearly suggested that the Swahili people were of Bantu origin and thus people of the general region of Eastern and Southern Africa whose livelihoods were mainly based in agricultural and fishing activities.

If language should be considered, it is interesting to note that linguists from the 1980s recognised that the Swahili people did speak a Bantu language (see Nurse and Spear 1985). Archaeologists had already established the existence of settlements of Early Iron Working people near the coast. These people were generally recognised by scholars as belonging to the early Bantu speakers (see Soper 1971). Historians had also, at this point, acknowledged that the people, who were reported by the Romans in the first centuries AD to have inhabited East Africa, at that time known as Azania, were agriculturalists and probably of Bantu speaking tradition (see Casson 1989). In the early 1990s I argued on the basis of my research, that the cultural tradition found to have formed the earliest horizon of the Swahili settlements was clearly related to that of the Early Iron Working (EIW) tradition dating back to the first centuries AD (Chami 1994). In some cases settlements of the Early Iron Working people and those of the so-called early Swahili, termed by this author as the Triangular Incised Ware (TIW) tradition, were found in the same location.[1] In some cases the latter was found superimposed over the former on the offshore islands and on the coastal littoral of the central coast of Tanzania (see Chami 1998, 1999a).

The confirmation of cultural continuity from the time of Christ, through the mid-first millennium AD, to the time of the foundation of the Swahili towns in the early centuries of the second millennium AD, has now been recognised by many scholars (see Kusimba 1999, Sinclair and Håkansson 2000, Spear 2000). Also those who disagreed with the gazetteering of the first set of evidence supporting this continuity have eventually recast their thoughts (see Horton 1996, Sutton 1998, Horton and Middleton 2000). Archaeological findings now confirm that the Swahili coast had been settled by agricultural and trading populations from the time of Pharaonic Egypt, 3000 BC, through the Greco-Roman period (for conspectus see Chami 2006a). Whereas the former was of the neolithic tradition the latter was of the Early Iron Working culture. Throughout these periods the Indian Ocean, just as later during the time of Islam, had brisk trade with communities of Asia, the Middle East as well as the Red Sea and the Mediterranean worlds. Ceramics and beads as evidence of trade from all these pre-Islamic trading periods have now been recovered from the islands of Zanzibar, Mafia and the Rufiji River Delta. Reports on the various findings have now

---

1. Pottery found at the Swahili site of Pujini on the offshore island of Pemba is in the literature known by two names, that is, Triangular Incised Ware (TIW) or Tana Tradition Ware. Triangular Incised Ware (TIW) is most closely associated with East African coastal sites dated to ca. the 8th–10th centuries, during the period of rapid Swahili expansion. It has also been located at interior sites.

been gazetted in various publications (for conspectus see Chami 1999b, 2006a).

The increasing amount of data about the origin of the Swahili towns necessitated a new research on the island of Kilwa. As already mentioned, Kilwa had been one of the earliest Swahili towns, and probably the largest of the early part of the second millennium AD. It was thus very necessary to document that Kilwa should be seen as part of the above mentioned ancient developments: that Kilwa evolved from the ancient cultural foundations. Research on Kilwa, which still awaits scientific reporting, includes remains of Early Iron Working pottery and those of the neolithic period – the earliest being related to those of the Nile valley dating back to 3000 BC (Plates 1–3). Mounds for iron smelting (Plate 4) have been discovered 2 km east of the stone town. Research now suggests that these could have belonged to the people of the Early Iron Working period. Other important items collected include pieces of Roman pottery and beads (Plate 5).

The significance of recent findings is that they confirm that nearly all the Swahili towns have formed part of an ancient continuity. Within this continuity, the emergence of Islamic communities in the first millennium AD produced political, economic and socio-cultural changes. This era should, however, not be understood as the 'source' of Swahili civilization. Yet, it is important to note that in the above mentioned era, the region was linked to a world system. People of the region adopted norms of the world order of the time and adjusted their culture in order to be able to take advantage of the new world order. Cosmopolitan towns like Kilwa received traders, missionaries and other visitors among whom some remained for a long time and others stayed on permanently becoming part of local affairs.

To conclude this section, a point echoed in several other publications of mine should be reiterated here. All visitors to the coast of East Africa during both what I call the Islamic period as well as in the Portuguese period reported that the people of the Swahili towns were of African background at least if we are to accept that the mentioning of black skin means 'African'. Some used the word black for the skin of the Swahili people. One can point out a few: Buzurg's comments on the King and the people he hijacked from the coast of Sufala and sold in the Middle East in the 9th and 10th centuries as Zanj, Ibn Batutta's jet black people of Kilwa, and the early Portuguese report of the Kilwa sultans being black. One can also add the 18th century Kilwa queen's letter to those who had fled the Omani control of Kilwa to Mozambique. In the letter the queen is asking them to come back because the Swahilis should not to be afraid of Arabs because they were all Muslims.

One may ask, if the Kilwa people were seen as, and saw themselves as being, Arabs as argued earlier by Chittick and others then the letter would have shown that Arabs had run away from fellow Arabs.

Some Cultural Aspects of the Swahili Towns

Regarding cultural orientation, the Swahili towns, as already suggested, should be seen as mainly African and Islamic, rather than Arabic. Yet, a substantial Arabic influence can be testified for the period after the 18th century when the Omanis started controlling and settling on the coast of East Africa. Furthermore, within the same period people from Asia arrived and settled along the Swahili coast. In the wake of these later migration processes Swahili culture and society were gradually accommodating the different life-styles, cosmologies and practices that migrating people brought with them.

The presence of Islam

Different Swahili people adopted Islam at different periods of time. Chinese and other records suggest that societies along the north coast were Islamic by the 13th century while societies towards the south were less so. Archaeological research suggests that mosques existed on the northern coast from about 800 AD. However, in most cases mosques are more common in the 14th century. Probably, most of the population along the coast continued practising rituals pre-dating Islam, integrating these into their wider Islamic cosmology, as is also seen today in the worship of spirits in caves on all the islands from Pemba, via Zanzibar to the Comoro islands and Madagascar. These practices could be seen as expressions of what is usually denoted as religious and cultural syncretism.

Most Swahili people are of the Sunni Islam and the Shafi'i law school. This suggests an early link with Southern Arabia. Large mosques had been built from stones from 1300 AD in every town on the Swahili coast. Some towns have several mosques, some being smaller for a clan or a family. *Qibla* walls or the north part of these mosques, were elaborately made: probably the one at Songo Mnara in Kilwa, I would hold, is the most elaborate.

One aesthetic tradition which seems unique to the Swahili towns is that of building large spectacular tombs. The tombs, with most of them concentrated around the mosques, were built using stones and lime. The walls of some of these tombs are more than two metres high with various decorative panels including impressed Chinese porcelain. Some tombs have high standing pillars reaching up to four metres above the tomb.

The above mentioned tradition of tomb construction is not common to Islamic communities in general. Muslims in most parts of the world are buried in humbler tombs rather than in monumental ones. Islam demands no material inclusion in graves or portrayal of wealth at the burials. That these spectacular tombs are also found attached to houses or are located in compounds where people were living has been used to suggest an African burial tradition which was blended with an Islamic burial tradition.

I have noted elsewhere (Chami 2002) that the above mentioned burial tradition has been said to form part of a cosmology where the living were supposed to live with the spirits of the dead within their houses or compounds or also within the settled landscape. This understanding is said to be based in African cosmology. The idea of burying around the tombs is also unique to the Swahili coast suggesting an African tendency to associate the dead with the holy (Othman Lali Omar, pers.com.). Like the ancient Egyptian tradition, the tradition of the Bantu speakers in general, says that the spirit should not be abandoned in the wilderness away from human warmth and food. A failure to observe this rule was and still is expected to bring bad omens to a family.

Reflections on Writing and Arithmetic

It is not yet known whether there existed a kind of pre-Islamic writing on the coast of East Africa. A Greek traveller in the 3rd century BC noted, however, a type of vertical writing (see discussion by Chami 2006a). I have also argued for the existence of some kind of schematic, geometric and amorphous script in the region in ancient times (Chami 2006a). In the Triangular Incised Ware (TIW) period we have abundant potsherds and stones grooved with geometric signs which most archaeologists have adopted as bead grinders. Most of these potsherds and stones like those excavated in Unguja Ukuu, Mpiji, Kiwangwa and the Kaole part of Tanzania (see Chami 1994, Juma 2004) are not associated with shell beads or any remains of bead making. This implies that the above mentioned finding cannot be used to support the interpretation provided by Chittick (1984) on Kilwa.

Early Islamic characters found at the Swahili settlements are Kufic[1] the earliest known being from the 11th century tomb of Kizimkazi on Zanzibar (Flury 1921). Later on Arabic scripts were used to write in the Swahili lan-

---

1. Kufic is the oldest calligraphic form of the various Arabic scripts and consists of a modified form of the old Nabatean script.

guage. These can be seen in many tombs post-dating 1300 AD and Swahili letters dating from 1200 AD. I must reiterate the point that when these Arabic scripts are seen on tombs or on coins such as the Kilwa ones, the tendency has been for scholars to use them as evidence for Arab settlements rather than Islamic influence.

Interesting to note is that in daily counting the Swahili people mixed Bantu and Arabic words. From this fact one may speculate whether counting may have followed Arabic in schools or official places, while an already existing African counting system was used in everyday life. Words such as *moja* (one), *mbili* (two), *tatu* (three) and so on are typical Bantu counting words and when one encounters words such as *saba* (seven), *ishirini* (twenty), *hamsini* (fifty) and so on these are Arabic counting words included in the Swahili language. Probably the Arabic influence was more intense after the Omanis re-established their control of the coastal towns from about 1837 AD.

Reflections on Architectural Structures

Peter Garlake (1966) studied the architecture of the Swahili town and in the wake of his work most of the interpretation of the Swahili architecture has followed (Chittick 1984, Sutton 1998). As was noted concerning the tombs, the architecture of the Swahili buildings is of Western Indian Ocean seaboard origin. This is a tradition that began and evolved within the region. The architecture is very much conditioned by available resources for building such as mangrove wood and coral rubble. The latter is made into walls with lime mortar and then plastered using the same lime mortar. Rarely were bricks and dressed stones used. The only dressed stone used for door and window frames, *mihrabs* and lamp chambers was porite. This is a coral cut from underwater while fresh and, then, dressed and decorated or inscribed while fresh.

Four storey houses' floor slabs were made by arranging mangrove or other hard wood across each other. Lime mortar, sometimes mixed with coral rubble, was spread on top. Some houses, especially mosques, had moulded roofs with the addition of decorative arches, domes and vaults. Most houses must have been roofed with wood and palm or grass. Swahili houses had large verandas and corridors for relaxation and cooking. The door frames and panels were decorated with carved panels.

Reflections on Livelihood in Coastal Societies

Swahili people have over time engaged in various economic activities which have formed their wider livelihood systems. I have argued that the Swahili societies were traditionally agricultural. In most cases people formed settled communities with vegetable gardens around their compounds and in areas only a few hours walk from towns. Allen (1983) characterized the Swahili as people who commute from town to the countryside for agricultural purposes. This seems to have been the situation from ancient times. Among crops cultivated are the most traditional ones such as rice, millet, beans and peas, bananas, coconuts, sugar cane, spices and fruits such as mangos, oranges. In recent history crops from America such as maize, cassava, sweet potatoes and tobacco have been added to the list.

Swahili people would have been farmers but they would also have kept chicken, cattle and ovicaprids.[1] Remains of these are well observed from archaeological records dating back to 3000 BC (Chami 2006a). The same records also show that they had dogs and cats and for the northern coast donkeys and camels (Horton 1996). Due to environmental variability the northern part of the Swahili coast would have been more pastoral than the south. In the north there has also been interaction between the more settled coastal people and people with nomadic livelihood adaptations in Somalia and northern Kenya.

Fishing must have dominated the activities of those living near the shore and on the island settlements as fish would secure the most reliable means of obtaining protein. The Swahili are the descendants of the people who must have conquered the ocean from ancient times through fishing and trading. They fished in the deep and shallower waters and there is much evidence indicating that there have been periods when the population consumed a lot of shellfish and land snails. These findings can be seen to suggest difficult times (Msemwa 1994). Mentioning fishing activities, these include not only marine, but also fresh water fishing. There are several large rivers entering the Swahili coast region from the interior and also a few lakes near the littoral which provide fish. Salting and drying fish facilitated transport to the interior.

Sailing, not only for fishing, but also for trade was probably the most prestigious activity of the Swahili man. Swahili towns were made up of people who had travelled far within and outside the region for the purpose of trade or prayers. Moreover, there were a lot of intermarriages between com-

---

1. Ovicaprids is the name of a group of animals, corresponding to sheep and goats.

munities and therefore households and families must have had relatives in areas relatively far from where they themselves lived. Oral traditions and chronicles such as the Kilwa one suggest that people were travelling to other towns for trade or other cultural purposes and that they even stayed on to marry. The pan-Swahili culture of the 12th–15th centuries clearly suggests that such a phenomenon could only be caused by regular interactions probably involving intermarriages.

More recent experiences do suggest intermarriages between men from the Middle East and Swahili women. Through such intermarriages further cultural and social integration could take place. The Seyyid Said children in Zanzibar and the subsequent dynasty, represent one form of such intermarriages. Records from ancient times, for instance, Periplus also suggest that when men from the Red Sea coast of Arabia travelled to the Swahili coast for trade they married women from the various local communities and learnt the language of the local people.

I have emphasized the importance of agriculture in the early coastal societies. Yet, the Swahili should also be seen as maritime people. Goods to be exchanged with those arriving from abroad had to be collected from the south or the interior. Such an activity must also have involved the distribution of the imported goods. So the Swahili towns were providing trade access for the larger part of Eastern and Southern Africa.

Consequently the Swahili people were also constructing sailing vessels. The Romans found the people of the Swahili coast already making sewn boats and also importing boats from abroad (Casson 1989). This technology grew tremendously and by the time of the stone towns the Swahili people must have been building large dhows used to cross the Indian Ocean to Arabia and India. In the ruined Swahili monuments one can observe early sailing vessels incised on the walls. In most of the Swahili towns today one can find at least one operating dhow or boat building yard suggesting a continuous tradition. Their technology included metal working, which was inherited from ancient times. Knowledge of and skills in metal working were necessary both for cultivation and boat making as wood had to be felled and worked.

Swahili Towns in Ruins

It was noted earlier that the realm of Swahili culture dwells in the period between 1200 and 1500 AD. After this hey day Swahili societies entered into a hectic period following the penetration of Europeans who wanted to conquer by destroying the large Swahili towns such as Kilwa and divert trade to the Atlantic Ocean. As discussed by Michael N. Pearson (1998), Portuguese aims in East Africa were set out at the beginning of the 16th century AD. There was, according to Pearson, no state-controlled trade in the region at the time when the Portuguese arrived, although it is known that the rulers of Mombasa and Kilwa levied high duties. During its presence in the region, Portugal wanted to force allegiance from local Swahili rulers to make them pay tribute. It also established a system where so-called legal trade was to be done in ships licensed by the Portuguese. Pearson argues that the Portuguese, in order to enforce this system, conquered most of the port cities of the coast. Moreover, they built forts at Sofala and Mozambique island and established factories on other coastal sites where some of them were fortified, for instance on Zanzibar (Pearson 1998:131–132). The monopoly of trade was, gradually, removed from the Swahili traders and put in the hands of European companies. Later on, after 1800 AD, most economic and political activities were dominated by Omani Arabs and Indians.

Before this period and until 1650, Portugal had dominated not only along the East African coast, but also on the coast of Oman. Gradually its domination diminished and around 1850 the Portuguese lost their last stronghold of Muscat. Following this event, the Omanis came even to East Africa to challenge the Portuguese. Oman, being the enemy of the Portuguese and other Europeans, started attacking Portuguese settlements on the East African coast and, eventually, this ended the Portuguese influence along the Swahili coast (Pearson 1998: 159). It should be noted, however, that the Swahili rulers had already invited the Omanis to exercise their Muslim responsibility to assist their Muslim brethren. The Omanis did not leave the Swahili coast after they accomplished the task of expelling the Portuguese. Rather, they stayed on and with time established dominance over most of the Swahili coast and thus the trading empire (ibid). Only petty trade was left in the hands of the Swahili. In some towns trade was left to the Swahili people, but they had to satisfy the masters of the new order.

In the new order, the towns of the Swahili, which had not given way to invaders, were suppressed to the extent that they fell into ruins. This was a consequence of the establishment of other prosperous settlements mostly controlled first by the new Portuguese and, then, by the Omani powers that emerged. It was to these towns that the new elite, whether foreign or local, would move (Chami et al. 2004). As Kilwa and other settlements of its type decayed, with only short periods of revival, previously unknown towns emerged from about 1700. Such towns included Zanzibar, Bagamoyo and Kilwa Kivinje. Mombasa also grew substantially. These towns, except Zanzibar, were founded by the British and German colonialists' enterprising.[1] From the 1890s these later Swahili towns were challenged by the new colonial towns such as Dar-es-Salaam, Nairobi and Kampala. An explanation of the rise and the fall of the Swahili towns has been attempted elsewhere (for further reading, see Chami et al. 2004).

Discussion

I have in this chapter re-conceptualized the Swahili world. This is not the first time I have done this (see Chami 1998, 2002), but then I reacted less to previous conceptions of the Swahili world and rather provided the now established, less controversial conception. The present chapter provides a summarized view of current knowledge which is the result of collation of data from history, archaeology, linguistics and architecture. Given recent research, new methodological approaches and interpretations, the Swahili coast which used to be seen as mainly non-African with regard to cultural history (Chittick 1974), can now, more clearly, be related to other African, especially Bantu, cultures. Today, we can show that Swahili societies which were previously claimed to have emerged with Islam, have had their roots in ancient times with settlements throughout all the historical periods and in nearly every part of the coast and islands (see Chami 2006b). I have earlier demonstrated this and the understanding is now widely accepted (see Sutton 1998, Kusimba 1999, Spear 2000, Horton and Middleton 2000 and Phillipson 2005) due to the incontrovertible data established recently by my work and that of my colleagues at Dar-es-Salaam University and the Ministry of Museums and Antiquities of Tanzania and Zanzibar.

New archaeological sites in the Bagamoyo region, the Rufiji Delta region, Zanzibar and Mafia islands have provided invaluable data which awaits further and better exploration. Furthermore, the examination of historical records from Egyptians to near modern times has been recast. Data and information that was either ignored or doubted by previous scholars concerning the cultural history and constitution of Swahili settlements and towns have been discussed and somehow rectified (Chami 2002b). When put together, the two categories of data mentioned above, have enabled scholars to re-examine other categories of data discussed above. Following

---

1. Zanzibar grew out of an invitation from the indigenous polity of Tumbatu to the Omanis to help the Zanzibaris to drive away the Portuguese. Following on from this, the pre-existing small fishing settlement at Shangani began to be settled by Omani elites in the 1690s.

on from recent knowledge and contrary to earlier interpretations provided mainly by Western trained researchers, it has now, in short, been acknowledged that the Swahili coast has had a long history and that the societies and cultures along the coast facing the wider Indian Ocean region grew, in the first place, from Africa and not from abroad. Important influences arrived from abroad as noted earlier, and forms of interactions were established across the ocean. However, it is crucial to bear in mind that societies along the Swahili coast were never only oriented towards the ocean, but also towards the interior of Africa.

The references made to Kilwa in this work have merely been used to assist in elaborating the conception of Swahili settlements and towns as being African based. Kilwa represents a significant source of information about the past, having played a major role in the coordination of 'the Swahili coast activities' especially during what can be seen as the hey-day of a more or less integrated Swahili culture. Yet, in a more recent period, when a new conception of the Swahili towns was being developed, Kilwa was left behind and, surprisingly, it was not re-excavated. Our understanding of Kilwa and its society was until recently based on Neville Chittick's work (1974). One major problem with Chittick's interpretation is that it, according to my view, can be said to represent the view of a Eurocentric scholarship. This view which was, perhaps, partly formed by political influences at the time seems to have affected both the interpretations of existing data as well as having also allowed other scholars to ignore important existing sources such as chronicles and oral narratives providing insights into, for instance, self-perceptions of the Swahili people. The historical analyses previously presented and which I re-conceptualize in my work, were, I argue, usually based on assumptions rather than research, claiming that Africa was a form of colonialist construct.

Hence, for me there were two main reasons why I thought that a re-examination of Kilwa would be essential in order to complete the new understanding of the Swahili coast as portrayed above. The first reason was that Kilwa must have been an important Swahili town. The second reason was that Chittick's interpretation remained unchallenged. My archaeological research in Kilwa from 2004 till today suggests that its history is similar to that of the region as a whole. This island had been settled continuously from the Stone Age until the Swahili period. Moreover, recent excavations and findings show that remains from all of the various historical periods of the Swahili coast and those of the rest of Africa known to us, can be found in Kilwa.

Archaeological research is not able to tell who the people settling in the various sites during the different periods were, but one aspect is clear: Kilwa island, like other parts of sub-Saharan Africa, developed Stone Age technology. And, so far, no scholar has suggested that the Stone Age was introduced to Africa through processes of migration from abroad. Furthermore, the neolithic period in Kilwa is similar to that of the Rift Valley, the Great Lakes region, the Nile and the Sahara. The ceramics being discussed in this chapter are typically African, with a round bottom, no handles or spouts and are coarse ware. No archaeologists from other continents have claimed this type of ware apart from existing early arguments arguing that it was from the Middle Eastern origins of domestication.

The Early Iron Working period is again the same as that found all over sub-Saharan Africa with people smelting iron and domesticating animals. In general, scholars so far have accepted that this tradition is African and thus even named it "Bantu". The subsequent Triangular Incised Ware period has clearly been demonstrated to have been derived, at least on the central and southern coast, from the Early Iron Working tradition. As I noted earlier this pottery's ancestral role in the Swahili culture of the second millennium AD is no longer doubted.

The Islamic period of Kilwa and that of the rest of the Swahili world followed other periods in a long history of cultural change, exchange and interaction. The main idea is that Kilwa's population over time was composed of people from the mainland as well as, especially later on, from other areas within the Indian Ocean region. The cultural history of Kilwa should be understood along the same lines: Kilwa derived most of its cultural and aesthetic orientation from within and, of course, received from the outside world as much as it had to offer. Although Swahili people interrelated and intermarried with traders and migrants arriving from abroad this can, nevertheless, not qualify an interpretation claiming that the cultural history of the Swahili should be understood with reference to places beyond the East African coast only.

In concluding, I wish to emphasize that here are no 'pure' populations on earth. When, or if, such a situation ever occurs we shall develop into human races. For now 'races' do not exist in human the species (Johanson and Edgar 1996) and the theories and intentions of those who have been forcing this concept onto African history have been critically discussed elsewhere (Chami 2006a).

Conclusion

Recent research on the culture and history of the Swahili coast has revealed new and significant information which has been used to modify and extend our knowledge about Swahili people. This clearly suggests that there is a need to continue to critically engage the previous scholarship in terms of its paradigm and research methodologies. As I have argued elsewhere, previous scholarship tended to claim that even in areas where complex social organizations were found to exist, such as along the Swahili coast and in Zimbabwe, these derived from people who hailed from outside Africa (Chami 2006a). Some of the reasons for what I see as a failure to understand the history of Africa and the way the continent was settled emanate from biases, including ethnocentric prejudices. These prejudices, I hold, come to the surface in cases when new discoveries are dismissed or rejected simply because, I argue, they challenge existing, preconceived ideas of Western based scholarship concerning African society and culture (Chami 2006a). Furthermore, it is also important to keep in mind that there has, so far, been limited research in sub-Saharan Africa, mainly in the area of archaeology. This fact could, however, be linked to the notion that there was no history to be discovered through excavation in Africa. An example worth mentioning is that the archaeology of later pre-history began in Eastern Africa only in the 1960s, under a British programme called Bantu Studies.

Yet, it has now been shown that the Swahili has had a long history dating back thousands of years. This history is, I contend, mostly an African history but an African history that must be understood with reference to the wider Indian Ocean region. The history of Swahili culture and society can help us learn how people from Africa engaged with the rest of the ancient world culturally and economically. Probably most histories in the world have been treated likewise, but, still, I hold, the Swahili and the rest of sub-Saharan Africa have lagged behind when it comes to developing and integrating the more recent findings and learning referred to above. The reason for this weakness has been discussed extensively elsewhere (Chami 2006a).

References

Abungu, George, 1994–5, "Agriculture and Settlement Formation along the East African Coast," *Azania,* vol. 29–30 pp. 248–256.

Allen, James, de V., 1974, "Swahili Culture Reconsidered", *Azania,* vol. 9, pp.105–38.

Allen, James, de V., 1983, *Swahili Origins*. London: James Curry Ltd.

Casson, Lionel, 1989, *Periplus Maris Erythreai*. Princeton: University Press.

Chami, Felix, 1994, *The Tanzanian Coast in the First Millennium AD*, Studies in African Archaeology 7. Uppsala: Societas Archaeologica Uppsaliensis.

Chami, Felix, 1998, "A review of Swahili archaeology," *African Archaeological Review* Vol. 15, No. 3 pp.199–218.

Chami, Felix, 1999a, "The Early Iron Age on Mafia Island and its Relationship with the Mainland", *Azania* vol. 34, pp. 1–11.

Chami, Felix, 1999b, "Roman Beads from the Rufiji Delta: First Incontrovertible Archaeological Link with Periplus", *Current Anthropology* vol. 4 no. 2, pp. 239–241.

Chami, Felix, 2002, "Kaole and the Swahili World", in Felix Chami and Gilbert Pwiti (eds), *Southern Africa and the Swahili World. Studies in the African Past 2.* Dar-es-Salaam: University Press, pp. 1–14.

Chami, Felix, 2004, "The Egypto-Graeco-Romans and Panchaea/Azania: Sailing in the Erythraean Sea", in Paul Lunde and A. Porter (eds), *Trade and Travel in the Red Sea Region*, BAR International Series 1269. Oxford: Archaeopress, pp. 93–103.

Chami, Felix et al., 2004, *Historical Archaeology of Bagamoyo: Excavations at the caravan serai.* Dar-es-Salaam: University Press.

Chami, Felix, 2006a, *The Unity of African Ancient History: 3000 BC to AD 500.* Dar es Salaam: E & D Limited.

Chami, Felix, 2006b, "The archaeology of Pre-Islamic Kilwa", in Jill Kinahan and John Kinahan (eds), *African Archaeology Network: Research in Progress, Studies in the African Past 5.* Windhoek: Dar-es-Salaam University Press, pp. 119–150.

Chittick. Neville, 1974, *Kilwa*, 2 Vol. Nairobi: British Institute in Eastern Africa.

Chittick, Neville.1975, "The Peopling of the East African Coast", In Neville Chittick and R. Rotberg (eds), *East Africa and the Orient: Cultural Syntheses in Pre-colonial Times.* New York: Africana Publishing Company, pp. 76–114.

Chittick, Neville, 1984, *Manda: Excavations at an Island Port on the Kenya Coast.* Nairobi: British Institute in Eastern Africa.

Flury, S., 1921, "The Kufic Inscriptions of Kisimkazi Mosque, Zanzibar, 500 H. (A.D. 1107)", *Journal of the Royal Asiatic Society of Great Britain and Ireland* vol. 21, pp. 257–264.

Fuwei, Shen, 1996, *Cultural Flow between China and Outside World Throughout History.* Beijing: Foreign Languages Press.

Galarke, Peter, 1966, *The Early Islamic Architecture of the East African Coast.* Oxford: British Institute in Eastern Africa.

Gibb, A., 1939, *Ibn Battuta Travels Asia and Africa.* London: George Routledge and sons.

Horton, Mark, 1987, "Early Muslim Trading Settlements on the East African Coast: New Evidence from Shanga", *Antiquaries Journal,* vol. 67, pp. 290–322.

Horton, Mark, 1990, The Periplus and East Africa", *Azania,* vol. 25, 95–9.

Horton, Mark, 1996, *Shanga: The Archaeology of a Muslim Trading Community on the Coast of East Africa.* London: British Institute in Eastern Africa.

Horton, Mark, 2006, "The Archaeology of Eastern Africa's Maritime Landscapes", paper presented at the conference *The Maritime Heritage and Cultures of the Western Indian Ocean in Comparative Perspective*, Zanzibar 11th–13th July 2006.

Horton, Mark and John Middleton, 2000, *The Swahili. The Social Landscape of a Mercantile Society.* Cambridge: Blackwell.

Johanson, Donald, and Blake Edgar, 1996, *From Lucy to Language.* New York: Simon and Schuster Editions.

Kusimba, Chapurukha. 1999, *The Rise and Fall of Swahili States.* London: Altamira Press.

Nurse, Derick, and Thomas Spear, 1985, *The Swahili.* Philadephia: University of Pennsylvania Press.

Msemwa, Paul, 1994, "An Ethnoarchaeological Study of Shellfish Collection in a Complex Urban Setting", unpublished Ph.D. Dissertation, Brown University, Providence.

Pearson, Michael, N., 1998, *Port Cities and Intruders: The Swahili Coast, India, and Portugal in the Early Modern Era.* Baltimore: The Johns Hopkins University Press.

Phillipson, David, 1977, *The Later Prehistory of Eastern and Southern Africa.* London: Heinemann.

Phillipson, David, 2005, *African Archaeology.* Cambridge: Cambridge University Press

Pouwels, Randal, 1987, *Horn and Crescent: Cultural Change and Traditional Islam on the East African Coast.* Cambridge: University Press, 800–900.

Pradines, Stephan, 2002, "La Bipartition des Cites Swahili: l' Example de Gedi", in Felix Chami and Gilbert Pwiti (eds), *Southern Africa and the Swahili World, Studies in the African Past 2.* Dar-es-Salaam: University Press, pp. 66–75.

Radimilahy, Chantal,1998, *Mahilaka.* Uppsala: Department of Archaeology and Ancient History.

Sinclair, Paul, and Thomas Håkansson, 2000, "The Swahili City-state Culture", in M. Hansen (ed.), *A Comparative Study of Thirty City-state Cultures.* Copenhagen: The Royal Academy, pp. 463–482.

Soper, Robert, 1971, "A general review of Early Iron Age of the Southern Half of Africa", *Azania,* vol. 5 pp. 5–37.

Spear, Thomas, 2000, "Early Swahili History Reconsidered." *The International Journal of African Historical Studies,*vol. 33 no. 2, pp. 257–290.

Sutton, John, 1998, "Kilwa", *Azania,* vol. 33, pp.113–169.

Wheatley, Peter, 1975, "Analecta Sino-Africana Recensa", in H.N. Chittick and R. Rotberg (eds), *East Africa and the Orient: Cultural synthesis in pre-colonial times.* New York: African Publishing House, pp. 76–114.

– CHAPTER 3 –

Towards a Paradigm of
Swahili Religious Knowledge
Some Observations

Farouk Topan

The Swahili are, by definition, a people whose source of identity is rooted in ethnic or racial diversity. Correspondingly, their 'knowledge' – i.e. a body of facts, information, philosophy and worldview through which and by which they lead their lives – also has its origins among diverse peoples, including Africans, Arabs, Persians, Indians and, more recently, Americans and Europeans from various nations. Thus, the scope of the subject is truly wide. However, in this paper, I confine my remarks to the religious knowledge of the Swahili, and, more specifically, to the premises of that knowledge forged through the interaction of indigenous culture with Islam, the dominant religion of the Swahili of the east coast of Africa.

Some basic questions prompt themselves when considering this topic: what are these premises? How do they, derived as they are from varied sources, cohere into what we might consider a working whole? Does this knowledge, or its premises, change – as Saleh would say, *kufuatana na wakati* 'going with the times' (2004:145–155)?

A huge amount of material related to Swahili knowledge, as well as knowledge of the Swahili, has been published over the past few decades by scholars seeking to understand Swahili identity, ideas, beliefs, rituals, practices, perceptions of history, and the role of communities and individuals in history. To be sure, not all studies address themselves directly to the epistemological aspect of the subject, as do those of Purpurra (1997) and Kai Kresse (2007). They have focused on various facets of Swahili knowledge and have thereby helped to construct a picture of what the Swahili 'know', 'believe' and 'perceive'. Jan Knappert's anthologies of Swahili Islamic poetry constitute a good example of such studies (1967, 1971); for, whatever their shortcomings, they nonetheless bring to the fore original material reflecting the premises upon which the poets base their knowledge. Some of the anthropological studies also highlight a useful tool of analysis in the study of Swahili knowledge: the dual concepts of *mila* 'custom' and *dini* 'religion'.

Mila has been conventionally understood as representing, or as expressing, customs that are largely indigenous to the Swahili, particularly on the coast. To some, *mila* represents 'African' customs, as, in some cases, the practices subsumed by this term are also found elsewhere on the African mainland. *Dini*, on the other hand, as the term implies, refers to the beliefs and practices that *are understood* as Islamic, i.e. brought to the coast by Arabs as the message of Islam. This neat and convenient distinction has been a useful tool in the analysis of facets of Swahili culture, especially in contexts where a high degree of interaction exists between the two in the same ritual. This paper provides an example of such a practice drawn from the phenomenon of spirit possession, a phenomenon whose premises are derived from *mila*, with significant adaptations from *dini*.

I begin by quoting from an article by Linda Giles in which she argues against the theory - propounded mainly by Lewis – that spirit possession cults are marginal to the society in which they occur. Giles refutes this, stating that the cults are not only central to the wider society but they form "one of its most illuminating expressions" (Giles 1987:234). In order to understand what these expressions are about, we need to study the phenomenon, not in isolation, but, as Michael Lambek suggests (1993:60), "within the wider system of meaning" of the society in which it occurs, in this case, the Swahili.

The question which then arises is applicable not only to the Swahili but to many other societies – Hausa, Somali, among them – which have had a deep and intensive interaction with Islam: does Islam provide a complete "system of meaning" for the people concerned? Theologically, the answer is a positive 'yes' since the teachers and practitioners of Islam view it as 'a complete way of life'. On the other hand, if we are to examine this question in terms of the culture of the people themselves, then the answer has to be 'no' or 'not quite'. To understand why not, we need to understand the general process of how Islam was accepted by the people among to whom it was taught. Wherever it spread, Islam was preached and taught, at least initially, within the pre-existing culture of the people. This is equally true of its beginnings; thus, even in Arabia of the 7th century, Islam was not preached nor received in a vacuum. Its teachings interacted in Mecca and the Hijaz with the pre-established culture of the so-called period of 'ignorance' (*jahiliyya*). And, as Izutsu has pointed out in his works (1964; 2002), among the features that Islam adopted from that culture were the notion of paradise and hell, the performance of the pilgrimage to Mecca (the *hajj*), and, concomitant with these, the central status and location of the Kaaba, the cubical building in Mecca in whose direction Muslims face in prayer five times a day (as *qibla*). These became major facets in the expression of Islamic theology.

A similar process took place in Africa. The difference – and it is a major, significant difference – is that, by the time Islam reached Africa, its core theology was already largely formulated, consisting of the 'five pillars': belief in one God (with Muhammad as His messenger), prayers, fasting, giving in charity (*zakat*), and the performance of the pilgrimage (*hajj*) for those who could afford it. But even this 'core' came encased in customs prevalent in the region in Arabia from which the preachers of the faith hailed. It was elements of this 'package' that interacted with local African customs and culture in a similar way that the core teachings had done with the culture of Mecca and the Hijaz. This would have resulted in an interactive dynamics of the two systems on the East African coast, the 'imported' Arabo-Islamic on the one hand, and the 'indigenous' African on the other. In that inter-action, some facets of the indigenous culture would have been modified to take account of, or to align them to, the teachings of Islamic theology, or even to Arab customary practices. We await archaeological and historical evidence to support this hypothesis, but clues from history do exist. For in-stance, it is said that there had existed long ago among the Swahili a system – some say a matrilineal system – in which women had occupied positions of influence and authority.[1] One such was the office of *mwana*, translated as 'queen'; Swahili coastal towns had a number of 'queens' mentioned in liter-ary texts. The 'queen' of Mombasa was Mwana Mkisi, of Zanzibar, Mwana Aziza. Thus, at the time of the Omani invasion of the East African coast, the Mombasan poet Muyaka bin Haji (d. 1840) appealed to the Zanzibaris as the 'children of Mwana Aziza' not to ally themselves with the Omanis against their kin in Mombasa, 'the children of Mwana Mkisi' (Abdulaziz 1979:129–131, 147). The system did not endure as the Arabs, being more patriarchal and patrilineal in orientation, gradually replaced the older sys-tem. It would be illuminating to know what other similar changes occurred in this respect but, unfortunately, the evidence at our disposal so far does not permit us to do so. Except, perhaps, in the case of spirit possession, where one can make some tentative observations.

Spirit possession is interesting in this respect as it also existed in pre-Islamic Arabia. We know from the Qur'an that this phenomenon was known to the Meccans during the life-time of the Prophet. And yet, unlike

---

1. This might have been connected to a matrilateral or matrilineal system then in existence (Shepherd 1977:344–358).

the *hajj*, the Kaaba, and notions of paradise and hell, it was not incorporated within Islamic practices. The reason for this exclusion seems to lie in the perception that a human being is possessed by an external entity other than the recognized divine authority. Indeed, some Meccans rejected the Message of the Prophet for that very reason, arguing that the Prophet was simply being possessed by a jinn, hence, *majnun,* one possessed, mad; and, further, that the recitations by the Prophet as poetry) were 'from' such spirits . The Qur'an explicitly denies this allegation (68:2; 81:22). To have then incorporated even the possibility of such an occurrence would have meant creating another source of the message and authority, parallel to the one recognized as divine and unique. As this would have created conflict, spirit possession had therefore to be placed outside of the accepted theology, of what is today called "orthodox" Islam. In other words, the principle underlying 'Islamic knowledge' (in this case, the recitations which formed the Qur'an) did not permit the existence of a dual source of knowledge and, by extension, of a fragmented divine authority.

In East Africa today spirit possession exists among both Muslims and non-Muslim societies. We do not know whether the phenomenon existed prior to the introduction of Islam in East Africa; it most likely did, and, as in Arabia, it was not incorporated in mainstream Islam on the East African coast. But it is also interesting that neither has spirit possession been discarded, the way 'matriliny' or its equivalent was. The phenomenon of spirit possession exists because it fulfills a need in Swahili society – a cultural, cosmological need – that is not being met by the teachings and practices of orthodox Islam. And, interestingly, this need is felt as much by ordinary Muslims as it is by teachers of Islam in the higher levels of the hierarchy.

Spirit possession has not been discarded but it has certainly been influenced as a result of its interaction with Islam. Put slightly differently, one can say that spirit possession has been modified or adapted to a degree that makes it 'practisable' by ordinary Muslims without a feeling of serious discomfort about its 'incompatability' or 'incongruity' with Islam.

The 'Charter'

One of the factors that makes spirit possession practisable by Muslims is its 'charter', a text that gives it its 'legitimacy' or rationale. The text, as quoted to me in Mombasa during fieldwork in the late 1960s, consists of verses from the Qur'an, 34:12–14:

12. And (We made) the wind (subservient) to Solomon; it made a month's journey in the morning and a month's journey in the evening; and We made a fountain of molten brass to flow for him. And of the *jinn* were those who worked in front of him by the command of his Lord. And whoever turned aside from Our command from among them, We made him taste of the chastisement of burning.

13. They (the *jinn*) made for him (Solomon) what he pleased, of arches and images, and bowls (large) as water-troughs and cooking-pots. Give thanks, O people of David, and very few of my servants are grateful.

14. But when we decreed death for him (Solomon), naught showed them his death but a creature of the earth that kept (slowly) gnawing away at his staff: so when he fell down, the *jinn* saw plainly that, if they had known the unseen, they would not have tarried in humiliating torment.
(Translation by Abdullah Yusuf Ali)

Let me hasten to add that not every Muslim practitioner of spirit-possession in East Africa quotes this verse, just as, indeed, not every practising Muslim quotes from the writings of Imam Shafi'i, the founder of the School to which most of the coastal Swahili belong. The practitioners of spirit possession borrow from the pool of knowledge essential to Islam, and through it, provide a rationale for the existence of the spirits, and, hence of spirit possession. Thus, *mila* draws on *dini* for its legitimacy and acceptance where appropriate.

The gloss on the story, which I received in Mombasa, was that, once the jinns realized that Solomon was dead, they spread all over the world; the most powerful of them went and settled in Pemba from where they travelled all over East Africa to possess people. The Qur'anic mention of spirits has also provided the Swahili - and probably other Muslim communities as well – not only with a rationale for their existence but also with a set of terminology which has now become part of the discourse on (and of) spirit possession, e,g, *jinni, shetani, ibilisi*. Interestingly, the Swahili name for spirits has been retained: *pepo*, which forms a generic term for the phenomenon as a whole, inclusive of spirits. Another term is *nyama* – animal, beast – which is used when referring to the undesirable behaviour of the spirit. The co-existence of the terms again points to a syncretic convergence of knowledge from the 'Bantu' and Islamic traditions.[1] But we need to go deeper than just to note this fact; there is now need to interrogate and explore the premises

---

1. Cf. the word for 'God' in Swahili (Frankl 1995, Topan 1992).

that underlie this syncretism, a process not dissimilar to that termed 'hybridity' by some scholars, most notably Bhabha (1994).

Another derivation from the Qur'an is from a chapter which is itself called "The Jinn" (Chapter 72). It opens with a statement from the Prophet that it had been revealed to him that a company of the jinns had listened to the Qur'an and found it a wonderful recital. After listening to the recitation, they became Muslim and believers. Similarly, among the Swahili, there are spirits who are Muslims and those who are not. But, being good or bad is not considered a prerogative of either. Just as among humans, so too, among spirits, there are those who are good and those who are evil among both Muslims and non-Muslims. There is an inter-play of roles in this respect between spirits and humans in relation to their characters: a good spirit can be controlled by an evil human – the *mchawi* (sorcerer) – and made to perform evil acts. The converse is also held to exist: that a good human is afflicted by an evil spirit. However, both do things that are *mambo ya kishetani*, 'diabolical actions', which only non-humans would do. Drinking the blood of a slaughtered animal is one such act, which, of course, is against the teachings of Islam. The given rationale is that it is not the human being who drinks the blood, or brandy in the Kibuki cult, but it is the spirit who performs such acts.[1] Here again we need to pose a question: what is the premise that lies behind this answer? What does it say of the relationship between *mila* and *dini* generally, or about the worldview of that individual or group? One thing it does is to point to conceptual areas where it is possible to re-negotiate a subject, or a deed, that has been considered taboo in society. Here *mila* gets around a taboo imposed by *dini*.

The relationship between the spirit world and the human world is such that one is a mirror-image of the other, i.e spirits are believed to have a world which is organized very much like that of the humans. They have gender - male/female; have families, clans and tribes, with leaders (*wazee*); they have dwellings - at sea and on land. In a sense, one can talk of a vertical continuum among the Swahili where the celestial world of God and the Prophet is at the top, with that of the spirits below them, and humans, with their frailties and weaknesses, below that of the spirits. God is omnipotent, and He is One; there is absolutely no compromise on the concept of *tawhid*, the oneness of God. In fact, some cults begin their singing sessions by a song addressed to God, or in reference to him. I give two such songs below:

---

1. The Kibuki spirit cult, popular in Zanzibar, is believed to have been brought there from the Comoros; its origins are said to be in Madagascar.

1.
Muombeleni Mngu.   You (pl.) pray to God
hata apoe   until she gets cured.

2.
Niombwe t'umwa   Let me pray to the Prophet
Na Mngu mwema   And to God, the good
Niombeleni waganga nao/   And you, *waganga*, pray to them
                                      for me
Waombeleni waganga nao   (variant) And pray for the
                                      waganga as well.
                                      (Topan 1996:119)

Closest to God in the divine hierarchy is the Prophet. Opinions differ as to who should be placed in closest proximity to the Prophet. The *'ulama* - the clerics - would put a pious and knowledgeable individual, an *'alim,* in that place; the Sufi would place a well-known devout Sufi in that position, and, in the case of the cults it is not surprising that the spirits and the *waganga* – their mediums – are placed there. Thus, individuals from the realm of *mila* also occupy the position of proximity to the Prophet.

Such elevated status focuses attention on the role of the *waganga* among the Swahili. The study of John Janzen (1992:193), based on Guthrie's classification, shows the wide geographical spread of the cognates of the term *nganga* in 'Bantu' language societies. Given the commonality of this term – and hence of the practice of healing over a wide geographical area – it is not surprising that there are many facets of what the Swahili called *uganga*. Although the basic notion refers to 'medicine' and 'healing', the way that the healing is practised differs from one society to another, sometimes in minor ways. More significantly, the knowledge on which healing is based also differs, and it is this which gives the phenomenon its *raison d'être* in that particular society. In the Swahili Muslim society, as we have seen, the Qur'an itself is made to provide the charter for the existence and presence of spirits in the area. To the Swahili, as to other peoples who practise *uganga*, the term covers a host of fields and skills. One who practises *uganga* – the *mganga* – is considered a healer, a herbalist, a leader of his/her group of followers (*kilinge*), a diviner, and a ritual leader. Each of these roles presupposes a certain kind of knowledge – be it of plants, of people, of ritual processes, of cosmology, etc, corresponding to, but not totally coinciding with, what Janzen calls the "varieties of knowledge within ngoma" (Ibid:1992:131).

There are both full-time and part-time *waganga* in Swahili society; the latter practise the craft/art while being employed in other professions. The full-time *mganga* is likely to have grown up in a family or in an environment where *uganga* is practised. He/she would have joined the cult after his/her initiation and perhaps would have been associated with it in some ways even before that. Another route is open to both men and women, but my impression is that it is mostly women who take it. A woman who has been initiated in the cult then becomes a *mganga* by moving through the hierarchy and, if she is able and successful, becomes a *mganga* and attracts a following. Yet another way, reported by Kjersti Larsen (2001:287–292), is through the spirits themselves where they 'teach' the rudiments of *uganga* (and also of *dini*) to the chosen medium, thus placing her on the path to becoming a *mganga*.

I found in the 1960s that female *waganga* in Mombasa were almost always subordinate to the male waganga; they had to have a male mganga officiate at a ceremony formally conducted and "owned" by them. By the 1980s, when Giles conducted her research, the situation had changed, and matters had moved on. Female waganga were officiating and conducting their ceremonies themselves[1]; they had a large following. This is now so all over the coast. The head of the popular Kibuki cult in Zanzibar was a woman; she held that position until her death. She thrived on the cult - she used to get invited to the Gulf to conduct her ceremonies there. The daughter of a mganga whom I had known in Mombasa has inherited her father's cult, and has a large following of her own.

It may be noted that some Qur'anic teachers are also waganga, either openly or secretly. This, in fact, represents a facet of what I have elsewhere called a "religious network" (Topan 1991) where an individual has roles within both uganga and the Islamic hierarchy of the transmitters of knowledge and blessings (*baraka*).

An important ceremony of the spirit possession cult is the *pungwa* which is, simultaneously, a healing and an initiation ceremony. Its duration varies: some are held for three, others for five and some for seven days. The aim is to get the spirit to come up to the head of the *mwele*, the initiate, (from her/his stomach) and to declare his/her name. Once this is done, the *pungwa* is said to have been successful. The spirit would then stop inflicting the illness or the condition on the *mwele* (literally, sick person) and the *mwele* her- or himself would now be initiated into the hierarchy of the cult. A cow or goat

---

1. Personal communication

is slaughtered during the early hours of the morning of the last day, and the blood is sipped by those present.

Two Islamic acts take place in the *pungwa* ceremony. The first day of the *pungwa* begins with the recitation of the Fatiha, the first chapter of the Qur'an. Incense is burnt while the recitation takes place, and the incense burner is then placed at the door of the room or place where the ceremony is to take place during the week. The spirit of the officiating *mganga* is then said to stand guard over the ceremony and to foil the attempts of rival waganga from "stealing" or "luring" away the spirit of the initiate from that place. Then follow songs of "prayers" which we mentioned earlier. Apart from these overt acts, there is little in the ceremony which one would say is theologically Islamic as such.

In view of the above, then, what conclusions do we draw regarding the perception of *mila* and *dini* within spirit possession? Or, if we may widen the question, what do we draw from the construction of the roles of *mila* and *dini* in the religious sphere of the Swahili? As stated earlier, the research of many scholars has made it possible now to start to explore the cohesion of Swahili knowledge and the premises that underlie it.

Generally speaking, knowledge in *dini* derives from the teachings of Islam. Though varied, it is divisible into the essentialist 'core' and, for want of a better term, 'general' other elements. The principle of *tawhid*, the unity, indivisibility and oneness of God, for instance, belongs to the core. It is acknowledged as such in the spirit cult, as the songs quoted above show. But the cult also reveals a hierarchy which is already present within the general teachings of Islam. The Muslim testimony of faith, the *shahada*, makes a categorical statement of the top two ranks of the hierarchy: 'There is no deity except God, and Muhammad is his messenger'. Different sects and groups in Islam have posited a third rank – perhaps not always in a formulaic and overt way - and placed their spiritual leaders in that position. Andrzejewski (1983:11-12), for example, cites a Somali verse in praise of Shaykh Uweys whose translation he gives as follows:

> O God, we turn to you through the intercession of our sheekh
> Our Uweys, beloved of the Qadiriyah disciples.
> In his name I invoke help in every calamity.
> Through his worthiness bring us relief in our concerns,
> Through his mysteries grant me success in my pursuits
> In this world and the world to come, and cure the disease of our hearts.

The spirit cults have followed that example. If a devout Sufi scholar and *walii* could be placed in the third position of the hierarchy close to the Prophet, then why not the spirits or the *waganga* in the spirit cults of Mombasa? As we have seen, some features of *dini* such as the burning of incense and the recitation of the Qur'an have been adopted in the ceremonies of the cult.

But the cult has also to be viewed in its own right as a vehicle of 'religious' expression operating through *mila* with its own essentialist core. Part of that core is built around the relationship between the healer (*mganga*) and her or his spirit, and between this pair and the client (*mwele*) and her or his spirit. This relationship, partly based on healing and also on the possibility of initiation into a cult, possesses its own reservoir of knowledge, encompassing fields related to herbs, astronomy, musical requirements, etc. Some of it is tapped from the general domain of *dini*, or from customs of the people whom the spirits represent (Arabs, mainland Africans, Europeans, etc). Most of it is from its own traditional sources of *mila*, passed by word of mouth, from generation to generation.

Perhaps the point to be made in conclusion relates to the position of the individual in society who is the focus of both *mila* and *dini*. Each of these concepts has its own essentialist core, supported by a heritage of knowledge from which it draws – a traditional corpus that is largely transmitted orally in the case of *mila*, and a formal ritual core with its canonical requirements and practices in *dini*. Also, the relationship between *mila* and *dini* is built upon premises that need to be 'acceptable' to society in general. However much the theologians might preach against the spirit cults, the latter fulfill a need in Swahili society. Their existence and even the presence of spirits within humans are not seen, as Larsen puts it, as "an abnormal situation" (2001:280). For, in the final analysis, *dini* and *mila* share a common goal for the individual in that both aim to preserve his/her well-being and that of the community to which the individual belongs. Only the boundaries and the means of achieving those aims differ. And it is the difference which forms the area of negotiation for Swahili men and women as they go through their daily lives.

References

Abdulaziz, M.H, 1979, *Muyaka. 19th Century Swahili Popular Poetry.* Nairobi: Kenya Literature Bureau.

Ali, Abdullah Yusuf, 1977, *The Holy Qur'an. Translation and Commentary.* American Trust Publications for the Muslim Students' Association of the U.S. and Canada.

Andrzejewski, B.W., 1983, *Islamic Literature of Somalia.* Hans Wolff Memorial Lecture. Bloomington: Indiana University.

Bhabha, Homi K.,1994, *The Location of Culture.* London: Routledge.

Caplan, Pat, 1995, "Law and custom: Marital disputes on Mafia island, Tanzania" in P. Caplan (ed.), *Understanding Disputes: The Politics of Law.* Oxford: Berg Publishers, 203–222.

Frankl, Peter, 1995, "The word for 'God' in Swahili: Further considerations", *Journal of Religion in Africa,* XXV, pp. 331–349.

Giles, Linda, 1987, "Possession cults on the Swahili coast: A re-examination of theories of marginality", *Africa* 57 (2): 202–211.

Horton, Mark and John Middleton, 2000, *The Swahili: The Social Landscape of a Mercantile Society.* Oxford: Blackwell Publishers.

Izutsu, Toshihiko, 1964, *God and Man in the Koran: Studies of the Koranic Weltanschauung.* Tokyo: Keio Institute of Cultural and Linguistic Studies.

――, 2002, *Ethico-religious concepts in the Qur'an.* Montreal: Ithaca, NY: McGill-Queen's University Press, 2002.

Janzen, John M., 1992, *Ngoma. Discourses of Healing in Central and Southern Africa.* Berkeley: University of California Press.

Knappert, Jan, 1967, *Traditional Swahili poetry: An investigation into the concepts of East African Islam as reflected in the Utenzi literature.* Leiden: E.J. Brill.

――, (ed. & tr.), 1971, *Swahili Islamic Poetry.* 3 volumes. Leiden: E.J. Brill.

Kresse, Kai, 2007, *Philosophising in Mombasa. Knowledge, Islam and intellectual practice on the Swahili coast.* Edinburgh: Edinburgh University Press, for the International African Library.

Lambek, Michael, 1993, *Knowledge and practice in Mayotte. Local discourses of Islam, sorcery, and spirit possession.* Toronto: University of Toronto Press.

Larsen, Kjersti, 1998, "Spirit possession as historical narrative: The production of identity and locality in Zanzibar Town" in Nadia Lovell (ed.), *Locality and Belonging.* London: Routledge, pp. 125–147.

――, 2001, "Spirit possession as oral history: Negotiating Islam and social status. The case of Zanzibar" in Biancamaria S. Amoreti (ed.), *Islam in East Africa: New sources.* Roma: Herder, pp. 275–296.

Lienhardt, Peter, 1968, "Introduction" in Hasani bin Ismail, *Swifa ya Nguvumali, The Medicine Man.* Oxford: Clarendon Press.

Middleton, John, 1992: *The World of the Swahili. An African Mercantile Civilization.* New Haven and London: Yale University Press.

Nisula, Tapio, 1999, *Everyday spirits and medical interventions: Ethnographic and historical notes on therapeutic conventions in Zanzibar town.* Transactions of the Finnish Anthropological Society, NRO XLIII. Sarrijavi: Gummerus Kirjapaino Oy.

Purpurra, Allyson, 1997, *Knowledge and Agency: The social relations of Islamic expertise in Zanzibar Town.* Ph.D dissertation, The City University of New York.

Saleh, Mohamed Ahmed, 2004, "'Going with the times': Conflicting Swahili Norms and Values", in P. Caplan and F. Topan (eds), *Swahili Modernities: Culture, politics, and identity on the East Coast of Africa.* Trenton, NJ: Africa World Press, Inc.

Topan, Farouk, 1991 "Réseaux religieux chez les Swahili" ['Religious networks among the Swahili'] in F. Le Guennec-Coppens and P. Caplan (eds), *Les Swahili entre Afrique et Arabie.* Paris: Karthala, pp. 39–57.

Topan, Farouk, 1992, "Swahili as a religious language", *Journal of Religion in Africa,* XXII, pp. 331–349.

Topan, Farouk, 1996, "Muslim Perceptions in a Swahili Oral Genre" in Kenneth Harrow (ed.), *The marabout and the muse.* Portsmouth (New Hampshire): Heinemann, pp. 116–123.

CHAPTER 4

Royal Ancestors and Social Change in the Majunga Area
Northwest Madagascar 19th–20th Centuries

Marie Pierre Ballarin[1]

Introduction

Focusing on the royal ancestors' cults, this paper will discuss how religious traditions are understood and reinterpreted by local communities in relation to social and political changes. First, the purpose is to provide some information about the Sakalava kingdoms, particularly the Boina, which have historically played an important role in the history of the Swahili area. Then the intention is to examine elements of royal symbolism and how they were integrated in the lives of the Sakalava people. Finally, this article will focus on how this knowledge, stemming from the symbolism of Sakalava kingdoms, has affected social and political fields from Independence to today and how ritualized responses have emerged in relation to these changes.

The Sakalava kingdoms flourished from the 17th to the 19th centuries in west Madagascar. They were organised into a series of monarchies that expanded northward, primarily in response to disputes over succession. They settled northward along the west coast, which had been an important area of exchange in terms of trade in the southwest Indian Ocean since medieval times.

In these kingdoms, organised hierarchically, the king was sacred and the universe revolved around him. The power of the king was symbolised by the remains of his ancestors, which were preserved as relics in a sacred place and were used to exercise power over the Sakalava people. The preservation of these relics and the cult around them (the ritual of the bath and the practice of spirit possession) allowed the king to make royalty sacred and to legitimate his power and his authority. This honouring of royal ancestors has been fundamental to the Sakalava culture up until today. At the bottom of the hierarchy were slaves from the maritime trade (mainly Makoa people

---

1. I am really grateful to Pat Caplan and Françoise Le Guennec for the time they took to look at this paper. Unless otherwise noted, all translations are my own.

from Mozambique and south Tanzania), who played an important role in ritual practices (Boyer-Rossol 2007).

Andriantsoly was king of one of these kingdoms, the Boina, in the Majunga area, on the northwest coast; in 1825 he lost his power with the invasion of the Merina kingdom from the highlands of Madagascar. Closely related to the traders from the Swahili coast (called Antalaotra in Madagascar); Andriantsoly converted to Islam and fled to the Comoro Islands, leaving the relics of his ancestors in the hands of the conquerors. However, Merina governors in Majunga controlled the population by keeping watch over the royal relics and the ritual practices and later, in the 20th century, the French colonizers did the same.

In the 19th century, the arrival of a Merina government, which developed rice growing in the prosperous plains along the Betsiboka River, had an important impact in Sakalava society. The main royal families settled further to the north and the people retreated with their cattle to less accessible places in the interior of the Boina. They had become a minority in the area of the former Boina kingdom at the time of independence. Migrants from the highlands and former slave lineages like the Makoa, cultivated land. During the period of colonisation, they competed to work on land owned by Europeans under the metayage system. By the end of French colonisation, societies of the Boina region were mostly composed of non-Sakalava migrants and native lineages that were considered as "possessors of soils". The majority of the Boina's inhabitants settled in towns like Majunga or agricultural centres like Marovoay or Ambato Boeni. After Independence, Andriantsoly's heirs have tried to restore economic and political power but without real success because, during colonisation, former slaves and migrants succeeded, economically, in gaining a new social status. As a result, royal families have had to compete with their former subjects in terms of economic development. This social context has led to the creation of new religious practices, such as the "mirror cult" in the Majunga area, which, despite its link to royal symbolism, is opposed to the former royal values involving the hierarchical system.

The Boina Kingdom, An Actor in Swahili Commercial Exchanges

Growth and loss of the Boina Kingdom

The Northwest coast of Madagascar is part of the Swahili trade zone where Islamic groups founded commercial centres in the Southwest Indian Ocean

Madagascar and the Swahili trade zone

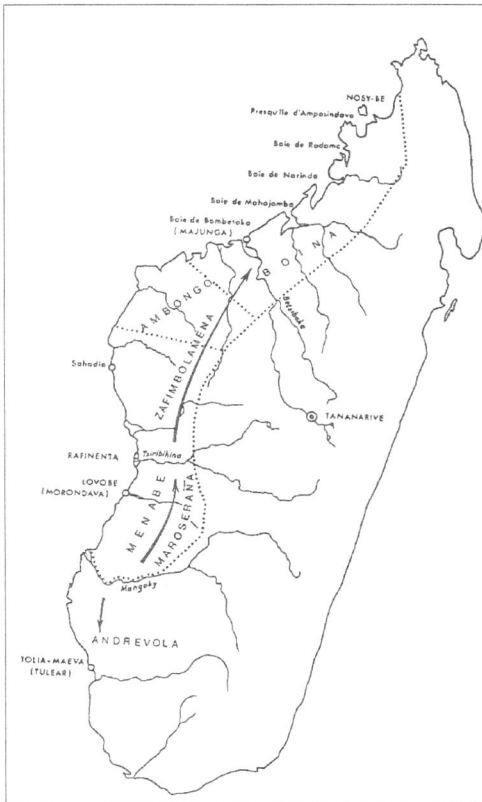

Map extracted from Lombard, 1988.

Since the 13th century, these groups have played an important role in terms of the economy, politics and religion. However, the wealth of Swahili culture of the Northwest coast never equalled that of cities along the East African coast. These traders, the Antalaotra, married Malagasy women and settled on the coast. When the Portuguese arrived in the 16th century, the Antalaotra founded independent commercial towns, which were governed by sheikhs and frequently contained mosques. Later, in the 17th century, Europeans tried to drive them out of these cities.

Conquering dynasties from the Southwestern coast were attracted to the Boina region for its rich pastures. Tsimenate, from the Menabe region further in the south, founded the kingdom of Boina when a conflict with his brother led to his secession. He brought with him relics of his royal ancestors, symbols and sources of power.[1] Then he founded the Zafimbolamena Dynasty, which spread north to Mahajamba Bay, and took control of the coastal trade. In the 18th century these Antalaotra centres were used as stopping points for the European trade and became central to the traffic of goods like fabrics, porcelain and glass, as well as slaves.[2] The Antalaotra founded the city of Majunga, and commercial exchanges became very important between the coast and inland, where the king lived. Majunga is still a cosmopolitan city where many different groups live together; not only Malagasy, but also Arabic and Swahili influences are present. Even today, ancestral cults and Islam exist side by side and most of the inhabitants are Muslim.

In 1780, when Queen Ravahiny took power, the kingdom of Boina was at its peak. However, the extinction of male descendants and quarrels within the Zafimbolamena dynasty weakened its power. In addition, Merina kings from the highlands of Madagascar arrived at the beginning of the 19th century and took control of the island with the help of the British and in 1822, Majunga was conquered. King Andriantsoly went to war, was defeated by the Merina king, Radama I, and fled to Mayotte.[3] His sister Ouantity stayed and settled further north with members of the royal family. Majunga was meanwhile left in the hands of Merina conquerors who took control of the royal ancestral cult, its relics, and thereby gained power. When Radama died, Andriantsoly, who had converted to Islam with the help of a Comorian family, tried to regain power from the Merina. He was defeated a second time by Queen Ranavalona I, fled for the last time to the Comoro Islands and became king of Dzaoudzi. The successive queens

1. These relics were those of Andriamisara, who was the brother of the king of Southern Menabe kingdom. He was a seer and a royal adviser. Tsimenate brought the remains of Andriamisara with him, which permitted him to a legitimate his power over the new territory. In the Menabe, we also can find relics and some of this Andriamisara's remains are kept there. However, the Andriamisara reference in the Boina kingdom is more important ideologically. See Lombard 1988, Ramamonjisoa 1976 and 1985–1986.
2. For more on the slave trade in the Southwest Indian Ocean, see recent work of Vernet 2003 and 2005. See also, Alpers 2001.
3. Noël reports that when Andriantsoly fled for the first time, he contacted the Sultan of Muscat and Zanzibar and advised him at the siege of Mombasa. He asked him for help against the Merina conquest. In return the Sultan demanded: the gift of the city of Majunga and part of the coast, as well as providing the troops with fresh supplies. A Zanzibari expedition on the West coast of Madagascar was detained due to the death of king Radama I (Noël, 1843–1844).

of the Boina kingdom reigned under the influence of the Antalaotra, who often became royal advisers and married the queens, becoming *biby*.[1] This Islamic influence became quite important in the Northwest of the island. The Muslim advisers did not have a direct role in the ancestral cult, but we do see the Swahili influence in the creation of the relics' shrines. When the Merina conquered the West coast, Islam became a means to escape their power, but it did not undermine the ancestors' cult, the medium of the Sakalava identity.

Relics shrines, means of power

Boina shrines hold the remains of four royal ancestors (Andriamisara, Andrianihanina, Andriamandisoarivo, Andrianambonarivo). They are called the "four Andriamisara" or "Andriamisara *efa dahy*" because of the name of the *ombiasy* Andriamisara,[2] who helped the king to conquer and found the kingdom. Silver and gold-plated shrines contain the relics, which were decorated by Arab jewellers. The reliquaries are decorated with coloured beads, coins and gold and silver metals. The power of the relics is like that of a talisman, protecting people from illness and misfortune and providing wealth; they are also the main protection during war. Coins adorn the exterior of the reliquaries and are also placed in the interior on a platter along with sacred water and white clay kaolin, called *tanimalandy* that is sprinkled on the participants of the ceremonies. Vegetable matter, such as wood, roots, honey or oil *(kinana)*[3] can be found within the reliquaries. Sometimes, like in the village of Besalampy, a face is represented or a little mirror, used in divination[4], is attached to the reliquary.

These reliquaries are kept in a miniature wooden house called a *zomba*. This word refers to a small building connected to the royal ancestors' cult. It is kept in a *doany*, a term used in the past for the king's residence. Today, this place, enclosed by a fence which delineates a profane "outside" and a sacred "inside", is reserved for Andriamisara relics and for the ritual that takes place in Majunga. One of the first accounts that speaks of the reliquaries

---

1. The term *biby* refers to a sakalava queen's husband, mainly in the Northwest of Madagascar. *Bibin'ny ampanjaka* means "Queen's animal". About the bemihisatra and bemazava monarchies of Northwest Madagascar, see the works of Baré 1980, Feely-Harnick 1991, Sharp 1996.
2. The term *"Ombiasy"* refers to a seer and a political adviser.
3. Pine kernel, *Jatropha curcas Euphorbiacées*.
4. This personification of the object referring to the king is common in Africa. This kind of mirror is a magical tool that we can find in spirit rituals or funerals. The purpose is to chase bad spirits away.

comes from the words of the captain of a Dutch ship, the *De Brack,* which was anchored in Majunga bay in 1741 during his visit to the royal residence of eastern Marovoay.[1]

> On nous a conduit dans une grande kaaba,[2] toute tendue de toile blanche, du toit jusqu'à terre, afin de la garantir du vent et de la pluie; à l'intérieur il y avait une riche collection de beaux et bons mousquets; nous en avons compté plus de cent; puis, des meubles et des coffres pleins, nous dit-on, de vases et d'objets en argent et un grand trône laqué et doré, tout orné de sculptures, reposant sur deux lions, que les Français ont fait venir spécialement pour lui de Chine et lui ont donné et enfin, le reliquaire royal, qui se compose de quatre écussons représentant chacun un des quatre aïeux du roi : Andian Mesorre, Andian Leyfoetse, Andian Chimenatte et Andian Tokaf : ces quatre "écussons", qui sont attachés chacun au haut d'un poteau, sont en or et en argent et portent quatre grandes dents en or semblables à celle des lamantins (ou plutôt des crocodiles); ils sont recouverts d'un carré d'étoffe de fabrication indigène, sur laquelle sont cousues des piastres et une grosse chaîne d'argent et, au pied de chacun d'eux, sont déposés par terre un collier de verroteries vertes et un vase à brûler de l'encens.

The captain describes the contents of the *zomba* and reports that along with the richly decorated reliquaries were found imported objects, such as rifles, vases, and a Chinese throne coming from the commercial exchanges between Antalaotra traders, Europeans and Sakalava kings.

---

1. Dutch descriptions in Grandidier 1906, *Collection des Ouvrages Anciens Concernant Madagascar* (C.O.A.C.M., T. VI) pp. 115–119. Manuscript of Rijksarchief-Kolonial Archief, 4127, Journal du voyage du navire "De brack" à Masselage ou Bombetok, in 1741.

   We were conducted into a big *kabaa,* hung with white cloth, from the roof to the ground, in order to protect it against wind and rain. Within the *kaaba,* there was a rich musket collection, more than one hundred; then furniture and full coffers with vases and silver objects and a big throne, lacquered and gilded, decorated with sculptures and built on top of two lions, which was imported from China by the French. Then, the royal shrine which is composed of four badges which represented each of the royal ancestors: *Andian Mesorre, Andian Leyfoetse, Andian Chimenatte* and *Andian Tokaf.* These four badges, tied at the top of a post, are in gold and silver metals and have four big gold teeth similar to those of crocodiles. They are covered by indigenous cloth on which are sewn piastres and a big silver chain and, at the bottom of each badge, are placed on the soil a necklace of glass beads and a censer.

2. It is probably the *zomba* but the captain confuses it with the square edifice that can be found in the centre of Mecca, which is covered by a black cloth during Ramadan, which results in a certain confusion between Islam and the relics cult in this area.

74

Sakalava Ideology

Between the 17th and 18th centuries, Sakalava kings created a dynastic cult that still exists today. In the 18th century, the king of the Boina was rich and powerful. He controlled trade, possessed a vast territory and was in charge of the ancestral cult. The king's force comes from God and his sacred ancestors and the religious side of power is expressed in cults. The king is at the head of the government, which is hereditary, and below them are free men and slaves.

To assume kingship, especially when sacred, the king must be unique, he has the *hasina*, which is a sacred force that is beneficial, but sometimes ill fated and potentially very dangerous.[1] The king is held responsible for the soil's fertility and he is preserved from death and impurity, although his own death provokes chaos. When the king is dead, he becomes an ancestor and speaks through possessed men and women. They are called *saha* which means spirit mediums. Possession by royal ancestral spirits, called *tromba* on the West coast, has a role as important as the relics in the exercise of power.[2] The role of *tromba* in social, political and economic contexts has been studied by a number of anthropologists. J.F. Baré (1980), G. Feeley-Harnik (1991) and L. Sharp (1996) showed that in the Northern bemihisatra and bemazava kingdoms the intervention of possessed people in secular activities has been unavoidable.[3] In the Boina kingdom, *tromba* and relics are linked and a means of power. They were used by natives before the growth of Sakalava dynasties and reinterpreted as a dynastic cult by kings. On the one hand, current social and political relations depend on social codes of ancestral cults and rituals: "*Les relations socio-politiques dans le présent se jouent sur le registre du rapport aux ancêtres...*"[4] and on the other, they also serve as a form of protest, especially when the power of the king has weakened. Later in this chapter, we will see the similar example of the mirror cult, which grew at the end of the colonial period in the Boina area, along the Betsiboka River. *Tromba* and religious practices permitted the Sakalava to communicate with the royal ancestors. The *Great Service*, which is the ritual of the bath, called *fanompoa*, gives the opportunity to reassert these links. This honouring of royal ancestors remains fundamental up until today.

---

1. The *hasina* is a mystical force of primacy and it is associated with high rank and royalty, but also the power of blessing in general. See Bloch 1986:41.
2. *Tromba* refers to the ritual, the spirit which is coming and the medium who embodies it.
3. See Baré 1980, Feely-Karnik 1991, Sharp 1996.
4. Lombard 1988:115, 123–130.

The ceremonial cycle lasts about six months and is composed of several steps. In February and March, two groups collect honey from the forest, which is used to bathe the relics during the *fanompoa*. In April and May, the two groups in charge of the honey bring their gifts. Also in April, the *doany*, the place where the ritual takes place and where the relics are kept, is cleared. In June, honey is prepared and cooked for the great *fanompoa*, which takes place just before the full moon. This ceremonial cycle finishes with the relics ritual. Several weeks before this ritual, emissaries are sent throughout the region to announce the date of the ritual and to collect gifts such as cattle and money from every village in the region of the former kingdom. At the beginning of the 20th century, in villages along the Betsiboka River, Sakalava came together to collect the great drum (*manandriabe*) and the key (*fanalahidy*) of the *zomba*.[1] The procession traversed several ritual places (*zombalahy*) which represented the former territory of the Boina kingdom. Voices of the possessed guided the participants accompanied by music, songs and *tromba*. The ritual place in Majunga, the *doany*, was the last stop. As far as we know, this journey is no longer made. Today, the key and the great drum (*manandriabe*) are probably kept in the *zomba* within the *doany*.

The ritual of the bath lasts about one week; the first days are devoted to the receiving of gifts and listening to the dialogue of all the Sakalava groups that participate in the ritual. Cattle are sacrificed within the sacred enclosure.

On the eve of the last day, moments of rapture are necessary to allow the royal order to be restored. In modern times, it is a festive night with popular dances. The following morning, women from the royal lineage collect seawater that will be used, along with the *tanimalandy* and the cooked honey, for the ritual bath. When the ritual begins, the main officiants and the royal family enter the *zomba*. Relics are cleaned with this mixture of *tanimalandy*, honey and sacred water[2] accompanied by the sound of the conch, rifles,

---

1. A protestant missionary, Henri Rusillon, described this route for the first time and his book is an important source of information on the subject. See bibliography. The map comes from Ballarin 2000:133.
2. This mixture is composed of several elements: gold and silver coins (*tsanganolona*), which were in the past *tahler* from France bearing the effigy of Austrian queen Marie-Therese. This queen symbolised the commercial exchanges between Europe and East Africa in the 18th century. Now others coins can be found (Malagasy money or Tanzanian shillings depending on the region). The sacred water is also composed of coloured beans, *tanimalandy* and a combination of medicinal herbs and roots. We can see the same mixture in the *kibuki* rituals in Zanzibar today.

The Fanompoa circuit

Source: Ballarin 2000.

shouts and singing. When it is finished, they leave the zomba and march within the enclosure; this is a moment of communion between the population and the royal ancestors. The ritual ends with the setting sun.

In his recently published book, Lambek (2002) gave a complete description of the Great Service and analysed how the Sakalava live in Majunga today with their symbolic past. The great *fanompa* appears to be a cult of life and prosperity, imparted by royal ancestors. The preservation of the royal relics and the cult around them (the ritual of the bath and the practice of spirit possession) allowed the king to consecrate his royalty and to legitimate his power and authority. It is important to evoke these elements of the Sakalava rituals because it appears that in Mayotte, some of them, mainly in the practice of *tromba*, were adapted for the historical reasons I mentioned above. Lambek worked on these religious practices in Mayotte in villages whose population speaks Malagasy. His works are fundamental to understanding the ways in which the Sakalava are deeply connected to the cultural and symbolic history of the Comoros Islands and the Swahili world. He dates the arrival of the trumba spirits from Andriantsoly's settlement in the first half of the 19th century. He reports that Andriamanavakarivo, Andriantsoly's posthumous name, is the leader of the *tromba* from Mayotte and his grave is the centre of the cult. In Zanzibar and Mayotte, the ritual is called rumbu.[1] Kjersti Larsen, as well as Linda Giles, have worked for a long time on spirit possession in Zanzibar and in particular on the kibuki spirits that come from Madagascar.[2] Larsen explains that these spirits are those identified by Lambek in the Comoros Islands but whose roots stem from "Damstarafadu in Dwani, Damizara" in Madagascar, thus directly from the *doany* Andriamisara in Majunga, which is the place where the royal relics are kept today. The kibukis' Sakalava origins seem to be genuine and to be descended from the Boina kingdom whose ideological foundation, the Andriamisara doany, is still in Majunga.

The Reinterpretation of Ancestral Values at the Time of Independence: The "mirror cult" of Majunga

As we have seen earlier, in 1825 Andriantsoly fled to the Comoros Islands, leaving the relics of his ancestors in the hands of the conquerors. Merina governors took command of the population in Majunga by taking control of the royal relics and the ritual practices, and, after them, the French colonizers. Sakalava, who were originally shepherds, still practised extensive agriculture. With independence, the idea emerged that the land belongs to the natives, mainly the great Sakalava lineages. The main reference is Sakalava and stems from the former Boina kingdom. Anyone who can prove a family link with a Sakalava prince could have rights to land (mainly former parts

---

1. See Lambek 1981 and 1993, Larsen 1995 and 1998, Giles 1989 and 1999 and their contributions in this book.
2. The word *Kibuki* comes from the way in which the Antalaotra traders called the Malagasy people: *"Les swahili de la côte de zanguebar appellent, en effet, l'île de Madagascar Bouki et ses habitants Oua-bouki."* Grandider 1914, volII, p. 158. He also mentioned the yearly visits of dhows "de nombreux boutres arabes, zanzibariens et comoriens..." fasc. 1, p. 163.

of royal lands and pastures). Because the identity of a man is symbolised by the grave of his ancestors, someone who has no reference to an ancestral tomb appears as non-native, like slaves who were buried in the grave of their owner. *"S'avouer 'sans terres' pour être un 'ayant droit' au regard de la puissance publique, c'est, implicitement, se reconnaître au plus bas de l'échelle sociale, 'sans droit' du point de vue de ses légitimités sociales."* [1] However, the social rise of these migrant and former slave lineages threatens the eminent Sakalava dynasties. They had to struggle to preserve their claims to local territory. As a result, royal families have had to compete with their former subjects who were actively engaged in economic development. This context has led to the creation of new religious practices, like the "mirror cult" in the Majunga area, which is linked to royal symbolism, but in opposition to the former royal values involving the hierarchy system. Sakalava identity then became a gamble for these lineages. With the example of the mirror cult we will see how this knowledge, stemming from the symbolism of Sakalava kingdoms, affected social and political fields from independence to today and how ritualized responses emerged in relation to these changes.

Dubourdieu, who conducted sociological research in the Boina region in the 1980s, discovered the mirror cult. She explained how in the 1950s Tsianindra, a prince of lower rank (his maternal lineage is Antalaotra) and founder of a village, legally took over the commune and a part of the royal herds. At the same time, he received a message from spirits whose origins predated the arrival of the Sakalava dynasties, before the 18th century. These spirits are known as ancestors of the *ombiasy* who gave Andriamisara, the main adviser and medium of the Sakalava kingdom of the Boina, the sacred force which permitted the founding of the royal dynasty. They are called the *Ndranahary agnabo*. [2]

The most important spirit ordered Tsianindra to build a zomba in which a togny is buried. This sacred element transformed the piece of land into a political territory. In this way, this spirit's power equals that of Andriamisara when royalty was founded. In addition, men who are possessed by these spirits did not have to participate in the ancestral cult in Majunga. Tsianindra rejected his duties as a subject of the Sakalava kingdom because the royal relics of Majunga were no longer the relics of his ancestors. New ritual practices were created to honour these spirits. However, the result was a failure. Tsianindra was chased out of his village by his nephews who re-

---

1. A slave is buried in the grave of his master and it marks his servile position. Dubordieu 1987.
2. *Ndranahary agnabo* are Spirits from the ombiasy who gave Andriamisara the *hasina*, permitting him to build the kingdom.

fused to acknowledge these new religious practices. Nonetheless, he later succeeded in a village, Ankaboka, which was ruled by an elder of a Makoa lineage, Tsimivony. These spirits possessed Tsianindra and Tsimivony. A new ritual was established around a mirror of Arab inspiration, considered prestigious, which came *an-dafy*, from outside the county, from the sea. It represents Makoa ancestors who were brought to Madagascar by dhow from Mozambique and it is related to the commercial exchanges in the Western Indian Ocean (Boyer-Rossol 2007). Mirrors play an important role in divination practices and this seers' cult replaces the dynastic cult. In this case, the saha, great mediums who practise this cult, were often rich owners of cattle and economically powerful.

The role of this mirror is equivalent to the role of royal relics in the Boina kingdom and the ritual practices are the same as those in Majunga. The mirror is bathed by the *tromba*, in the same way as the relics by Sakalava princes. Ideologically, we can see a break with the former royal values involving the hierarchical system. The cult is founded on the knowledge of the *tromba*, but also expresses the claims of men threatened by a new political order during independence and the first republic of Madagascar. Tsimivony broke his allegiance to the former royalty and imposed a new order dominated by men who kept economic and ideological power in their hands: they are owners of cattle and land but born of Makoa or lower ranking lineages. This example illustrates new social relations and a re-interpretation of royal Sakalava symbolism relating to political changes. Those who were excluded by the king, who gave the land, invented a cult as powerful as that of the royal ancestors' cult, which gave them the right to land.

By Conclusion

Sakalava *tromba* possession was a key mechanism of political legitimization in the Sakalava kingdom. The cult was connected with the foundation of royalty and marked the territory of the king, which has a strong relevance in the present. Different kinds of power (political, economic) could have been legitimated by the cult as well. And, up to today, the royal cult has been reinvented and transformed by social actors. From the 18th century, the possession of the relics and the control over the place where they are still kept have been represented as a stake for all the political governments which followed one another. Since independence, the relics of Andriamisa have been representing all the political changes of the Malagasy society through a lawsuit concerning their control which began in 1957 and which has not found a solution up to today (Ballarin 2000).

Ancestral cults represented a stake in which ambitions, expectations and sometimes fears of the society were expressed. The fanompoa is still celebrated but a lot of tensions exist within royal families in Majunga, which people are less tolerant of these days. In Majunga, ceremonies are performed in private places, in order to collect money to celebrate the big ritual, the Great Fanompoa. In the 1980s, Tsimivony passed his knowledge on to his nephew, who was himself possessed by the spirits Ndranahary agnabo. When the two founders of the cult died, other officiates competed to control this cult. One of them, very rich, decided to build another zomba, thereby breaking away from the Ankaboka cult. This shows that these cults could still be considered as a means to conquer land and control social relations. A small group in recent Boina society can appropriate Sakalava ancestral knowledge and exploit it in relation to political and economic changes.

At present, the cult has become significant for other Malagasy and forms a part of the common Malagasy history and culture that is used by politicians. In the 90s, it emerged clearly that the great fanompoa was an important element of the national history, which had to be emphasized and promoted towards tourists, foreigners and locals (Ballarin 2000: 397–410. See also Lambek 2002:11–14; Blanchy et al. 2006). The relics are still bathed annually, shrines regularly maintained and new spirits appearing after the death of a king. The *mpanjaka* Désiré, who had ruled over the Boina since 1971, died a few months ago and was given the name of Andrianahavitaniarivo; his spirit will probably become apparent one day during a ritual performance. His children are competing for his succession, involving politicians as has always been the case in the Sakalava kingdoms (Ballarin 2000). In 2007, the Great *fanompoa* was celebrated on behalf of the fight against AIDS, which was an interesting innovation and anchored the cult a bit more within the national modern context.

Thus, in spite of many changes in the Great *fanompoa* and in the practice of spirit possession amongst the Sakalava of the Boina area, this ritual is the most significant annual ceremony in the region, attracting thousands of people from the whole island and also from abroad (mainly Mayotte but also La Réunion where emigrants from Madagascar continue to orient themselves to the *doany* and the Andriamisara shrines. (See Dumas-Champion 2001). Moreover in the 90s, one of the *manantany* (guardian of the *doany* in Mahajanga) was possessed by Andriamisara and proudly pretended to have an international clientele coming from parts of the East

African coast and Saudi Arabia (Lambek 2002:40–41). In Mayotte and Zanzibar, as observed by Lambek and Larsen, these cults have apparently lost their legitimating power but are still efficient ideologically. It appears that the migration and historical connections provided some elements used in ritual practice, which are actually quite different from that of the Sakalava in Madagascar. Locally the cults evolved according to their own dynamics and logic. In Comoros and Zanzibar, royal ancestors are the chief source of blessings and prosperity but they do not legitimise the authority of rulers neither on individual nor local levels. The ritual moved into a healing mode and has lost its power of legitimization, but is ideologically effective and has an important social significance as K. Larsen and M.A. Saleh show in their work. In all of the places where the *tromba* spirits are invoked (Mayotte, north-west Madagascar, Zanzibar) men and women sing, laugh and chat, request drinks (beer or rum) and perform the ritual with accordion music and dancing. Everyone is splashed with clayed water and drinks from the dish in the same way, which is done during the Sakalava royal ritual and *tromba* performances. Beyond the ritual, the performance has revealed different kinds of identities, which can be ethnic, religious or sexual, performing a different role and allowing people to negotiate status in individual ways. These same issues are still important up to the present and permit us to understand how rituals contribute to the creation of social practices and identities in African and Malagasy societies from the West Indian Ocean.

References

Alpers, Edward A., 2001, "A complex relationship: Mozambique and the Comoro Islands in the 19th and 20th centuries", *Cahiers d'Études Africaines,* vol. 41, n°161, pp. 73–96.

Althabe, Gérard, 1982, *Oppression et libération dans l'imaginaire.* Paris: Maspero.

Amselle, Jean Loup, 2001, *Branchements. Anthropologie de l'universalité des cultures.* Paris: Flammarion.

Appadurai, Arjun, 2001,. *Après le colonialisme, les conséquences culturelles de la globalisation.* Paris: Payot. Originally published as *Modernity at Large. Cultural Dimensions of Globalization,* 1996.

Balandier, George, 1967 (1995), *Anthropologie politique.* Paris: Quadrige, P.U.F., 54.

Balandier, George, 1992, *Le pouvoir sur scènes.* Paris: Balland.

Ballarin, Marie Pierre, 2000, *Les réliques royales à Madagascar: source de légitimation et enjeu de pouvoir.* Paris: Karthala.

Ballarin, Marie Pierre, 2007, "Empreintes africaines dans les royautés sakalava de l'Ouest malgache ; ancrages sakalava aux Comores (XVIIe-XXe)" in D. Nativel, F. V. Rajaonah (dir.), *Madagascar et l'Afrique. Permanences et mutations de liens complexes.* Paris: Karthala, pp. 337–357.

Baré, J.F. 1980, *Sable rouge: une monarchie du Nord-ouest malgache dans l'histoire.* Paris: L'Harmattan.

Blanchy, S., J.A. Rakotoarisoa, P. Beaujard, C. Radimilahy, 2006, *Les Dieux au service du peuple.* Paris: Karthala.

Bloch, Maurice, 1986, *From Blessing to Violence, History and Ideology in the Circumcision Ritual of the Merina of Madagascar.* Cambridge: C.U.P.

Bloch, Maurice, 1997, *La violence du religieux.* Paris: Odile Jacob.

Boyer-Rossol, Klara, 2007, "De Morima à Morondava : contribution à l'étude des Makoa de l'ouest de Madagascar au XIXe siècle", in D. Nativel, F. V. Rajaonah (dir.), *Madagascar et l'Afrique. Permanences et mutations de liens complexes.* Paris: Karthala, p. 183–220.

Dubourdieu, Lucile, 1987, " Le culte du mirroir dans la basse Betsiboka. Son rôle dans la compétition foncière", *Recherches pour le développement, série Siences de l'Homme et de la Société*, no 4, Ministère de la Recherche Scientifique et Technique pour le Développment, Tananarive, p. 53–112.

Dumas-Champion, F., 2001, "À propos des lieux de cultes chez les Réunionnais d'origine malgache", *Études Océan Indien* 30 :171–190.

Feeley-Harnick, Gillian, 1991, *A Green Estate. Restoring independence of Madagascar.* Washington: Smithsonian.

Giles, Linda, 1987, "Possession cults on the Swahili coast : A re-examination of theories of marginality", *Africa* 57 (2), p. 234–258.

Giles, Linda, 1989, *Spirit possession on the Swahili coast : peripheral cults or primary texts*? PhD dissertation, university of Texas at Austin.

Giles, Linda, 1999, "Spirit Possession and the Symbolic Construction of Swahili Society", in Behrend, Heike and Ute Luig (eds), *Spirit Possession, Modernity, and Power.* London: James Currey, p. 142–164.

Glassman, Jonathon, 1995, *Feasts and riots. Revelry, rebellion and popular consciousness on the Swahili coast, 1856–1888.* Social history of Africa, Nairobi: Heinemann, James Currey, E.A.P. Dar es Salaam: Mkuki na Nyota.

Grandidier, Alfred and Guillaume, 1903–1920, *Collection des ouvrages anciens concernant Madagascar et les îles voisines.* Paris, 9 tomes.

Guillain, Charles, 1845, *Documents sur l'histoire, la géographie et le commerce de la Partie occidentale de Madagascar.* Paris: Société Ethnologique de Paris.

Guillain, Charles, 1856–1857, *Documents sur l'histoire, la géographie et le commerce de l'Afrique orientale.* Paris: Société Ethnologique de Paris, 2 tomes.

Hobsbawm, Eric and Ranger, Terence (eds), [1983], 1992, *The Invention of Tradition.* Cambridge University Press.

Lambek, Michaël, 1981, *Human spirit : A cultural account of trance in Mayotte.* New York: Cambridge University Press.

Lambek, Michaël, 1993, *Knowledge and practice in Mayotte : Local discourses of Islam, sorcery and spirit possession.* Toronto: University of Toroton press.

Lambek, Michaël, 2002, *The weight of the past. Living history in Mahajanga, Madagascar.*Contemporary Anthropology of Religion. Boston University: Palgrave Macmillan.

Larsen, Kjersti, 1995, *Where humans and spirits meet. Incorporating difference and experiencing otherness in Zanzibar town.* PhD dissertation, Oslo: University of Oslo.

Larsen, Kjersti, 1998, "Morality and the refection of spirits: A Zanzibar case", *Social anthropology,* vol. 6:1, pp. 61–75.

Larsen, Kjersti, 1998, "Spirit possession as historical narrative: The production of identity and locality in Zanzibar Town" in Nadia Lovell (ed.), *Locality and Belonging.* Routledge, pp. 125–147.

Lombard, Jacques, 1988, *Le royaume Sakalava du Menabe. Essai d'analyse d'un système politique à Madagascar. 17ème–20ème.* ORSTOM, Travaux et Documents, no. 214, Paris.

Martin, Jean, 1983, *Comores: quatre iles entre pirates et planteurs. T. 1 Razzias malgaches et rivalités internationales (fin 18e-1875);Genèse vie et mort du Protectorat 1875–1912.* Paris: L'Harmattan, p. 612.

Noël, Vincent, 1843–1844, "Recherches sur les Sakalava", *Bulletin de la Société Géographique de Paris,* 2ème série, 1843; t. 19, p. 275–295 ; 1844, t. 20, p. 60–64, p. 286–306.

Ottino, Paul, 1965, "Le Tromba, Madagascar", *L'Homme,* vol. 4, no. 1, Paris: La Haye Mouton, p. 83–94.

Raison, Françoise (ed.), 1983, *Les souverains de Madagascar: l'histoire royale et ses résurgences contemporaines.* Paris: Karthala.

Ramamonjisoa, Susy, 1976, "Questions sur Andriamisara : un exemple de critique historique à propos de traditions culturelles influencées par l'islam bantouisé à Madagascar", *Omaly sy Anio,* vol. 3–4, pp. 251–266.

Ramamonjisoa, Susy, 1985–86, "Symbolique des rapports entre les hommes et les femmes dans les cultes de possession de type tromba à Madagascar", *Bulletin de l'académie malgache,* t. 663/1–2, 1985–86, pp. 99–110.

Rusillon, Henri, 1912, *Un culte dynastique avec évocations des morts. Le Tromba.* Paris: Picard.

Saleh, M.A., 2007, "Les Comoriennes de Zanzibar et le culte des esprits kibuki malgaches in D. Nativel, F. and V. Rajaonah (eds), *Madagascar et l'Afrique. Permanences et mutations de liens complexes.* Paris: Karthala, 425–437.

Saleh, Mohamed Ahmed, 1995, "La communauté zanzibari d'origine comorienne. Premiers jalons d'une recherche en cours", *Islam et sociétés au sud du Sahara,* vol. 9, 1995, Maison des Sciences de l'Homme (M.S.H), Paris, pp. 203–210.

Sharp, Lesley, 1996, *The possessed and the dispossessed.* University of California Press.

Vernet, Thomas, 2003, "Le commerce des esclaves sur le côte swahili, 1600–1750", *Azania,* vol. 38, pp. 69–97.

Vernet, Thomas, 2005, *Les cités-etats swahili de l'archipel de Lamu, 1585–1810. Dynamiques endogènes,* Doctorat d'histoire, Université Paris I-Panthéon Sorbonne.

CHAPTER 5

Societal Change
and Swahili Spirit Possession

Linda L. Giles

This paper surveys the effects of recent ideological, economic, and political changes on Swahili spirit possession. It summarizes many of the observations I have made on this topic in past publications[1] but also adds new points and considerations. Moreover, it incorporates and makes comparisons with some of the more recent published and unpublished observations made by other scholars on this subject.

Most of the fieldwork for this paper was conducted during doctoral research on Swahili spirit possession from 1982 through 1984, supplemented by short visits in 1992 and 2001. My field sites were located in various areas of the Kenyan and Tanzanian coast – primarily in Mombasa, Vanga and Wasin in southern Kenya, the Tanga and rural Pangani areas in northern Tanzania, the city of Zanzibar, and the Wete and Chake Chake areas in Pemba. Although much of my research focused on the Swahili, I also studied spirit possession among the Giriama, Digo, Duruma, and in some mixed Shambaa/Bondei spirit guilds in Tanga, which provided useful comparisons with Swahili spirit beliefs and practices.

Political Economy, Modernity, Urbanism, and Islamic Attitues

There have been a number of scholars who have related spirit possession throughout the world to societal change. Many have suggested that spirit possession expresses contact with alien peoples, concepts, and objects, either as a means of acquisition, accommodation, control, or resistance.[2] Many have also analyzed how spirit possession reacts to economic, political, and socio-cultural dislocations, often caused by state, colonial, neo-colonial, and global exploitation during the last two centuries (e.g., Fry 1976, Lan

---

1. Giles 1987, 1999, and especially Giles 1995.
2. This aspect has been noted in many studies of specific possession complexes (e.g., Lindblom 1920, Boddy 1989, Kenyon 1995) and is one of the main thrusts of Kramer's comparative analysis (1987/1993) as well as Lewis' definition (1971) of "peripheral" possession.

1985, Ong 1987, Smith 1991, Sharp 1993 and 1995, Stoller 1996). In the case of the Swahili, noted historian Edward Alpers (1984) has analyzed certain Zanzibari possession cults during the 19th century as reactions to increased subordination of women under the Busaidi state with its associated emphasis on the literate tradition of *sharia* law. Alper's analysis, however, tends to reduce Zanzibari spirit possession to a mere reaction to a stressful and oppressive societal change. Whereas I agree that spirit possession, among the Swahili and elsewhere, reacts to various types of societal change, I believe that in most cases it cannot be explained solely in these terms. In many societies, a cultural tradition of spirit possession preexists, and continues long after, any specific societal change. In regard to the Swahili, I believe that spirit possession has a long history in the coastal region which is firmly rooted in Swahili tradition.[1]

Another interesting point is that, contrary to many expectations, spirit possession in Africa and elsewhere has not disappeared during the last century as societies "modernize".[2] The Swahili coast is no exception. During my fieldwork in the early 1980s, I found that spirit possession as well as possession guilds (*vilinge*, or *vyama*) were still present in many Swahili areas. I suggested, however, that participation in most spirit possession guilds seemed less extensive than in the past, especially in regard to male membership and their public possession. I also found that the role of spirit possession in community-wide activities had declined significantly.[3] The prevalence of various types of possessive spirits and the guilds dedicated to them also changes significantly over time, in reaction to societal and cultural changes, especially in regard to the influence of various peoples and life styles on Swahili society, as I will discuss briefly at the end of this paper.

During my fieldwork I found Swahili possession guilds to be thriving more in modern urban sites such as Mombasa, Tanga, Zanzibar, as well as

---

1. Nisula makes a similar assessment in his 1999 study.
2. See the 1999 edited volume by Behrend and Luig (eds), *Spirit Possession: Modernity and Power in Africa* for an exploration of this point in the African context, and the earlier edited volume by Comaroff (eds), *Modernity and its Malcontent* (1993), which extends the argument to African ritual in general.
3. Whereas formerly towns and villages conducted spirit rituals associated with the monsoons, the agricultural cycle, bull-baiting ceremonies (in Pemba), the Swahili (solar) New Year, and held other periodic ceremonies in honor of community guardian spirits, only remnants of these practices can still be found, often in remote locations (Giles 1995, 2006). The best known of these is the Swahili New Year ceremony in Makunduchi, Zanzibar, but other villages in the more isolated areas of Pemba and the Mrima coast (northern Tanzania) also continued to conduct community spirit rituals during the time of my fieldwork in the 1980s.

the smaller town of Wete in Pemba, than in many rural areas. I have suggested several reasons for this: the greater access to cash and goods needed for ceremonies, the organizational benefits of a densely populated area, as well as the need for a social network and support group in heterogeneous urban communities (Giles 1995). Hence I would suggest that increasing urbanization and increased migration of diverse peoples into urban sites may well continue to encourage spirit possession guilds and activities. However, it should be noted that I did not find this urban association true of Mijikenda spirit possession ceremonies, which I found almost exclusively in rural areas and small villages.

Another reason for the vitality of Swahili possession guilds in urban settings may relate specifically to the opportunities that they give to women, who often form the majority of possession guild membership. Urban Swahili communities have historically shown greater concern for Islamic constraints on female roles and behavior, especially for the upper classes, than in rural areas. Under such situations, activities and associations that provide women with opportunities for social interaction, support, status, and power beyond the domestic setting take on added importance (Strobel's research (1979) on the popularity of women's dance associations in Mombasa, and more recent research by Fair (2001) and Askew (2002) on female dance societies as well as female participation in *taarab* music bands in urban Tanzania). Moreover, spirit possession ceremonies are one of the few public arenas where women and men not only often participate together in non-segregated groups but also have equal opportunities for status positions[1] (although Topan believes that female possession guild leaders did not have the same degree of power as their male counterparts until after the 1960s, see his chapter). However, gender roles have been changing in recent times, with more Swahili women receiving Western secondary and post-secondary education and pursuing careers (often as office workers or

---

1. *Taarab* musical bands and performances are another such arena, as are older traditions of mixed gender competitive "dance" (*ngoma*) societies. Both of these latter arenas, however, have undergone increasing gender segregation during the twentieth century, although assessments of the extent and timing vary. Askew (2002:83) notes that dance societies became segregated by colonial times, but Fair (2001:183) observes that women in Zanzibar still participated in mixed gender activities, including both *taarab* and *ngoma*, during the 1920s and 30s. I found mixed gender dance societies still thriving in the isolated Vanga area on the Kenyan border as late as the 1980s. Fair (2001:99) observes that Zanzibari *taarab* bands became gender segregated during World War II, though Askew (2002) still writes about (and participated in) mixed gender *taarab* bands on the Tanzanian mainland in Tanga in the early 1990s.

shopkeepers) in the public arena, especially in urban areas. These changes may decrease participation in more traditional public female realms such as spirit possession ceremonies and dance associations, for certain segments of the population.

One must remember, however, that people do not join possession guilds because of social benefits. They join because they have been diagnosed with possessive spirits who want them to join a spirit guild. Such possession is not voluntary and usually not wanted, and people often try to avoid joining a possession guild. The social benefits of spirit guilds may thus help keep people, especially women, active in the guilds once they have already joined, and also be important for women who have not been initiated into the spirit guild but assist and support its activities.

In addition to affecting women's roles, Islamic attitudes also obviously impact the acceptance of spirit possession itself, as Topan explores at length in his chapter. The impact is by no means all negative, since Islam acknowledges the existence of spirits (see Topan's discussion) as well as healers using Islamic methods (*waganga wa kitabu*) to treat cases of spirit possession. The most orthodox Islamic authorities, however, oppose spirit possession guilds and other activities that accommodate spirit relationships. In spite of this opposition, many Swahili turn to healers who utilize possessive spirits (*waganga wa pepo*, also called *waganga wa shetani* or *waganga wa kichwa*) and often also agree to establish spirit relationships themselves when illness or misfortune does not respond to other forms of treatment. As Topan notes, spirit possession " ... fulfills a need in Swahili society ... that is not being met by the teaching and practices of orthodox Islam". Moreover, Topan and I both stress that spirit possession practices are framed within a larger Islamic context, not only through initial invocations to Allah and his Prophet (see Topan's chapter) but also through incorporating Islamic spirits and ritual practices. Thus I have argued, together with other scholars of the last several decades (Lambek 1981 and 1993,[1] Larsen 1998b and 2001, Nisula 1999) that spirit possession is part of local Islamic practice. This is not to say, however, that concerns for Islamic orthodoxy have not adversely affected possession guilds and activities at certain times and locations. I was told that strict Islamic attitudes had greatly reduced spirit possession guilds in Lamu long before my research period. I also found that no spirit ceremonies were al-

---

1. Lambek's research focuses on Malagasy-speakers on Mayotte in the Comoro Islands. However, the Comoro Islands have strong connections with Swahili communities and the Swahili spirit possession complex is prominent even among Malagasy-speakers, together with the *trumba* possession complex derived from the Malagasy Sakalava.

lowed in the town of Vanga for the same reasons (which was ironic because I had originally intended it as my research site). Researchers have noted recent increases in fundamentalist movements for stricter interpretations of Islam in other Swahili localities, especially in Zanzibar town (personal communication from Allyson Purpura, Larsen 1998b noting Parkin), after my fieldwork period. (See also Bruinhorst's comments about the *Ansaar Sunna* movement in Tanga, Tanzania, in this volume.) However, these movements appear to have been limited and thus do not seem to have been successful in significantly discouraging spirit possession among the general population (cf. Larsen 1998 in regard to Zanzibar). In Zanzibar town, for instance, both Larsen and Nisula have recently found that spirit possession is still part of everyday life.

Governmental Attitudes and Policies

Governmental attitudes, of course, have also affected spirit possession guilds and public spirit ceremonies. European colonial governments often discouraged spirit ceremonies, partly because of an ethnocentric attitude that viewed all such activities as witchcraft but also because they were regarded as backward, and inimical to public order and morality. The British colonial government banned spirit dances in Mombasa along with many other social dances that were said to lead to "debauchery and excess" (Strobel 1979:168). My Mombasa informants did not report that this law wiped out spirit possession ceremonies but it no doubt drove them more underground.The law was no longer enforced during my fieldwork period in the 1980s, but there were governmental measures to regulate spirit healers and other traditional healers (all of whom are subsumed under the Swahili term *waganga*). All *waganga* in the Kenyan coastal area were required to pay for licenses to practice traditional medicine and also apply for permits to hold each spirit ceremony. These regulations would naturally reduce the number of practicing *waganga* as well as the number of ceremonies they held, especially in the urban areas where ceremonies could not be easily performed without detection.[1]

British colonial administrators in Zanzibar had similar negative reactions to indigenous public dances and ceremonies to those in Mombasa, citing the impact on labor of all-night dances (Depelchin 1991:26). However, contrary to Kenya, the most drastic measures against spirit guilds took place

---

1. Most Mijikenda *waganga* that I encountered in the rural areas did not apply for permits to hold public spirit ceremonies, and thus there was always a danger that their ceremonies would be broken up by police.

after independence when the revolutionary government of Karume banned all spirit ceremonies. My informants reported that this ban had a drastic effect on spirit possession guilds, especially in Zanzibar town. Even on the island of Pemba, far away from the Zanzibari seat of government, informants reported that ceremonies had to be held surreptitiously without drums in order to escape detection.

Nisula has recently suggested that this ban did not adversely affect spirit healing ceremonies in Zanzibar town but only communal spirit activities (1999:45). Perhaps he believes this because at the time of his research he found spirit healing ceremonies common. During my fieldwork period in 1984, however, the Zanzibari government was just starting to emerge from its revolutionary socialist period. The ban on spirit ceremonies had been relaxed but informants reported that many types of spirit guilds that had been active in the past were either gone or barely existent. During the several months that I spent at various times in Zanzibar town, I found ceremonies for a few types of spirits (e.g., *bwengo/rubamba, ruhani*) but these were small healing sessions for individual clients. The *Habeshia* spirit guild was still alive but ceremonies were rare. Its decline was not surprising due to its associations with the former Arab ruling class, many of whom had fled or been killed during the revolution. The only spirit guild that appeared to be thriving was the *kibuki* guild, whose members told me that they were the one spirit guild that Karume allowed to continue during the ban because they had impressed him with their abilities.

During the 1980s, the Zanzibari government was beginning to take an interest in spirit performances, not as healing and ritual activities but as folkloric national culture.

In Pemba, I found several local government researchers who were studying spirit possession, but focusing their efforts on collecting the texts of spirit possession songs. When I first arrived, instead of directing me to practicing *waganga* and spirit ceremonies, government officials took me to several villages where they assembled the villagers together and told them to perform spirit songs for me and answer my questions, assuming that this artificial and coerced performance would satisfy my research needs. I later learned that a similar approach had been used prior to my arrival when a research team from Guinea came to help the Zanzibari government document its folkloric traditions by traveling from village to village and asking the occupants to perform spirit dances. I also heard rumors of a plan to have spirit possession songs and dances performed at a new government tourist facility. At this time the tourist industry was virtually non-existent in Pemba and just beginning in Zanzibar town. With the subsequent growth of Zanzibar, especially Zanzibar town and other sites on the island of Unguja, as a major tourist destination, it would not be surprising if elements of spirit possession traditions were reproduced as performances for tourists, though I have no information about this.[1] Although I tend to view such performances as robbing ritual beliefs and practices of their meaning and function,[2] I also realize that this need not always happen. Cohen (1988) has pointed out that tourism can also facilitate the preservation and revitalization of cultural traditions that still retain local meaning, as others have asserted for certain locations (e.g., Shackley 1999 (Nepal), especially Bali (McKean 1977, Noronha 1979, Picard 1996).[3] Moreover, as Simpson (1993:180) has noted, though tourism often empties meaning from cultural practices, it can also create new meanings for them. He further observes that tourism can help legitimize cultural traditions that the local elite have previously viewed as backward, unrefined, or sacrilegious (1993:171).

The attitude toward spirit practitioners and other traditional healers on the Tanzanian mainland during my research period was much more cooperative than that found elsewhere. Local officials were surveying traditional healers in order to discover what types of illnesses they could cure and what medicines they used, in the hope that these healers had useful skills and medicines that could be combined with modern biomedical practice. Government aims, however, did not seem to coalesce with those of most *waganga*. Many of the *waganga* that I interviewed in the Tanga area were not anxious to share their medical knowledge, especially in regard to the medicines used, which they regarded as their professional secret that they had acquired through apprenticeship, payments, and spiritual guidance.

In her recently published study, Erdtsieck (2003) provides a useful historical overview of governmental attitudes and policies toward traditional healers in mainland Tanzania. Of particular note are the several attempts in the last few decades to formally organize traditional healers, including the recent National Organization of Traditional Healers and Midwives formed in 1994 under the Ministry of Health. Erdtsieck points out, however, that

1. Cf. the controversial performance of the *unyago* dance used in female puberty rituals as cultural entertainment at an international conference, as reported by Larsen (2000).
2. Similar critiques appear frequently in the academic literature on tourism, echoing MacCannell's analyses (1973, 1976) of "staged authenticity".
3. See also the interesting National Geographic film, *Bali: Masterpiece of the Gods* (1990), where performers and artists who re-create ritual objects and performances for the tourist market reported that these developments had actually revitalized their religious traditions outside of the tourist context.

these organizations have had limited success. Nonetheless, in the city of Tanga, German student Lisa Mackenrodt (personal communication Feb. 8, 2004) recently reported that every *mganga* whom she contacted there during several months of research in 2003 was not only licensed but also belonged to an association of *waganga*. Of course this does not imply that the association was very effective aside from licensing, or pervasive in other regions, especially in rural areas.

Socioeconomic Factors

In addition to governmental attitudes, socioeconomic conditions, which themselves are often linked to government policies and actions, can have a major impact on spirit possession, by making spirit ceremonies and of-ferings less affordable. This was very evident during my fieldwork period in Tanzania, when the national socialist economy was at one of its lowest points. There were severe shortages of even the most basic goods and very high prices on the black market. Many items needed for spirit activities, including the luxury items often desired by spirits and the food needed to feed those attending spirit guild ceremonies, were unavailable locally, espe-cially in the rural areas (Giles 1995:92). Conditions were particularly dire in Pemba. Although Pemba is famous throughout the Swahili coast for its spirits and witches (cf. Topan's chapter), I did not find elaborate spirit cer-emonies comparable to those in Mombasa, or even the Tanzanian main-land. Nor did I find them in Zanzibar town, except for the *kibuki* guild, which still managed to find the luxury goods, including imported brandy, needed for its ceremonies. This ability of the *kibuki* guild may have been due to the economic position and international connections of the leader of the main guild.

After my fieldwork period ended, the economic contrast between Kenya and Tanzania reversed itself. Economic conditions steadily worsened in Kenya, which I would expect to have a negative impact on spirit ceremo-nies, at least in regard to their degree of elaborateness and economic costs. In Tanzania, however, the period of economic socialism ended and the na-tional economy improved, which I believe probably led to a revival of spirit guild activities. Such economic gains within a capitalistic system, however, do not reach all levels of society, and lead to widespread inequalities. Thus in Zanzibar town, which developed a thriving capitalist economy connected to its booming tourist market, some local friends tell me that life is even harder than before, for although a wide array of goods are now available, they cannot afford to buy them. Hence, for many Zanzibaris as well as mainland Tanzanians, participation in spirit activities may still be hampered by economic difficulties.

Geographical Mobility and Westernized Education

Another factor affecting spirit possession is geographical mobility. Ever since the period of the caravan trade, which was most pronounced in Tanzania, Swahili spirits and healing methods have traveled inland and affected the spirit illnesses, relationships, and healing complexes of interior societies (Koritschoner 1936, Feierman 1974, Thompson 1999, Erdtsieck 2003). The reverse process, however, is also true. Swahili society has always been cosmopolitan, where different peoples and cultural influences intermingle. As a result, various spirit traditions influence each other, relationships with various peoples and cultures are expressed in terms of possessive spirits, and individuals who are absorbed into Swahili society bring their spiritual traditions with them. The Arab-Swahili slave trade brought many interior cultural elements into Swahili society (cf. Strobel 1975, on women's puberty rites and dance associations), including spirit types and ritual techniques. After the slave period, ongoing labor immigration, marital and non-marital sexual relationships, and socio-cultural assimilation into Swahili society continued the process. New modes of transportation also facilitated mobility, and it became easier for the better-off members of society to come to the coastal region to seek the services of Swahili healers. During my fieldwork, for instance, I was surprised to find a university-trained archaeological student coming from Nairobi to seek treatment from a Swahili spirit medium. Moreover, some clients were coming from the Middle East to seek out Swahili healers. The Middle Eastern connections were especially prominent in the case of the main *kibuki mganga* in Zanzibar, who traveled herself to Oman for extended periods.[1]

On the other hand, for part of my fieldwork period the border between Tanzania and Kenya was closed, thus greatly inhibiting the movements of *waganga* and patients between the two countries. Even after the border opened, traffic across it was limited and beset by bureaucratic difficulties. It was also not easy to travel between Zanzibar, Pemba, and the Tanzanian mainland, hence limiting the influence of Zanzibari and Pemban *waganga* and the ongoing exchange of spiritual knowledge. (Despite this basic transportation problem, however, local people still traveled rather extensively via

---

1. Also noted by Topan in his chapter in this volume.

local boats.) Subsequently, travel to and between Zanzibar and Pemba has become much easier, as has that between Kenya and Tanzania, which has probably had a positive effect on the practice of spirit therapists.

Whereas one might think that the growing impact of Western education and cultural influences would be detrimental to spirit possession, this is not necessarily true, as the case of the Nairobi university student noted above attests. I found other cases of individuals who had been well-educated in Western-style secondary or post-secondary schools, not only seeking spirit therapies but also becoming members of spirit guilds (cf. Topan's chapter). One of these was actually a man who had been educated overseas and had embraced a Western secular lifestyle before succumbing to spirit possession and eventually becoming a professional *mganga*. I have suggested reasons for this phenomenon elsewhere (e.g., 1989, 1995), including the fact that possession is not a voluntary decision, is often inherited, and is deeply rooted in Swahili cultural traditions. Several individuals even noted that they had not believed in spirit possession prior to their own spirit afflictions (cf. Larsen 1998a:39). Hence even conscious belief is not necessary for spirit possession to take place.

The Impact of Western Biomedicine

Nisula (1999) focuses his recent Zanzibar study on another factor affecting spirit possession, i.e., Western biomedical practices. He points out that Western biomedical intervention was never very successful in East Africa. Moreover, from its start until the present, it focused on curative rather than preventative medicine, unlike spirit therapies which focused on both aspects (1999:13 & 198). Thus spirit therapy remained a popular treatment option. After independence and the subsequent Zanzibar revolution, Nisula points out that the biomedical system has deteriorated further, with shortages of medicines in public institutions and a breakdown in hospital care (1999:270). This assessment agrees with my own experience during the mid-1980s. There were considerable problems with delivery of biomedical treatment in coastal Kenya, especially for rural and poorer segments of the population, but the situation in Tanzania, including Zanzibar, was much worse. Here even urban and well-off segments of the population had problems obtaining proper medicines and medical care. Nisula notes that the prestige of biomedicine and public health care depends on access to pharmaceuticals, and thus has suffered in Zanzibar (1999:255). Under these conditions, alternative therapies, including those involving spirits, continue to

94

be popular. Moreover, like myself and many other recent researchers, Nisula (1999:196) points out that treatment through spirit therapies often is sought after biomedical treatments have failed, which happens frequently.

Nisula suggests that an efficient biomedical system could threaten the position of possessive spirit healers but that this did not take place in Zanzibar because of a lack of medical authority and control together with the declining state of biomedical health care (1999:46). This seems to imply that the spirit possession complex could, or even, would, lose its appeal under the proper standards of biomedical care. I believe that this is not very likely, however, because of many reasons which have been well discussed in the scholarly literature.[1] 1) Medical therapy, especially in non-Western settings, is essentially pluralistic. 2) Biomedicine is never totally successful in diagnosing and curing illness. 3) Spirit-based therapies are often more effective in cases of mental illnesses than modern Western medicine. 4) Western-based biomedicine is not as effective in treating the mind-body connection as many non-Western therapies. 5) Spirit possession therapies also deal with a range of problems and misfortunes besides illness and other physical problems (reproduction, etc.). 6) Biomedicine does not provide for many non-medical human needs therapies based on spirit possession do. Explanations based on spirits (as well as witchcraft and sorcery) are often more cognitively satisfying than those given by biomedicine, (not only as to causal agents but also, as Evans-Pritchard pointed out long ago in his classic study of Azande witchcraft, as to why the particular individual, family, or community was affected) and also provide a psychologically satisfying means of action for dealing with problems. Likewise, indigenous therapies dealing with spirits or witchcraft/sorcery address the social as well as the

---

1. Many of these points have been succinctly discussed in the introduction to the section on ethnomedicine in the readings collected by Lehmann and Myers and the various articles within, e.g., Arthur Lehmann, "The Eyes of the *Ngangas:* Ethnomedicine and Power in Central African Republic"; Thomas Bass, "Traditional African Psychotherapy: An Interview with Thomas Adeoye Lambo"; C. Levi-Strauss, "The Sorcerer and his Magic"; Robert Edgerton, "A Traditional African Psychiatrist"; and (in another section) E.M. Pattison, "Psychosocial Interpretations of Exorcism". Many of these points are likewise made in Worsely's review article (1992), though he also stresses the diversity between and within non-Western medical practices. See also, among others, Gonzalez (1966), Waxler (1977), Kleinman (1980), Hepburn (1988), Helman (1994:70), Offiong (1999), Connor and Samuel, eds (2001) (especially the article by Hunter), Micozzi (2002), Reiff et al. (2003), as well as the many other studies that note the psychotherapeutic benefits of shamanistic, spiritual, and other forms of symbolic healing; the importance of medical pluralism in various non-Western areas, and the emphasis on therapy managing groups rather than a single patient in non-Western medical practice.

cultural context of the patient, involving relationships within the domestic and community setting and utilizing cultural beliefs, forms of expression, and ritual actions. Nisula himself acknowledges that spirit possession therapy is not just a medical therapy but also a means of social manipulation, an expression of personal and social identity, and a form of cultural knowledge, including historical consciousness (1999:12, 257, 285), all points that have been stressed by recent Swahili and other African possession studies (e.g., Lambek1981, Boddy 1989, Lambek 1993, Sharp 1993, Giles 1995, Stoller 1996, Larsen 1998a and b, Giles 1999, Larsen 2001). For all these reasons, continuing existence of spirit possession is not a mere function of the state of biomedical practice.

Historical Changes in Spirit Types and Representations

I have previously discussed historical changes in the types of spirits found among the Swahili (1995, 1999), as has Larsen (1998a). The following provides a brief summary of some of the major points. Spirits have long been divided along the same two dimensions: pagan and Islamic, and coastal and inland, but specific spirit types within these broad divisions have varied as have their representations. The number of spirit types seems to have decreased since colonial times (e.g., cf. Koritschoner 1936). Most spirits in recent times represent human ethnic or regional groups, often with associated Islamic or non-Islamic identities, whereas those of former times include more animalistic and individualized pagan spirits. In current times Islamic Arab (*kiarabu*) and pagan Swahili spirits from the island of Pemba (*kipemba*, sometimes called *bwengo*) are the most widely found. In Mombasa, I found a significant minority of Mijikenda (*"Nyika"*) and Masai spirits, plus a smattering of other spirit types. A decade earlier, Topan (1971) found more cases of these latter spirit types, hence suggesting that a decrease in spirit types was still ongoing. In my other field sites, several other categories of spirits took on local significance, including Nyamwezi and Shambaa spirits in Pemba, and, as already noted, Malagasy *kibuki* and Ethiopian *Habeshia* spirits in Zanzibar town, with the latter in decline. European spirits, which were prominent during colonial times, were quite rare.

One can often find historical reasons for the popularity of spirits during certain time periods and in certain locations, depending on what ethnic groups and cultural traits impacted local Swahili society. The emergence of new spirit categories is often easy to correlate with new historical contacts and situations. The persistence or decline of spirit types is less straightforward. In his influential study of African art and spirit cults, Kramer (1987/1993), who sees spirits as representing the exotic Other (Larsen 2000), suggests that such spirit representations will disappear once the possessed person gains practical experience with the people or objects represented. This might explain why European spirits have declined among the Swahili, whereas Masai spirits, which still seem exotic, have persisted in certain locations. However, it does not explain why Islamic Arab spirits have remained important as possessive spirits, nor why spirits that are categorized as "Swahili" (i.e., *kipemba* spirits) would be a possessive spirit category at all. Contrary to Kramer, I view Swahili spirits as representing not only the exotic Other in opposition to the Self, but also different aspects of one's own personal and cultural identity (Giles 1995, 1999). From this perspective, I suggest that both the Arab Islamic spirits and the pagan Swahili spirits can be viewed as different and opposing aspects of Swahili identity (Larson 1998a). Moreover, I see the persistence or decline of various spirit types as relating to the degree of importance they hold for the formulation of personal and cultural identity, through representations of aspects of both Other and Self. The ongoing importance of Islamic Arab spirits and pagan Pemban spirits hence indicates that they still form the dominant discourse about the construction of identity and historical consciousness in Swahili coastal society, whereas the importance of other spirit types in other localities reflects more localized discourses.

Of course changes or lack of change in the enacted representations of specific spirit types are also revealing. In comparison with earlier descriptions of *kiarabu* spirits, current representations show more Islamic orthodoxy in regard to ritual, costume, and musical instrumentation. Some of the most objectionable ritual practices associated with non-Islamic spirits have also been abandoned, or at least better hidden from view. Thus, whereas Topan notes in his chapter the practice of drinking the blood of a sacrificial animal during possession, guild members usually told me that they no longer do this although the spirits themselves continued to do so. Similarly, those possessed by Mijikenda ("*Nyika*") spirits in the Mombasa area noted that they would not accede to the spirits' wishes for drinks or food objectionable to Islam, i.e., palm wine or rats. On the other hand, however, those possessed by *kibuki* spirits in Zanzibar not only provide the imported alcoholic beverages that many of these spirits relish but also consume them during possession ceremonies.

The *kibuki* cult, which has also been described by Larsen, is not typical of Swahili possession guilds. It is an adaptation of the *tromba* spirit possession complex for royal Sakalava ancestors, which originated in north-western Madagascar and was subsequently brought to the Comoro Islands (Lambek 1981, Sharp1993). *Kibuki* spirits thus represent a non-Islamic and non-Arab domain of power. In contrast to most Islamic spirits, *kibuki* spirits are arrogant and hedonistic, and attracted to Western material culture. Younger male spirits are especially undisciplined, throwing brandy about and chasing after women in the audience. They are very similar in behavior to the playboy spirits that Sharp (1995) notes as new formulations of *tromba* spirits among urban youth in northwestern Madagascar. Erdtsieck has also recently suggested that there is a growing trend in urban areas throughout the Tanzanian coast for possessive spirits to be more modern in character and demand more expensive objects and rituals (2003:49).

More Recent Changes and New Studies

During my brief visits in 1992 and 2001, I found signs that spirit guilds were still alive and well in several of my field sites. I sought out members and leaders of the *kibuki* spirit guild in Zanzibar town during both years, and during my 1992 visit actually found them in the midst of a spirit ceremony. I received the impression that the guild was still thriving. Similarly, when I visited my primary informant spirit guild leader in Wete in 1992, I also found him conducting a spirit ceremony for various clients. In Mombasa, I found a very elderly female guild leader still alive but very frail in 1992. Family members told me that her son, however, was becoming more involved in the guild, and after his mother's death in 2001 he was reported to be the new guild leader.[1] Furthermore, during my 1992 visit, his mother informed me that Mombasa's Swahili community was revitalizing the communal Swahili New Year's ceremony, including the reintroduction of spirit dances.

The reports of recent researchers also suggest an increase in spirit activities and guilds. Whereas, as noted above, the only frequent large public spirit ceremonies that I encountered during my 1984 research in Zanzibar town, were those of the *kibuki* spirits, Larsen (personal communication, April 2, 2005) found numerous public ceremonies for a variety of spirits during her research period from 1990–1992. Nisula (1999) also observes that in 1992/1993 many possession guilds were thriving in Zanzibar town.

---

1. During a 2006 visit, I found him in the midst of practicing spirit *uganga*, giving advice to a number of clients while possessed by one of his spirits. He told me that he had indeed succeeded his mother and had many followers, but that he did not hold *ngoma* (spirit ceremonies with drums and dancing held for non-Islamic spirits) like his mother had.

In regard to Tanga, although I had found a number of different types of *waganga* in the 1980s, it seems the number had increased by 2003, when Mackenrodt reported (personal communication, Feb. 8, 2004) that she had found "hundreds" of *waganga* there. She also noted that one of the non-Swahili spirit possession *waganga* that I had worked with extensively had become extremely prominent.

Although Erdtsieck's recently published study (2003) focuses on healers in the southern inland area of Tanzania, she also offers observations about *waganga* on the coast during the mid- to late 1990s. However, Erdtsieck's observations are rather hard to relate to specific coastal healing traditions because she tends to conflate coastal, urban, and Swahili practices in her discussion. It is also often unclear if she is referring to non-Swahili *waganga* who have incorporated Swahili healing techniques into their healing repertoire or to *waganga* who are ethnically Swahili.[1] Moreover, it is hard to discern if some of her remarks about coastal *waganga* as a generalized group apply to *waganga* wa pepo/sheitani (healers using possessive spirits). Erdtsieck points out that coastal *uganga* has been commercialized and that most *waganga* are male, often with no spirit inspiration and specializing more on protection than healing (2003:377). During my earlier research period, I also noted many male *waganga*, especially in urban areas, who seemed mostly interested in the commercial benefits of their practice, and some of them were no doubt charlatans. However, I found many female *waganga* among spirit healers. Whereas spirit *waganga* charged for their services, most, especially the women, felt that their spiritual services were more of a calling and that they should not charge large fees.[2]

Erdtsieck also observes that, in contrast to the southern inland area, few coastal healers practiced musical healing, and that those who did were usually in spirit guilds, which were themselves in decline. I found this assessment rather surprising, since I had worked with many coastal *waganga* from various ethnic groups (Swahili, Mijikenda, Bondei/Shambaa) who used musical healing therapies. Albeit they were *waganga* who treated spirit afflictions by calling up the spirits involved, but not all of them were associated with spirit guilds and some were actually Qur'anic *waganga* (*waganga*

---

1. Throughout her study she seems to characterize all coastal *waganga* as "Swahili" even when she notes their non-Swahili ethnicity.
2. The two female *waganga* for *kibuki* spirits in urban Zanzibar, however, seemed to be somewhat of an exception. People often talked about the fees that they charged as excessive and pointed to their desire to enrich themselves from their practice.

wa kitabu).[1] The musical element, however, is indeed most pronounced in the ceremonies of the spirit guilds, which emphasize dancing and often add various types of instruments. Erdtsieck's point about the decline of coastal spirit guilds agrees with some of the data from my research a decade earlier, but, as noted above, I found that this decline should not be overemphasized, for possession guilds seemed to be far from disappearing.

Conclusion

Swahili spirit possession has been affected by many societal changes throughout its history, and also reflects such changes within its spirit cosmology and ritual practices. Contrary to many expectations, recent societal and cultural changes do not necessarily lead to the demise of possession beliefs or possession guilds. Some scholars have suggested that spirit possession is actually on the rise in other areas of Eastern Africa, especially in urban areas (Kenyon 1995, Sharp 1995, regarding northern Sudan and northern Madagascar respectively), and throughout much of the world (Behrend & Luig, 1999, introduction). Whereas most studies on the Swahili coast do not point to a recent increase in spirit possession, they do suggest that spirit possession as well as possession guilds continue to show vitality and still relate to people's current concerns. In some cases one may even find an increase in Swahili spirit activities, especially due to recent liberalization of political ideology and/or economic policies in post-socialist Tanzania, especially in the case of Zanzibar.

One reason for the tenacity of spirit possession is that it is both multifunctional and polysemic (capable of carrying various and even opposing messages). It provides a fluid medium of expression, social action, and therapeutic strategy for various individuals and segments of society, which can incorporate both continuity and change as well as acceptance and critique. It thus remains relevant to current as well as future Swahili societal contexts.

Considerations for Further Research

All of these factors make spirit possession on the Swahili coast a fertile topic for further research. Functions, messages, societal participation, as well as the numbers and social categories of guild members all change depending

---

1. These use specific rhythms and songs, but limited instrumentation (handclapping, clapping objects, and sometimes tambourines).

on place, time, and social context. The same is true of spirit types, representations, and ritual expressions, as well as guild organization. Whereas surveys and assessments of public opinion can be useful, the information gained may be suspect and superficial, and thus must be coupled with in-depth and long range studies of spirit possession in specific localities, individuals, and guilds.

In this chapter I have also noted a number of specific trends and topics that require further study. Two of these are 1) changing gender roles within possession activities and guilds as well as the effects of such changes in the wider society and 2) the incorporation of new generations into possession activities and guilds. The latter is related to 3) the need for long term studies that follow and restudy specific guilds, individuals, and families that have already been studied, in order to not only examine changes through time but also to gain a better general perspective on possession itself. Other research topics mentioned include 4) the effect of Islamic fundamentalist or reformist movements; 5) the incorporation of spirit possession songs, dances, and rituals into non-ritual forms as affirmations of cultural heritage as well as social entertainment for local people, tourists, and other visitors; 6) the interaction of Western-inspired biomedicine and indigenous spiritual forms of healing, including cooperative efforts and their effects; and 7) forms of official organization and their effectiveness among *waganga*. Another interesting topic is 8) the movements of *waganga*, their clients, and possession beliefs across local and international borders in the past and present, especially with recent increased opportunities for travel. The travel of clients from, and *waganga* to, the Middle East, especially Oman, is an important facet of such movements. A related area for needed exploration is to what degree Swahili-inspired possession activities and guilds have emerged in the Middle East, India, and other areas of the world among Swahili immigrant communities. Another area for further research is 9) the reaction of possession practices and guilds to economic and political changes, one special case being the increasing capitalism and tourism in Zanzibar.[1]

---

1. A similar situation is also occurring in the Lamu area of Kenya (see Amidu in this volume). My few Lamu area informants in the early 1980s suggested that spirit possession guilds were not very active in Lamu town but that incidences of spirit possession still occurred. This assessment as well as the situation in the more rural areas warrants further study, since possession practices and guilds are often not readily evident or acknowledged. Moreover, the rapid social and religious changes since that time suggest that the situation regarding spirit possession may have undergone significant changes.

10) The two unusual possession guilds still found in Zanzibar town, *kibuki* and *Habeshia*, require more research, including their relations to Malagasy, Comorian, and Ethiopian *zar* possession complexes and cultural heritage.[1] 11) Also, there are many areas of the Swahili coastal area where possession has not been well studied, including the northern and southern extremes – the Benadir coast of Somalia and northern Mozambique respectively.[2] 12) More study also needs to be done in Pemba, rural Zanzibar, and the mainland coast of Tanzania, where older forms of spirit practices still prevail but are disappearing.

13) The entire history of spirit possession and possession guilds on the coast is not well understood. The origins and timeframe of possession guilds needs special attention. The fact that no written sources are known prior to European contact does not mean that spirit possession guilds did not exist on the coast. European and other written historical accounts also need to be interpreted more critically, and not simply taken at face value. Much more collection and examination of oral spirit traditions needs to take place, especially as these are disappearing. Some of these traditions can also enlighten other aspects of coastal history.[3]

14) Finally, the past and ongoing history of the interaction of Swahili spirit beliefs and rituals with other spirit traditions is an ever-present research topic. This includes research on the penetration and incorporation of Swahili spirit beliefs and practices into the interior, where researchers with in-depth knowledge of Swahili possession on the coast are needed in order to avoid misunderstandings and ambiguous terminology.

Swahili spirit possession thus remains an important research topic which can not only further our knowledge of an important aspect of Swahili society but also provide a revealing window on ongoing cultural, societal, and religious change.

---

1. Two contributors to this volume, Mohamed Saleh (of Comorian ancestry) and Marie Pierre Ballarin, have started to investigate the Comorian and Malagasy connections of the Zanzibari kibuki. Ballarin has even been able to trace the names of some of the kibuki spirit "kings" to specific historical Sakalava kings (personal communication, 2007).
2. The current political situation of course makes research in Somalia difficult. One researcher who has studied possession among several groups (including non-Somali) in Somalia, Francesca Declich (see her contribution to this volume), has also begun initial inquiries in northern Mozambique (personal communication, 2007).
3. For example, see Giles 2006 for spirit traditions regarding various pre-colonial local rulers (*majumbe*) in the Pangani region of Tanzania.

References

Alpers, Edward, 1984, "Ordinary Household Chores: Ritual and Power in a 19th-century Swahili Women's Spirit Possession Cult", *International Journal of African Historical Studies*, vol. 17, no. 4, pp. 677–702.

Askew, Kelly, 2002, *Performing the Nation: Swahili Music and Cultural Politics in Tanzania*. Chicago: University of Chicago Press.

Behrend, Heike and Ute Luig (eds), 1999, *Spirit Possession, Modernity, and Power in Africa*. Madison: University of Wisconsin Press/James Currey.

Boddy, Janice, 1989, *Wombs and Alien Spirits: Women and Men in the Zar Cult in Northern Sudan*. Madison: University of Wisconsin Press.

Cohen, Erik, 1988, "Authenticity and Commoditization in Tourism", *Annals of Tourist Research*, vol. 15, pp. 371–386.

Comaroff, Jean, and John Comaroff (eds), 1993, *Modernity and Its Malcontents: Ritual and Power in Postcolonial Africa*. Chicago: University of Chicago Press.

Connor, Linda, and Geoffrey Samuel, 2001, *Healing Powers and Modernity: TraditionalMedicine, Shamanism, and Science in Asian Societies*. Wesport, Connecticut/London: Bergin & Garvey.

Depelchin, Jacques, 1991, "The Transition from Slavery 1873–1914", in Abdul Sheriff and Ed Ferguson (eds), *Zanzibar under Colonial Rule*. London: James Currey, pp. 11–35.

Erdtsieck, Jessica, 2003, *In the Spirit of Uganga: Inspired Healing and Healership in Tanzania*. Amsterdam: AGIDS.

Evans-Pritchard, E.E., 1937, "The Notion of Witchcraft Explains Unfortunate Events", in *Witchcraft, Oracles, and Magic among the Azande*. Oxford: Clarendon Press.

Fair, Laura, 2001, *Pastimes and Politics: Culture, Community, and Identity in Post-Abolition Urban Zanzibar, 1890–1945*. Athens/Oxford: Ohio University Press/James Currey.

Feireman, Steven, 1974, *The Shambaa Kingdom*. Madison: University of Wisconsin.

Fry, Peter, 1976, *Spirits of Protest: Spirit-Mediums and the Articulation of Consensus among Zezuru of Southern Rhodeia*. Cambridge: Cambridge University Press.

Giles, Linda, 1987, "Possession Cults on the Swahili Coast: A Re-examination of Theories of Marginality", *Africa*, vol. 57, no. 2, pp. 234–258.

——, 1989, "Spirit Possession on the Swahili Coast: Peripheral Cults or Primary Texts?", PhD dissertation, University of Texas at Austin.

——, 1995, "Socio-Cultural Change and Spirit Possession on the Swahili Coast of East Africa", in Susan Kenyon (ed.), *Possession and Social Change in Eastern Africa*, special issue of *Anthropological Quarterly*, vol. 68, no. 2, pp. 107–120.

——, 1999, "Spirit Possession and the Symbolic Construction of Swahili Society", in Heike Behrend and Ute Luig (eds), *Spirit Possession, Modernity, and Power in Africa*. Madison: University of Wisconsin Press/James Currey, pp. 142–164.

——, 2006, "The Role of Spirits in Swahili Coastal Society", in Beatrice Nicolini (ed.), *Magical Practices, Witchcraft, and Warfare in the African Continent*. Lampeter, U.K.: E. Mellen Press, pp. 61–85.

Gonzalez, Nancie, 1966, "Health Behavior in Cross-Cultural Perspective: A Guatemalan Example", *Human Organization*, vol. 25, pp. 122–125.

Helman, Cecil G., 1994, *Culture, Health, and Illness: An Introduction for Health Professionals*, 3rd ed. Oxford: Butterworth-Heinemann.

Hepburn, Sharon J., 1988, "Western Minds, Foreign Bodies", W.H.R. Rivers prize essay (1986), *Medical Anthropological Quarterly*, vol. 2, no. 1 (NS), pp. 59–74.

Hunter, Linda, 2001, "Sorcery and Science as Competing Models of Explanation in a Sasak Village", in L. Connor and G. Samuel (eds), *Healing Powers and Modernity: Traditional Medicine, Shamanism, and Science in Asian Societies*. Westport, Connecticut/London: Bergin and Garvey, pp. 152–170.

Kenyon, Susan, 1995, "Zar as Modernization in Contemporary Sudan", in Susan Kenyon (ed.), *Possession and Social Change in Eastern Africa*, special issue of Anthropological Quarterly, vol. 68, no. 2, pp. 89–120.

Kleinman, Arthur, 1980, *Patients and Healers in the Context of Culture: An Exploration of the Borderland between Anthropology, Medicine, and Psychiatry*. Berkeley: University of California Press.

Koritschoner, Hans, 1936, "Ngoma ya sheitani", *JRAI*, vol. 66, pp. 209–219.

Kramer, Fritz, 1993, *The Red Fez: Art and Spirit Possession in Africa*. Translated from German by Malcolm R.Green. London: Verso. Originally published as *Der Rote Fes: Über Besessenheit und Kunst in Afrika* by Athenaum Verlag, 1987.

Lambek, Michael, 1981, *Human Spirits: A Cultural Account of Trance in Mayotte*. Cambridge: Cambridge University Press.

——, 1993, *Knowledge and Practice in Mayotte: Local Discourses of Islam, Sorcery, and Spirit Possession*. Toronto: University of Toronto Press.

Larsen, Kjersti, 1998a, "Spirit Possession as Historical Narrative: The Production of Identity and Locality in Zanzibar Town", in Nadia Lovell (ed.), *Locality and Belonging*. London: Rutledge, pp. 125–146.

——, 1998b, "Morality and Rejection of Spirits: A Zanzibari Case", *Social Anthropology*, vol. 6, no. 1, pp. 61–75.

——, 2000, "The Other Side of 'Nature': Expanding Tourism, Changing Landscapes, and Problems of Privacy in Urban Zanzibar", in V. Broche-Due & Richard Schroeder (eds), *Producing Nature and Poverty in Africa*. Uppsala: Nordiska Afrikainstitutet, pp. 198–219.

——, 2001, "Spirit Possession as Oral History: Negotiating Islam and Social Status: The Case of Zanzibar" in Biancamaria S. Amoretti (ed.), *Islam in East Africa: New Source*s (International Colloquium Rome 1999), pp. 275–294.

Lehmann, Arthur, and James Myers, 1993/1997, *Magic, Witchcraft, and Religion: An Anthropological Study of the Supernatural*. 3rd & 4th eds. Mountain View, CA: Mayfield Publishing.

Lan, David, 1985, *Guns and Rain: Guerrillas and Spirit Mediums in Zimbabwe*. London: James Currey.

Lewis, I.M., 1971, *Ecstatic Religion: An Anthropological Study of Spirit Possession and Shamanism*. Harmondsworth, U.K.: Penguin.

Lindblom, Gerhard, 1920, *The Akamba in British East Africa*. 2nd ed. New York: Negro Universities Press.

MacCannell, Dean, 1973, "Staged Authenticity: On Arrangements of Social Space in Tourist Settings", *American Journal of Sociology*, vol. 79, no.3, pp.589–603.

——, 1976, *The Tourist: A New Theory of the Leisure Class*. New York: Schocken Books.

McKean, Philip, 1977, "Towards a Theoretical Analysis of Tourism: Economic Dualism and Cultural Involution in Bali", in Valene Smith (ed.), *Hosts and Guests: The Anthropology of Tourism*. Philadelphia: University of Pennsylvania, pp. 93–107.

Micozzi, Marc S., 2002, "Culture, Anthropology, and the Return of 'Complementary Medicine'", *Medical Anthropology Quarterly*, vol. 16, no 4, pp. 398–403.

Nisula, Tapio, 1999, *Everyday Spirits and Medical Interventions: Ethnographic and Historical Notes on Therapeutic Conventions in Zanzibar Town*. Transactions of the Finnish Anthropological Society, NRO XLIII. Sarrijavi: Gummerus Kirjapaino Oy.

Noronha, R., 1979, "Paradise Revisited: Tourism in Bali", in E. de Kadt (ed.), *Tourism: Passport to Development*. Oxford University Press, pp. 177–204.

Offiong, Daniel, 1999, "Traditional Healers in the Nigerian Health Care Delivery System and Debate over Integrating Traditional and Scientific Methods", *Medical Anthropology Quarterly*, vol. 72, no. 3, pp. 118–130.

Ong, Aihwa, 1987, *Spirits of Resistance and Capitalist Discipline: Factory Women in Malaysia*. Albany: State University of New York Press.

Picard, M., 1996, *Bali: Cultural Tourism and Touristic Culture*. 2nd ed. Singapore: Archipelago Press.

Reiff, Marian, Bonnie O'Connor, Fredi Kronenborg, Michael Balick, Patricia Lohr, Maria Roble, Adriane Fugh-Berman, and Kimberly O. Johnson, 2003, "Ethnomedicine in the Urban Environment: Dominican Healers in New York City", *Human Organization*, vol. 62, no. 1, pp. 12–26.

Shackley, Myra, 1999, "Cultural Impact of Religious Tourism in the Himalayas", in M. Robinson and P. Boniface (eds), *Tourism and Cultural Conflicts*. Wallingford: CABI Publishing, pp. 95–111.

Sharp, Lesley, 1993, *The Possessed and the Dispossessed: Spirits, Identity, and Power in a Madagascar Migrant Town*. Berkeley: University of California Press.

——, 1995, "Playboy Princely Spirits of Madagascar: Possession as Youthful Commentary and Social Critique", in Susan Kenyon (ed.), *Possession and Social Change in Eastern Africa*, special issue of *Anthropological Quarterly*, vol. 68, no. 2, pp. 107–120.

Simpson, Bob, 1993, "Tourism and Tradition: From Healing to Heritage", *Annals of Tourism Research*, vol. 20, no. 1, pp. 164–181.

Smith, James H., 2001, "On Spirit Possession and Structural Adjustment Programs: Government Downsizing, Education, and Their Enchantment in Neo-liberal Kenya", *Journal of Religion in Africa*, vol. XXXI, no. 4, pp. 427–456.

Stoller, Paul, 1996, *Embodying Colonial Memories: Spirit Possession, Power, and the Hauka in West Africa*. London: Routledge. See also *American Anthropologist*, vol. 96 (1994), pp. 634–648; and *Ethos*, vol. 12, no. 2 (1984), pp. 165–188.

Strobel, Margaret, 1979, *Muslim Women in Mombasa, 1890–1975*. New Haven: Yale University Press.

Thompson, Barbara, 1999, "Kiuza Mpheho (Return of the Winds): The Arts of Healing among the Shambaa Peoples of Tanzania". PhD dissertation, University of Iowa, Iowa City, Iowa.

Topan, Farouk Mohamedhussein T., 1971, "Oral Literature in a Ritual Setting: The Role of Spirit Songs in a Spirit-Mediumship Cult in Mombasa, Kenya". PhD thesis, University of London.

Waxler, Nancy, 1977, "Is Mental Illness Cured in Traditional Societies? A Theoretical Analysis", *Culture, Medicine, and Psychiatry*, vol. 1, pp. 233–253.

Worsley, Peter, 1992, "Non-Western Medical Systems", *Annual Review of Anthropology*, vol. 11, pp. 315–348.

CHAPTER 6

Contested Interpretations of Muslim Poetries, Legitimacy and Daily Life Politics

Francesca Declich

Introduction

In Somalia the translation and interpretation of *qasiidooyin* commonly re-cited and sung within the celebration of *nabi-ammaan* are considered mat-ters not "pertaining" to all. Regardless of this, participants in the ceremo-nies hold their own views of their actions within the ritual and behave consistently with their understanding. More than once, when asking for translations of complete songs from common people they would refuse and suggest that we refer to a more knowledgeable person, notably a *sheekh* or a *khaliifa* they would mention; and yet, they seemed never to be sure which one would be best for the task and, often, after further enquiries, they re-alised he or she was in fact not the best and another person was called onto the scene. On the other hand, university level educated people would agree to engage in literal translations while declaring their ignorance on the is-sues concerned; yet, if the recordings of the *qasiidooyin* come from rural areas where certain dialects are spoken (usually, not their own) then they often express derision and scorn towards the contents of the verses, a disdain which is extended to those who recite such poetry. Alternatively, if the verses come from the part of the country they originate from, literal translations would be provided, yet with the clarification that they did not necessarily express the more profound contents related to those texts.

It is not surprising that religious poetic texts have different levels of readings, ranging from merely literal to a highly complex metaphoric one. However, in this specific context one seems to be facing a pattern of know-ledge management where some almost secret domains of knowledge ex-pressed in poetry are believed to only pertain to experts.[1] The focus of this reflection is thus on the social dynamics of exclusion and inclusion lying be-hind the legitimation of the recognised capacity to offer the best translation and, consequently, the moral teachings brought about by such legitimate

---

1. See also Bledsoe and Robey 1984 and Murphy 1980.

capacity. One matter at stake is who can offer these recognised interpretations in a daily life context and on the basis of which source of authority. Elsewhere I have discussed the role of the *sheekhs*, the *khaliifa* and the community surrounding them.[1] In daily life contexts, however, people do not refer continuously to those considered proper *sheekhs* living in the specific *jamaac* villages, nor to the village *sheekhs* acting as *qadi* (court judges) nor to the *khaliifa,* and they resort, obviously, to their own knowledge and lived experience. It is within this level of discourse that this essay examines the contents of the religious poetry and its interaction in defining and reproducing moral codes of socially acceptable individual behaviour and conduct.

I believe that a number of changes in the moral code concerning what is considered good demeanour for a woman and for a man are partly negotiated through the interplay and negotiation, which takes place in this arena. It is on the possibility of asserting one's own legitimacy in interpreting, and having one's assertions accepted, repeated, given credit and echoed that the power over the results of such negotiations lies. It goes without saying that since television started being broadcast on a larger scale in Somalia, approximately a decade ago, this power is being progressively and inexorably taken away from common people who are voiceless in this media communications system.

Yet, considering that nomadic lifestyle implies living for long periods of the year away from electric power, and therefore far from visual broadcasting instruments even if occasionally close to radios (in many Somali agricultural villages and towns electricity is not widely available to the villagers), negotiation over legitimacy on interpretation of religious issues still lies in an arena where literacy in Arabic, education and belonging to a certain social stratum play major roles.

Another relevant factor to this argument is that until now the majority of the people in rural Somalia are not literate either in Arabic or in Somali. Yet, their own interpretations of the *qasiidooyin's* words, and of the more general meanings and understanding of the entire performance of the *nabi-ammaan* are the basic foundation for their attachment to the celebrations, even if they are not usually asserted publicly as legitimate and correct.

I do not intend to argue here that the literal meanings of the stanzas are the basically important aspects of the celebration, but that multiple layers of meanings, including the significance of the verses as well as the experiential ones, interact at the same time within different sections of the audience. The meanings people express when asked to translate the stanza, especially when

---

1. Declich 1996, 2000b and 2001.

they do not literally translate the words contained in the verses, might be considered those particularly cogent to the speakers themselves.

A woman may attend a performance ascribing certain meanings and reasons for her attendance, while outsiders may believe she is participating out of other motivations. Motivations for participating may therefore be different and support given to the celebration by men and women may be endowed with diverse intentions. Such intentions are diverse in men and women whose expectations in life, needs, wishes and desires follow different lines. Yet, in the interaction of different motivations the performance takes place repeatedly every week following the same pattern as well as on the other prescribed occasions, although the contents may slightly change from one performance to the other, depending on the leaders' will.[1] All this constitutes an arena of negotiation where a number of actors may participate and interact with their own agency. Moreover, men and women show significant differences in the way they see their participation in Muslim celebrations and how they interpret hymns and prayers. In other words, religious performances are gendered experiences and produce gendered views and interpretations of themselves. Such different *positional understandings* are gendered. Men and women explain differently what is at stake in the ritual. Women seem to attend for the need to share difficulties with others who supposedly have the same problems, hoping to find, or at least to seek to bring about, a solution. Men, who largely do not know much about the entire *nabi-ammaan* celebration, since it is a "women's matter", may think of it as a context that helps in moralising women's lives. The usual sexual segregation of the ritual space of the *nabi-ammaan* fosters and facilitates the production and reproduction of different, gendered religious discourses within Muslim celebrations; yet, an interaction between such discourses through performance occurs when, as in Somali sufi pilgrimages, circles of feminine *dikri* are performed publicly in the squares of the *sheekhs'* community villages.

To give evidence for my argument I shall discuss a number of cases of translations of the prayers for Hawo and Faduumo (Eve and Fatima) sung as hymns during *nabi-ammaan* celebrations. I shall first present one case showing one kind of conflict of authority over the religious meanings of Sufi celebrations which take place in Somalia nowadays. This example reflects how higher education and ethnic belonging can be played out to exercise authority over recognised models of moral codes claiming new moral codes as pertaining to "correct" and real Islamic teachings.

---

1. Declich 1996.

I shall then offer a second case concerning the different translations provided by a man and a woman, Osman and Amiso, of the same prayer for Faduumo. This shows that although only women attend the celebration, men also have expectations about the outcomes of the performance and these may be different from the women's hopes. A man expects it to reinforce what he considers the women's "good" demeanour in the community and towards her husband, which he tends to represent as the demeanour Faduumo used to attain. A woman sees the celebration as a context where she can share difficulties of life with other women, she can identify with important personalities who have already passed through such difficulties and pray for success in her endeavours. In so doing, of course, she also represents a number of moral models she expects women should arrive at by conscious efforts.

In general the two cases illustrate different levels of negotiation over meanings and moral codes where Muslim religious attachment is claimed to legitimise the proposition of particular moral codes concerning women's behaviour and demeanour. The fact that most people in rural Somalia are illiterate makes it easier for educated people to claim higher authority over others even on matters concerning Islam.

While the study of Islam in East Africa has often been concerned with the study of the production of norms, theological and, possibly, political issues fashioned by ulamas, or schools of thought concerned with spreading Islam in certain territories, as well as with the authority they gained over people, I intend to focus on the way ordinary people perceive certain features of Islam as locally expressed in their contexts. This paper is not about theological or political disputes, but about daily life negotiation of meanings and the arena in which such meanings are debated. Of course this arena of negotiation is a locus where individuals and groups can exert political control through the manipulation of moral meanings in daily life contexts.

The Field

The argument put forward in this paper stemmed from the many observations I registered during an initial two-year-long fieldwork carried out in Somalia in between 1985 and 1988 and on the many occasions offered by follow-up research carried out during the last twenty years on and off in Somalia and among Somali Bantu refugees in Kenya, Tanzania and the USA. The specific material presented in this essay comes from several recordings gathered among Somali Bantu[1] refugees in Tanzania in 1996 and 1997 as well as on two visits paid to the country of the Somali speakers in July/August 1997 and in February 1998. The latter visits were paid respectively to Beled Weyne, the town of the important cattle market of central Somalia, and to the town of Borama, in the northwestern area of the country of the Somalis – today (2007) Somaliland. In both cases I had an opportunity to attend *nabi-ammaan* sessions organised by female local leaders. In Beled Weyne women belonging to the *tariqa* used to hold such sessions every Friday afternoon. These visits though brief sufficed to prove that these kinds of celebrations are not peculiar to the southern riverine areas of Somalia but are common all over Muslim Somalia. The performances witnessed between 1986 and 1988 along the Juba River are, therefore, not directly connected with legacies of the traditional rituals the Bantu speakers performed along the Juba River since they are also executed, sometimes with different songs and prayers, depending on the dialect spoken by the performers, in many Somali regions.

Part of my concern was to record mystic hymns devoted to female personalities of the Qur'an in order to compare them with other hymns recorded in Somalia. Moreover, I wished to gather a number of different points of view on such celebrations.

While previously I had the hymn contents described by local people and then also translated by literate and educated people, this time I decided to attempt to also obtain real local translations if this were at all possible. In fact, the widespread illiteracy creates an ambiguity about the evidence used. Although, in ethnographic terms, the comments and discussions on the text given by local people would be part of the evidence, together with a formal translation, the formally correct translation of poetry one has to offer to readers of an article, must be revised by specialists who may not be available in the area where the poetry has been collected. This very mixture of sources is problematic from an ethnographic point of view because the meanings ascribed to religious poetry by their users may not be the same that learned people and specialists offer for them; therefore, the very act of

---

1. Since the outbreak of the civil war in 1990 and the consequent flight of many refugees from Somalia to northern Kenya the new ethnic label "Somali Bantu" has been coined (Declich, 2000a). This indicates a number of different groupings of people who used to live in southern Somalia in riverine and interriverine areas who were mainly united by the fact of being marginalized by the main Somali clans: their marginalization was often based on the assumption that they were descendants of slaves. Some of the people nowadays referred to as "Somali Bantu" speak Bantu based languages such as, *Kizigula* and *Kibajuni*. On options and life strategies concerning the Somali Bantu in exile see also Declich 2006a and b.

transcribing poetry in a journal, which implies that it has been read and translated by a number of literate people in order to provide the most correct possible written version and translation of the poetic form, entails losing much of the significance it arouses among people when recited "in context". Yet, one peculiarity of poetry is exactly the ability, through the combination of words, to provoke feelings and allusions at meanings otherwise not easy to convey. Also, any original combination of words in verses may open the way to interpretations, suggestions and expression of feelings. The material presented at the end of the process of transcription always becomes, therefore, a mixture of viewpoints difficult to disentangle. For this reason, this time I wanted to record in the field many more local translations and perspectives on the poetry.

The search for a local translation, finally, proved to be an interesting aspect of the research because beyond the meanings, negotiation concerning authority became evident in the exercise.

Audience and Negotiating Interpretation

The first "exercise" implied putting together three people, two women (Mariamo and Deko) and a man (Omari), to listen to the recordings of the hymns in order to elicit their meanings for me. They all lived in Beled Weyene, the women belonging respectively to the Jijele and Gaaljeel clans while the man was a Makanne. Only Mariamo had studied until grade twelve so that she had a fair command of the written Somali language. The other two were almost illiterate in the Somali language. All were adults between 30 and 50 years of age.

Listening to the recordings kindled a number of types of behaviour among the three, which are worth describing. While playing, the recording seemed to help them to bring back memories; they sometimes looked as if rapt in wonder by certain verses; other stanzas they mimicked, showing the action described in them.

One of the hymns, for instance, is dedicated to Zeynab, the daughter of the Prophet, and the women singers plead with Zeynab to take them with her in the boat, which is a metaphor for heaven, teaching them to walk there as children. The verses (i and l) say "Let us go to the boat, Zeynab. Daughter of the Prophet, we follow you while you hold us by our hands". While translating and singing softly they imitated the scene of Zeynab teaching how to walk by extending both their arms in front of them as if they were helping a one-year-old baby to try its first steps. The same hymn contains soliciting help from each other when wearing a turban on their heads. While humming this part of the hymn they almost automatically mimed the act of making a *dub* (turban) on the head of a companion. When attending parties women in Somalia often twist a *garbasaar* (i.e. the coloured light veil they use loosely to protect their heads from the sun) on their heads, as if it were a turban. This is placed over the black scarf made of a sort of hairnet married women use to tie up their hair:

a) *Abbay dubkey dubka*	Sister I make to you a *dub*
b) *Annay dubkey dubka*	You make me a *dub*
c) *Abbadey dubkey dubka*	Sister, make her a *dub*
d) *Dub harirey dubka*	Make me a silk *dub*
e) *Donnidai isar dubka nasar*	Take us to the boat
f) *Ankuddahdane*	We would like to dance
g) *Anku din barane*	We learn to read religion
h) *Donnida inana sar*	Let us go to the boat
i) *Deynabo rasule*	Zeynab. Daughter of the Prophet
l) *Allah ddaddeheye*	We follow you while you hold us by our hands
m) *Gabal wadahaye*	It is late now
n) *Soddo baalo*	Go
o) *Nacam*	Yes!

The meanings of another poem called Abbay Sittidey, namely, "Sister Fatima", provoked long debates. For the translation of many verses the three occasional translators engaged in passionate discussions about the real significance of the stanzas, finally agreeing on a version and being happy about conveying it to me. I kept wondering why the verses provoked such discussions as texts usually have a finite range of possible translations. Although there may be many metaphoric meanings offered by poetic verses the three people ended up by proposing very descriptive translations of them featuring the images depicted in the poems.

A sort of answer to my wondering came up when a well-educated (graduate) man Ali, from a Galjeceel Somali clan, who was considered a *sheekh* as he had also done his Hajj to Mecca, intervened in the group translation. Rather than just engaging in passionate discussion about the real meanings conveyed by the verses, he showed a derisory attitude and burst into laughter whenever the three came up with translations, asserting that they were just stupid. In particular, he considered unacceptable the translation of a verse describing the journey towards Medina (g) where a panorama of mountains is illustrated before reaching the town. He laughed at length apparently unable to stop while absolutely rejecting this description. Mariamo and Omari became upset at the derision and Mariamo contested that, however often they listened to the recordings, this could not but be the translation: "Mountains will be seen, the *bun* (fried coffee beans) will be prepared when one goes to Medina". Yet the three of them had been fascinated until then at seeing in their mind's eye the mountains one would have to glimpse first from far away and then cross before reaching Mecca, and they had been gazing almost in contemplation at this image they seemed to be visualising. Only later, confidentially, did Ali mention to me that the verses probably refer to earlier journeys to Medina, when people would have to walk for days or months with a caravan before reaching the place instead of flying. In the public discussion, however, he was asserting the authority credited to him for the very fact of having been on a pilgrimage to Mecca.

Another translation Ali laughed at for several minutes, concerned verse (q) when my interpreters' descriptive translation depicted the Morning Prayer as "illuminating the women who execute it". Only later, again in private, did he tell me why he had laughed: he would rather interpret the stanza in metaphoric terms. The Morning Prayer can help to reach a certain benevolence, and benevolence is represented as luminosity. According to his interpretation, the purpose of the stanza is therefore to incite women to perform the Morning Prayer to achieve this state.

The group of three much less educated persons who were kindly "translating" for me perceived in particular the illustrative, almost pictorial aspect of the poetic expressions, which appeared to encompass them with evocative effects. They were inclined to describe figurative images of the situations described in the verses and to emphasise sentiments and passion towards them. While describing some of the actions or mimicking the scene portrayed in them, they gazed into the distance as if they were trying to visualise at that very moment what they were enunciating.

Another discussion showing the strong emotions evoked by the verses arose, for instance, when talking about verse (d), which says: "I deeply long for her, the last day she will give us happiness". The three interpreters together insisted that it was all about profound love and nostalgia for Mariamo while Ali would not endorse this version in front of them. He may not have been certain of the metaphoric meaning of this verse and did not want to assert something he was not sure of. Yet, he would not express his uncertainty in public, thus letting disrespect and derision fall on the group of three. The day after, he discussed the verses again with me; as he could not find other interpretations, he agreed that the translation might just as well be the one the occasional interpreters had given.

And yet Ali Haji, who was considered authoritative in that context, discredited in public everything they said or seemed to feel.

The text in point is the one of Abbay Sittidey as recorded during one performance:

Refrain *a)*	*Abbay sittidey*	Sister my Lady	
	Nurki Muktar	Light of Mukhtar	
	Batula Nabi	the Holy Batula	
b)	*Imaanka salaad*	She has great will for *salaad*	
	Sekeeda, sonkadka hijap	*zakat* fasting and doing the *hajj*	
	Abbay sittidey	Sister my Lady	
c)	*Baanka bismillahi*	I start with the name of God	
	bataya nabow mahadole	and after that I continue to	
	abowquey alloh Nabié	eulogise the Prophet	
d)	*Beder nuur badané*	I deeply long for her	
	badanka helaia behi		
	bankaaga bishaara na si	the last day she will give us happiness	
e)	*Minimki awka berrigi*		
	la gelaayo		
	Imaanka (allow nabiow)		
	Abbay Sittidey	Sister my Lady	
f)	*Abbay Nabiow*	Sister, of the Holy,	
	Dinti awka musliminti galeyso	for the Muslim religion of the Prophet	
	Abbay Sittidey	Sister my Lady	
g)	*Beri la ggaha bur bur la korà*	Mountains will be seen the bun (fried coffee beans) will be prepared	
	Bun bishara le kora Medina daià	when one goes to Medina	

h) *Bashar la naca bashar*   [In Medina] there are not plays and dances

    la naca beri kairle   it is a blessed day

    salama Allah nabiow   I pray God, (of the) Holy

i) *Ballanki awka barakoi*   The pledges taken by the

    alkada or (ballanka   Prophet towards his followers

    abbadia ba)

l) *Dintada tilman sodkaada*   The directions you gave us with

    shafea Dintada mistijaaabo   your benevolent voice, God wel-

    allah nabié   comes them

    Abbay Sittidey   Sister my Lady

m) *Towhidka xqiiji*   Understanding that God is only one

    Nabiow salamo   Prophet we ask for safety

    Abbay Sittidey   Sister my Lady

n) *Dintada la wa diya*   The recurrence of the Muslim

    bismillahi   religion

    La hubaa xuuskaga ramadan is the month of Ramadan

    Hassanow amin   Prophet, Amen

o) *Rihanta nabow*   The Prophet himself was scented

    Araftiza madaxa   the scents he held must be considered

    Suro wa

p) *Saladda adke son wa rahma*   Pray and fast

    Sonka sbar wa   and you will enjoy indulgence

    Abbay Sittidey   Sister my Lady

q) *Luxwa nurkaga*   The morning prayers

    Saladdo luxuhaa   Will illuminate you [You will

    badankaaga la maana   obtain benevolence (luminosity)]

    Abbay sitiyay   Sister my Lady

r) *Arafa la baha*   During the Arafa month one

    adana la mara asii   goes, one passes via Aden (the Red Sea)

    Abbay sittidey   Sister my Lady

s)	*Tugow la gala*	One prays God
	Sakawa la baga	One pays the *zakat*
	Bur bura la gala	if you do not, you will have problems

t)	*La kaca la kufa*	When you pray you stand up and bend down
	La kafara gudà	But you need to pay the kafara
	Kulonkin nabigen	Too meet the Prophet
	Abbay Sittidey	Sister my Lady

u)	*Luuxha la digà*	Those who will meet the Prophet
	Shecerki nabigen	
	Nabadallo gaga	will have to be pardoned by God first

The basic difference in understanding these hymns between my group of interpreters and the *sheekh* Ali was one of perceiving metaphoric and symbolic meanings as prescriptions. *Sheekh* Ali tended to interpret and translate every stanza in terms of the "teaching bit" contained in it; he was inclined to abstract concepts and teachings from concrete descriptions of actions and scenes. For instance, for verse (u) he did not provide any literal translation but only the didactic and moral meanings he assumed to be enclosed in the phrase. After listening several times he said: "It signifies that 'Those who shall meet the Prophet are those whose sins have been pardoned by God'".

Yet, Omari, was not able to give a comprehensive interpretation of the same verse saying for instance: "When praying one bends down and stands up to request mercy from God (or meet the Prophet)" or "if you say bad words, for instance, to your mother, go to the *sheekh*, tell him what you have done and have him read the Qur'an and the right words over you". He was particularly concerned about explaining what a *kafara* mentioned in stanza (t) is, namely a fine one has to pay to the *sheekh* in the case of bad mistakes such as, for instance, insulting one's wife.

Probably the *sheekh* was more knowledgeable about symbolic meanings ascribed to different aspects and figures proposed in the verses. Yet, the interaction of the *sheekh* with the group was one of complete disregard, arrogance and derision. The three people would not have considered themselves in a position to defend their own interpretations if it were not for the fact that I myself was inciting them to say what they thought was correct. Two were women and one was a man from a clan considered the very lowest in the Somali social stratification;[1] moreover Ali was an educated man with a university degree in addition to having made the pilgrimage to Mecca. A conflict of authority was enacted in front of me and seemed to reflect the local social stratification existing at the time: women were considered less important together with individuals regarded as descendants of slaves. Nevertheless, the values given to strata may change and women, as occurred in Mombasa with female *waganga* and verified by Farouk Topan and Linda Giles (Topan this book chapter 3), may acquire authority in the future, although there seem to be no signs of this kind of change now. On the contrary, the negotiations seem to be disempowering women at present in the wake of trends and fashions for completely covering clothing.

Perhaps, there would not have been any real dispute over who could give the most authoritative interpretation of those verses if I had not been present and shown my obvious confidence in the three occasional interpreters. The *sheekh* would have been ascribed the first reliability and trustworthiness as he was well educated, he came from Mogadishu, he was a man, he was not from a disregarded clan, he had been to Mecca.

In spite of the embedded authority he held because of his position in the social stratification, as he talked he revealed a lot of stereotypical ideas about the celebration of the *nabi-ammaan* for Hawo and Faduumo together with disregard for people of Bantu origins, considered as ex-slaves at the bottom level of the Somali social ladder. He started by asserting that this kind of celebration is common particularly among the people of southern Bantu origin and among people of the *tariqas*, whose leaders were initially mainly of Bantu origin. Yet, considering that the *nabi-ammaan* for Hawo and Faduumo is also practised in northern Somalia, he was, in fact, casting a negative stereotype usually ascribed to the Bantus on something he himself did not consider a good practice, the *nabi-ammaan* for Hawo and Faduumo.

He continued summing up a number of reasons why he did not agree with this kind of performance since, he said, women should behave differently. According to his idea of correct Muslim female behaviour, firstly, they should not raise their voices in front of many people; secondly, they should pray at home and not outside; thirdly, they should answer straight-forwardly without talking much in order to avoid somebody with bad intentions taking advantage of their kindness. In other words, his discontent over a certain kind of women's behaviour he disapproved of was transferred to women who, according to the teachings of the "Bantu" charismatic religious leaders, learn to pray in public and perform these celebrations.

---

1. See Cerulli 1957 and Luling 1971.

Unlike the stereotypes expressed by the authoritative man, in describing the meanings of the verses the three occasional interpreters showed the meanings and motivations of their attachment to the *nabi-ammaan* and, therefore, to what they consider their relevant features in the Muslim religion. Omari recalled being moved and cherishing the memory of women singing the hymns when he had set himself apart in a corner to cry on one of the seven days of mourning after his uncle's funeral. He said he is still moved to tears when he hears the songs and thinks of that day.[1] In other words, following the line of thought suggested by Gerard van de Bruinhorst (this book chapter 7) he was manifesting what he considered both the "performance" and the "spiritual" meaning of those *nabi-ammaan* hymns, probably reflecting local discourses concerning Islamic practices behind the texts.

Different Interpretations and Different Concerns

It is clear that, despite the fact that in the first instance everybody tries to escape taking on responsibility for a "correct" translation of the hymns, their interpretation becomes an arena for negotiation on moral discourse in the wake of changing material and ideological circumstances.

The dispute and negotiation in meanings played out in front of me revealed other important issues worthy of notice. In the first place, for none of the onlookers the translation of the *qasiidooyin* was evident at first. Indeed, the words of the *qasiidooyin* were not commonly shared and even after having listened to the recordings some verses were not clear to all of them. Different translations could be given as the words could get mixed up. Probably a leader of the feminine *nabi-ammaan* could have provided a clearer wording; yet, it is worth noticing that the people who simply partici-

---

1. If a digression is allowed, the motivation expressed by Omari for the attachment to certain Muslim performances reminded me of a reflection Assia Djebar presents in her book "L'amour, la fantasia" (Assia Djebar, *L'amore, la Guerra*, Ibis, Pavia, 1995: 189–190). She discusses the way she remembers the *Id of the Ram* of her childhood, when the Abraham lament used to be broadcast continuously in long Arabic songs. The lament describes Abraham tormented on the night God demanded the sacrifice of his son Isaac; later his wife Sara accompanied him, unaware of what was about to occur, and Isaac advanced up the mountain, innocent in his openness. The description within the song produced vivid emotions in Assia. Abraham's wife could have been her mother when recounting her premonitions; Abraham could have been her father who did not speak to express his emotions although he could have done so; she was caught up in emotion at the son Isaac's submissive attitude … A number of memories related to the stories of Abraham and Mohammed which she heard from relatives when she was a child, identifying herself in the situations described, are capable still today of provoking in her a sudden desire for Islam.

pate in the celebration, such as the three occasional interpreters, also have an imprecise idea of the literal meaning of what they recite neither do the moral concerns brought up in the poems seem to be generally understood and shared.

Though, this may not be not particularly surprising considering that much of the Somali population is barely literate, this fact points out to a number of considerations. First, despite the wide range of possible under-standings of the meanings of these songs, the women who sing them and participate in the celebrations are anyhow caught up almost in rapture by the performance; second, it seems obvious that each participant in the per-formance reproduces only those words he or she understands and remem-bers, especially the figurative images he or she likes most; third, as the meanings of the *qasiidooyin* are somewhat shifting, the celebrations take on as many meanings as those ascribed to them by the participants.

The teachings Ali Haji assumed to be obvious in the *qasiidooyin*, were not so obvious for the less educated local audience. Rather, the emotional attachment to some of these verses and contents and their body mimicking seemed more important to them. Emotional attachment and nostalgia for the atmosphere of the *nabi-ammaan* celebrations were shown by the occa-sional interpreters towards what each of them thought was the sense of the qasiidooyin performed, including the supposed luminous aura given to a woman by the Morning Prayer.

Male and Female Interpretations

Another case shows what seems to be at stake for ordinary people who par-ticipate in the celebrations praying for Hawo and Faduumo and the extent of negotiation involved. Often these prayers have a lot to do with what is considered a bad and a good woman or, in other words, with moral aspects concerning the construction of gender behaviour. It is worth noticing that women and men may see the performance from quite different perspectives. Examples of this point are the meanings of some *nabi-ammaan* hymns dedi-cated to Faduumo as related by a man and a woman, both literate in the Somali language, native *kizigula* speakers, able to speak simple *kiswahili*, and write in basic Italian. I asked both, in separate settings, to translate the same prayer to Fatima sung in the Somali language by a woman living in their village. Interestingly enough, while the men stressed the moral behav-iour of Faduumo as a good wife, the woman emphasized the plea women reiterated to the dead daughter of Mohamed to help them during delivery.

To clarify this latest point, one of the occasions when the *nabi-ammaan* is performed is before a woman's delivery in order to avoid problems and pray for a good childbirth. In addition such celebrations are usually held in contexts where no public health services are available so that women risk haemorrhages and even death from delivering. Yet, as explained elsewhere, the *nabi-ammaan* for Hawo and Faduumo is held on many other occasions when women would like the support of other women in their endeavours.

It is striking how different the interpretations given by the two of the same verses were. The man (Osman) mentioned a number of important aspects as if they were verses of the hymns:

Faduumo was never tired, she was a really good Muslim woman, she prayed and worked day and night because she loved God, she was not jealous, she was clean, she would use henna on her feet and hands before meeting the husband because he liked it, she used black powder (*ind khul*) to paint her eyes, she never said a bad word to her husband, she was not a liar or one who speaks to manipulate situations, her husband had two wives but she was not jealous, the two wives did not live together, she once fought with her husband to make the other wife happy, she never went to the husband of another woman, she never stole anything, she did not pay attention to gossip about things she did not witness, she once gave her *jijimo* to the second wife of her husband and told her to stop fighting with him until he could find money to make another one for her, she did not go around to gossip, on the contrary she spent time praying, she used to cut her nails and clean them very well, when she finished working she spent time with her husband and the children to make them happy.

It may be that the man did not understand the Somali poetry of the hymns and did not want to reveal it. Or that, as he knew I am his wife's friend, he wanted to send reprimands to his wife concerning how she should behave, according to a "speaking" scheme of communication as analysed by Duranti (1992:53). According to this frame an act of communication can be directed to both the audience and the addressee and this may occur when there is a social or affective relationship between the two. (Sometimes anthropologists find that people do not do precisely what they are requested to!) However, what he said instead is important anyway: he gave a number of rules women have to follow in order to make their husbands happy and not to fight with their second wives! He evidently thought it was perfectly plausible to ascribe this moralising function to the hymn for Faduumo and in line with the rationale of the celebration addressed to her. Here, instead, are the meanings as reported by the woman (Amiso):

> *Faduumo, when we are in labour pain, we pray to you to have the child come out smoothly, when we are in labour pain we must run to the eldest sister Faduumo, when we feel the labour pain Faduumo is there with us, we are to make the madax-shub as she did it, Faduumo is kind with everybody, the one who celebrates the xuus (i.e. annual memorial prayers) for her will find everything, if we do pray together Faduumo is there too, if one becomes pregnant one must pray to Faduumo, Faduumo was good at talking with everybody, Faduumo now I feel the pain of the labour, Faduumo please pray that the labour keeps on so that the child can come out, Faduumo also had the black hairnet on her head, you must be careful about talking good things to people, which is important to avoid difficulties during the delivery, Faduumo got along with other wives of her husband, Faduumo is our mother, those who have problems must call the name of Faduumo, Faduumo is sweet as honey.*

The meanings given by the woman to the verses include some of the same contents pointed out by the man, yet, she emphasises completely different aspects. The woman interprets each verse as related to the help Faduumo can give to a pregnant woman. Even having bad discussions with somebody can jeopardise a good delivery, therefore Faduumo is depicted as the woman who always spoke gently with everybody. Alternatively, for the man the emphasis is on the fact that Faduumo was not jealous of the second wife of her husband and was not a gossiper.

The result of this exercise seems amazing and one starts wondering what these celebrations really are about and what sort of issues are truly debated within them. Both the man and the woman were mainly *kizigula* speakers, the Somali language was their second language (although the woman was a teacher of Somali in primary school) and the chanted verses reproduced by a tape recorder are not always perfectly clear; we may therefore assume that both could not understand the verses very precisely. However, possibly for this very reason, the exercise revealed all the more the wishes and hopes for the resolution of the daily problems the man and the woman projected on the performance of a celebration for Hawo and Faduumo. I can testify, having known both for years, that the man always had trouble with his wife who has a difficult character and is particularly jealous of his second wife; on the other hand, the woman greatly feared deliveries although she had borne nine children: more than once the labour cramps stopped during childbirth and she feared that the baby could choke and die because of this. In this specific case the man believed or expected the songs to be about the demeanour a Muslim woman has to keep within marriage, especially in the case of conflict between two wives of the same husband and concerning the bringing up of children. The woman described, rather, the celebration as a place where women can share their fear about delivery together with the other participants projecting onto Faduumo the possibility to foster its success.

Osman and Amiso's translations were very different from each other and suggest that the man and the woman ascribe different significance to the hymns and that they hold different expectations concerning the outcome of the celebrations. By inferring that their behaviour reflects a more general trend, I would think that when a man offers money to his wife to buy the food needed to organize her child-bearing banquet for a *nabi-ammaan*, he might also expect that his role as husband in a polygamous household, honoured and respected by both wives, will be reconfirmed through the celebration. The wife, on the other hand, by sharing her fears with other women, expects to get through the delivery smoothly.

This means once again that the entire celebration does not have a univocal sense for all and, on the contrary, is a real arena where multiple expectations are brought in by participants and a number of moral issues are spelled out though not necessarily understood and appropriated by all. Rather, this evidence seems to show the existence of *positional understandings* individual participants have of prayers and ritual songs, which is precisely what gives rise and space to negotiation, as well as sustaining possible different Muslim and gender identities. To put it in terms of the ethnography of the language of daily life (Duranti, 1992:58) it is clear that the literal meanings of the poetic communication within the celebration may convey in reality completely different or unexpected messages when analysed within the sociocultural context in which they are expressed. There may in fact be a separate and practically parallel communication among women and men, especially when the social context of the reproduction of the prayers and songs is strictly monosexual. Men and women can develop completely separate contexts, especially meaningful to them. In particular, the celebration of the *nabi-ammaan* organised separately by the women constitutes a space for negotiating meanings about their role in society and succeeding in sharing them, as shown elsewhere, (Dechlich, 1996) despite what might be expected of them. The verses can contain and diffuse among women ideas and meanings about women's demeanour which are not controlled by the men.

Some Conclusions

By way of concluding, poetic forms sung communally in Somalia open up space to a number of interpretations, revisions of meanings and denials; the intended moral and practical didactic meanings are not necessarily understood in the same way by everyone even when the language is the one spoken by the audience, let alone when the audience hardly knows Arabic – the original language of the Islamic texts.

These cases show that the ideal of close connection with what is considered "really Muslim" and the moral teachings related to "being Muslim" are not fixed once and for all, but negotiated in different daily life contexts. In other words, paraphrasing Bledsoe, who used it to assert that literacy in Arabic among the Mende was used to conceal information rather than make it more accessible "literal meanings of the words may be less important than negotiated claims about their meanings – if indeed, these literal meanings can be determined reliably" (Bledsoe and Robey, 1984: 206). The result of the negotiation is a matter of power, and power in this ethnographic case is marked by a number of social criteria that have not much to do with the Qur'an itself or the links with the Prophet's life or descent. Should the woman *khaliifa* of the *nabi-ammaan* I recorded be present at the discussion with the three occasional interpreters, a different analysis of the moral issues encompassed in the different songs would have been elicited. Perhaps, *sheekh* Ali would have dared to contradict her interpretations, maybe not, and probably the three occasional interpreters would have sided with her. Certainly, when no male and well-educated person who has visited Mecca is present, a woman *khaliifa* asserts her interpretation and she is credited for this. Much may depend on the availability of contexts where such a woman can affirm her position.

Contexts of this kind, however, seem to be restricted nowadays. Certainly, a number of prohibitions due to the sensitive and peculiar situation of the town of Beled Weyne at the time I visited it might have discouraged the *habitués* of the *nabi-ammaan* celebrations from continuing to participate thereby delegitimising the interpretation given by the women *khaliifa*. Omari told me that *dikri* and *nabi-ammaan* performances were a bit restricted in those days (1997) due to new radical Muslim groups who arrived in the town and did not approve of the celebrations. Some of these groups requested women to wear a black all-covering chador in exchange for a subsistence allowance. Although he would not allow his wife to do so, Omari very much regretted that other women had accepted in order to be able to "eat enough". "All of those women are fat, and even their faces are fat for they have plenty to eat", he said "but I love the *dikri* too much for accepting this offer". Being fat in Somalia is a matter of prestige: it shows wealth and good health. Moreover, having plenty of food seemed a sort of joke for those women all the more because, at the time, it was not easy to arrange *dikri* celebrations in town for lack of food and money to organise the prescribed meal for the participating people.

Authority, in this Somali daily life context is also based on the existing boundaries of the local social stratification and criteria of inclusion/exclusion; belonging to a certain clan may enhance the voice of somebody's opinion in comparison to others; having visited Mecca is another decisive factor involved in providing people with authority. In some ways, education too is an important criterion.

Far from being a rationally discussed active participation, acceptance[1] and attachment to Muslim celebrations and rituals are also expressed as an emotional attachment. Omari showed that his personal attachment was also related to the fact of having individually marked difficult moments in life (such as death or other forms of loss) with memories of socially recognised representations. Socially recognised representations would range from communally held rituals to communally recognised narratives such as the Book or the poetry sung in the celebrations. Yet, even the sort of passionate and mimicked descriptions the two women gave of the verses seemed to show a sort of emotional attachment to the celebrations, marked by the pleasure of miming. It seemed as if miming the events mentioned in the verses helped them to mentally enter into the atmosphere of those descriptions and revive, even if in their imagination, the same experiences and feelings of the people depicted in the verses. Moreover, miming also favoured an intercommunication of those supposed feelings through bodily gestures, thus conveying a sense of communally sharing the same experience. The entire communication setting was evidently pleasurable and enjoyable.

References

Bledsoe Caroline H. and Robey Kenneth M., 1984, "Arabic Literacy and Secrecy among the Mende of Sierra Leone", *Man*, 1984:202–226.

Cerulli, Enrico, 1957, *Somalia*. Roma: Istituto Poligrafico dello Stato.

Declich, Francesca, 1996, "*Nabi-ammaan*: poesia religiosa femminile in un contesto rurale della Somalia", *Africa*, 1.

---

1. I like to talk about "active participation in" and "acceptance" as different from conversion as argued by Lambek, 2000:65.

Declich, Francesca, 2000a, "Fostering Ethnic Reinvention: Gender Impact of Forced Migration on Bantu, Somali Refugees in Kenya", *Cahiers d'Études Africaines,* EHESS, 157, LX.

Declich, Francesca, 2000b, "Sufi experience in rural Somalia: A focus on women", *Social Anthropology*, 3, 8, 1–24.

Declich, Francesca, 2001, "Oral and written among Muslim Somalis: Religious poetry and feminine poems between dialects and Arabic", *Islam in East Africa*, B. M. Scarcia Amoretti (a cura di), Roma: Herder.

Declich, Francesca, 2002, *I Bantu della Somalia. Etnogenesi e rituali mviko*, Milano: Franco Angeli.

Declich, Francesca. 2006a, "Somali 'Bantu' in diaspora: Options and concerns", paper presented at the Workshop of the Nordic Network *Diaspora and State Formation in the Horn of Africa*, Helsinki, 11–14 May 2006.

Declich, Francesca. 2006b, "Can boundaries not border on one another?", paper presented at the Workshop *Divided they stand: The affordances of state borders in the Horn of Africa*, Max Plank Institute, Halle, 7–8 September, 2006.

Djebar, Assia, 1985, *L'amour, la fantasia*, J.C. Lattès, Paris. Trans. It.: *L'amore, la guerra*. Ibis, Pavia, 1995: 189–190.

Duranti, Alessandro, 1992, *Etnografia del parlare quotidiano*. La nuova Italia Scientifica, Roma: 40–41 and 53.

Kaptejin, Lidwien with Matiam Omar Ali, 1996, "*Sittaat:* Somali Women's Songs for the 'Mother of the Believers'", in Harrow Kenneth W. (ed.), *The Marabout and the Muse. New Appraches to Islam in African Literature.* London and Portsmouth: Heinemann & James and Currey.

Lambek, Michael, 2000, "Localising Islamic Performances in Mayotte", in Parkin, David and Headley Stephen C. (eds), *Inside and Outside the Mosque: The Anthropology of Muslim Prayer Across the Indian Ocean.* Curzon, pp. 63, *Islamic Prayer across the Indian Ocean.* Richmond, Surrey: Curzon, pp. 63–97.

Luling, Virginia, 1971, *The Social Structure of Southern Somali Tribes.* London: University of London, PhD thesis.

Murphy, William P., 1980, "Secret knowledge as property and power in Kpelle society: Elders versus youth", in *Africa*, 50, 2, 193–207.

– CHAPTER 7 –

Siku ya Arafa and the Idd el-Hajj
Knowledge, Ritual and Renewal in Tanzania

Gerard C. van de Bruinhorst

Introduction

On Sunday 4 March 2001 thousands of Tanzanian Muslims commemorated the victims of two clashes between the riot police and citizens: Mwembechai (February 1998) and Zanzibar (January 2001). In the Islamic lunar calendar it was the day of Arafa (Swahili: *siku ya Arafa*), the 9th Dhul Hijja, one day before the holiday '*id al-adha* (Swahili: *Idd el-Hajj*). Both days derived their name and significance from the *hajj*: the annual pilgrimage to the sacred centre of Mecca. The demonstration was a joint product of two organizations: the Baraza Kuu la Jumuiya na Taasisi za Islam (Supreme Council of Islamic Organizations and Institutes) and the Islamic Propagation Centre (IPC). The Baraza Kuu was established in January 1992 as a rival organization to the official Supreme Council of Tanzanian Muslims, BAKWATA. After 23 years of 'repression and injustice', according to the founders of Baraza Kuu, it was high time to launch an Islamic institute defending the rights of Muslim citizens.[1] In the same year the IPC started to publish their newspaper an-Nuur. Both Baraza Kuu and IPC have similar goals: emancipation of Tanzanian Muslims as citizens who make use of their civic rights and are equal to their Christian compatriots and the boosting of Islam as a framework for political action. Both organizations foster close links and the same names appear in both circles. Both have connections with the opposition party Civic United Front (CUF).[2] Their means to achieve their goal are twofold: education and political participation.

The Arafa demonstration must be seen as painted on the canvas of a wider historical/political background. As Cameron and Caplan describe in this volume from a Zanzibar and a Mafia perspective, trust in the ruling party CCM (nicknamed "Catholic Church Movement") seems to have diminished during the last decade. The IPC and Baraza Kuu discourse blames

---

1. "Baada ya kudhalilishwa kwa miaka 23 hatimaye," *an-Nuur* 6, January 1992.
2. Every five years an-Nuur publishes the CUF election programme in full.

the government for destroying those elements within the civil society that helped Muslims to get an equal share of the development cake. According to both groups rather than being unrelated historical incidents this marginalization must be attributed to a deliberate plan directed towards safeguarding the Christian political hegemony. The ban on the East African Muslim Welfare Society (EAMWS) and the creation of the government controlled Muslim council BAKWATA (1968), the extradition of the writers collective Warsha ya Waandishi (1982) and the prohibition of the NGO al-Haramayn (2002) are presented as illustrations of a continuing trend. Among the coping strategies and counter-narratives as described by Caplan and Cameron Islamic religious ritual should also be considered.

In this paper I will highlight some of the elements that made the Arafa meeting a powerful ritual to deal with a deeply felt social and political unease. I will argue that

1)   textual knowledge of Islamic ritual is essential but only as one of the sources that contribute to the significance of the Arafa demonstration (section 2)
2)   the *hajj* within the IPC discourse is a powerful symbol for the renewal of the Muslim moral community in Tanzania (section 3)
3)   the significance of the day of Arafa is intimately connected to the symbols and (sacrificial) rituals of the following day of the *Idd el-Hajj* (section 4)

Knowledge and Ritual Practice

"Muslims shape their religious rituals to local cultural concerns and to universalistic scriptural imperatives" John Bowen states in his article on Muslim sacrifice (Bowen 1992:656). Despite the truism of this statement, many anthropological analyses of Islamic rituals still either overstate their so-called scriptural base or totally neglect the influence of trans-local scriptural discourse. In the case of the *'id al-adha* this distortion takes on the shape of an almost total neglect of the link between the *hajj* rituals as performed in Saudi Arabia, and the rituals simultaneously carried out elsewhere. Although the Arabic word for the celebration *'id al-adha* (Sacrificial Feast) or *'id al kabir* (Major Feast) is extensively used all over the world, local Islamic communities often indicate the holiday with their own term in a vernacular or popular transcription such as *Bakri Eid* (India, Bangladesh, Pakistan) or *Kurban Bayram* (Turkey). By neglecting these local names as is often done in favour of the 'real' Arabic word for the ritual (cf. Trimingham

1964 passim), important information necessary to understand its local practice and meaning gets lost. On the other hand focusing purely on local aspects of an Islamic ritual betrays the existence of any relationship between local practice and global discourse. The Tanzanian case shows a few of the complex, changing and subtle connections between local and global 'textual' ritual.

Swahili discourse employs five different words for the celebration on the tenth of the month of Dhul Hijja, each highlighting different semantic cores:

- *Idd el-Hajj* (festival of the *hajj*)
- *Idd ya mfungo tatu* (the *Idd* of the third month after Ramadan)
- *Id-ul Adh'ha* (derived from the Arabic word for *hajj* sacrifice *adha* and *udhiyya*)
- *Siku ya kuchinja* or *Idd ya kuchinja* (day or feast of immolation)
- *Siku ya vijungu* (day of the dishes)

The first two names are by far the most popular. *Idd el-Hajj* obviously refers to the pilgrimage to Mecca, and connects the local festivity with the ritual in Saudi Arabia. It implies a connection between the annual pilgrimage 'out there' and the activities of those believers left behind in Tanzania. The second word cluster *Idd ya mfungo tatu* is very common among mainstream, non-reformist Muslims and its semantics focus on the time of the festival, rather than on the sacrificial act itself. The name *mfunguo* refers to the month of Ramadan and the subsequent 'releasing' (*funguo*) of the spirits chained in the holy month. Here the Sacrificial Feast is positioned between the *Idd el-Fitr* or *Idd ya mfungo mosi* (first month after Ramadan) and the birthday of the Prophet in the sixth month (*mfungo sita*). The Arabic *Id-ul Adh'ha* I usually read in 'higher' Islamic discourse: textbooks, reformist pamphlets and theological discussions in newspapers. Finally *siku ya kuchinja* is a literal translation of the third term and is not very common. The verb *kuchinja* carries the same brutal overtones as the English 'to slaughter', and once I heard a preacher defend the peaceful nature of the ritual despite its cruel name. 'Although Muslims slaughter animals they are not butchers (*wachinjaji*) as the enemies of Islam assume,' he said. Finally the expression *siku ya vijungu* refers to the traditional practice of communal meals in commemoration of the deceased, in the nine days before the *Idd*. The popularity of the name *Idd el-Hajj* (even the reformist Ansaar Sunna movement prefers the word) suggests that in the Tanzania discourse the *Idd* is more intimately linked with the *hajj* than is generally the case.

To explain such a link between the Tanzanian *Idd* and the Arabic *hajj* with reference to authoritative texts and textual knowledge of Arabic theological discourse is rather unsatisfactory. The *Idd* is indeed one of the final rituals of the *hajj* marking the end of the rites connected with this fifth pillar of Islam. Yet, Islam is not an essentialized monolithic system of beliefs exercising equal influence on all Muslims everywhere throughout history. In each case the influence of particular texts should be established and proven. The mere existence of an Arabic written discourse on a particular subject cannot act as a proof of influence.

Although I find Woodward's subtle analysis of the Javanese ritual meal slametan quite convincing, his attempt to transcend the normative/popular, dini and mila (Topan, this volume), distinction of Islamic ritual by a more complex typology is not very helpful for the Tanzanian context (Woodward 1988:87–89). As will become clear, the *Idd* as performed by many Tanzanian Muslims contains elements from all his categories: 'universalist, essentialist, received and local Islam'. Woodward presents the *hajj* and the *Idd* celebration as examples of universalist Islam being 'rites specifically enjoined by universalist texts' (Woodward 1988:89). Yet his strong focus on the exclusive importance of textual knowledge in the interpretation of these two rituals can become a barrier to seeing other aspects of the Tanzanian *Idd el-Hajj*. It is seldom the text that provides a priori the incentive to start a practice, although texts offer a 'charter' to justify behaviour as Farouk Topan (this volume) states with respect to spirit possession. In Swahili discourse the *Idd el-Hajj* is usually justified by a single Qur'anic verse: 'Pray to your Lord and sacrifice (Q 108:2). The major problem for believers is that the verse appears in a Meccan Sura, too early to be connected with the commonly accepted later introduction of the *Idd el-Hajj*. It would imply that Muhammad ordered participating in a pagan sacrificial rite long before this had become Islamized! But no Muslim would deny the 'orthodox'/ textual foundation of the ritual, which is in this case derived from more recent prophetic traditions.

Claiming that the Arafa demonstration in Dar es Salaam lacked any textual foundation does not enhance our understanding of the ritual. Not because this statement is not true, but because the Islamic discourse on ritual is not only concerned with narrow, specific expectations (for example praying five times a day) but also with the broad, vague expectations of behaviour (for example it should not compromise the principle of *tawhid*). "Specific expectations involve narrow ranges of behaviour that require little interpretation [but] general expectations ... are quite different and call for elaborate interpretation of behaviour in assessing whether they have been met" (Swartz 1991:11). Discussions on the legitimacy of Islamic rituals are more often on the level of general expectations.

To overcome the false dichotomy between global/local, normative/popular practices, Talal Asad proposed an approach to Islam as 'a discursive tradition' (Asad 1986). This concept is particularly useful in pointing out the coherences and continuities of particular ideas and rituals, rather than their reformations and renewals (Schielke 2006:242–246). A unique event like the 2001 Arafa demonstration cannot be understood without exploring the discursively constructed connections between the acts of the demonstrators and those of the pilgrims. In this vein I will analyse the IPC discourse discussing the meaning of the *Idd el-Hajj* as constructed between local understandings and global textual imperatives. I will make a distinction between three different paradigms: the hajj as performance, focusing on the acts of the pilgrims and their experience. This first paradigm is closest to what is usually understood by 'textual knowledge'. Secondly I describe the *hajj* as a spiritual meaning behind the bare acts and finally I will show how the *hajj* in Swahili discourse is presented as endangered by forces from outside and within.

Presentations of the Pilgrimage

The hajj *performed*

How to perform the *hajj* is the subject of videos, audiocassettes, books, articles and booklets. Its main stages (circumambulation of the Ka'ba building, running between the two hills Safa and Marwa, standing on the plains of Arafa, stoning of three pillars and sacrificing an animal) are explained at special meetings to prepare the pilgrim for this occasion. A good example is the booklet *Muongozo wa Hijja* (Guide to the *Hajj*) used by the largest *hajj* organization and written by the Zanzibar author Muhammad Salim Zagar.[1] The 51 pages of the book are divided in useful sections which can easily be consulted during the *hajj*. After the explanations of the rites the book concludes with three appendices: the farewell sermon of the Prophet, the translations of all the Arabic supplications and a complete overview of all the religious performances ordered by time and place. The bulk of the literature in Swahili describes the *hajj* as Zagar does: a laborious endeavour

---

1. Zagar performed the *hajj* at least four times. The author also wrote a forword in Saleh al Farsy's *Masuala ya dini* (1992).

with long lists of prescriptions and potential mistakes.[1] From the perspective of these guides textual knowledge is essential to find your way in the bewildering throngs. They seem to suggest that there is only one proper way to perform the 'visit to the House of God'.

However, from the moment of arrival in Mecca the pilgrim experiences that different interpretations of *hajj* rituals exist but are not allowed by Saudi officials. The Saudi ministry of *hajj* is embodied in the local guide (*mutawwif*). The power to enforce the rules as understood by the Saudis is also illustrated by the behaviour of police and soldiers during the *hajj*: a Shi'ite pilgrim comments on a Swahili website: "These Wahhabiyya assail the pilgrims with any kind of persecution (*mateso*) and prevent them from praying (*kutaburuku*) and kissing the tomb of the Messenger and you will see time and again they grab their stick and have them ready in their hands to attack every *hajji* who dares to pray to or kiss the grave of the Messenger."[2] This reveals that, despite the generally acknowledged textual status of the *hajj* on the practical level of performance, Muslims can discuss, contest and condemn practices. For example within Swahili discourse one can find discussions on the legal status of the rites, the recitation of Arabic supplication instead of Swahili, how to keep the veneration of the Prophet within the proper monotheistic boundaries and how and when to shave the hair after the accomplishment of the *hajj* (cf. Bousquet 1949:104).

The hajj *as edification*

The *hajj* is not only a divine command to be obeyed as well as you can, but also a lofty enterprise with a high spiritual meaning.[3] The holy places in and around Mecca bring the pilgrim both in spirit and in action close to God. The Ka'ba is a faithful copy of God's House in heaven, the *hajj* rituals equal those of the angels,[4] and the Black Stone is the hand of God. Several of the rituals are linked to well known historical paradigms, specifically those of the prophets Ibrahim and Muhammad. Thinking about God's behaviour towards these prophets will encourage the Muslim to imitate them.[5] The effect of the *hajj* is therefore highly edifying. Most of the major lessons (*mafunzo makubwa*) a pilgrim should learn from the pilgrimage can be classi-

1. See for example "Ibada ya Hijja," (*Istiqama*, January 2002, p. 24) listing six different categories of mistakes.
2. "Uchunguzi Juu ya Uwahhabi," at: http://www.al-islam.org/kiswahili/uchunguzi2/23.htm (accessed 16 August 2006).
3. See "The Hajj Pilgrimage," *al-Islam* 1977, p. 12–24.
4. See "Historia na falsafa ya Hijja," *Maarifa* (3), 16 January 2002, p. 6.
5. "Ibada ya Tawaf," *an-Nuur* 332, 2 March 2001.

fied in five categories: awareness of the global Muslim community (*ummah*), obedience to God, preparedness for self-sacrifice, continuing remembrance of the final Judgement and the willingness to revive, defend and protect the Islamic religion.

In the first place the *hajj* reminds the Muslim of the fact that he is part of God's *ummah*. The plain, seamless *ihram* clothes in their simplicity stress the equality of all believers, they remove all traces of discrimination and jealousy. Love, equal treatment of all races, brotherhood, equality and 'communitas' (*kushikamana*) are exalted.[1] Being shoulder to shoulder in performing the *tawaf* (circumambulation), the *saa'y* (running between the two hills) standing at Arafa and stoning the pillars represent the unity, brotherhood and equality (*umoja, udugu, usawa*) of all believers from all corners of the world.

Obedience to God (*kumtii Allah*) is a second theme in the *hajj* discourse. The sole reason of the hajj is that Allah has ordered the sacred journey in his Book, and that all the prophets from Adam to Muhammad have performed the ritual.[2] Donning the ihram, chanting the ritual formula talbiya and abstaining from all kinds of normal acts like clipping nails or covering your head, offer in their apparent triviality an exercise to obey God in all things.[3] Running between the hills of Safa and Marwa shows the believer's agility in obeying God's commands. If everything is done to the law and with the true intention then the believer really becomes God's representative on earth (*khalifa wa Allah*).[4]

A third spiritual fruit of the pilgrimage is abnegation, self-sacrifice and willingness to give up all earthly possessions including one's life (*kujitoa muhanga*).[5] Staying in tents and abstaining from comfort makes the Muslim like a soldier willing to fight and die for God's sake. Slaughtering in the name of God is explained in the same mental framework of martial obedience and self-denial: the believer is willing to give up everything, even his life and the life of his loved ones. The IPC describes in their text book the

---

1. Poem "Nendeni salama mahujaji," *Nasaha*, 36; "Vazi la Ihram," *an-Nuur* 331, 27 February 2001; "Ibada ya tawaf," *an-Nuur* 332, 2 March 2001; "Saudi Arabia isipotoshe lengo la Hija," *Nasaha* 14, 13 February 2002.
2. Poem "Wanusuru Mahujaji," *an-Nuur* 246, 24 March 2000, p. 6.
3. IPC, *Maarifa ya Uislam* (III), 70.
4. IPC, *Maarifa y Uislam* (III), 68; Khalifa as equivalent for pilgrim is also found in the poem "Nendeni salama mahujaji, *Nasaha* 36 and "Ibada ya tawaf," *an-Nuur* 332, 2 March 2001.
5. IPC, Maarifa ya Uislam (III), p. 66.

final three days of the *hajj* as a soldier's rest after battle and as the apex of the pilgrimage.[1]

The *hajj* should also remind the pilgrim of the final gathering on judgement day when all creatures will stand before God awaiting their trial.[2] Standing at Arafa before God's presence, remembering Him, listening to the religious sermon and praying for the forgiveness of sins is like standing before God's throne on the Day of Reckoning (*siku ya Hesabu*), or the Day of Payment (*siku ya malipo*).[3]

Finally the *hajj* offers an opportunity to realize the defence, renewal and revivification (*kuihuisha*) of religion. Praying for the Kingdom of God to come here in this world (*kusimamisha ufalme wa Allah S.W. hapa ulimwenguni*) should be an important part of the pilgrim's supplications.[4] Throwing stones at the ancient pillars is directed at all enemies of Allah, (and not someone's bad habits). The image of the soldier, often used in these edifying articles, is meant as a warning to foes.[5] At the same time the authors make clear that 'real' Islam does not use violence. As an example, the peaceful entry of Mecca in the year 6 Hijra is used. Without weapons, by sheer force of their unity, and supported by God's promises the first Muslims performed their Lesser Pilgrimage (*'umra*). They fought with the names of God (*tahlili* and *takbiri*) without use of physical weapons. The enemy was terrified and they conquered the city without one drop of blood being shed.[6] The peacefulness of the ideal Muslim is presented in stark contrast with the aggression of their enemies. The IPC *hajj* discourse emphasizes the protection of Islam rather than private piety, suggesting that inimical forces not only threaten the *hajj*, but also the whole Islamic moral community.[7]

> It is the Muslim's responsibility (*jukumu*) to recognize the enemies of their religion, to recognize their plan (*mbinu*) and the weapons these enemies use in assailing Islam and to be ready to fight them fiercely (*kupambana nao vikali*) with their possessions and their soul.[8]

---

1. IPC, *Maarifa ya Uislam* (III), pp. 73–74.
2. IPC, *Maarifa ya Uislam* (III), p. 68. In Islamic theology both 'standings' are indicated with the same Arabic name *wuquf.*
3. "Ibada ya tawaf," *an-Nuur* 332, 2 March 2001.
4. IPC, *Maarifa ya Uislam* (III), p. 73; "Ibada ya tawaf," *an-Nuur* 332, 2 March 2001.
5. "Vazi la ihram," *an-Nuur* 331, 27 February 2001.
6. "Vazi la ihram," an-Nuur 331, 27 February 2001.
7. "Zingatieni lengo la hijja," *an-Nuur* 191, 5 March 1999.
8. "Ibada ya tawaf," *an-Nuur* 332, 2 March 2001.

The hajj *endangered*

Both from outside and inside enemies attack, corrupt and slander the fifth pillar on which the Islamic moral community rests. For example non-Muslims try to talk their way into this holy religious duty ("even their names are not Islamic!").[1] The possibility of the Pope visiting Mecca is discussed in a 1992 article.[2] The American president George Bush is said to have suggested this as an opportunity for East and West to meet each other. The writer perceives this proposal as a natural result of the fact that more than a half million non-Muslim soldiers were already stationed in Saudi Arabia for the Gulf War. After a de facto military invasion of the Islamic heartlands, the spiritual appropriation and destruction of Islam will be the next step. In this article three important icons of hostility show their eagerness to attack Islam: the president of the Great Satan, the head of the Christian Church, and the corrupt Saudi keepers of the holy places.[3]

Another threat involved coverage of the *hajj* by non-Muslim Swahili press. In 1997 a daily newspaper charged the vice president Dr. Omar with giving Muslim leaders the opportunity to use the government's plane to visit Mecca to perform their devotional duties. An-Nuur immediately responded by comparing this case with a similar one two years earlier of a Christian minister going to a religious leaders conference, without being accused of spilling the 'sweat of non-Catholics'.[4] Instead of focusing on the sacred Islamic institution of the *hajj*, Christian newspapers allegedly single out the bad behaviour of some believers in order to 'vilify' the whole of Islam. Other instances of wrong representation of *hajj* rituals by non-Islamic press are also presented as examples of *kashf* (slander). The clothes of the pilgrims are, according to a non-Muslim journalist, to better endure the heat of Saudi Arabia, instead of being a divine command. "What aim has this kind of misleading," an-Nuur rhetorically asks.[5] According to the IPC discourse in schoolbooks Muslim pilgrims are depicted as hypocrites. An-Nuur quotes: "As a good Moslem going to Mecca I can't take beer with all those fellows looking at me. But at home, you know, I do take pombe and beer, if I can get it. But here, just buy me a cup of coffee."[6]

---

1. "Wasio waislamu wadaiwa kwenda Hija," *an-Nuur* 332, 2 March 2001.
2. "Papa kwenda Hijja" *an-Nuur* 9, April 1992.
3. Complaints about the Saudis are a recurrent theme in the long violent history of *hajj* demonstrations in Mecca (van Leeuwen 1991).
4. "Tuhumu za hijja kwa ndege ya serikali," *an-Nuur* 94, 17 April 1997.
5. "Upotoshaji huu una lengo gani?" *an-Nuur* 17, April 1998.
6. "Wizara yaidhinisha kutukanwa Uislam," *an-Nuur* 580, 10 September 2004.

Just like Caplan (this volume) explains, different discourses on the moral community attributing blame to external and internal factors co-exist simultaneously. According to the IPC the major threat is not coming from the outside, but from within the bosom of Islam itself. Without the proper spiritual intention and leaving behind sinful behaviour like *riba* (usury), *uongo* (falsity), *rushwa* (corruption) the *hajj* will not be a crown (*taji*), but a mere tourist trip.[1] An anonymous Muslim leader is presented as talking badly about fellow believers and creating turmoil during the sacred *hajj* (...*zungumza manano machafu na kufitinisha watu kwa aliyehirimia Hija*).[2] From the IPC perspective 'BAKWATA Muslims' are particularly apt to use the *hajj* only as a pretext to achieve the religious title *Al-hajj*.[3]

The abuse of the *hajj* title is a recurring theme in the discourse on the pilgrimage. Calling oneself a Muslim or *Al-hajj* while at the same time going against the doctrine of *tawhid*, is a clear case of hypocrisy (*unafiki*) and is an example of fearing human beings more than God (*kuogopa watu zaidi kuliko Mwenyezi Mungu*).[4] Going on *hajj* with the intention to carve a seal with the title *Al-hajji* is only a joke (*kufanya riyya*) in the eyes of God.[5] An anonymous person in Songea blames an equally anonymous Muslim of the wanting to bring a certain mosque under the wing of BAKWATA. Although the accused calls himself *Al-hajji* the letter writer is sure "he is not influenced at all by the *hajj* because his actions do not resemble true Islam."[6]

Summarizing the three different presentations of the *hajj* in the IPC discourse it becomes clear that the link between authoritative texts and ritual practice is strongest on the level of performance. Almost every step of the *hajj* is orchestrated and supervised by the Saudi religious establishment. Yet, for the meaning and significance of the ritual, textual knowledge is not very helpful. For example weeping is recommended at some stages of the *hajj*, but this does not mean that the emotional response is dictated by the authoritative text. The spiritual value of the pilgrimage as described in an-Nuur articles is not a reiteration of classical texts, but more a reflection of the current sense of marginalization felt among Tanzanian Muslims. The pilgrimage to the historical site of Islamic prophets, is presented as a source for spiritual

---

1. Warsha, *Nguzo ya tano*, p. 44; "Ukamilifu wa ibada ya hijja," *an-Nuur* 142, 27 March 1998.
2. "Hija ya wengine kuruku patupu," *an-Nuur* 331, 27 February 2001.
3. "Ukamilifu wa ibada ya hijja," *an-Nuur* 142, 27 March 1998.
4. "Alhaj mgeni rasmi Tusker, mara kwa Mahujaji," *an-Nuur* 332, 2 March 2001.
5. "Waislamu watakiwa kutangaza kashfa ya Mwembechai," *an-Nuur* 195, 2 April 1999; see also "Ibada ya hijja," *al'Istiqama*, January 2002, p.24.
6. "Ukamilifu wa ibada ya hijja," *an-Nuur* 142, 27 March 1998.

renewal, not primarily individual but above all social. More than any other Islamic ritual the *hajj* provides the imagery of the ideal moral community. The imagined *hajj* community in Mecca allows the Tanzanian Muslims to reflect on the shortcomings of their own society in the last decade. The association of the *hajj* with soldiers, battle and weaponry is already present in sources predating Mwembechai (as well as in non-Tanzanian pilgrim accounts; cf. Trojanow 2004:27, 30, 105), but after 1998 the frequency of the war metaphors seems to increase. It is these images that dominate the discourse around the day of Arafa and the *Idd el-Hajj* in 2001.

The Day of *Arafa* and the Day of the *Idd el-hajj*

The awareness of the *hajj* rituals and their influence on daily life in Tanzania is evident. Muslims buy xeroxed leaflets extolling the virtues of each of the first ten days of the *hajj* month Dhul Hijja, and imitate the *ihram* status of the pilgrim by not clipping nails and cutting hair during these days.[1] Two days of the *hajj* deserve extra attention: the day of Arafa (9 Dhul Hijja) and the day of the *Idd* (10 Dhul Hijja). Both of them have equivalent rituals performed by non-pilgrims (fasting on the Day of Arafa and sacrificing on the Day of the *Idd el-Hajj*) in order to connect "those on the *Hajj* with those elsewhere."[2] These ritual practices of fasting and sacrificing are firmly rooted in authoritative texts, but their meaning and evaluation is constructed in a process of tacking back and forth between text and practice in a socio/political reality. In the following section I describe how the *hajj* discourses on the Day of Arafa and the *Idd el-Hajj* almost completely merged in a massive protest meeting in March 2001.

The Day of Arafa

Undoubtly the standing on the plains of Arafa is a highly spiritual and emotional experience as many pilgrims explicitly state.[3] Both Arabic texts and witness reports are clear about the higher status of Arafa compared to the following Day of Sacrifice. Authoritative Islamic texts affirm "there is no *hajj* without Arafa".[4] The Qur'an mentions Arafa as an important place to

---

1. Pamphlet "*Siku kumi bora mwezi wa mfungo tatu (dhul hijja)*"; Cf. "Funga za sunna na fadhila zake," Maarifa (3), 16 January 2002.
2. Aramco, *The hajj: Special issue*, 1974.
3. See for example "Ibada ya hijja," *al'Istiqama*, January 2002; Aramco, *The hajj: Special issue* 1974; (Wolfe 1997: passim).
4. "Mamilioni wasimama Arafa," *an-Nuur* 94, 17 April 1997; *Guardian*, 20 February 2002; Bachoo, *Ufafanuzi*, p. 112.

ask forgiveness (2:198–199). Within the period of the pilgrimage the day of the *Idd* is not seen as the most important moment despite many secondary sources claiming just that. Standing on the plains of Arafa is compulsory, and not doing it or not standing at the right time, nullifies the *hajj* and the pilgrim's effort will not be accepted by God.[1] At Arafa past, present and future are conjoined. The final pilgrimage of Mohammed is re-enacted here,[2] the Muslim assembly clad in the same clothes resembling the white clothing of newborn children and corpses represents the *ummah* and their equality before God, and it reminds the pilgrim of the final gathering of mankind on the Day of Judgement.[3] The status of the day of Arafa is on a par with Friday and the month of Ramadan as the three most sacred times in Islam.[4] This theological opinion is echoed by Muslim experiences as published in numerous pilgrim reports.

The importance of Arafa is therefore not something specific to the IPC discourse. But all groups that make use of the emotional and religious potential of 'Arafa' do so in specific ways for specific reasons. For example the *Ansaar Sunna* movement in Tanzania exploits the value of Arafa and turns it into an important identity marker, a justification to celebrate the *Idd el-Hajj* one day earlier than mainstream Tanzanian Muslims (van de Bruinhorst 2002). According to the *Ansaar* modernists the Day of Arafa is so important, that all Muslims worldwide should fast on the same date as Saudi Arabia. There is only one God, one moon, and one Arafa. The Saudi author of a book on the proper date of the *Idd el-Hajj* gives as the main reason for writing it: "… it has to do with one of the *arkan* of the Islam: the *hajj*. Yes, it has to do with the most important pillar that is with the *wuquf* at Arafa."[5] The importance of this day and in general the link with Saudi Arabia might have induced the organization to give their primary and secondary school in Tanga the name of Arafa. On the day of Arafa, 21 February 2002, a radio reporter from Saudi Arabia was connected to the six large speakers on top of the Ansaar Muslim Youth Centre (AMYC) mosque to give an impression of the event over there. The message that 'Arafa' is determining the day of the *Idd el-Hajj* was driven home the next morning during the festival

1. According to the Shafi'i school of law: cf. Al-Amin bin Ali Mazrui, *Hidayatu al-at-fal*, p. 57; Khamis Abdurahman, *Mwezi ko-ongo*, p. 19–20; other schools recognize only four compulsory acts of the *hajj* (Lemu, *Tawhid*, p. 164).
2. Khamis Abdurahman, *Mwezi ko-ongo*, p. 20.
3. Lemu, *Tawhid*, p. 181; the whole of *hajj* is "a glimpse of the Day of Judgement"; bin Yusuf, *The hajj experience*.
4. Siddiqi, *Does the burial in Madinah pave way to paradise?*
5. Ibn Rajab, *Ahkam al ikhtilaf fi ru'ya al-hilal Dhul HIjjah*, p.6. Cf. Muhammad Nassor Abdullah al-Qadiry, *Kitabu Arafa*, p. 10–13.

prayers when the imam stated: "Brothers, Muslims, today all the Muslims in the world celebrate the Sacrificial Feast, except maybe some Muslims from BAKWATA." In the AMYC's monthly paper distributed the same day the leading article repeated the message in capitals "LEO NI IDD" (today is the *Idd*).

To give an indication of the importance of Arafa in Swahili writings: Ally Mohamed Mtawazi[1] devotes one complete chapter (out of five) in his 20 page book to the fasting on the 'siku ya Arafa'; Mohamed Omar Dumila published in two editions an Arabic book and its Swahili translation on the same topic. The latter had reached its third print in 1999. Sheikh Muhammad Nassor Abdullah al-Qadiry published in 1998 his 87 page explanation on the 'most important pillar of the *hajj*: Arafa'. Also on the popular level in a non-religious context the notion of Arafa is present: on 5 February 2003 the author SAH on the Swahili forum Youngafrican.com wishes all Muslims worldwide not a happy *Idd*, but a happy *'siku ya Arafaa* 11/02/2003'.[2] None of these authors are associated with the Ansaar or other reform groups; some of them are even declared enemies.

All of the additional religious practices recommended to Tanzanian Muslims on the days preceding the *Idd el-Hajj* could be performed in private such as fasting, praying additional prayers and supplications at specific times and recitation of recommended Qur'anic parts. However, because the *siku ya Arafa* is connected to the sensitive issue of the 'correct' *Idd el-Hajj* date,[3] notions of Arafa are increasingly perceived as constitutive of social identity. Public references to Arafa therefore are potentially powerful symbols. I have already mentioned the direct broadcasting from the Arafa plains by radio, broacast by the AMYC in Tanga. The global imagined community with Arafa as its focal point is not only comforting, but also empowering vis a vis the threatening attacks of government and non-Muslims. The Arafa congregation is a strong image of a united community devoted to the worship of God and willing to defend true Islam. The translation of this spiritual image towards a more practical attitude in daily political life is necessary according to IPC. Not surprisingly *an-Nuur* fiercely criticised

---

1. Imam of the Masjid Irshad at Tandika/Chiota (Dar es Salaam); arrested in September 1999 on the accusation that he had invited Shaykh Mbukuzi, a well known preacher who was also arrested for referring to the Mwembechai incident.
2. www.youngafrican.com/forum/topic.asp?topic_ID=4113 (accessed 20 February 2003).
3. Although the Arafa demonstration took place on 4 March, most participants continued to celebrate their *Idd el-Hajj* according to the local lunar calendar on Tuesday 6 March (and not on Monday 5 March simultaneously with Saudi Arabia).

the Saudi position to restrict the *hajj* solely to its spiritual meaning. Against the ban on all political expressions during the pilgrimage, the *an-Nuur* author claimed that it is to the favour of Islam to discuss all matters during this spiritual ritual (*ibada ya kiroho*). And that should include politics. Worth mentioning is the publication date of this article: a few weeks after the Mwembechai incident.[1]

Since 1998 the victims of this vicious clash between state and Islam (as perceived by Muslims) were remembered annually on February 13, the solar date of the event. When in January 2001 another confrontation took place between government and Muslims on Zanzibar and Pemba (cf. Cameron this volume), Muslims decided to integrate the commemoration of both events at a single political/religious meeting. 4 March 2001 the day when the pilgrims in Saudi Arabia assembled for their holy duty on the plains of Arafa was taken as a public day of demonstration, mourning, fasting and standing in remembrance of the casualties from Mwembechai and January 2001.

The ritual showed a careful orchestration grafted on the well known Arafa practice of the *hajj*. Just like the *hajj* which is often sponsored by home communities, Muslims from other provinces collected money in order to send a few of them to the Dar es Salaam 'Arafa' demonstration. The reason for the meeting was explained to the public as 'joining the pilgrims in spirit and in action' (*kuungana kwa nia na kwa vitendo*). Both congregations were standing on the plains (*viwanja vya Arafa* and *viwanja vya Jangwani*). Their action was described in the same words: *kusimama*: 'standing'. Both groups listened to high ranked religious, male speakers: on Arafa the Grand Mufti of Saudi Arabia addressed the pilgrims and in Dar es Salaam the preacher Maalim Ali Bassaleh lectured to the Tanzanian congregation. Both groups simultaneously started their ritual activity: in Dar es Salaam the protestors headed for their field around 10 a.m. (*saa nne asubuhi*) about the time the pilgrims left Mecca in the direction of the Arafa fields. In the same way as the Arafa pilgrims constructed their moral community in prayer (invoking God's blessings for loved ones and God's wrath for the enemies), so the Tanzanian mirror congregation told God their complaints and listed all the names of victims killed by hatred and injustice.[2] These Arafa prayers by pilgrims always include family, friends, loved ones as well as those who have already passed away.[3] The tsunami victims in Asia were remembered

---

1. "Mahujaji wailaani Marekani, Israel," *an-Nuur* 144, 10 April 1998.
2. "Mwanza wahimiza jihad," *an-Nuur* 333, 6 March 2001, p. 3.
3. In Tanzanian reports these prayers for the deceased loved ones are often present:
   '...na walio fika huko, kina baba warehemu, ya Rabi Mola Karimu, wanusuru

by Tanzanian Muslim pilgrims in 2005. At the same time these prayers also construct the boundaries between who belongs to this moral community and who has no right in there. In a letter to the editor of *an-Nuur* Ali Juma asks the *hajjis* not to forget the victims of Mwembechai and Chechnya, and blame their murderers on Arafa.[1] Whereas in normal years pilgrims include Tanzanian state officials and important persons in their prayers on Arafa, they refused to do so during the *hajj* in 2001 and 2004.[2]

The organizers of the Arafa demonstration in Dar es Salaam emphasized this symbolic representation of the Arafa ritual as an icon of the whole Islamic *umma* and therefore urged women and children to join them.[3] Pictures of the demonstration show mainly women to balance the male overrepresentation at this kind of event. People were asked to come in a state of ritual purity, further stressing the ideal of a pure and sanctified moral community. The Dar es Salaam Muslims already left where the pilgrims stood waiting for the signal to leave after sunset, before the afternoon prayer to perform a procession (*zafa*) through town to be ended in the Mtambani mosque. Praying together and jointly breaking their fast (*futari*) concluded the Dar es Salaam ritual emphasizing the community by commensality.

On the western side of the country, in Mwanza, a similar event took place on the day of Arafa, 2001. There Muslims chose for their remembrance another symbolically laden site: the Aqswah-Buzuruga mosque. In 1984 the grassroot law and order organization *sungusungu*, forced Muslims "to worship the sun and beat them with parts of the Qur'an'".[4] What in particular angered the Islamic community in the aftermath of this incident was the comment of the BAKWATA mufti Sheikh Hemed that it was not

---

Mahujaji' poem "Wanusuru mahujaji," *an-Nuur* 246, 24 March 2000.

1. Ali Juma, "Hijja Mabrur," *an-Nuur* 243, 3 March 2000; Majid Hamza "Dua zenu ya Hujaj," *an-Nuur* 243, 3 March 2000.
2. "Mahujaji watakiwa kuomba dua watakaposimama Arafa," *an-Nuur* 328, 16 February 2001, p. 1, 3; "Mahujaji wagoma kumuombea Mkapa," *Nasaha* 238, 14 January 2004, p. 1 (in January 2004 the president was in hospital with pneumonia (*baridi yabisi*). An Ahmadiyya poem suggested *hajj* prayers for all Tanzanians: 'If the pilgrim arrives at the Ka'ba, he prays to the Lord, let us receive our desires, all of Tanzania' ("Maka afike salama," *Mapenzi ya Mungu*, June 1972).
3. "Hija ya wengine kuruka patupu," *an-Nuur* 331, 27 February 2001, p. 4; "Waislamu kusimama Jangwani Jumapili, *an-Nuur* 332, 2 March 2001, p. 1, 3 ('pamoja na watoto wao'). 'kila Muislamu anatakiwa kujiandaa yeye pamoja na familia yake kuhudhuria' (*an-Nuur* 332, 2 March 2001, p. 7).
4. "Mwanza wahimiza Jihad; Dar wasema kisasi ni haki," *an-Nuur* 333, 6 March 2001, p.1, 3. In a Tanga class room I witnessed a discussion on this incident as part of the lesson in Arabic, standard VI, 17 April 2002. For a more detailed and contextualized description of the affair see Chande (1998:151–152).

the Qur'an but 'only' sura Yasin. All over the country Muslims remembered a string of similar incidents: the abolishment of the 'Muslim' East African Muslim Welfare Society in favour of the 'state owned' BAKWATA (1968) the slandering of the Qur'an in Dodoma (1988); the pork riots after the responsible authorities turned a deaf ear towards complaints of Muslims (1993). The day of Arafa offered a good occasion to remind Muslims of the clear pattern: "enemies of Islam continuously attack our religion, our possessions and our lives."[1] Enemies are in this case Christians; one of the banners carried on the Arafa demonstratioen read *"Mfumo Kristo ndio kiini cha mauaji Mwembecahi na Zanzibar"* (the Christian system is at the heart of the Mwembechai and Zanzibar killings).

The question is why *siku ya Arafa* takes on this political meaning, rather than any other Islamic calendrical festival like the *Idd el-Fitr* or the *mawlid*. What seems important here is the association of Arafa with the Prophet Muhammad rather than Ibrahim who is the hero of the *Idd el-Hajj* sacrificial myth. Most of the *hajj* rituals are explained with reference to the history of Ibrahim: the building of the Ka'ba, the running between the hills, the stoning of the pillars and the animal sacrifice. However the day of Arafa is more closely linked with Muhammad, his first revelation on the Jabal al-Nur, his cave on mountain Hira where he used to go in retreat and especially his final sermon during his farewell pilgrimage (*hija ya kuaga*). This address contains the final Qur'anic verse revealed to Muslims (Q 5:3) "Today I have completed your religion" and could be read as the Prophet's legacy. Reference to this sermon is not something specifically Tanzanian, but probably its dominant presence in the Mwembechai discourse is remarkable.[2] This farewell sermon offers many possibilities to politicize the *hajj*, to link everyday events in the social reality to an underlying paradigm and to give meaning to the terrible predicament of Mwembechai and January 2001. In fact the Arafa sermon "is the first declaration of Human Rights" (*hilo likawa ndilo tangazo la kwanza la Haki za binadamu*).[3] An additional advantage of the Muhammadan historical paradigm is the possibility it offers to name personal enemies with names of the Prophet's adversaries.[4]

---

1. "Tahariri," *Nasaha* 90, 7 March 2001.
2. "Ujumbe wa mtume Arafa: Iheshimiwe Damu ya WaIslamu isimwagwe ovyo," *an-Nuur*, 2 March 2001.
3. "Saudi Arabia isipotoshe lengo la hijja," *Nasaha* 140, 13 February 2002.
4. For example Abu Lahab and Abu Jahali mentioned in *an-Nuur* 26 February 2002, p. 3. The AMYC director Barahiyan is described as Abu Bakr from the outside, Abu Lahab within.

One of the themes picked up from the Prophet's sermon and elaborated in the discourse surrounding the *siku ya Arafa* 2001, is the inviolability of human life (*utakatifu wa uhai*). Muhammad linked this sacredness of all living things to the holiness of the day of Arafa, to the month of Dhul Hijja and the town of Mecca. According to the IPC authors this not only means the sanctity of life in general, but it explicitly gives Muslims the responsibility to defend their life and property against anyone who wants to destroy it. The application to the current situation is clear: because the government kills Muslims at random (*ovyo*), the Prophet's message justifies any defensive action.[1] Instead of contemplation and personal piety usually stressed in the Arafa worship, the Dar es Salaam gathering used the word revenge. The *hajj* will not be of any significance if Muslims go on *hajj*, stand at Arafa, listen to the sermon of an Islamic leader, and not listen to the Prophet's words spoken on this plain and not be moved by fellow Muslims being shot in the head on the Day of Congregation (*yaumul Jumua*). Those having a grain of faith (*chembe ya imani*) should listen to the meaning of the day of Arafa and the inviolability of life. Is it possible for one Muslim to neglect this important message, which Muhammad asked God Himself to be witness to (*Ewe Mwenyezi Mungu shuhudia*) and still call himself a Muslim?[2]

Summarizing my argument so far: *siku ya Arafa* is a very important part of the *hajj* as religious experience (pilgrim's reports) and as Islamic doctrine. However, there is no compelling necessity to push this day forward for non-pilgrims as is done in Tanzania. The false dichotomy between orthodox and local Islam is clearly inadequate in explaining this phenomenon. The ritual standing at Jangwani is justified by a textual charter and grafted on a 'canonical' *hajj* ritual but cannot be reduced to texts only. Tanzanian Muslims are able to defend the importance and some of the practices of *siku ya Arafa* by referring to Qur'anic verses and prophetic reports accepted by large parts of the Muslim community. On the other hand the practice of *kisimamo* (standing) in a field to commemorate victims of a political clash is very much a local expression of Muslim political views and emotions. Tanzanians do not emphasize the individual salvation to be achieved in Arafa as expressed in the *hadith:* "There is no other day on which Allah relieves more people from Hell fire then he does on the day of Arafah," but rather solidarity and concern with the whole Islamic community. Defence, opposition (*kupinga*), revenge (*kulipiza kisasi*), and anger are stressed more than personal piety. Yet, this Arafa ritual in Dar es Salaam is not *based on,*

---

1. "Ujumbe wa mtume Arafa," *an-Nuur* 332, p. 2.
2. "Watakiwa kukemea ukandamizaji," *an-Nuur* 333, 6 March 2001, p. 8.

or *derived from* these texts, but rather shaped by actors and local cultural foci. In a different socio/political setting it could even be imagined that some Muslims found fault with the Tanzanian practice because Arafa rituals should not be performed in other places than the prescribed ones.[1]

The Day of Sacrifice

Although the Arafa demonstration was clearly non-violent, its temporal location one day before the Day of Sacrifice, suggested more aggressive interpretations. Sometimes the IPC articles explicitly hint at a more violent course of action, derived from sacrificial symbols.[2] On the prescriptive level of *hajj* manuals and educational publications, there is an important difference between the Arafa rituals and the day of the Sacrifice: the first one is a 'pillar' (*rukn*) and essential for the divine acceptance of the *hajj*, the other 'only' a meritorious act. The discourse on sacrifice, dealing with narrow, specific expectations, contains more quotations and references to authoritative texts than the discourse on Arafa (which is more spiritual and deals with broader expectations). Killing an animal on the 10th Dhul Hijja "signifies that all that one possesses actually belongs to Allah and should be willingly given away for His sake."[3] It is clearly linked to the Ibrahimian paradigm: Ibrahim's slaying or Ishmael's eagerness should be part of one's willingness to obey Allah. Hardly any of the sources fail to refer to the Qur'anic story of Ibrahim's love for God.[4] The spiritual value of the sacrifice is straightforwardly established by the Qur'an in Sura 22:37: "The flesh and blood of the animals does not reach Allah, but what reaches Him is (the spirit of) your piety."[5] Supplications and sacrificial formulae before, during and after the immolation are duly mentioned in the handbooks and school material. Other subjects in Swahili sacrificial discourse are the condition of the animal, number of persons allowed to share it and the distribution of the meat.

While Tanzanian practice seems to suggest that the *siku ya Arafa* is both on the symbolic and emotional level more important than the *Idd el-Hajj*, some Arabic texts put forward the opposite. There are many elements in authoritative texts which might be interpreted to such an extent that 10th Dhul Hijja is really the religious summit of the *hajj*. Foremost is the following *hadith*: "O people, do you know what day it is? They answered: God

---

1. See "Bida in Hajj 2" (www.adimin.Muslimsonline.com/~bern/hajjbida2.html) accessed 15 February 2005, condemning the "imitation of the people of Arafah".
2. "Tutajitoa muhanga staili ya Wapelestina," *an-Nuur* 547, 26 February 2004.
3. *an-Nuur* 95, 25 April 1997.
4. IPC, *Maarifa ya Uislamu* (III) p. 73.
5. IPC, *Elimu ya dini* (3): p. 136.

and the prophet know it. He stayed silent [...] and than he said: is it not the day of slaughtering?"[1] What is interesting is that *an-Nuur* uses this report in an editorial comment underscoring the importance of the *siku ya Arafa*. However, quite a lot of the Arabic and other non-Swahili sources attribute this narration to a speech held on the day of the *Idd*.

> Once the Prophet was riding his camel and a man was holding its rein. The Prophet asked, "What is the day today?" We kept quiet, thinking that he might give that day another name. He said, "Isn't it the day of Nahr (slaughtering of the animals of sacrifice)?" We replied, "Yes." He further asked, "Which month is this?" We again kept quiet, thinking that he might give it another name. Then he said, "Isn't it the month of Dhul-Hijja?" We replied, "Yes." He said, "Verily! Your blood, property and honor are sacred to one another (i.e. Muslims) like the sanctity of this day of yours, in this month of yours and in this city of yours. It is incumbent upon those who are present to inform those who are absent because those who are absent might comprehend (what I have said) better than the present audience." [2]

Some versions continue this report with the sentence "this is the day of the Greater Pilgrimage" (*hajjul akbar*), thus distinguishing it from the Lesser Pilgrimage or the *umrah*. Apparently we have here an early instance of a contest between the day of Arafa and the day of Sacrifice or at least a blurring of the boundaries between them. The expression "like the sanctity of this day" is used in Swahili discourse as evidence for the significance of the *siku ya Arafa*,[3] while it could also justify the claim of sacredness for the Day of Sacrifice.

In contrast to the emotional significance of the Day of Arafa, the actual experience of the *hajj* sacrifice is smaller than the extensive discourse suggests. Probably because of the improved abattoir facilities in Saudi Arabia most of the sacrifices take place behind closed doors. Bin Yusuf, a Zanzibari pilgrim, writes on his experiences on the Day of Sacrifice: "...while the rest of the Muslim Ummah celebrates Idd al-Hajj, those performing the actual Hajj do not even realize that it is a day of celebration." [4] My interviews with Tanzanian pilgrims corroborate the view that animal slaughter is a relatively unimportant part of the *hajj*. Slaughtering is hardly practised at all by Tanzanian pilgrims. The official video shown to *hajj*-candidates at the

---

1. "Ujumbe wa mtume Arafa," *an-Nuur* 332, p. 2.
2. Translation from MSA *hadith* database http://www.usc.edu/dept/MSA/fundamentals/hadithsunnah: Bukhari, *Volume 1, Book 3, Number 67.*
3. "Saudi Arabia isipotoshe lengo la hijja," *Nasaha* 14, 13 February 2002.
4. Bin Yusuf, *The hajj experience.*

Tanzania Muslim Hajj Trust devotes only 58 seconds of the 90 minute play-ing time to the slaughtering practice. The director Jabry even said that he discouraged the performance of the sacrifice for Tanzanians who went for the first time on *hajj*, thus limiting the number of possible mistakes.

The non-involvement of the Tanzanian pilgrims in personal sacrifice is paralleled by a relatively low concern with sacrifice in Tanzania itself. In a survey (399 questionnaires) less than half of the Tanga households indicated they had sacrificed an animal in 2002 or 2001 at *Idd el-Hajj*. Many among them chose a chicken instead of the prescribed four-legged animal.[1] This casual attitude is attacked in Swahili discourse suggesting that Tanzanian Muslims should look at their "West-African brethren". The Ansaar also mention among the long lists of innovations the lack of interest in sacrifice (*'watu kupuuza kuchinja Udh-hiya siku ya Idi Alhajj'*).[2] The imam of an-Nisa mosque in Tanga expressed his incredulity that people could not save 15,000 Shillings a year to accomplish this divine duty.[3]

Despite the authoritative texts, the widespread knowledge about and the attractiveness of sacrifice as one of the 'grandes pratiques' of Islam (Bousquet 1949), analysis of the *Idd el-Hajj* should take into account the concomitant rituals like the Arafa day. Swahili sources mention the importance of the sacrifice on this Islamic holiday as derived from *siku ya Arafa*. For example it is not uncommon to read about the *Idd* that "people in Tanzania slaugh-tered an animal after the day of Arafa".[4] Not surprisingly after Mwembechai and especially in 2001 the meanings of *siku ya Arafa* and *siku ya kuchin-ja* increasingly seemed to overlap in many politico/religious meetings in Tanzania. The significance of the *siku ya Arafa* as a mourning ritual, social protest and expression of popular anger, spilled over to the *Idd el-Hajj*. In the Baraza la *Idd el-Hajj*, 1999, the sorrow for Mwembechai was more im-portant than the joy on this day of celebration, the bookseller Masoud in Tanga remarked.[5] The same year Muslims in Dodoma watched the vide-otape of the Mwembechai killings at the *Idd el-Hajj*. Here also the link was explicit to the day of Arafa rather than the day of Slaughtering: "to re-

---

1. For the number and species of animals sacrificed on the occasion of the *Idd el-Hajj* in 2001 in Tanga see van de Bruinhorst 2007:393-401. I thank the anonymous reviewer for pointing out that the Ngamia mosque on Zanzibar has been ritually sacrificing a camel every year at the *Idd* since 1999. The Qadiriya zawiya in Dar es Salaam usually kills a camel to celebrate the birthday of the Prophet Muhammad (*an-Nuur*, 209, 9 July 1999).
2. *al-Fikrul Islami* 37, p. 5.
3. *Idd el-Hajj* sermon, 23 February 2002.
4. *An-nuur* 93, 11 April 1997.
5. "Korogwe washuhudia mauaji ya Mwembechai," *an-Nuur* 196, 9 April 1999.

mind them of the Prophet's speech he spoke there on Arafa: your blood and your possessions are sanctified commodities you should not allow anyone to play with."[1] The message was to unselfishly sacrifice (*kujitoa muhanga!*) life and possessions to protect the integrity of the Islamic moral community. A commentator from Shinyanga wrote: "In a prayer on the day of Arafa and yesterday the day of the *Idd* in the al-Farouq mosque, the philosophy of slaughtering on the day of the *Idd* was explained urging the believers to be ready to sacrifice themselves in order to protect life."[2]

Conclusions

In order to understand the religio/political meeting in Dar es Salaam during the *hajj* in March 2001, I made a distinction between three different levels of *hajj* discourse. In each of them the *hajj* was associated with different elements from textual knowledge, local politics or personal sentiment. From the experience of pilgrims performing the *hajj* it is clear that the day of Arafa has a much more profound, emotional impact than the sacrifice itself which is performed (if at all) behind closed doors. Practices performed by pilgrims on the day of Arafa (praying for forgiveness, meditating) and by non-pilgrims (fasting, remembering God and deceased community members) closely match the themes of mourning and the wish for renewal of the religion, expressed in the Jangwani protest movement. Knowledge of the correct performance of the *hajj* clearly influenced this meeting and provided powerful imagery. However, there is no direct Prophetic precedent or textual injunction urging Muslims to perform protest demonstrations modelled on Arafa rituals. On the other hand the Prophetic example and detailed instructions for animal sacrifice on the day of the *Idd* are mostly ignored by Tanzanian Muslims.

On the level of edification and spiritual lessons, the *hajj* is a visit to the House of God. Personal renewal should only be the first step in a new life dedicated to the defence and renewal of Islam. The solemn activities at Arafa emotionally remind the Muslim of the Day of Judgement and his social duties towards fellow members of the Muslim community. Arafa is both the most important day of the *hajj* and also one of the few *hajj* rituals shared by all pilgrims. The sacrifice on the other hand is relegated to the margin of the *hajj* and largely taken over by the mechanisms of modernity.

---

1. "Kanda ya mauaji Mwembechai yaliz wanawake Dodoma," *an-Nuur* 196, 9 April 1999.
2. *an-Nuur* 333, 6 March 2001.

Finally the *hajj* is put forward as an illustration of the endangered Muslim moral community. Polluted from within by fellow Muslims with the wrong spiritual dispositions, and attacked from the outside by enemies, the *hajj* (as a metonym for the Islamic moral community itself) should be defended against evil forces. The meaning of animal sacrifice within the Ibrahimian model (giving up everything and willingly surrendering to whatever God will send) is not so popular in the current Tanzanian climate. Arafa and its clear reference to the Muhammadan paradigm with all his enemies, his battles and victories, is meaningful in the IPC and Baraza Kuu discourse where the *hajj* is presented as threatened. Blaming the shortcomings of outsiders is understandable in a political environment where Muslims are perceived as a marginal social group. The Arafa paradigm offers the idiom to express complaints in religious terms. It offers clear answers on the question of who is to blame for the current predicament, and it offers a model for action. It belongs to the moral narratives of the opposition that 'may increasingly serve as an ideology which provides cohesion, justification, counter-critique' (Cameron, this volume). The religious narrative adopted in the Arafa demonstrations enables Muslims to redefine their social identity in terms of membership of the global Muslim community; temporally disconnecting themselves from the problematic, national and secular Tanzanian community.

Failure to properly distinguish between the different elements of these discourses on the *hajj* can lead to serious misunderstanding of social reality. The too often taken for granted textual base of Islamic ritual, focusing on coherence and continuity, is to be interrogated rather than assumed. In political rallies like the one in Jangwani the global textual elements like the Prophet's farewell sermon, remembering the dead on Arafa etc. are harnessed to local ends. The continuous slippage between text and practice seems to be essential in all ritual Islamic practice, even in such an 'universalistic' one as the *hajj*.

References non-Swahili sources

Asad, Talal, 1986, *The Idea of an Anthropology of Islam*. Washington: Centre for Contemporary Arab Studies.

Bin Yusuf, M., 1995, "The hajj experience: a personal story," www.baalawy.freeyellow.com/hajj.html

Bousquet, G-H, 1949, *Les Grandes Pratiques rituelles de l'Islam*. Paris: Presses universitaires de France.

Bowen, John R., 1992, "On Scriptural Essentialism and Ritual Variation: Muslim Sacrifice in Sumatra and Morocco", *American Ethnologist* vol. 19 no. 4, pp. 656–671.

Bruinhorst, Gerard C.van de, 2007, *Raise Your Voices and Kill Your Animals: Islamic Discourses on the Idd el-Hajj and Sacrifices in Tanga (Tanzania)*. Amsterdam: University Press.

Bruinhorst, Gerard C. van de, 2002, "Muslims, Moons and Modernity. Recent Islamic Discourses on 'id Celebration in Swahili writings with special reference to Tanzania", Paper presented at the Graduate Student Symposium "Local Modernities: Islamic Cultural Practices as Sites of Agency, Mediation and Resistance, Cambridge Massachusetts, MIT.

Chande, Abdin N., 1998, *Islam, Ulamaa and Community Development in Tanzania*. San Francisco: Austin & Winfield.

Chelhod, Joseph, 1955, *Le sacrifice chez les Arabes*. Paris: Presses Universitaires de France.

Combs-Schilling, M.E.,1989, *Sacred Performances: Islam, sexuality and sacrifice*. New York: Columbia University Press.

Delaney, Carol, 1990, "The hajj: Sacred and secular", *American Ethnologist* 17 (3), pp. 513–530.

Delaney, Carol, 1998, *Abraham on Trial: The Social Legacy of Biblical Myth*. Princeton: University Press.

Knappert, Jan, 1971, "The Function of Arabic in the Islamic Ritual on the East African Coast," *Actes du Vieme congres d'arabisants et islamisants*, pp. 285–296.

Lazarus Yafeh, H.,1981, "Modern Muslim attitudes towards the Ka'ba and the Hadjdj", in H. Lazarus Yafeh (ed.), *Some religious aspects of Islam*. Leiden: Brill, pp. 106–129.

Leeuwen, Marianne van, 1991, "Politiek geweld in Mekka", in Willy Jansen and Huub de Jonge (eds), *Islamitische pelgrimstochten*. Muiderberg: Coutinho.

Lemu, B. Aisha, 1988, *Tawhid and Fiqh*. Minna: Islamic Education Trust.

Loimeier, Roman, 2006, "Perceptions of marginalization: Muslims in Contemporary Tanzania," B. Soares and R. Otayek (eds), *Political Islam in Subsaharan Africa*. Paris: Karthala.

Maudoodi, Sayyid Abdul A'la, 1977, "The Hajj Pilgrimage", *Al-Islam*, pp. 12–23

Peters, F.E., 1994, *The Hajj: The Muslim Pilgrimage to Mecca and the Holy Places*. Princeton & New Jersey: Princeton University Press.

Schielke, Samuli, 2006, "Snacks and Saints: Mawlid Festivals and the Politics of Festivity, Piety and Modernity in Contemporary Egypt". Unpublished dissertation.

Swartz, Marc J., 1991, *The Way the World Is: Cultural Processes and Social Relations among the Mombasa Swahili.* Berkeley: University of California Press.

Trimingham, J.S., 1964, *Islam in East Africa.* London & Oxford: Oxford University Press.

Trojanow, Ilija, 2004, *Zu den Heiligen Quellen des Islam.* Munchen: Piper Verlag.

Wolfe, Michael, 1997, *One thousand roads to Mecca. Ten centuries of travellers writing about the Muslim Pilgrimage.* New York: Grove Press.

Wolfe, Michael, 1998, *The Hadj: An American's Pilgrimage to Mecca.*

Woodward, Mark R., 1988, "The Slametan: Textual Knowledge and Ritual Performance in Central Javanese Islam", *History of Religions,* vol. 28 no. 1, pp. 54–89.

CHAPTER 8

Narratives of Democracy and Dominance in Zanzibar

Greg Cameron

The Genesis of Zanzibar's Contemporary Crisis

An integral part of the Swahili Coast, the island-state of Zanzibar, is currently locked in social and political struggles the intensity of which have increasingly blurred the line between non-election 'normality' and electoral 'upheaval'. In this chapter I seek to analyze the mechanisms by which Western capitalist democracies (henceforth the Western bloc) have channelled the democratic transition in Zanzibar to a status quo situation in favour of the incumbent *Chama cha Mapinduzi* (Party of the Revolution, in Swahili and henceforth CCM) regime in Tanzania.[1] A cursory outline of Zanzibar's historical lineages is crucial in understanding the contemporary authoritarian dénouement. Zanzibar comprises approximately one million inhabitants and two primary islands: Unguja and Pemba. Under Omani Arab rule before becoming a protectorate of Great Britain in 1890, Zanzibar's de-colonization journey in the mid-20th century was a rough road pitting mainly the pro-Arab settler class Zanzibar Nationalist Party (ZNP) against the pro-African labouring class Afro-Shirazi Party (ASP). The majority indigenous peasantry was roughly split between the two parties, with the pro-ZNP peasantry concentrated mainly on Pemba and the pro-ASP peasantry on Unguja. Independence in December 1963 saw the ZNP coalition narrowly defeat the ASP coalition. January 1964 ushered in the murky and bloody events known as the Zanzibar Revolution, which overthrew the ZNP coalitional government. Almost immediately after seizing power, Abeid Karume's ASP government rapidly moved to a union with Julius Nyerere's Tanganyika African National Union (TANU), independent since 1961. Due to anti-communist concerns about leftist elements within the ASP regime, the US supported the hastily written Articles of Union

---

1. CCM emerged from the TANU-ASP merger of 1977. Henceforth I refer to the defunct ASP as 'CCM Zanzibar' and the defunct TANU as 'CCM Dodoma' (the capital of the United Republic of Tanzania).

between Karume's Zanzibar and Nyerere's Tanganyika, with no popular mandate from the Isles' peoples. Controversial to this day, it remains the sole remaining union between two hitherto sovereign states in contemporary Africa. Throughout the 1970s a growing number of Zanzibaris began to view the 1964 Union as an instrument to keep the Isles politically prostrate. *Ujamaa* (African socialism), based on communal villages, state control of the commanding heights of the economy, self-reliance, and an ascetic political elite, was the bedrock locking mainland and Zanzibari society into the vision and embrace of a 'benign authoritarian state'. However, CCM's economic kingdom never arrived. Yet how does the contemporary post-*ujamaa* CCM state 'see' and 'narrate'? After 40 plus years in power it is far less benign than the younger version of the 1970s (Scott 1998: 223–261). Leaner and meaner, its developmental 'punch' has been emasculated by the collapse of the Eastern bloc, International Monetary Fund/World Bank structural adjustment policies, economic regression, and the introduction of competitive party elections in 1992. This same authoritarian state still stands these days, but one less interested in erecting communal villages, than in mapping, engineering, and managing the socio-political grids of multiparty politics in the United Republic's increasingly tortured political landscape.

Building on earlier empirical work (Cameron 2002a,b; 2004a,b) this paper seeks to theoretically conceptualise a political conjuncture that may have far reaching consequences for Zanzibar, the United Republic of Tanzania, and East Africa's Swahili Coast sub-region. Rather than analyzing yet another electoral debacle on the Isles, the 2005 general elections, I believe analysis must go beyond the fact that the CCM regime is clinging to power. For the modalities of global power frame not only how dominant and dominated groups and classes speak about politics but, crucially, the local forms of social organization available to the contending political forces. The global can both stabilize and undermine the local/national/regional political status quo. I seek, therefore, to relate the theme of 'knowledge, renewal and religion' to the globally generated changes that are politically, economically, and ideologically sweeping the Swahili Coast. In the first section I provide a summary of key (neo)Gramsican tenets. It argues that there is a general pattern of global and national convergence in an ever-deepening neo-liberal environment, albeit of an unequal nature between core Western states and peripheral African states like Tanzania. The second section examines the internal political conjuncture on Zanzibar and the ways in which the CCM regime situates the opposition in historical, ethnic, and religious discourses and the way global narratives come into play. The third section analyses the oppositional response to the Western-CCM bloc(s) symbiosis, sketching the possibilities of Tanzania's popular forces moving beyond the limitations of Western neo-liberalism.

The Hegemonic Convergence Between the West and CCM

The Swahili coast shares a long common history. It also forms at least two modern nation-states, which are subject to its laws, policies and political processes. A crucial similarity is that East Africa is a relatively stable region in comparison to the regions surrounding it: whether the Great Lakes region of Burundi, Rwanda, and the Congo; the Southern Africa region, notably Mozambique and Zimbabwe; or to the north, the Horn of Africa , where collapsed states, 'new wars', warlordism, shattered societies, successful breakaways, Islamic insurgencies, and precarious peace processes hang in the balance. This stability is emphasized by all sides of the political equation in Tanzania and reflects a certain national pride. At the same time, while parliamentary democracy and structural adjustment programmes are common to both Tanzania and Kenya, these global forces have articulated with their respective social formations differently (Caplan 2004: 4). The defeat of Moi's Kenya Africa Nationalist Union (KANU) by Mwai Kibaki's National Rainbow Coalition (NARC) government also adds to a sense of stability and pro-Western reforms where, despite a change of party, poverty and corruption remain deeply embedded, and Western corporate predation is ongoing (e.g. importation of EU subsidized milk powder and its deleterious damage to the Kenyan dairy industry).[1] Democracy in East Africa is increasingly about the management of discontented populations.

In this section I apply a simplified (neo)Gramscian framework to understand political events in Zanzibar. Tanzania's turn to Western style 'reforms' led to an inter-hegemonic convergence between governing elites at global, regional, national and local levels, which a (neo)Gramscian international approach allows us to view as a totality, but one that is not pre-determined by purely structural and/or class forces (e.g. classical theories of imperialism) and therefore leaves autonomy for global, state and social actors.[2] In his classic work *Prison Notebooks* (Gramsci 1996) the Marxist revolutionary and theoretician, Antonio Gramsci, addressed the nature of power in

---

1. "EU Set to Milk East Africa with Subsidised Goods?" *Inter Press Service News Agency* 15 November 2007 (accessed 23 November 2007).
2. I am indebted to Ngai-Ling Sum for this framework. For details see Sum (2004).

the post-World War 1 West. Gramsci sought to elucidate the ways in which power manifested itself at all levels of Western European social formations compared to the way revolution had unfolded in Russia in 1917. Gramsci was concerned with opening new analytical avenues based on theoretical solutions, and hence new practical possibilities, for the left by rethinking strategic options and tactical alliances (Merrington 1978: 148). More recently, and building on Gramsci's key concepts, a plethora of (neo)Gramscian writings have sought to understand both local contexts and broad historical patterns (Morton 2000:257). A central concept in the Gramscian tradition is hegemony which refers to the means by which ruling classes obtain the consent of subordinate groups to their own domination (McLellan 1979: 185). Hegemony is in turn materialized in a 'historic bloc', that is, the economic, social, and ideological forces that combine in temporary unity to change a society. The ideas of the historic bloc are diffused by organic intellectuals who represent these dominant classes. Organic intellectuals seek to make the subordinate classes embrace the ideas of the dominant classes as their own, or as the common sense way of social being. Key here, therefore, in understanding this global/national hegemonic quest by the Western bloc is the concept of discourse analysis, which is concerned with the role of meaningful social practices and ideas in political life; it suggests ways in which systems of meaning or 'discourses' shape the way people understand their roles in society. Discourse analysis attempts to understand how the discursive practices which structure the activities of social agents are produced, how they function, and how they are changed (Howarth 1995: 115). Competing interpretations are part of social struggles in and through which participants seek to control the discourse and their subsequent actions (Sum 2004:5). The greater the range and depth of sites, the greater is the potential for effective institutionalisation and integration of the dominant discourse. Thus the 'common sense' of neo-liberalism, (open markets, a minimal state, foreign investment) seeks to merge the subordinate and elite interests through propagating neo-liberal discourses ad infinitum in the mainstream global, regional and national media. Behind this 'common sense' is the effort to create a 'collective popular consensus' around these ideas, whether these sites be in the workplace or in the community. The aim is to produce structured coherence that supports continual accumulation (Sum 2004:14). Often regional/national/local notables are materially and psychologically rewarded for the ways in which they successfully embed or facilitate the percolation downwards of the 'common sense' of neo-liberalism locally (e.g. CNN news, UNDP seminars, working papers on 'reform', international conferences). Adjusting to this neo-liberal world, and its 'machinery of surveillance' (World Trade Organization, IMF, World Bank), is a trial and error process of what is and is not possible in the pursuit of local-level hegemony. It is a complex dialectic anchored in negotiation, 'winks and nods', backroom deals, quid pro quo arrangements, and material incentives.

Certainly there are tensions within the Western blocs (e.g. French, Nordic, EU; US and Anglo Saxon). The EU sub-bloc, given some of its members' colonialist past in Africa, as well as the calamitous 'Thirty Years War' (WW1 and WW2), is less openly imperialistic than the US. Yet overall, corporations and Western states also 'see' and what they eschew is instability. Instability creates a poor business environment for investments in sectors such as tourism and, crucially, mining. Likewise there are tensions within the CCM party-state. Bakari notes that there are fundamental differences within CCM, in part based on there being two founder parties, ASP and TANU. For instance the Zanzibar group has continually tried to reassert its position as an independent political organ within CCM. But what binds the mainland and Zanzibar sections together is their mutual security concerns: the Union provides security guarantees toCCM Zanzibar despite its low domestic legitimacy; and Dodoma, in turn, makes hard concessions in areas such as the trans-shipment of goods from Zanzibar to mainland, tolerates Zanzibar's unpaid share of Union expenditure, and accepts over-representation in parliament and party (Bakari 2001:176; Maliyamkono 2000; Anglin 2000:41). In sum, factions notwithstanding, all wings of the contemporary CCM state espouse a common narrative of neo-liberal development buttressed by post-socialist authoritarianism. Just as earlier Eastern bloc political traditions were partially indigenized (e.g. fusing of Chinese Maoism and African socialism into the concept of *ujamaa*), indigenization of the liberal democratic narrative remained the only option for the CCM state given that the Eastern bloc had passed into history and the Islamic bloc was not so close to the mainland-dominated CCM (in the early 1990s the CCM Zanzibar state's overtures to the Organization of the Islamic Conference (OIC) , was overturned by the Union state, led by Julius Nyerere and mainland Christian MPs). Thus it was the Western bloc that had the resources (e.g. debt relief, aid) and the political conditionalities of a 'take it or leave it' kind. In response, CCM intellectuals have sought to apply Western governance concepts to the local level. A Tanzanian scholar has cited key factions within the post-*ujamaa* CCM: a) party political elite, b) party bureaucratic elite (e.g. party secretariat), c) state party elite (top civil servants), and d) CCM Zanzibar (one could add the Tanzanian army officer corps). He aptly notes that Tanzania's externalization to the global economy had put CCM on the ideological defensive to the extent that it was unclear as to whether the party stood for socialism, capitalism, or something in between (Maliyamkono 2003:148–9). Seeking a synthesis, and viewing 'democracy' as an institutional arrangement with checks and balances and a strong civil society, Maliyamkono maintained that such a model should take into account the racial and historical dimension of Tanzania (Maliyamkono 2000). What this meant in practice was that Western neo-liberalism became welded to 1964-style ethnic African nationalism and Union pan-nationalism – a potent elixir meant to refinance and reconstitute the previously diminished CCM.

Western media reports have noted the close movement of the CCM regime to the Western bloc. One business magazine, for instance, notes how the 'socialist mind-set' is succumbing to a free wheeling capitalist system, the rule of law, poverty reduction, and a free and fair general election, "marred only by a localized Zanzibar power struggle" (Vesely 2000:12). This convergence can be seen at the elite level around both political and economic issues. For example, Western powers (the 'Paris Club') held out to Mkapa the 'handsome reward' of nearly $1b in development assistance if he were to sign the terms of the Agreed Memorandum on the Commonwealth agreement in the late 1990s (Anglin 2000:48, 55, 58). President Mkapa being chosen by the New Labour government of Prime Minister Tony Blair to sit on its Price Commission on African development may be interpreted as another incentive. The UK's New Labour's Price Commission rewarded two of Africa's leaders, President Mkapa of Tanzania and Prime Minister Meles of Ethiopia, with appointments to address Africa's development problems. This may be interpreted as part of the 'special relationship' with the Anglo-Saxon sub-bloc (US, UK, Canada). This inter-elite convergence saw former radical socialists mixed with ex-politicians, a former IMF director, African entrepreneurs, and an ex-pop star despite both leaders having overseen deeply mismanaged elections. Mkapa was also the darling of the international development complex during his presidential tenure. At a World Economic Forum meeting in Davos Switzerland, dubbed by an observer as the 'International of Capital' (Robinson 2004:128), Mkapa, during the plenary on poverty, made an appeal for help in tackling malaria in Tanzania. Hollywood star Sharon Stone, moved by Mkapa's appeal, donated US$ 10,000, while cajoling corporate delegates to contribute over US$ 1 million to the Global Fund to fight aids, tuberculosis, malaria.[1] In this particular instance, such a public discourse on 'Third World poverty' underlied the structural impotence of a hitherto radical nationalist regime that had now become exposed to the full force of the global economy, while increasingly being aid dependent and unable to undertake even basic social provision for its citizenry. Certainly the Tanzanian government has fought hard at times in the WTO against the neo-liberal 'free' trade agendas of Western governments, working to develop 'Global South' positions in the WTO rounds. Invariably, however, Tanzanian trading positions have come under the pressure of bilateral concessions to Western interests in exchange for debt relief. For example, after the Doha Round, the IMF/WB announced external debt relief of US$ 36 billion for Tanzania, though at the same time there was a drop in commodity prices of cotton and coffee and therefore an actual rise in the country's debt. To take another example, in February 2002, Canada announced the cancellation of a further US$80 million under the Canada Debt Initiative for Tanzania. Subsequently Tanzania was accredited to a pro-business framework, AGOA, after 18 months of anxious waiting by the local Tanzania business community (Jawara and Kwa 2004:180–81). It is therefore not surprising that even were the Tanzanian government truly committed to 'South-South' alliances in WTO forums, it would be pressured 'through the back door' not to take overly radical stances vis-à-vis Western trading and investment practices. The foreign investment priorities of Western countries can be seen in the visit of Stephen Harper, Prime Minister of Canada, a former neo-liberal organic intellectual. Despite Canada's lamentable foreign aid profile vis-à-vis other OECD countries, especially the Nordic sub-bloc, Harper toured a primary school where he hailed the Canadian-led programme to save 'One Million Lives' through the reduction of child and maternal mortality rates, which was partially funded by the Bill and Melinda Gates Foundation and other agencies.[2] Almost right away, Harper then met directly with officials of the controversial Canadian mining giant Barrick Gold, and during a sensitive time when the company's miners were on strike at its Bulyanhulu site. Both At the end of the visit, Prime Minister Harper and President Jakaya Kiwete praised the mining sector and stressed the importance of a stable environ-

---

1. "Sharon Stone Follows 'Basic Instinct,'" at Davos 2005', http://www.ruggedel-egantliving.com/a/003445.html (accessed 22 November 2006).
2. "Canada to help reduce child, maternal deaths," *IPP Media*, 27 November 2007 (accessed 27 November 2007).

ment for building further foreign investment and the continued support of the Canadian government.[1]

Mention should also be made of the local 'efforts' at implementing global neo-liberalism upwards to domestic constituencies in Western countries. A newspaper article, to take one instance, situated Tanzania's poverty reduction strategy within the UN Millennium Development Goals, expounding a profoundly technical (devoid of social content) and anti-historical (claiming that these recent initiatives are a 'first-time' effort) discourse on poverty reduction campaigns (agriculture, social provision, infrastructure), good governance (human rights, transparency), streamlined and accountable donor-government cooperation, the effectiveness of service-NGOs, and income generating projects and school uniforms for poor women, all with a renewed and 'clearer' vision on good governance in the 'new age of liberalism'. Such framing by international media create 'blank slates' upon which the story of 'free market democracy' can be written The socialist past in such cases is consigned to the historical dustbin (Pitcher and Askew 2006:3). This particular article shows pictures of joyful girls in the Paje area of Zanzibar at the Madrasa Muawanat primary school, and another of women from Kidati who make coconut soap for tourist hotels. Another case in point concerns international funding of local NGOs on Zanzibar. The Aga Khan NGO Resource Centre, funded by the Canadian International Development Agency (CIDA, has been recognized for a number of initiatives including helping fishermen at Nungwi whose fish hauls have been depleted by large fish trawlers, running coral reef and other types of conservation projects, and improving government-market-civil partnerships. Yet an alternative viewpoint would critique such programmes as palliative because only the social and political effects of global integration are being addressed rather than the nature of the ongoing integration itself.[2] Such simple narratives transmitted to already politically passive Western societies may reinforce images of African dependency, as well as the status quo of core-peripheral state relationships.

How did the collapse of African socialism impact local Zanzibari communities? Ethnographic contributions are important not only in revealing the human meaning of concepts such as 'structural adjustment', 'privatization', 'market reform', but also how "the reconfiguration of these particular social and religious worlds can be grasped as alternative transformations of

---

1. "PM meets with Barrick as Tanzanian strike continues," *The Star* (www.thestar. com 27 November 2007 (accessed 27 November 2007).
2. *The Weekender,* 13 February 2005 "New era dawns in foreign aid", Tanzania Road to Progress, Special Report.

a shared, wrenching global process".[1] Subjected to neo-liberal shock treatment from the mid-1980s, thousands of Zanzibari households' livelihoods were scrambled by currency devaluation; de-industrialization; deteriorating social services like electricity especially on Pemba; subsidy removals on imported staple foodstuffs like rice and sugar, and on agricultural inputs like fertilizer; chronic shortages; ecological degradation of common property institutions; the privatization of essential services in health and education; pro-market land tenure 'reform'; civil service retrenchments; predatory behaviour by public officials; non-operational extension services that left more and more villages isolated, and so on - all of which accelerated rural-urban migration, expanded the precarious informal economy, and deepened social inequality. For the primary co-operatives there was absolutely no political or economic preparation around what potentially lay in store for their members' local communities concerning land tenure changes, foreign and local investors buying up beach front, factory fishing by fleets of foreign trawlers, and the need to form economic unions to confront these forces. While with the Co-operative College of Moshi, Pemba Wing, my Zanzibari colleague and I belatedly urged a group of fishermen to consider these issues at the close of a training seminar in 1993. There was no response from the men who silently listened and then departed for home; and we certainly did not have the means to facilitate such a process even had there been a momentum for immediate self-organization. It would be the calm before the storm (Cameron 2002a:161).

The neo-liberal conjuncture, like elsewhere in radical Africana, reordered not only property relations (Pitcher 2006:4), but social relations, values, and even culture. During my years on the islands I heard few Zanzibaris of any political persuasion express the view that economic reforms would ameliorate living standards or provide employment. Even when 'on-the-ground' in the form of hotel projects and Economic Processing Zones, like in Fundo Unguja, such investment projects rarely positively impacted on their local communities. Similarly Caplan notes the disjuncture between macro-economic indicators (i.e. GDP growth rates) and the realities the inhabitants of Mafia Island must grapple with (Caplan, this volume). Caplan's study found that local people criticized government leaders for selling off national assets such as beach frontage even while they suffered from ex- acerbating food insecurity, corruption and health user fees. Perhaps Mafia's greater isolation, weaker historical identity, and non-constitutional status, in contrast

---

1. Editorial, "Mal-Adjustments: Ritual and Reproduction in Neo-Liberal Africa", *Journal of Religion in Africa*, XXXI, 4, p. 367.

to Zanzibar, may explain the greater internalization of *maisha magumu* (the difficult life) and corrosion of community trust compared to the oppositional groundswell in Zanzibar.

CCM-Style Democracy in Zanzibar

In 1990 a Zanzibari friend recounted a speech to me how a CCM leader had claimed that the likelihood of multiparty politics coming to Tanzania was equivalent to 'the sun rising in the West and setting in the East'. But the reality rather was that the single-party system itself was facing its sunset. With the advent of multiparty politics in the early 1990s, Zanzibari nationalism found its institutional expression in the Civic United Front (CUF). CUF represents a coalition of urban intellectual and business interests, and the vast majority of rural peasantry on the second island of Pemba, as well as growing support on the main island of Unguja. CCM Zanzibar's stronghold rested on the peasantry of the main island of Unguja, and the resident mainlander population, many of whom are Christian. Given the sequence of electoral events since political liberalization in 1992, most recently the 2005 elections, it is now manifest that Tanzania's CCM regime has extinguished the promise of political pluralism in Zanzibar: it refuses to leave office constitutionally if defeated at the polls, and more seriously, resorts to repression against the Isles' constitutional opposition, the CUF. Multiparty 'democracy' on the Isles appears to have become a lugubrious game of performative politics: endless prevarications, manipulations, and diversions to prevent the separation of party and state; an electoral machinery under regime control (ID cards, voters' registration); rallies where opposition supporters are assaulted by para-military hooligans; a state-dominated media; voting day as a kind of military campaign; electoral verification as a ritual of both sides citing different observer missions' (not) 'free and fair' declarations; the subsequent constitutional closure for five years with a swift swearing in ceremony of the new president; promises by the newly 'elected' CCM president to serve all citizens regardless of political affiliation; protests and repression by the Union and Zanzibar security apparatus; Western human rights reports calling for the CCM state to investigate its security apparatus; legislative boycotts by the opposition of the Zanzibar House of Representatives; 'aid-rattling' by Western institutions; and inter-party accords in the lead up to the next general election. A concrete example of the Western bloc's 'application' of a macro-level narrative that bolstered the public image of the CCM Zanzibar was a UNDP's expatriate job posting for a 'Governance' advisor. The expatriate post holder would be mandated to formulate pro-poor policies and accountability within the Tanzanian and Zanzibar governments' poverty reduction and good governance policies.[1] This post holder would be accountable to Ahmed Hassan Diria, Minister for Constitutional Affairs and Good Governance. Not only did the opposition oppose the appointment, alleging Diria directed and actually publicly flogged people when he was Wete District Commissioner in the mid-1960s, but it employed a human rights frame of reference, copying the correspondence to Amani Karume, diplomatic missions, media, and human rights organizations.[2] Diria was also considered by some election observers as having helped to orchestrate the behind-the-scenes electoral machinations in 2000.

CCM hegemony is consent ('democracy') armoured by 'revolutionary' coercion (dominance). For the CCM Zanzibar state overseeing this neoliberal 'new word order', the failure of pro-market development to take root is invariably the fault of others, not of itself: merchants should invest in productive enterprises to reduce unemployment; traders should not engage in black market activities that denies the state much needed revenue[3]; peasants should pick more cloves at lower wages; donor training seminars must equip the unemployable for vocational occupations in the burgeoning informal sector. There are vague promises of new fishing nets, small scale credit, and agricultural tools (to those that need 'to develop'). Indeed CCM Zanzibar has the penchant to award itself a 90 per cent grade in implementing its election manifestos, with any shortcomings due to aid boycotts by donors (*wafadhili*) in cahoots with the opposition, since lifted after the 2005 general elections. Boastful quoting by CCM Zanzibar leaders of growth rates culled from its statistical toolkit communicate a rosy narrative of 'trickle down' economics that no doubt clashes with the perceptions of ordinary Zanzibaris. And though poverty rates in urban Tanzania are decreasing on target to reach the Millenium Development Goals for 2015; rural Tanzania, despite some progress, will not reach the goal of decreasing the proportion of people living in extreme poverty by half (1990–2015) (Sahn and Stifel 2002:11). According to the World Bank, roughly sixty percent of Tanzanians continue to live on US$ 1 per day.

1. UNDP, Governance Advisor (Zanzibar) www.devnetjobs.org (accessed 29 January 2005).
2. CUF letter dated 28 September 2004 to Human Rights Watch.
3. *"Karume awaasa wafanyabiashara kuhusu magendo,"* "Karume warns businessmen about the blackmarket," *Guardian* (Tanzania), 26 September 2005 www.ippmedia.com (accessed 10 October 2005).

If consent is not forthcoming the final alternative against a recalcitrant population remains the resort to brute force. Over the course of three multiparty general elections, rationalist political dialogue in the form of multiparty party political programmes, manifestos, rallies and so on has become increasingly empty in relation to the underlying sub-texts of violence and domination. Indeed in a political environment where multiparty elections are akin to fictive (and increasingly less fictive) warfare, while simultaneously spawning cargo-cult-like visions among anti-regime Zanzibaris of a plentiful life in a post-CCM world, many political actors of all persuasions have undeniably tended towards essentialism about the origins of the 'other' (e.g. employing labels like 'Persian', 'Arab', 'African') through moral economic claims to indigenousness. Despite this, the ethnicization/historicization of multi-party politics can be largely attributable to the CCM regime's explicit project of creating essentialist 'African' and 'Arab' identity markers anchored to the bloody imaginings of the 1964 Zanzibar Revolution (see Mapuri 1996). Through 'ethnoscapes' (Appardurai 1990) the CCM regime (Dodoma and Zanzibar wings) has sought to divert attention from a de-legitimized post-colonial governance whereby ineffective state-socialism and structural adjustment policies have failed to better the lives of Zanzibar's majority.

The resort to force, however, can be a great sign of weakness, and consent remains the goal of all ruling groups. When force is required, "the attempt is always made to ensure that force will appear to be based on the consent of the majority, expressed by the so-called organs of public opinion – newspapers and associations – which therefore, in certain situations, are artificially multiplied" (Gramsci in Merrington 1978:154). This can be seen in Mkapa congratulating the police force and talking a 'rule of law' narrative, cheered along by pro-government newspapers (*Daily News*) and commentators. Violence, in the state's version, stems from 'troublemakers' (*wachocezi*) intent on causing 'disorder' and breaking the rule of law; or even killing of police, as Mkapa said in the wake of the January 2001 'disorders'.[1] Hence protestors have only themselves to blame for the stern reaction by the security forces and militias. Indeed both wings of the party-state feel chagrin at an ungrateful society and opposition elite, the latter having been 'brought up' by the CCM leadership over its 40 plus years of rule. Opposition complaints to Western embassies further embarrass and anger the regime. Both states, being under the same party, can be indis-

---

1. "Zanzibar riots were a blot on my presidency – Mkapa," *Guardian* (Tanzania) 14 September 2005 ippmedia.com (accessed 30 September 2005).

tinguishable. The Dodoma and Zanzibar states turn on and off the tap of their relationship to fit the political moment: the margins become blurred and fluid during threatening moments such as the transfer of Union security personnel and funds to the Isles in order to bolster CCM Zanzibar's election machine; and at other times the borders are 'air tight', such as the constitutional 'my-hands-are-tied' stance of the Union government when international protests ensue over electoral fraud allegations. Only in the wake of the 1995 elections was there a charismatic mediator, Julius Nyerere, who could rise above the corporate interests of CCM Dodoma and CCM Zanzibar to instead articulate a national interest, in this case, urging Salmin Amour's CCM Zanzibar to form a national unity government with the opposition. The half-hearted effort did not cut it with the Amour group. The death of Julius Nyerere, remarked upon with foreboding by some observers, further removed any constraint against the employment of lethal force, as revealed by the January 2001 massacres. International censure of the CCM government has not gone beyond a mild aid boycott of the Isles, removed since the 2005 general elections. A local Zanzibari man once remarked to me that he had little truck with the effectiveness of a donor aid boycott of the Zanzibar government as CCM Zanzibar would 'just draw the water from the mainland' (*'watachota maji kutoka Bara'*).

Both the Dodoma and Zanzibar states have become increasingly militant in the ways that they frame the opposition within a particular moral universe that serves to justify repression when certain 'lines in the sand' are crossed. One cannot underestimate the fear inflicted upon communities by 'neutral' Weberian-like state organs when the reality is that the lines are blurred between judicial and extra-judicial violence (Gledhill 2000). On the Isles, the Union armed forces are not portrayed as occupiers but rather as 'protectors', ensuring electoral fair play and the safety of citizens, according to the regime. Besides, CCM Dodoma perceives that were a CUF government to come to power on the Isles it would demand renegotiation of key articles of the Union even though the opposition remains adamant that it seeks to reform not to break up the Union. And modern African history demonstrates that central regimes, no matter their ideological self-appellations, will ferociously resist even partial territorial dismemberment, as Biafra and Eritrea demonstrate. CCM Dodoma as the 'Guardian of the Union' argues that a federal system as proposed by CUF would break the Union: 'something that will never be allowed to happen', said President Mkapa during the 2000 general elections, hinting at the expulsions of mainland-based Zanzibaris back to the Isles and the seizure of their properties were the two-government union to collapse (Cameron 2002b). Claims by Anglin that inter-island relations appear to assume the character of incipient civil war between Pemba and Unguja (2000:40) obfuscates the deep power imbalance between the two islands, and the coercive power of the Union forces, of which some units are based on Pemba Island at Vitongoji. To put it in local Pemban idiom: *wao wanashika mpini na panga na sisi ukali wake* (they grip the handle of the machete and we its blade).

CCM Zanzibar maintains that the CUF opposition elites seek an 'Arab Restoration', with CUF's followers, many being Pembans, considered fellow travellers with these opposition elites. Hence the CCM Zanzibar cannot even entertain the notion of the opposition sharing power in a national unity government, even as a junior partner; multiparty democracy requires an opposition for effective parliamentary governance, argues CCM Zanzibar. Another element of intimidation are CCM Zanzibar's militia and irregular units, termed the *Janjaweed*. Many opposition communities in Zanzibar fear that the security forces may exploit 'zones of disorder' in order to attack non-party members, loot property, and violate women. Undoubtedly many of the youth who join CCM Zanzibar para-military units are frustrated by unfulfilled consumerism as seen on the satellite TV images of 'Westworld'. More ominously, CCM Zanzibar's references to the metaphorical machetes (*mapanga*) of 1964, that they are only in storage with keys in hand, is evocative of 'Hutu power'.[1] Mamdani argues that failure of the Rwandan Nationalist Revolution of 1959 to transform post-colonial society and its racial narratives led to the deepening of the political project known as the Interahamwe movement (Mamdani 2003: 174–175). Similarly the rhetoric of 'permanent revolution' (*'mapinduzi daima'*) and of 'to overturn' (*'kupindua'*), is evocative of the ethnic pogroms of 1964 and of what is yet still a possibility (it is importantn to recall that the Zanzibar indigenous majority are neither mainland Africans nor settler Arabs): as an untransformed way of thinking, it is the fundamentalist politics of a failed state.

In the wake of '9/11' in the US, the Tanzania Union government promulgated the 2002 Prevention of Terrorism Act, following namesake legislation in other countries such as the UK and India. The Act gives the Union government considerable latitude since the legislation does not clearly define 'terrorism', but rather lists acts that include, among other things, at-

---

1. An alleged example of this rhetoric occurred in a speech delivered by Zanzibar President Amani Karume 26 September 2005. *Zanzibar Election Update* No. 7, 6 October 2005.

tacks upon a person's life, kidnapping, and serious damage to property.[1] This deepening securitization of Tanzanian society can again be seen in the presence of the Chargé d'Affaires, Michael S. Owen, of the US Embassy in Dar es Salaam, when he addressed members of the Zanzibar House of Representatives on 24 January 2004.[2] Owen sang the praises of globalization while warning against illicit financial transactions by terrorist networks:

> The terrorist attacks on the American Embassy in Dar es Salaam on August 7, 1998, and the subsequent attacks on the World Trade Centre and the Pentagon on September 11, 2001, could not have been carried out without the necessary financing from overseas sources ... We want to join hands with you and work together to do everything possible to ensure that such violence and destruction never come to Zanzibar. Zanzibar and the United States are partners in a global coalition that is united in its resolve to fight terrorism ... [3]

The 1964 Union, anti-communist in orientation, had paradoxically become perceived as a way to contain the 'threat' of radical Islam. CCM Zanzibar's 1964 'time honoured' Anti-Arab narrative had become latched onto the Bush regime's '9/11' 'war on terror' narrative: a symbiosis of local and global narratives that now framed the Orwellian conflict waged against the Isles' democracy movement.

Popular Social Forces in Zanzibar Society

Gramsci sees civil society both as a space for the consolidation and normalization of domination, and as a sphere of resistance potentially spearheading counter-hegemonic projects. Important here are how discourses mediate the production and contestation of hegemony (Sum 2004:12). For hegemony, however seemingly dominant, must face the counter-discourses of the oppressed and marginalized, ranging from 'everyday forms of resistance' to growing economic-corporate awareness, from parliamentary opposition to extra-parliamentary struggle. Counter-hegemonic challenges may be rooted in class, social movements, popular culture, and may be led by organic intellectuals based in community organs like co-operatives, trade unions, movement-based NGOs (one should note that the Union NGO Act passed in

---

1. *Freedom House* – Tanzania (2007) www.freedomhouse.org (accessed 19 November 2007).
2. "Blood Money: Financing Terrorism in the Global Era", *Tanzania.usembassy.gov*, 24 January 2004, accessed 19 November 2007.
3. Ibid: p. 2.

2002 restricts NGOs around compulsory registration, and prohibits national networks and coalitions), oppositional political parties, academia, mosques, churches, or even the local market. Such challenges may deploy 'wars of position' (a long period of struggle) and/or 'wars of movement' (capturing state power) to resist and replace hegemonic control. Despite the fact that the historic ruling class bloc may seek the absorption and cooptation of independent social forces, the quest for hegemony is never complete given that such a system, which privileges certain dominant interests in a 'new word order', shuts out the voices of 'others', whether they be ethnic-, gender-, class-, or place-based (Sum 2004:16). The resultant forms of governance are asymmetric with the effect that uneven power relations remain (e.g. class, gender, ethnicity, religion, region) and hence continue to be contested (Sum 2004:11). This is not to say that economic crises alone (e.g. massive unemployment) cause counter-hegemonic challenges to automatically emerge. This is because organic intellectuals, who represent counter-hegemonic movements, are potentially prone to neutralization and cooptation by grants, institutional recognition, partnership, and "invited visits to the global heartland of 'worldview' production" (Sum 2004:16). Cooptation of political party leaders on Tanzania's mainland since the introduction of the multiparty system would be a case in point. Thus revolutionary success is not guaranteed: "it may be ruled out that immediate economic crises of themselves produce fundamental historical events; they can simply create a terrain more favourable to the dissemination of certain modes of thought, and certain ways of resolving questions involving the entire subsequent development of national life" (Gramsci in McLellan 1979:187).

A key role of organic intellectuals who represent the marginalized must be to distinguish between *conjunctural* (day-to-day problems such as unemployment and corrupt leaders) and organic crises (which give rise to socio-historical critique). Whether a crisis is conjunctural or organic will influence whether a 'war of movement' or a 'war of position' will be adopted (McLellan 1979:190).

Indeed the application of (neo)Gramscian theory to particular regions of the 'Global South' has revealed the complex and inter-connected dominant power relations facing the popular sectors. Morton, for example, examines the complex of international institutional organization and the state/society complex of the Institutional Revolutionary Party (PRI) of Mexico (overseeing many decades of dominant party rule before its defeat in 2000). Even in Mexico, powerful popular forces – *campesinos*, indigenous peoples, agrarian Marxists, the popular church, gender activists, North American solidarity organizations – must deepen their 'war of position' by further developing organizational capacity to establish a rival historic bloc in order to resist both pro-NAFTA (North American Free Trade Agreement) forces as well as the Mexican state's assault on communal land tenure (Morton 2000: 270). The authoritarian turn of Robert Mugabe's regime's, after having expended its revolutionary legitimacy through class compromises and elite entrenchment, and risking Western bloc open hostility for seizing white farms, likewise, presents formidable challenges to its democracy movement (Saul and Saunders 2005). What of the Tanzanian context, where compared to Mexico and Zimbabwe, the popular sector is weaker (e.g. weak anti-capitalist groupings and trade unions)? CCM has in fact been perceived as a kind of 'East African PRI' among opposition Zanzibaris: a once revolutionary party gripped by an iron law of oligarchy, one which shuts out even its own members' contribution to party policy; but a party that one day, despite the appearance of unassailable dominance, may be defeated at the polls. This raises the question of the nature of the parliamentary opposition in Zanzibar and whether it can organize a counter-culture within civil society as a long term strategy, as opposed to merely conducting politics at the formal level (e.g. elections, legislatures).

Where Swahili coastal society drifts may depend on two sets of processes: a) electoral prospects for substantive democracy on the Isles; and b) an ever-enlarging zone of piety where cultural critiques against secular nationalism and capitalism deepen (Pasha 2000:248). Parliamentary democracy in Tanzania and Zanzibar was meant to be the basis of popular sovereignty in the transition from a radical nationalist regime to a neo-liberal pluralist state. Yet sovereignty remains embedded more than ever in the CCM executive of the party-state bureaucracy. At present CUF is mired in the trappings of a newly-installed political system forged at the interfaces of the global/regional/national levels. CUF's 'war of movement' against the CCM regime is largely on a constitutional terrain fully to CCM's advantage. CUF may in fact be suspended in perpetuity to permanent opposition in order to showcase the successful 'workings' of liberal democracy in Zanzibar. This point can be modified in that tensions may exist around the extent of the 'passive revolution' (i.e. economic reform within existing social relations, formation of national unity government, freedom of the press, ethical dimension to rights, social provision within the UN Millennium Decade, Zanzibar Vision 2020 and the Zanzibar Poverty Reduction Plan (ZPRP) and so forth) In other words, there are possible tensions between CCM's 'revolutionary legitimacy' and Western human rights narratives, which therefore cautions one not to draw the conclusion that the Western bloc uncritically supports CCM. CUF's constitutionality, coupled with CCM Zanzibar's periodic extremism, may have saved CUF from being left to its own devices by the Western bloc. The Tanzanian security apparatus might have long ago crushed the CUF were it not for CCM's interfacing with Western powers, especially the EU sub-bloc with its human rights orientation. There may also be the fear of instability in East Africa were this to occur.

In its parliamentary 'war of movement' CUF has sought to exploit these tensions between the Western bloc and the CCM regime. CUF Zanzibar's leader, Seif Shariff Hamd, for instance, on the premise that the CCM is 'socialist' (the Western media often refers to Mkapa as a 'former socialist') narrates the need for Zanzibar to move away from "a socialist, state controlled economy. Rather, CUF would liberalize the clove economy, privatise government owned businesses and create a truly attractive climate for business and investment" (CUF 2005). Whether CUF could structurally resolve underdevelopment within this neo-liberal paradigm is questionable. Nevertheless, this counter-narrative is a message to Western interests that a future CUF government on the Isles would be market-friendly. Analogies to successful protest movements in the Balkans and, more recently, the Ukraine, are appeals to the Western liberal consciousness of the role of non-violence in the toppling of dictatorial regimes. Yet in Eastern European countries the role of the security forces, and the separation of powers, are of a different order than in agrarian-based African social formations where security forces usually do not distinguish between peaceful and armed protest, and where society is less organized. Crucially these pro-Western protests in East European 'transitional' states are invariably supported by the Western bloc against its hegemonic rival, Russia. And the more CUF appeals to the Western bloc, the more succour it gives to CCM to play the nationalist trump card, locally, against a 'traitorous' opposition.

Common to issues around globalization in academic circles is whether the state can be a target of counter-hegemonic power, the point being that resistance now slices across geopolitical boundaries and various identities, not just class but nationality, race, ethnicity, religion, gender (Chin and Mittleman 2000:43; Sum 2004:16). Geopolitically, CUF has sought to tap the sympathies of global civil society by employing the internet to disseminate the speeches of its leadership, and to circulate pictures of human rights abuses perpetrated by CCM's security forces. In this vein, resistance may cut across global, regional, national and local levels such as the Swahili Diaspora in Europe and the Middle East. For example, advocacy work in the West on human rights, including internet activist sites in the Swahili Diaspora, like Zewatch Zacomed and Zanzibar Watch Election Update, play a strong advocacy role, while at the same time circumventing Zanzibar government print and radio media. It is unclear if this focus affects the hold of the CCM regime in any way. The state is still the paramount site of struggle. CUF itself realizes this and has pointed to the possibility of instability in 'stable' Tanzania if there was a third flawed election, "which may well turn out to be a real ground for terrorists to exploit the ensuing political chaos and frustration within the numerically larger Muslim community" (CUF Press Release 18 November 2004). In return, CCM claims CUF is a front for extremist Muslim groups, supporters of Arab sultans, and terrorists in general. No doubt such accusations are meant to strengthen CCM's hand in deepening its consensual relationship with the Western bloc over the so-called 'fundamentalist' threat.

Looking beyond CUF, who are the organic intellectuals that may emerge if Zanzibari society makes a significant shift to a more intensified 'war of position'? The role of teachers may be pivotal. Teachers' remuneration comes from the state; in this sense they are civil servants. Nonetheless they live in the most isolated communities as underpaid civil servants obliged to help their poorer *jamaa* (community), who expect this of them. Moreover teachers must do this with salaries continually declining in real terms. In this sense they have committed 'class suicide'. Teachers see the problems of their people in a most immediate way: listless malnourished children unable to concentrate; lack of school desks and chairs; outdated teaching materials like books and laboratory equipment; and poor career prospects, especially for politically 'polluted' *wachochezi* (agitators). Where teachers stand out vis-à-vis other locally-based civil servants is the role they play as intelligentsia: they are not mere technicians like medical assistants, police, or extension workers, but are peddlers of ideas. They are trained to think critically and have a wide-ranging generalist knowledge of the world. They feel they should – as the 'educated' in their communities – and do challenge state propaganda. And in one instance prior to the 1995 election, allegedly shouted down the CCM zealot and Education Minister at the time, Omar Mapuri, during a school inspection on Kisiwa Panza Pemba. Teachers are highly respected in Tanzanian society, as evidenced in their title of *maalim* or *mwalimu*. Julius Nyerere, before being anointed 'Father of the Nation', was known simply as *'Mwalimu'*. Teachers are not 'pure intellectuals' peddling 'meta-narratives' like Marxism or neo-liberalism separated from the people; on the contrary, teachers are organically linked to their communities through praxis, living in the incessant grind of extreme poverty. Gramsci noted the crucial mediating role of teachers in bringing the peasantry into contact with the state apparatus; that though such intellectuals represented the aspirations of the poor peasantry, strata such as teachers, doctors, and priests were at the same time objects of anger and envy (Gramsci 1996:15).

It is possible that the dialectic of a new governance may supersede the system of multiparty politics and its sponsors due to the deteriorating political situation, economic crisis, deepening cruelty, and erosion of security. Aside from individual survival strategies such as migration to the mainland, and the wider Swahili Diaspora by the fortunate few, extra-constitutional resistance may take form collectively. The extent to which political Islamicic currents will be indigenised in a Zanzibar where moderate Sunni Islam flourishes in a non-sectarian and multicultural society, and where both regime members and opponents are Muslim, is unclear. Without a doubt religious scholars are becoming more prominent politically on both mainland and the Isles, though the leadership dynamics remain in need of further research.[1] Gerard C. van de Bruinhorst (this volume) has observed that the sacred day of *Arafa* has become a politicized day of remembrance of the Tanzanian Muslim community (*jamaa*), for those massacred by the regime's security forces in January 2001, and, in Dar es Salaam, for the victims of the Mwembechai riots. On the Isles, media reports suggest that CUF may be outflanked by two Islamic organizations called the Islamic Propagation Organization (IPO) and the Imams' Association of Zanzibar.[2] The IPO's critiques range from government corruption, electoral fraud and the culturally corrosive effects of uncontrolled tourism,[3] to the Tanzanian government's Prevention of Terrorism Act as well as the US occupations of Islamic lands.[4] This growing fault-line, moreover, may override specific nation state contexts where Swahili peoples reside. Media reports suggest that Western officials are watching developments to prevent what they call extremists from gaining more footholds on the African coast. A geo-political area of concern to the Western bloc and its mainstream media is in Somalia

1. "Tanzania: Zanzibar Vote Spells More Trouble," *Africa Reports* No 46, 16 November 2005 http://www.iwpr.net/index.pl (accessed 15 December 2005).
2. Zanzinet Forum Uamsho's Report 2005 www.zanzinet.org (accessed 8 November 2007).
3. "Islamic groups in Zanzibar want strict enforcement of Ramadan rules," *International Herald Tribune* 21 September 2006 (accessed 8 November 2007).
4. "Discontent Brews in Zanzibar," *Los Angeles Times* 30 October (accessed 5 November 2007).

where the US and another regional ally, Ethiopia, hunt al Qaeda suspects allegedly connected to bombings in Tanzania and Kenya (similar media bites talk about the Zanzibar origins of other al Qaeda suspects implicated in the US embassy and Mombasa bombings), while also fighting an insurgency against a home-grown Islamic Somali nationalist movement led by the Islamic Courts Union (ICU), and supported by Eritrea.[1] From a counter-hegemonic perspective the reality is different, however, and more accurately reflects the attempts by the US-led Western bloc to militarise the African continent (e.g. the new US Africa Command) vis-à-vis both hegemonic newcomers (China) as well as local anti-imperialist social movements.

In a vacuous context where secular identities have experienced loss of meaning in a post-socialist era, political Islam may increasingly serve as an ideology that provides cohesion, justification, counter-critique, an alternative vision, and an integrative mechanism against an authoritarian nationalist regime's failure to relinquish power or halt economic regression. Pasha argues that globalization increasingly marginalizes the popular social sectors by decreasing welfare provision, and, crucially, by the growing numbers of educated unemployed, as well as the spawning of informal forms of education like the *madrasa* (Islamic schools) (Pasha 2000:247). Resistance in the Islamic world has been conceptually homogenized by globalization purveyors as an anti-Western and atavistic reaction to modernization. This position assumes that globalization is an ongoing uniform process, rather than an uneven and contradictory one. Rather for Pasha, Islamic politics represents multi-layered historical forces that challenge and resist secular and Western regimes over issues of governance (Pasha 2000:241–254). In contradistinction Amin questions the anti-imperialist, and more pointedly, the anti-capitalist credentials of political Islam because of its exclusive emphasis on culture. Amin argues that political Islam eliminates from every sphere of life the real social confrontations between the popular classes and the globalized capitalist system that oppresses and exploits them:

> The militants of political Islam have no real presence in the areas where actual social conflict takes place and their leaders repeat incessantly that such conflicts are unimportant. Islamists are only present in these areas to open schools and health clinics. But these are nothing but works of charity and the means for indoctrination. They are not means of support for the struggles of the popular classes against the system responsible for their poverty (Amin 2007:1).

---

1. "The War on Terror's Newest Front," by David Case *dehai.org* 4 December 2007 (accessed 5 December 2007). For other great power parallels between Tanganyika/Zanzibar and Ethiopia/Eritrea see Cameron (2004b).

Amin's position is perhaps too class-reductionist, not exploring in sufficient detail the ways in which culture, religion, nationalism, and class intersect. Moreover Amin's position does not explain why the US-led Western bloc so vehemently opposes political Islam, which has been in evidence even on the Swahili coast as note above. Examining the Tanzanian context further, it is not clear to what extent a resurgent yet independent Tanzanian left can credibly add its anti-capitalist critique independent of the voice of political Islam. Many Tanzanians are weary of CCM-style socialism And no opposition party dares occupy ground left of the CCM, knowing the opprobrium it would receive from the Western bloc (the closest in terms of a left sounding name in the party political opposition appears to be the Tanzanian Labour Party). How can Islamic and secular forces unite so that popular aspirations and alternative economic and political mechanisms are rooted in Tanzanian realities? As more and more people must use one another as the means to survive poverty and exploitation, and where resistance to some extent has become cultural in form in an individualized post-socialist world, perhaps Islam for growing numbers remains a communitarian pillar, a kind of holding fast to a certainty. Tentatively speaking, I would concur with Amin that political Islamists are not actually anti- capitalist per se. For instance, an alternative economic model for the Isles away from tourism and cloves does not appear to be well formulated. It is less clear, however, as to whether Islamic activist have anti-imperialist credentials. On the one hand, Zanzibar Islamic organizations have reportedly called for increased local control over the economy, a call that speaks to nationalist quarters on the Isles. On the other hand, the leader of the IPO has been reported as advocating rule by Shari'ah law for Zanzibar.

Zanzibari popular forces must avoid being sucked into the vortex of the 'Clash of Civilization' project. Throughout its modern history Zanzibar's politics – British/Omani colonial rule; ASP post-revolutionary authoritarianism; neo-liberal authoritarianism – has been a cycle of destructive binaries: 'Arab/African'; *'Mzungu/Mwafrika'*; 'Revolutionary/ Counter-Revolutionary'; 'Christian/Muslim'; 'Secularist/Fundamentalist'; 'Unguja/Pemba'; 'Zanzibar/Mainland'; *'Wazanzibara/* *'Wazanzibari'*; 'Security Official/Terrorist'; 'Believer/Non-Believer'. If the primary binary of 'Dominator/Dominated' is to be resolved (see Matustik 1995) then Tanzania's political traditions must empathize with and respect their very differences while, at the same time, sharing common normative perspectives and programmes that move beyond political fundamentalisms (nationalism, religiosity, sectarian socialism, possessive individualism). The issue must be to build horizontal density in order to strengthen oppositional society over the medium term, while maintaining pressure on the parliamentary system on the Isles and on the mainland. CUF's engagement in the sterile alternative of participation/abstentionism in the Zanzibar House of Representatives should be replaced by active engagement with both the political process and the wider social dynamic, which no doubt is occurring. Yet neither CUF nor any other political or civil force can capture power on its own. The militant robustness of the CCM regime in blocking, repressing, or co-opting popular challenges must not be underestimated. For, in the end, the Zanzibar question will be settled on the mainland. If this premise is correct it stands to reason that the popular movement must cross the Zanzibar channel and encompass the spiritual and class identities of all Tanzanian communities facing the deleterious consequences imposed on them by the dominant historic bloc (Western and CCM blocs). Organic intellectuals representing all popular forces must expose the oppressive and exploitative side of this dominant historic bloc. Until an emergent popular movement becomes anti-capitalist and moves towards an alternative socio-economic popular order – rooted in, but transcending, the Tanzanian national tradition of community, unity, peace and mutuality – it will remain grounded down in a 'war of position' against the CCM regime. Tentatively speaking, such a counter-hegemonic popular movement must debate the appropriate balance of state, market, collective forms, and community, while linking with movement-based community organizations and NGOs on these issues locally, nationally, regionally, and globally: above all, avoiding violence as a tool for political change, knowing that in the process, even where successful, new authoritarianisms emerge. How the matrix of 'position' and 'movement' plays itself out will depend upon these outcomes. Perhaps not a pleasant conclusion, but one in which Swahili studies must engage with if it is to link the micro-analytics of cultural dynamics to the wider political challenges confronting the contemporary Swahili Coast.

References

Amin, Samir, 2007, "Political Islam in the Service of Imperialism," *Monthly Review* www.monthlyreview.org, (accessed 7 December 2007).

Anglin, Douglas G, 2000, "Zanzibar: Political Impasse and Commonwealth Mediation", *Journal of Contemporary African Studies*, 18, 1.

Appadurai, Arjun, 1990, "Disjuncture and Difference in the Global Cultural Economy", *Theory, Culture and Society* 7, pp. 295–310.

Bakari, Mohammed Ali, 2001, *The Democratisation Process in Zanzibar: A Retarded Transition,* Hamburg: Institute of African Studies.

Cameron, Greg, 2002a, "Protest and Cooperation in Post-Revolutionary Zanzibar," PhD thesis, SOAS, University of London, London, UK.

Cameron, Greg, 2002b, "Zanzibar's Turbulent Transition," *Review of African Political Economy* 29, No. 92 (July): 313–330.

Cameron, Greg, 2004a, "Political Violence, Ethnicity and the Agrarian Question in Zanzibar," in Pat Caplan and Farouk Topan (eds), *Swahili Modernities: Culture, Politics and Identity on the East Coast of Africa*, Trenton, New Jersey: Africa World Press, pp. 103–119.

Cameron, Greg, 2004b, "Authoritarian Federalism in the Dock: An Historical Comparison between the Ethiopia-Eritrea Federation and the Tanganyika-Zanzibar Union", *Journal of Eritrean Studies*, Volume III, Number1 (May): 1–25.

Caplan, Pat, 2004, "Editor's Introduction," in Pat Caplan and Farouk Topan (eds), *Swahili Modernities: Culture, Politics and Identity on the East Coast of Africa*, Trenton, New Jersey: Africa World Press.

Chin, Christine and James Mittleman, 2000, "Conceptualizing Resistance to Globalization," in Barry K. Gills (ed.), *Globalization and the Politics of Resistance*, N.Y.: Palgrave, pp. 29–45.

CUF Press Conference by Secretary General and Zanzibar Presidential Candidate Seif Shariff Hamad 2005, "Zanzibar: The Ukraine of East Africa in the Making?", at the internal launch of the 2005 general election campaign at the Jacaranda Hotel Nairobi, 7 September.

CUF Press Release by CUF National Chairman Prof. Ibrahim Lipumba 2004, "CUF welcomes the hosting of the International Conference of the Great Lakes Region and calls for preventive measures to avoid potential conflict in Tanzania", 18 November.

CUF letter to Human Rights Watch, dated 28 September 2004.

Editorial, 2001, "Mal-Adjustments: Ritual and Reproduction in Neo-Liberal Africa," *Journal of Religion in Africa*, XXXI, 4. Freedom House.

Gledhill, John, 2000, *Power and Its Disguises: Anthropological Perspectives on Politics*, London: Pluto Press.

Gramsci, Antonio, 1996, *Selections from the Prison Notebooks*, Hyderabad: Orient Longman Ltd.

Howarth, David, 1995, "Discourse Theory," in David Marsh and Gerry Stoker (eds), *Theory and Methods in Political Science*, London: MacMillan Press Ltd., pp. 115–136.

Internet, "Sharon Stone Follows 'Basic Instinct' at Davos 2005", http://www.ruggedelegantliving.com/a/003445.html (accessed 22 November 2006).

Jawara, Fatoumata and Aileen Kwa, 2004, *Behind the Scenes at the WTO: The Real World of International Trade Negotiations*, London: Zed Books.

Maliyamkono, Ted and F.E. Kanyongolo, 2003, *When Political Parties Clash*, Dar es Salaam: Tema Publishers Company Ltd.

Maliyamkono, Ted, 2000, "Zanzibar's Financial Benefits From the Union", in T.L. Maliyamkono (ed.), *The Political Plight of Zanzibar*, Dar es Salaam and Kampala: Tema Publishers Company Ltd., pp. 213–244.

Mamdani, Mahmood, 2003, "Making Sense of Political Violence in Post-colonial Africa," in Leo Panitch and Colin Leys (eds), *Socialist Register* (Fighting Identities: Race, Religion and Ethno Nationalism), London: Merlin Press, pp. 159–183.

Mapuri, Omar, 1996, *Zanzibar the 1964 Revolution: Achievements and Prospects*, Dar es Salaam: Tema Publishers.

Matustik, Martin J. 1995, "Towards Radical Democratic Multiculturalism," in *Constellations* Volume 1 No. 3 January 1995, pp. 386–387.

McLellan, David, 1979, *Marxism after Marx. An Introduction*, New York: Harper and Row.

Merrington, John, 1978, "Theory and Practice in Gramsci's Marxism," in New Left Review (ed.) *Western Marxism A Critical Reader*, London: Verso, pp. 140–175.

Morton, Andrew, 2000, "Mexico, Neoliberal Restructuring and the EZLN: A Neo-Gramscian Analysis," in Barry K Gills (ed.), *Globalization and the Politics of Resistance*, N.Y.: Palgrave, pp. 255–279.

Pasha, Mustapha Kamal, 2000, "Globalization, Islam and Resistance," in Barry K Gills (ed.) *Globalization and the Politics of Resistance*, N.Y.: Palgrave, pp. 241–254.

Pitcher, M. Anne and Kelly M. Askew, 2006, "African Socialisms and Postsocialisms", *Africa* 76 (1), pp. 1–14.

Robinson, William, 2004, *A Theory of Global Capitalism Production, Class, and State in a Transnational World*, Baltimore: John Hopkins University Press.

Sahn, David E. and David C. Stifel, 2002, 'Progress toward The Millenium Development Goals in Africa.' on line mimeo June.

Saul, John S. and Richard Saunders, 2005, "Mugabe, Gramsci, and Zimbabwe at Twenty-Five", in John S. Saul (ed.), *The Next Liberation Struggle Capitalism, Socialism and Democracy in Southern Africa,* Toronto: Between the Lines, pp. 129–145.

Scott, James C., 1998, *Seeing Like a State How Certain Schemes to Improve the Human Condition Have Failed*, New Haven: Yale University Press.

Sum, Ngai-ling, 2004, "From 'Integral State' to 'Integral World Economic Order': Towards a Neo-Gramscian Cultural International Political Economy". Cultural

Political Economy Working Paper Series, Working Paper No. 7, Institute for Advanced Studies in Social and Management Sciences, University of Lancaster.

Terdman, Moshe, 2006, "Project of the Research of Islamic Movements (PRISM)", *Islam in Africa Newsletter* Volume 1 (2006), Number 4 (August).

UNDP, Governance Advisor (Zanzibar) www.devnetjobs.org 29 January 2005.

Government of the United States, *Tanzania us embassy.government website*.

Vesely, Milan, 2000, "Tanzania Rise of a New African Star", *African Business* December No. 260.

Zanzibar Election Update, No. 7, 6 October 2005.

Newspapers

Afrcia Reports

Guardian (Tanzania).

International Herald Tribune.

Inter Press Service News Agency.

IPP Media.

Los Angeles Times.

The Toronto Star (Canada).

The Weekender (Canada).

Zanzinet Forum.

– CHAPTER 9 –

Baraza as Markers of Time in Zanzibar

Roman Loimeier

Introduction

Space and space related terms such as sphere (public sphere) or scape (land-scape, seascape, ethnoscape, etc.) have been in the centre of anthropologi-cal attention for some time and the concept of "scapes" as formulated by Arjun Appadurai, in particular, has been expanded to many different con-texts in recent years. When discussing "space" we still have to take into ac-count, however, the concept of the "public sphere" as developed by Jürgen Habermas (1962/1989/1990), who defines "public sphere" as a "Form von bürgerlicher Öffentlichkeit" (a form of civilian publicity) which allows for the free circulation of information and ideas, outside the control of the state (Habermas 1990: 86ff). This concept was taken up by Robert Launay and Benjamin Soares in their discussion of an "Islamic sphere" in French colo-nial West Africa and defined as "a space conceptually separate (though obvi-ously not entirely autonomous) from *particular* (my emphasis) affiliations... but also from the colonial (and later the post-colonial) state", a space that was consequently hotly contested, in particular, with respect to the defini-tion of public ritual, the fixing of dates and religious holidays and the public modes of prayer, or "Islam" as such (Launay and Soares 1999:468ff; 483), and became, thus, space for the negotiation of influence and power, in the struggle for "Deutungshegemonie", the power to define religious, social or political issues in a hegemonic way. The idea of thinking societies in spaces has diverted, however, the attention from another, equally important per-spective, namely that of thinking societies in times, and to then link (social) time with (social) space, although there is a small group of neo-marxist au-thors such as David Harvey who have thought exactly along these lines. In addition, Anthony Giddens has contributed considerably to the discussion on times and spaces by introducing the concept of time-space-distancia-tion (Giddens 1997: 28ff). In the following deliberations, I would like to focus on this idea of linking space and time by presenting a case study from Zanzibar, where I was led to discover the *baraza* as a major place for the ne-gotiation of all kinds of things. Before approaching the *baraza* as "markers of time", it is necessary, though, to explore the vast array of meanings of the term as such and to present the social setting of the *baraza* in Zanzibar.

The Space, Place and Time Dimensions of the *Baraza*

The term *baraza* (*baraza/mabaraza* pl.)[1] as such has many different meanings, yet, the term has so far not really been discussed in the academic literature, and to the best of my knowledge, only Marc J. Swartz (1991) and Mohamed Ahmad Saleh (2004) have provided first academic definitions of the *baraza* by defining it as "a place of public audience or reception, a veranda, a stone seat in the entrance hall, a bench against the wall outside a house or a raised platform with stone seats and sometimes roofed over in front of the house, for receiving visitors, holding an audience, transacting business, for gossiping, where men gather on a fairly regular basis, usually between *magharibi* and *isha* prayers. It is a male place of socialization par excellence[2] with contrast to *ua*, the courtyard, where female members of the society get together (*uani*) for their talks and their domestic activities" (Swartz 1991:317; Saleh 2004:16).[3] Mw. Ramadhani Kututwa has added to this definition by remarking that there also are, in rural (*shamba*) areas, *baraza* in the form of (public) sheds in either the village or along the roadside, often wooden, sometimes mud or concrete constructions (*kibanda, makuti*) with benches (*magogo*) and mats (*mkeka, gamvi, busati*) to sit on (Mw. Ramadhani, 2 August 2004). The oldest Kiswahili dictionary of Krapf (1882) defines the *baraza* as "a stone seat or bench table, either outside of the house or in the hall, where the master sits in public and receives

---

1. Mohamed Ahmed Saleh has pointed out that the plural of the term *baraza*, namely *mabaraza*, is applied only when referring to "meetings of a council" and other forms of organization that are not necessarily linked with a specific place. When referring to the *baraza* as a place, people would form the plural by saying, for instance, "he is sitting in three barazas", i.e. *anakaa katika baraza tatu*. In my text, I will follow this rule instead of applying the grammatical plural *mabaraza* (Mohamed Ahmed Saleh, 2 April 2005).
2. In contrast to Saleh's and Swartz's definitions of the *baraza*, there are, however, numerous women's *baraza*, both in Zanzibar Town, in particular, the different Ng'ambo quarters, as well as the rural areas (see below). For a more detailed presentation of the gender aspect of *baraza* see Loimeier 2007.
3. Swartz's definition of the *baraza* was developed in the context of his research on the Bena in Tanzania, where the term *baraza* means, as in many other mainland societies, a "session to settle disputes" (Swartz 1991:317). We have to be aware of the fact that the term *baraza* has acquired, in different societies and at different times, different meanings. I am grateful to Pat Caplan for directing my attention to Marc Swartz' work.

his friends; hence the public audience held by the Sultan and the council then held; meeting of a council" (quoted in Haugerud/Njogu 1991:8). The Arabic root of the term, namely *b-r-z* (to jut out, to protrude, to stand out), actually points to an architectonic meaning of the term which defines the *baraza* as a platform which protrudes from a building. The term *majlis* (council, meeting) would, thus, be a better translation of the term into Arabic, at least with respect to the social meaning of the term. Also, *majlis* would point to a corresponding social institution of communal sitting and communicating in, for instance, south Arabian cultural contexts.[1]

The term *baraza* essentially points thus to three different dimensions of interpretation, namely the *organizational, spatial*, as well as *temporal*, i.e. time-linked notions of the *baraza*. All of these notions should be seen as to reflect a spectrum of possibilities:

I. in *organizational* terms, a *baraza* may represent different degrees of formality/informality, institutionalization and abstractness. A *baraza* might be a simple (informal) meeting of people, but also a council, or, in historical times, the audience of the Sultan of Zanzibar, which was described as a *barza* (Ruete 1998:125), or, finally, a huge range of clubs, unions or associations such as the *Baraza la kiswahili la Taifa* (National KiSwahili Council), the *Baraza la Musiki za Taifa* (National Council of Music), the *Baraza la Sanaa la Taifa* (National Board of Industry), the *Baraza Kuu la Waislamu wa Tanzania* (Supreme Council of Tanzanian Muslims), or the *Baraza Kuu la Jumuiya na Taasisi za Kiislamu* (Supreme Council of Islamic Organizations and Institutions in Tanzania), organizations, where membership is defined in more or less formal terms;

II. in *spatial* terms, the *baraza* represents a spectrum of places where people meet, such as the verandah in front of a house (see above);[2] or, in particular, in shamba areas, a place near the local mosque. Inside a house, a *baraza* would be a parlour for receiving visitors such as, again, the audience chamber of the Sultan of Zanzibar; such an "inside" *baraza* would also correspond to the above mentioned *majlis*. In Zanzibar, the Sultan had several baraza, the most important being the *baraza al-ʿīd* or *al-ʿīd* which met each morning after the *ʿīd al-fiṭr* (ie. at the end of Ramadan) at 10am, and then continued as a state reception until dinner in the evening (ZNA AB 10/83).

1. Corresponding institutions may be found in many societies, such as the majlis in Arabia, the *shadow tree* in the West African savannahs, the *Bangwe* in Rwanda/Burundi, the *piazza* in Italy, the German *Stammtisch*, the Bavarian *beergarden* or the *café de commerce* in France.
2. As discussed in Garth Myers (2003).

In addition to these meanings of the term, any kind of place, where people would meet in different functions, could acquire the notion of a *baraza,* agency being, thus, the defining issue. Globalization (*utandawazi*) has finally added another dimension to the spatial notion of the *baraza*, namely the cyber-baraza which should be seen, according to Farouk Topan, as the e-mail networks and chat-rooms, i.e. the electronic forum of the global Zanzibari diaspora as well as of those globalized Zanzibaris who are united in one virtual baraza, "Zanzinet" (Topan 2006:65).[1]

III. in *temporal* or time-linked terms, a *baraza* is connected with the specific times of the day when its members meet, such as the *baraza za wazee*, the "old men's *baraza*", at Jaws' Corner which is frequented daily between *ʿaṣr* and *maghrib* prayers. In fact, a single *baraza* (in the spatial sense of the term) could be occupied, in the course of a day,[2] by different groups. In addition, each *baraza* is linked, as has been mentioned above, with the stories of that specific place and its people, and, thus, with local history. It would be possible, in fact, to write a social history of Zanzibar by recording the histories of the different *baraza*.[3]

In more abstract terms, the *baraza* could be characterized as "inscribed places", spaces which have been defined in meaningful terms by the people of a specific place, and the way people have transformed *undefined space* into *defined place* (Low/Lawrence-Zuniga 2003:13). A *baraza* may be regarded, thus, as *space* (Raum) which has come to life as a *place* (Augé 1992/2000: 79ff). Consequently, a *baraza* has stopped being "something in between", i.e. pure (undefined) space, and has become "something", namely a distinct *Platz*, a place, which is known for the stories associated with it, for its specific history, as well as for the people meeting there. These notions of *place* (Platz) and *space* (Raum) have not only been discussed prominently by Low/Lawrence-Zuniga and Augé, but also by Smith (1987) and Harvey (2004/1996) who support, in their respective work, Low and Lawrence-Zuniga's definition of space and place. Smith, following Yi-Fu Tuan, thus defines the space-place continuum as:

---

1. It would be interesting to see whether other forms of virtual *baraza* exist as well, such as, for instance, a *baraza* of the spirits (*wapepo*).
2. A day in Zanzibar would be divided into *siku* (day-time), from 6am, 7am being the first hour of the day, or, in "Swahili time", *saa moja asubuhi* (one o'clock in the morning), until 6pm (*saa kumi na mbili*, twelve o'clock); and *usiku* (night-time), starting from 6pm, 7pm being the first hour of the night, until 6am (*saa kumi na mbili usiku*).
3. Georg Deutsch has started to do this with his history of Soko Mohogo street (publication forthcoming).

> Space is more abstract than place. What begins as undifferentiated space be-comes place as we get to know it better and endow it with value...If we think of space as that which allows movement, then place is pause; each pause in movement makes it possible for location to be transformed into place...When space feels thoroughly familiar to us, it has become place. Thus, abstract space, lacking significance other than strangeness, becomes concrete place when it is filled with meaning (Smith 1987:28).

David Harvey, while stressing that "place, in whatever guise, is like space and time, a social construct", also maintains that place, much more than space is connected with "permanences" (Harvey 1996:293), linking, thus, space/place and time. Such permanences (i.e. all kinds of human agency) come to occupy, "a piece of space in an exclusive way (for a specific period of time) and thereby define a place – their place – (for this period of time)" (Harvey 1996:293). The concept of place is thus intrinsically linked with concepts of time, namely the concepts of time of those who transform, through their permanences, space into place, when they meet at specific times at specific places. While space may exist in an independent way, place is always situated in a time-continuum, namely the time-continuum of those, who frequent specific places. As soon as these temporal perma-nences cease, place stops to be place and turns again into undefined and non-used space. Places are consequently spaces where time has "condensed" through the permanences of specific persons or groups. In places such as a *baraza*, time becomes, as a consequence, "visible" (Harvey 1996: 294). Places are, thus, in the end:

> ...constructed and experienced as material ecological artefacts and intricate net-works of social relations. They are the focus of the imaginary, of beliefs, long-ings, and desires. They are an intensive focus of discursive activity, filled with symbolic and representational meanings, and they are a distinctive product of institutionalized social and political-economic power (Harvey 1996:316).[1]

In this context it has to be added, finally, that *baraza* are not the only form for the organization of places and spaces known in Zanzibar. There are, for instance, the numerous clubs and associations, in particular of the young, often football fans who meet in their own spots (*kijiwe*), marked, in Zanzibar, by little flags, often a shed as protection against the sun. In addition, there are the so-called *maskani* associations, the meeting places,

---

1. As such, the baraza even seems to fit into Heidegger's definition of place "as the locale of the truth of being", "der Ort, an dem sich Sein vollzieht und darstellt" (M. Heidegger, 1971: *Poetry, Language, Thought;* as quoted in Harvey 1996: 299).

usually simple sheds with benches, of the supporters of a specific party which started to form in the early 1990s in Zanzibar in the context of the emergence of a multiparty system (Crozon 1998:41ff). The Zanzibari ruling party even equipped some of its *maskani* with a TV-set in order to attract people (Mohamed Ahmed Saleh, 2 April 2005). In contrast to the *baraza*, the *maskani* are associated, however, with specific aims and they have a more formal character than a *baraza* (for a detailed discussion of the political background for the development of the *maskani* see Bakari 2001:189ff). Finally, there are the *kikao*, the "places to sit", where specific agendas are discussed, *kikao* representing, thus, rather formal meetings (Mw. Idris, 27 July 2004). It should also be mentioned in this context that *baraza* have been spreading, in recent decades, on the mainland under the influence of Nyerere's politics who supported the *baraza* as an instrument to propagate his ideas of social reform in mainland Tanzania (Mw. Idris, 19 July 2004).

The Phenomenology of the *Baraza*

Baraza seem to represent a rather broad spectrum of different forms of organization, as well as different notions of place and space which are again defined in different temporal terms. *Baraza* may consequently appear to represent a rather vague notion of the organization of *Öffentlichkeit*, the "public sphere" as well as "public times", in Zanzibar. Yet, *baraza* are not entirely amorphous, they rather follow a distinct set of rules and are linked with a distinct code of behaviour which we could call the *baraza*-etiquette. These rules and codes of behaviour also apply to the form of the *baraza* I would like to highlight in my paper, namely the Zanzibar Stone Town street *baraza*.[1] At the same time, I would like to stress that I will not discuss for-

---

1 It should be mentioned here that the island of *Unguja* forms, together with the island of Pemba and some smaller islands such as Tumbatu or Uzi, the Zanzibar archipelago. *Unguja* could again be structured into three socio-geographical zones: Zanzibar Stone Town proper, the historical and political centre of Zanzibar (c. 20,000 inhabitants as of 2002); Ng'ambo, the urban areas of Zanzibar Town on the "other side" (*ng'ambo*) of the "creek" that almost cut off Stone Town from the rest of the island until being filled up in the colonial period, today, a major urban agglomeration (c. 390,000 inhabitants) which consists of numerous quarters such as the different "Miembes" (Miembeladu, Miembeshauri, etc.), Kikwajuni, Kisiwandui, Saateni, Kilimani, Jang'ombe, Mwanakeregwe, Gulioni and others; as well as the rural and farm areas (*shamba*) with a population of about 200,000. The island of Pemba would have about 350–400,000 inhabitants, but, apart from some smaller towns like Chake and Wete, no urban agglomeration comparable to Zanzibar.

mations of the *baraza* in Ng'ambo or *shamba* (farm) areas which may acquire different forms. Ng'ambo *baraza*, for instance, seem to be more mixed in age than those in Stone Town.

Walking through Stone Town,[1] we immediately realize that *baraza* seem to meet virtually everywhere. Major concentrations of *baraza* are to be found in the Darajani (market) area, but also in Mkunazini: from Vuga street down to Mskiti Jibrin (Jibrin mosque), at least nine or ten *baraza* are located at different times of the day, and Jaws' Corner in the very centre of Stone Town alone accounts for at least six *baraza*. Other concentrations of *baraza* are to be found in the different parts of Baghani, Vuga, Kokoni, Malindi, Kiponda and Hurumzi. Hamamni, Kajifijeni and Shangani, by contrast seem to have only a few *baraza*, while Forodhani is rather a place for picnicking and tourist activities, and, thus, not really a place for *baraza* but for family evenings.

It has to be pointed out, here, that even if *baraza* have existed in Zanzibar, in particular in *shamba* areas, for a long period of time, they are a comparatively recent feature of many parts of Stone Town, and started to develop, essentially, only after the revolution in 1964. This rather astonishing development is connected with the fact that Stone Town had been, until 1964, an area for the rich and aristocratic, who would never sit "in the street" as they had their indoor *majlis*. Sitting "in the street" (in a *baraza*) was, thus, until 1964, a feature of the poor (in Stone Town) or of the "Africans" living in Ng'ambo or Shamba areas. *Baraza* were, thus, confined, before 1964, in Stone Town, to the market areas (i.e. Darajani, Mkunazini and Kokoni), to the mosques (such as Mskiti Ruta) and to public places, or the poorer and popular quarters in Stone Town, such as Malindi. *Baraza* were, thus, and are, until today, spatial expressions of the social context in which they are situated (E. Meffert, 7 August 2004). The development of *baraza* has to be seen, consequently, as a feature of social change (and development), which could be characterized, for some parts of Stone Town such as Shangani, where *baraza* scarcely existed before 1964, as a development from "*majlis* to *baraza*" (i.e. from meeting inside the house to meeting outside the house).

---

1. Stone Town (or "Mji Mkongwe", the "old town") is defined here as the old and densely settled area of Zanzibar Town west of Creek Road between the Mnazi Mmoja hospital in the South and Fungoni in the North, comprising the quarters of (from north to south) Malindi, Kiponda, Kokoni, Darajani, Hurumzi, Forodhani, Hamamni, Mkunazini, Soko Mohogo, Baghani, Vuga, Kibogoni and Shangani, an area of approximately one square kilometre (3 km north–south, 200–1,000 metres in east-west extension) and it is a maze of narrow alleys of more than 20 kilometres in length.

In a broader sense, a change in social context will consequently also influence the social character of the *baraza* of a specific locality.[1]

When walking through Stone Town, it is rather easy to come across *baraza* "in session". In fact, it might be said, that virtually every house in Zanzibar (Stone Town, Ng'ambo and *shamba* areas) has its own *baraza*. Most of these *baraza* are, however, *baraza* for the house and the people of the house only, and thus, not public. Only a few baraza have become real communal or public *baraza*, although even their number may add up, in Stone Town alone, to more than 3–400 (see map), even though the number of famous public *baraza* is smaller, probably between 50–60. It is necessary, thus, to differentiate again between "house" *baraza* and public as well as communal *baraza*, although boundaries would be fluid. Most house *baraza* would be attended, however, only by those people, men and women,[2] who actually live in a specific house, or some passers-by who greet somebody from the house who happens to be sitting in his *baraza*. Communal *baraza*, by contrast, would no longer necessarily be associated with a specific house, but be situated at strategic places such as small openings in an alley or at an intersection of several alleys, and consequently attract more people from diverse backgrounds, although, still the neighbourhood, who would come at specific times of the day, night or week to sit in their *baraza*. Public *baraza* would subsequently denote all those *baraza* which would attract people from an even greater geographic background. For these public *baraza*, residency would no longer constitute a defining factor. Also, public *baraza* would be situated at strategic places, such as one of the small places in Stone Town, as, for instance, "Jaws' Corner" in Soko Mohogo or the place in front and around the "Spice Inn" in Kokoni. In terms of numbers of members, communal and/or public *baraza* would normally unite groups of more than two (but often less than ten) persons, such as, in Zanzibar Stone Town, the *baraza* of the *wazee* of Jaws' Corner, which regularly unites from two to six or seven members.[3] Finally, there is a small number of (male) indoor *baraza* such as the one in the Masomo bookshop, where local politicians meet, or the one in Tembo Hotel which unites members and friends

---

1. In that context, it has to be added that *baraza* in *shamba* and *Ng'ambo* areas did not necessarily have a social function. Often they were built only to protect houses against heavy rainfall (E. Meffert, 7 August 2004).
2. Sitting in *baraza* is, so far, gendered. I have not seen any mixed *baraza*, although women may sit, during different times of the day, on the same spot as men (see Loimeier 2007).
3. *Baraza* in Zanzibar Stone Town thus seem to be smaller than corresponding *baraza* in Mombasa (see below).

of the Muzamil family.[1] These contemporary indoor *baraza* are character-ized by the fact, however, that access is not open to everybody, that *baraza* discussions are often on sensitive issues such as politics or business, and that one has to be invited to become a member of such a *baraza*, even for a short term period of time.[2]

Some of the public/communal *baraza* have acquired particular fame, such as, in historical times, the *baraza* of the Sultan mentioned above; the *baraza* of the *qāḍīs* of Zanzibar which met, in the 1890s, each day (ex-cept Fridays) from 4–5 pm. in front of the clock tower (Norbert Oberauer, 28 September 2004); the different *baraza* at Mskiti Ruta;[3] the *baraza* ya Khamis Machungwa in Majanini; the Passing Show Hotel *mbao* players *baraza* of Nassor Bubek in Malindi; the *baraza* of Bwana Mkelle (the "po-ets" *baraza*); the *baraza* of Sayyid Ba Wazir close to Mskiti Barza; the Baraza ya Hollis Road (in Malindi); the *Ice Krim Klabu* in Darajani; the Mizingani Baraza *kwa Mr. Lasi*; or even famous Ng'ambo *baraza* such as the *baraza ya six four* (in Michenzani), the *baraza ya msikiti Nambani* and the *baraza ya msikti Mchangani* (Mw. Idris, 19 July 2004); or, finally, *baraza* which be-came famous in the early years of the revolution such as "Bright Brother", "Peace Lover" and "Jaws' Corner" (established 1974) (Burgess 2002:293). At least some of these historical *baraza* continue to exist until today, and have been complemented, since the early 1980s, by other popular *baraza* such as the *baraza* of the fans of Manchester United in Kokoni, the businessmen's *baraza* close to the Cash&Carry supermarket in Darajani, the intellectuals' *baraza* close to the Manispaa (the Municipality), the fishermen's *baraza* in Funguni, the *hamali* (porters and riksha pushers) *baraza* in Mkunazini and Darajani as well as the taxi drivers' *baraza* in lower Vuga street, Shangani, Forodhani and Darajani, and numerous others, all around Stone Town. These *baraza* have become known for different occupational, communal and religious orientations and quite a number of *baraza* are even known for their distinct political affiliations, like some of those in Jaws' Corner which have become famous for their sympathies for the Civic United Front (CUF), Zanzibar's major opposition party.

Communal *baraza* are characterized now by the fact, that they are all situated in rather public and strategic places which serve many purposes,

---

1. Abdalaziz Lodhi, 2 April 2005.
2. In my paper, I concentrate on communal and public *baraza* and exclude the multi-tude of purely private *baraza*, even though these *baraza* would represent up to 90% of all *baraza*.
3. Which is also shown in the documentary film "Jeder Wind hat seine Reise", Bavar-ian TV and ARTE, produced by *Along Mekong Productions*, Heidelberg, 2002.

such as the market area (Darajani) or well frequented alleys with many shops (Mkunazini, Kokoni, Gizenga);[1] Many *baraza* are also in the vicinity of a mosque (such as Ruta, Istiqāma, Malindi); or, finally, at important places such as Jaws' Corner where we would also find a coffeemaker,[2] *mbao* and domino players, a TV set, a sugarcane-juice maker or the notice board for public announcements of the area.[3] Consequently, these places would attract specific *baraza* such as a particular group of morning coffee drinkers. Morning coffee drinkers would indeed come to a specific place and their *baraza* from even far away places to get their morning coffee (or night coffee, as in Gizenga) from a specific coffee-maker. In addition, major places and their *baraza* would also attract film watchers (in the evening) or groups of card, domino or *mbao* players (usually in the afternoon). In recent times, the character of evening *baraza* has been changing, however, as an increasing number of families have acquired private TV sets and are connected, by satellite dish, to the numerous TV programmes offered by different providers. As a consequence, video shops are closing and only those who cannot afford a TV set still meet in the evenings in front of the communal TV set. These public video evenings are still financed, however, by the *baraza* of the film watchers, who usually pool funds to rent a film.[4]

Jaws' Corner, for instance, is today the home of numerous *baraza*, and during most parts of the day it would be possible to simultaneously meet at least five or six *baraza* as different *baraza* would meet at different times of the day on the same spot. However, the most permanent *baraza* are the old men (*wazee*) of the area: scholars, teachers, retired bureaucrats as well as some traders from the northern Baghani quarter (i.e. Lebanon brothers corner); the businessmen of upper eastern Soko Mohogo, mostly local traders of "Arab" origin; the business men of upper western Soko Mohogo, mostly local traders of "Indian" origin; the young drop-outs and rascals of

---

1. Those *baraza* are frequented, consequently, only during business hours.
2. There are, in fact, quite a number of coffee-makers in Stone Town, such as in Jaws' corner, in Gizenga Street (corner Cathedral street, but only in the evening), at the Cash&Carry Supermarket in Darajani, in Narrow Street/Malindi, at the Passing Show Hotel in Malindi, at Mskiti Ruta, those close to the former Empire and Majestic Cinemas, at Muzammil's store in Darajani as well as in Mlandege market. In former times, these coffee-makers were mostly itinerant and moved from place to place to sell their coffee. In recent times, they have become more attached to specific places and try to attract customers to their places (Adam Shafi Adam, 2 April 2005).
3. Such as "what is on tonights' TV", "Who is going to give what kind of lecture in Barwani mosque", "how Manchester United played against Liverpool", etc.
4 Muhammad Ali, 31 July 2004.

the area; the pious affiliated with Soko Mohogo (Barwani) mosque and its *imām*; as well as the residents of the neighbouring houses in the northern outlet of Soko Mohogo towards Darajani. Finally, there are always some passers-by who come to Jaws' corner to drink coffee and chat, play cards or *mbao*, in addition to all those who pass through this area on their way to work and business, and who would perhaps stop for a moment to chat and exchange greetings.[1]

With respect to the social character of the Zanzibar Stone Town *baraza*, we have to note that membership may appear to be rather informal: there is in fact no formal membership, and there are no membership fees or membership cards as in more formal associations, parties or unions. Yet, membership is defined all the same: everybody may, thus, theoretically join any *baraza*. As each *baraza* has a specific character, some *baraza* may, however, be more open than others.[2] Thus, some *baraza* may be perceived as rather hermetic and the members of such a *baraza* will probably stop their conversation, possibly on sensitive issues, such as politics, when an unknown person tries to join such a *baraza*: one would have to be invited, essentially, to become a permanent member of such a *baraza*.[3] Recruitment into such a *baraza* is thus a process of conscious inclusion, to be initiated by the members of the respective *baraza*. Living in a specific neighbourhood, regularly passing by a certain *baraza* and respectful greeting,[4] sticking to the rules

---

1. As Georg Deutsch has been working on Soko Mohogo and Jaws' Corner, in particular, I refer here to his work for detailed information.
2. Some *baraza* may develop specific strategies to keep outsiders away. Thus, the "intellectuals' *baraza*" close to the Manispaa (Municipality) excluded a nightguard of a neighbouring building who was suspected to be a government informer. The members of the *baraza* knew that this nightguard was afraid of death and diseases and consequently started to chat about these topics each time he came to sit down with them, until he eventually gave up (Abdul Sheriff, 22 July 2004). Another *baraza* (of Comorians) in Kisimamajongoo would even dissolve when unknown people approached (Bi Saada Meffert, 4 August 2004).
3. Hassan Mwakimako, 20 April 2004 and Mw. Idris, 20 May 2004.
4. I was invited to become a member of the *baraza za wazee* in Jaws' Corner, as I had passed by this particular *baraza* regularly and greeted the *wazee* with the seemingly religious formula of "as-salāmu ʿalaikum", triggering a debate among the *wazee* whether a non-Muslim such as me was actually allowed to employ such a form of greeting. When their search in the compilations of Prophetic traditions (*aḥādīth*) as well as their inquiries through the local *imām* had confirmed the correctness of my greeting, an invitation to join their *baraza* came forth quickly. The search of the *watu wa barazani* for religious legitimization of my greeting had, in fact, led to a *ḥadīth* which claimed that if a non-Muslim greeted a Muslim or a group of Muslims by saying "as-salāmu ʿalaikum", at least one member of the group was constrained to respond. Otherwise, the curse of God would fall on the whole group.

of *heshima* (respect) and *adabu* (proper and good manners), the established rules of public as well as *baraza*-etiquette, having a friend or friends in the *baraza*, or having similar occupational, religious or political interests and orientations may help to speed up the process of being invited to eventually join a specific *baraza*, but are not an automatic bridge from non-membership to membership, from exclusion to inclusion.

Most *baraza*, are open, however, and would welcome any non-member to join, either on a permanent or a temporary basis, even for short slots of time, although some degree of continuity of residence in a specific area may help to speed up integration into a specific *baraza*. The varying open/closedness of *baraza* shows that it is very difficult to translate the concept of the *baraza* into one of Max Weber's ideal types (Idealtypen): most of what is said about the *baraza* may be true for most *baraza*, but not necessarily for all. Due to the semi-public, semi-formal, and semi-open character of the *baraza*, the *baraza* escapes efforts of categorization: *baraza* may, in fact, be described to be "semi" in many respects.

The semi-character of the *baraza* is also reflected in the character of *baraza* conversations, the *mazungumzo ya baraza* (or *kupiga soga*, i.e. chatting), which are semi-public, i.e. not official, yet, in any case, not really private either. In addition, *mazungumzo ya baraza* are different from formalized forms of public discourse such as, for instance, a *mihadhara*, a public lecture (for a further discussion of the *mihadhara* as another form of organization of the public sphere see below). With respect to the *baraza* etiquette in Mombasa, Swartz mentions that members of *baraza* avoid gossip:

> Each man is greeted on arrival by everyone already there with a handshake and a greeting consisting minimally of 'salaam aleikhum' (sic) and generally of a considerably more elaborate sort. This is true even when the gathering is very large. Thirty or forty men were the most I ever observed at a *baraza*, with five to eight being more usual, but whatever its size, greetings occupy a good deal of the group's time. The tone of the *baraza*s I attended, whatever their particular content might be, was decorous, dignified, and restrained. The participants were invariably good humoured and agreeable in their relations with one another... (Swartz 1991:251).

Mazungumzo ya baraza are not necessarily chatty, thus, even if men in Zanzibar do not necessarily reject a "good chat" as they seem to do in Mombasa. Usually, *baraza* conversations focus on specific topics of conversation which are then discussed, by the members of the *baraza*, in a more or less structured way, even if topics may again vary widely, from politics and marriages to new forms of fashion or the effects of aphrodisiacas.[1] An important feature of *baraza* conversation, however, is that discussions have to follow the established rules of *baraza* etiquette which privileges the elderly (*wazee*) over the younger members of a *baraza*. This does not mean that the young are excluded from *baraza* conversations. Often, the question of age does not even come up as members of a baraza are of roughly the same age.

Baraza may acquire, thus, a multitude of forms (*aina*) who have in common that members of the *baraza* usually are a group of people who follow specific rules of conduct that are binding for all members of the *baraza*. As such, *baraza* are natural networks of people who have known each other for some time and trust each other. As a consequence, *baraza* have acquired manifold functions: they provide security, and members of a *baraza* may vouch for each other and even grant credit in case of need. Thus, Shaykh Masoud b. Alî ar-Riyâmî was well-known "to stand for any who entered his *baraza*" (Aley 1994, n.p.). Also, *baraza* would go out and organize picnics in the *shamba* areas, especially in the month of Ramadhan, either for a day or even a weekend, and collect money for such purposes. Money could also be collected, of course, for the needy, for burials, for *maulidi* ceremonies, for parties and marriage ceremonies (*arusi*), and members of the *baraza* would usually also be the first to be invited to such festivities (Mw. Idris, 19 July 2004). *Baraza* may be seen, thus, as *lieux de sociabilité*, an important social institution, which finally also provide education, not only in the direct sense of *wazee* helping school-children with their homework, but also in a broader sense as places where the rules of social life are practised as, for instance, with respect to the different ways of solving communal problems (Valcke 1999:338).

As *baraza* are usually groups of people (mostly men) who chat and discuss all kinds of seemingly banal things such as neighbourhood affairs or marriage arrangements, or comment on people passing by, a *baraza* may not even be perceived by outsiders as such an important *lieu de sociabilité* or as "a basic cell" of Zanzibar's social and political life, or, if perceived at all, *baraza* are possibly seen as a group of men sitting "idly" and, thus, a lingering handicap for any kind of economic development. The manifold if hidden (or better: not very spectacular, visible) functions of the *baraza* for Zanzibar's social, political and economic life possibly explain, however, why the *baraza* has so far not come under attack from, for instance, the

---

1. Abdul Sheriff, 19 June 2004.

anṣār as-sunna, the local activist Muslims,[1] or some development-minded technocrats, as an awful waste of time and as a "typical expression of the men's laziness".

Baraza as Markers of Time

Baraza are not only bodies of social coherence and control, of political and religious discussion, of communal inclusion and exclusion, i.e. bodies for the organization of space and social relations but also, as has been mentioned above, bodies for the organization of time. First of all, *baraza* do not take place day in, day out, but only at specific times of the day. Thus, only few *baraza* meet in the late morning, before *zuhr* (noon) prayers. In fact, the only major *baraza* known to meet in the morning, before noon, was the *baraza* of Shaykh ʿAlī (b.) Maṣʿūd al-Riyāmī, the son of Shaykh Maṣʿūd (b. ʿAlī) al-Riyāmī, also known as "Bwana Udi"(master of incense), one of the richest Zanzibaris of Omani origin in pre-revolutionary times (see Aley 1994, np.). Also, only a few *baraza* tend to meet after *zuhr* or after evening (ʿishāʾ) prayers, while most would meet between ʿaṣr (afternoon) and *maghrib* (evening) prayers or between *maghrib* and ʿishāʾ prayers, such as the "intellectuals'" *baraza* in Malindi, close to the Tourist Office,[2] which meets from *maghrib* to ʿishāʾ prayers (Fatma Alloo, 11 March 2003). Also, the *baraza za wazee* in Jaws' Corner is occupied by at least three different *baraza* in the course of a day: the *wazee* in the evening between ʿaṣr and *maghrib* prayers, on a daily basis except Saturdays and Sundays, when they meet before *zuhr* prayers; a group of old school friends, mostly retired, living in different parts of the town nowadays but still meeting in Jaws' Corner, in the late morning, for their chat; as well as, finally, another group of residents who meet in the afternoon but who are not members of the *wazee* group.

As specific *baraza* meet at specific times of the day, it is rather easy to meet a particular member of a *baraza*, who is known to be sitting in his *baraza* at a specific time. A *baraza* is, thus, not only a sort of German *Stammtisch* but also a kind of semi-public office. In that context it has to be mentioned, however, that old men and pensioners spend much more time in their *baraza* than those who have got to attend to business or work, even if they see their friends in their own *baraza* in the evening, or on a Saturday or Sunday. To some extent "sitting in a *baraza*" may thus be interpreted as

---

1. Who are also called *watu wa bidaa*, the "people of the innovations", as they tend to attack alleged un-Islamic innovations as *bidʿa*.
2. Abdul Sheriff being a member.

a manifestation of affluence in time, in particular, leisure-time, which is not devoted to other purposes but to the cultivation of the social life of an individual person as well as his/her community.

The fact that most *baraza* meet between the afternoon and evening prayers is due to the fact that time between these prayers is regarded as rather "short" to do "something of substance", or to go home between prayers and come back to the mosque after only a short period of time, i.e. one and a half or two hours. Thus, men often decide to spend this time in between (prayer) times, which is also regarded as being "long enough for a good chat", in their respective *baraza*.[1] Prayer times, thus, provide the major structure for meeting in a specific *baraza*, while other markers of time, such as the "modern *adhān*" (call for prayer)[2], i.e. the Zanzibar siren which can be heard every morning, afternoon and evening at 7.30 am, 15.30 and 18.30 pm, to signal the beginning and the end of the working day, are secondary markers of time for *baraza* meetings.

While walking around Zanzibar and passing by the different *baraza*, I realized that *baraza* might also be seen as "islands of time" which allow us to observe how people move at different speeds at different sets of time. In the end, I came to understand that sitting in a *baraza* may not necessarily be a very speedy occupation, but one that allows major insights into the organization of time in Zanzibar. All members of "my" *baraza* (i.e. the *baraza* of the *wazee* in Jaws' Corner, the *baraza* of Bw. Saleh Saloum in Darajani as well as the *baraza* of Mw. Idris in Shangani) actually agreed that you see more while sitting. With respect to the different speeds that may be observed from a *baraza* perspective, there is, first of all, the "speed" of those sitting, who have the time to watch and to properly greet any passer-by and to exchange some words with anybody who "takes the time" to stop and greet them. Extended greeting may, in fact, also be seen as a strategy to stretch, win or create time in order to give both parties to a greeting the chance to develop an opinion on the conversation which is eventually going to develop after the greeting has been concluded.

Secondly, there is the speed of those who are on their way to work, and will probably greet only briefly, as *heshima* and *adabu* demands, and then pass by, or even try to pass through some back alleys, where no *baraza* are known to exist, so people may thus pass quickly without violating the laws of *heshima* and *adabu*.

---

1. Abdul Sheriff, 19 June 2004.
2. Muhammad Haron, 21 April 2004.

Then there is the speed of those working in Stone Town, for instance, *rik-sha* pushers, who have to fight, in certain months, a heroic struggle against clusters of tourists blocking whole alleys while gaping and taking pictures.

Finally, there is the hectic speed of those tourists who have lost their way in the maze of alleys and get increasingly nervous when they realize that they have been passing by a specific place several times already and seem to be unable to find their way out again. These poor creatures contribute, however, greatly to the amusement of some *baraza*, as members of these *baraza* bet on how often a specific *mzungu* (a white person, literally, a person who is not circumcised) will go wrong again at the next corner and come back, inevitably, sooner or later, to the same place, being, thus, lost in time and space.

The different speeds of moving in Stone Town, as well as the central role of the *baraza* for the organization of time in Zanzibar point to another aspect of Zanzibari everyday life which is intrinsically linked with the organization of time, sitting in *baraza* and speed, namely the importance of social norms such as politeness, good culture, good manners and proper behaviour (*adabu, heshima*), in short, *baraza* etiquette. In Zanzibar Stone Town, these norms are still very important. It is a "must", for instance, to greet properly, not only friends and relatives, but also neighbours, and all those one knows, in general, from walking through Stone Town, day after day, year after year, on the way to work, to the market, to pay a visit or to go to one's *baraza*. Although it is theoretically possible to cross Stone Town from east to west, from Forodhani to Darajani, in five minutes, when walking fast, provided one knows the shortcuts, and to cross Stone Town from north to south, from Malindi to Shangani in about 15–20 minutes,[1] walks through Stone Town usually last much longer as one usually meets somebody, and often several people, who have to be greeted properly. Proper greeting, now, takes time, and a short walk of 500 meters or five minutes from Mkunazini to Shangani via Jaws' Corner may, thus, last more than two hours, and may even include sitting and chatting in a *baraza* on the way. The constant "delays" that build up, thus, in the course of a day, are, however, not really problematic, as everybody is delayed, and, thus, more or less "in time" again.

The calculation of "time-budgets" gets, however, problematic, when Zanzibari (Stone Town) concepts of time, speed and good manners are confronted with "Western" concepts of time, speed and good manners which

---

1. Theoretically, it would be possible, of course, to walk for hours, in Stone Town, as the total length of Stone Town alleys exceeds 20 kilometres.

usually stress speed and punctuality more than good manners. When such mixing of different concepts of speed, time and good manners occurs, irritation and confusion usually follow, as Westerners accuse Zanzibaris of being "too late", while Zanzibaris usually perceive Westerners as rude and impolite. However, I do not want to essentialize here Zanzibari (or Western) concepts of time, speed and politeness, as Zanzibaris are themselves well aware of the importance of time-budgets. Zanzibari time-budgets differ though from "Western" time budgets as they are to a large extent defined by social, and not by economic factors. As a consequence, Zanzibaris are also familiar with the notion of "time is pressing", and they are in a hurry when late for the important (social) events of their life.

In order to escape time-consuming procedures of polite greeting, Zanzibaris have developed strategies to evade certain *baraza* by taking back alleys, where they are sure that they will not meet, during this specific time of the day, people they would have to greet properly. Distances and the respective time-slots that are necessary to reach point B from point A are calculated, thus, in Zanzibar not in actual distances (metres, yards, feet) or the amount of time, one needs, when walking anonymously (as a foreigner, for instance), but in terms of social time (distances): one knows that it will take about ten minutes from Hoteli Flamingo to Mskiti Shangani when walking through Vuga, as it is rather unlikely to meet anybody in these back alleys, except those who also "hurry", as there are virtually no *baraza*; yet, it would take about two hours to walk from Hoteli Flamingo to Msikiti Shangani when walking through Soko Mohogo and Jaws' Corner, as there will be numerous acquaintances and friends on the way, plus the *baraza* in Soko Mohogo and Jaws' Corner, in Baghani and Gizenga. In addition, "speeding" through Soko Mohogo and Jaws' Corner would also not only be terribly impolite, as one would violate local codes of *adabu* and *heshima* when not even quickly responding to the numerous *karibus* (welcomes) on the way, but would show that the person is largely ignorant with respect to the social geography and the geography of time in Zanzibar. Such a person obviously does not know the back alleys where it would be possible to hurry like a *mzungu*.

Finally, *baraza* could be seen as focal points for the production of history, as places where agency and events are transformed and translated into "stories told", and thus integrated, on an abstract level, into historical discourses. *Baraza* are, thus, by extension, laboratories of history. And even if events and agency that come to form history are often not connected with a specific *baraza* (although they might be), *baraza* are places where history is commented, interpreted, told and retold, and, in that process, shaped. If we now translate, into literary terms, basic events as well as acts of human agency which, so to speak, "start history" (or a specific chapter in history), we could, by analogy, describe an original event as a basic text, a "mother-code", or, in Arabic, a *matn*. Consequently, we could also interpret *baraza* discussions on such a specific historical event (be it important or banal) as a commentary, a *sharḥ* on the *matn*, which would finally be translated by historians, orientalists, sociologists or anthropologists into a super-commentary, a *ḥāshiya*. Such a super-commentary would again be commented upon, in the context of conferences, and, thus, be adorned with glosses and, finally, complementary notes, *taqārīr* and *taʿālīq*. These complementary notes would then, sometimes at least, be passed back to the *baraza* and fed into local lore in the way in which my own research about the *baraza* was discussed in some *baraza* when I presented my first small publication on the *baraza* (Loimeier 2005) to local friends in Zanzibar in 2007.

By Way of Conclusion:
How I Became a Member of a *Baraza*...

Having passed by numerous *baraza* during my stay in Zanzibar in the summer of 2002,[1] and having been chatting with some of their members for some time, I was rather surprised, when I was, one day, invited by a member of the *baraza za wazee* in Jaws' Corner to join them. Having passed by every day at least twice for a couple of weeks, having greeted respectfully all the members present, and told them about the events of my day, my work in the National Archive, the interesting and curious things I had found there, the questions that had come up and my problems with *Kiswahili,* I had got the impression that I had been a welcome break in quotidian routines but not more. As soon as I was invited to join the *baraza* of the *wazee*, I became aware, however, that to be informed about anything going on in Zanzibar, or the world, I only had to sit in my *baraza* and to listen.

At the same time, I was, of course, still welcome to pass on bits and pieces of information about Zanzibari history which I had got in the archive and which turned out to be important for the *wazee* and their interpretation of local history. In addition, I constituted a further source of information to feed the curiosity of my fellow *baraza* members with respect to things going on in Europe, and was surprised to learn, how well informed these

---

1. As well as before that, in early 2001, and later, in the spring and summer of 2003, as well as the summer of 2004 and 2007.

truly cosmopolitan *wazee* were. I realized, thus, that sitting, watching and listening made the *wazee* of my *baraza* the true sociologists of their quarter, and by extension, quite knowledgeable with respect to all kinds of worldly and un-worldly affairs. In the end, I probably learned more about Zanzibari society by sitting and listening in a *baraza*, than by sitting and reading in the Zanzibar National Archive.

References

Aley, Juma, 1994, *Enduring Links*. n.p. Zanzibar.

Appadurai, Arjun, 1996, *Modernity at Large. Cultural Dimensions of Globalization*. Minneapolis: University of Minnesota Press.

Augé, Marc, 1992/2000, *Non-Places: Introduction to an Anthropology of Supermodernity*. Verso, London.

Bacuez, Pascal, 2001, *De Zanzibar à Kilwa. Relations conflictuelles en pays swahili*. Peeters, Louvain.

Bakari, Muhammad, 2001, *The Democratization Process in Zanzibar: A Retarded Transition*. Afrika-Institut, Hamburg.

Burgess, Gary, 2002, "Cinema, bell bottoms, and miniskirts: Struggles over youth and citizenship in revolutionary Zanzibar", in *The International Journal of African Historical Studies*, 35, 2–3, 287–314.

Crozon, Arielle, 1998, "Les maskani et le parti: une alliance sans entente", in F. Le Guennec Coppens and D. Parkin (eds), *Autorité et Pouvoir chez les Swahili*. Karthala, Paris, 41–60.

Deutsch, Jan Georg, 2002, "The Indian Ocean World and a very small place in Zanzibar", in Brigitte Reinwald (ed.), *Space on the move. Transformations of the Indian Ocean Seascape in the 19th and 20th century*. Klaus Schwarz Verlag, Berlin.

Fair, Laura, 2001, *Pastimes and Politics. Culture, Community and Identity in Post-Abolition Urban Zanzibar, 1890–1945*. James Currey, London.

Giddens, Anthony, 1997, *Konsequenzen der Moderne*. Suhrkamp, Frankfurt.

Habermas, Jürgen, 1962/1990, *Strukturwandel in der Öffentlichkeit*. Campus, Frankfurt.

Habermas, Jürgen, 1991, *The Structural Transformation of the Public Sphere: An inquiery into a category of Bourgois society*, Transl. Thomas Burger, U.K. The MIT Press.

Harvey, David, 2004/1996, *Justice, Nature and the Geography of Difference*. Blackwell, Oxford.

Haugerud, Angelique and Njogu, Kimani, 1991, "State voices in the countryside: Politics and the Kenyan Baraza", *Working Papers in African Studies*, 159, African Studies Center, Boston University, Boston.

Krapf, Johann Ludwig, 1882/1958, *A Dictionary of the Suahili Language*. London: MacMillian.

Kresse, Kai, 2003, "The Swahili Baraza: Socializing intellectual practice in Old Mombasa Town". Paper presented at departmental seminar, University of Edinburgh, October 17th, 2003.

Launay, Robert and Soares, Benjamin, 1999, "The formation of an 'Islamic sphere', in French Colonial West Africa", in *Economy and Society*, 28, 467–89.

Loimeier, Roman, 2005, "The Baraza: A grass roots institution", in *ISIM review* (International Institute for the Study of Islam in the Modern World, Leiden), 16, 26–27.

Loimeier, Roman, 2007, "Sit local, think global: The Baraza in Zanzibar", in *Journal for Islamic Studies. Thematic issue: Islam and African Muslim Publics* (ed. A. Tayob), 27, 16–38.

Low, Setha M. and Lawrence-Zuniga, Denise (eds), 2003, *The anthropology of space and place*. Blackwell, Oxford.

Myers, Garth, 2003. *Verandahs of Power: Colonialism and Space in Urban Africa*. Syracuse University Press, Syracuse.

Ruete, Emily, 1998, *Memoirs of an Arabian princess from Zanzibar*. The Gallery Bookshop, Zanzibar.

Saleh, Mohamed Ahmed, 2004, "Going with the times (Kwenda na wakati). Conflicting Swahili Norms and Values Today", in Pat Caplan and Farouk Topan (eds), *Swahili Modernities*. Africa World Press, London, 145–56.

Smith, Jonathan Z., 1987, *To Take Place. Toward Theory in Ritual*. University of Chicago Press, Chicago.

Swartz, Marc J., 1991, *The Way the World Is. Cultural Processes and Social Relations among the Mombasa Swahili*. California University Press, Berkeley.

Sheriff, Abdul, 1995, *The History and Conservation of Zanzibar Stone Town*. James Currey, London.

Topan, Farouk, 2006, "From coastal to global: The erosion of the Swahili 'paradox', in R. Loimeier and R. Seesemann (eds), *The Global Worlds of the Swahili. Interfaces of Islam, Identity and Space in 19th and 20th Century East Africa*. LIT, Hamburg, 55–66.

Valcke, Sandrine, 1999, "Entrepreneurs. Business à Zanzibar", in Catherine Baroin and François Constantin (eds), *La Tanzanie contemporaine*. Karthala, Paris, 335–48.

Material from the Zanzibar National Archives

ZNA AB 10/83: Id al-Fitr Baraza

ZNA AD 5/52: Baraza za Uchumi

ZNA AD 5/63: Baraza la Taifa la Lugha ya Kiswahili

ZNA AD 12/35: Minutes za Baraza-conference: Mkutano wa Baraza kuu Idara ya Futboli

My partners in conversation (in Zanzibar and beyond) were:

Adam Shafi Adam, Bi Fatma Alloo, Bi Marloes van der Bijl, Dr. Duchi, Muhammad Haron, José Kagabo, Ramadhani Kututwa, Abdalaziz Lodhi, Dr. Erich and Bi Saada Meffert, Mw. Muhammad Idris Muhammad, Hassan Mwakimako, Muhammad Ali Said, Mohamed Ahmad Saleh, Saleh Saloum, Abdul Muhammad Hussein Sheriff and Issa Ziddy.

– CHAPTER IO –

The Impact of Religious Knowledge and the Concept of *Dini Wal Duniya* in Urban Zanzibari Life-Style

Mohamed Ahmed Saleh

Introduction

The phrase *Dini wal Duniya* (literally 'religion and the world') is commonly used by the Zanzibaris, most particularly the urban dwellers, in defining their way of seeing and their meaning of life. It is attributed to the tradition of the Prophet: *"Qala Rasulullahi Salalwahu Alahim Wasalam, Amalu Duniyaka Taanak Taishu Abadan, Waamalu Akheraka Taanaka Tamutu Ghada"*, which literally means "Prepare your life in this World as if you would live forever, and prepare your life-hereafter as if you would die in the next minute". It indicates a flexibility of Islam as a religion, and encourages Muslims to strike a balance between their temporal and spiritual life. This tradition of the Prophet is generally interpreted in the sense of "Enjoy your temporal life while at the same time preparing for your life-hereafter: *akhera*".

However, it is common among Muslims to deviate from their religious teaching by seeking to present a contradictory interpretation of this tradition of the Prophet. Such is the case with some Zanzibari urban dwellers.[1] They consider their religion with a lot of philosophy and interpret the Prophet's tradition in such a way that they have a pretext to take a break in their spiritual life and make the best use, to the fullest, of their temporal life, in total contradiction to Islamic teachings.[2] This happens especially during a particular period of their life cycle, notably when they are in their early twenties and continues into their mid-forties or early fifties. They later return to the strict religious observance and purity of the original religious interpretation as they grow old and approach death. Taking into account

---

1. It is not very much the case with the Zanzibari rural inhabitants.
2. There are many other religious quotations which are interpreted out of their context. For instance people who are inclined towards a homosexual relationship would interpret in their own way the following quotation *"vitoweni hivyo mnavyovipenda"* meaning "provide that which is the most precious for you", implying "one's bottom".

that the life expectancy in the society under study is around 52 years, they are likely to turn in their late forties.

This study aims to reconstruct this reality and look at the religious knowledge that Zanzibaris acquire in the process of their socialisation and the impact that it has on the conceptualisation of urban Zanzibari lifestyle. It focuses on the Zanzibaris of the generation that grew up during the post-second world war period (mid-1940s) right through the period of the Zanzibar independence struggle *'zama za siasa'*[1] (1950s–1963) and the aftermath. It covers the epoch when it was still said, *"when one blew the trumpet in Zanzibar the whole of Africa up to the Great Lakes danced"*, and continues up to the present period when the opposite is also said: *"when a whistle is blown in Tanganyika the Islanders dance to the tune"*. The analysis focuses on the pre-revolutionary period – before the post-revolutionary major brain drain – when Zanzibar was one of the important regional learning centres, and the archipelago extensively relied on its own elite, religious and secular scholars. It is a period when there was much religious tolerance in the country when the orthodox Muslim majority cohabitated in perfect harmony with other religious denominations and sects, as well as minority groups such as homosexuals. The latter had their space without having to fight for it. The society was neither encouraging them nor subjecting them to any kind of persecution.

Nevertheless, the situation has dramatically changed during the last three decades. This is particularly since Zanzibar lost its own secular and religious scholars and had to rely on foreign countries to assure the training of its religious elites. This was the result of the brain drain that the country experienced after 1964, following the civil war that led to the revolution, overthrowing the Sultan and the first post-independence democratically elected coalition government[2] of the Zanzibar Nationalist Party (ZNP)[3]

---

1. It was a period of open politics when Zanzibar had a veritable multiparty system and anti-colonial agenda. The Islands had more than six political parties: (1) Zanzibar Nationalist Party (ZNP) led by Mr. Vuai Kitoweo; (2) Afro Shirazi Party (ASP) led by Mr. Abeid Amani Karume; (3) Zanzibar and Pemba People's Party (ZPPP) led by Mr. Muhammed Shamte; (4) Umma Party (Comrades) led by Mr. Abdulrahman Mohamed Babu; (5) Zanzibar Communist Party (ZCP) led by Mr. Abdulrahman Mohamed Hamdani (Gae); and (6) Human Rights led by Mr Mmanga Said Abdulla (Bamanga) and Jimmy Ringo.
2. Zanzibar obtained its independence from Great Britain on 10 December 1963: two years after Tanganyika and two days before Kenya. It became full member of the United Nations Organisation on 16 December 1963.
3. Issued from a peasant movement, which started in the early 1950s, Zanzibar Nationalist Party was created in 1956.

and Zanzibar and Pemba People's Party (ZPPP).[1] The main parliamentary opposition party, the Afro Shirazi Party (ASP),[2] which took over power by the barrel of the gun, arrows, spears and machetes on 12 January 1964, imposed a dictatorship, which was openly against intellectuals, secular or religious.[3] The first post-revolutionary government under the leader, Abeid Amani Karume, who ruled the Islands with an iron fist, forced Zanzibari secular and religious scholars to go into exile.[4]

Subsequently, Zanzibar suffered a great deal. The lack of adequately trained and enlightened religious scholars capable of articulating their religious discourse within the context of the Swahili culture led to the standard of education dropping dramatically. So much so that Zanzibar had to rely on the importation of foreign scholars to assist it in this field. The alien ideas brought into the country ignored the previous socio-geographical and cultural factors, which used to serve as the backdrop of understanding. At present, the country is experiencing more and more radicalisation of religious discourse and practice. The past tacit understanding that guaranteed the rights of minorities, such as those of homosexuals so long as they gave no open "provocation"[5] started to be challenged. Today, most of the religious

1. It was formed by the group that seceded from the Afro Shirazi Party: to avoid the over-control of the party apparatus by people of mainland origin. The leader of this party Mr. Muhammed Shamte became the first Prime Minister of independent Zanzibar, and was the one who took the country to the United Nations on 16 December 1963.
2. It was formed in 1957 from a union between the African Association (regrouping Africans of mainland origin) and Shirazi Association (regrouping indigenous Zanzibaris). In 1977, the Afro Shirazi Party (ASP) united with the Tanganyika African National Union (TANU) of Mr. Julius Nyerere to form Chama Cha Mapinduzi (CCM), the ruling party.
3. One could recall a number of cases of violation of human rights committed against Muslim scholars in terms of arbitrary arrests, beatings or shootings in the mosques. The most dramatic shooting that still remains in the memory of many Zanzibaris was the one committed by Karume's lieutenant, Muhammad Abdulla Kaujore on 9 September 1964 on a group of worshippers in a Shia mosque at Kiponda in the Stone-town. He shot dead a number of them for no reason at all. Five were killed outright. One of them a boy of eight was called Abbas Kassim. Others were Sayyid Abdul-Muttalib Hashim, Sayyid Ali Asghar, Haji Abdul-Husain Tejani and Babu Haji.
4. Sheikh Al-Habib Seyyid Omar bin Sumeyt, Sheikh Seyyid Omar Abdallah (Mwinyi Baraka) and Sheikh Abdalla Saleh Farsy are three examples among many others of Zanzibari scholars who ended their lives in exile, far from Zanzibar. The first two ended their days in the Comoros and the third one started in Kenya and later on ended his life in Oman.
5. For example, the organisation of a public parade of homosexuals, like Gay Pride. This does not mean that they were not free to organise their get-together. One

leaders, even those who would be considered as moderates, would preach for religious purity with particular emphasis on correct religious practice and ethics. They would rather take a stand against social and religious deviance as well as political corruption, and fiercely condemn the impact of tourism instead of remaining neutral, as they used to.

The Socio-Geographical and Cultural Context

Situated at the crossroad between Africa and Asia, Zanzibar belongs to that string of islands extending all along the east African coast, from Lamu to the Comoros and adjacent hinterland, where for many centuries Swahili culture and civilisation took shape and flourished.[1] It is by all standards a cosmopolitan society, with a very rich mixture of people originating from the four corners of the globe,[2] and most particularly the Indian Ocean basin who intermingled throughout history and formed what is now a homogenous Zanzibari Swahili culture. The latter is fundamentally Islamic, although some other non-Islamic cultural elements have also contributed in enriching it. The Islam of Zanzibar has its own particularities, specificities and history. Like in many other Swahili localities the expansion of Islam in Zanzibar took place through commercial and social contacts. It was not imposed on the population with a sword. This non-radical and tolerant Islam has left its imprint in all aspects of Zanzibari social and cultural life. This is so much so that a good understanding has developed between different religious denominations in Zanzibar to such an extent that even the non-Muslim Zanzibaris would consciously or unconsciously use common Islamic terminologies in their day-to-day conversations. For instance, it is very common for Zanzibaris belonging to the Christian faith or Hinduism to use Muslim/Arabic lexical terms such as *Asalamu Aleikum*

---

of the well known homosexual gatherings in Zanzibar was organised around the traditional dance *"bomu"* quite often at Gongoni in the Ng'ambo area of Zanzibar. They were dressed in female clothes with artificial breasts and wore lipstick and eye make-up. The homosexuals *"bomu"* used to take place in late evening at the time when the children would be in bed.

1. The Swahili cultural influence extends about 3 000 kilometres all along the east African coast, from Brava (Somalia) down to Sofala (Mozambique), including adjacent islands, notably Lamu, Mombasa, Pemba and Unguja (Zanzibar), Mafia, Kilwa and the Comoros. See Middleton 1992, Saleh 1996, 2002 and 2004.
2. This reality is allegorically reflected in the diverse number of different types of bread existing in the Islands, from *mkate wa Ajemi* to *mkate wa Kingazija* "from Persian bread to Comorian", one can count more than ten types of bread in Zanzibar, representing different regions of the world.

to greet their fellow Zanzibaris, *Alhamdulillah* to express their gratitude or *Inshallah* to express their hope. They would respect the Ramadhan month of fasting by abstaining from eating outside, in public. They would always attend religious functions such as *maulid* "celebration of the birth of Prophet Muhammad", weddings, funerals and *hitmas* "post-funeral prayers", taking place in the mosques despite their religious faith or philosophical stance. The contrary was also true. The Muslims would take part in Christmas celebrations or the Birthday of Great Buddha without any complex (Al Barwani 1997:32). Furthermore, the existence of different branches of Islam in the Islands was never seen as an obstacle but rather as an enriching element of the society. Shia, Ibadhi and Sunni Muslims would congregate and do their prayers together without considering that they were in Ibadhi, Shia, or Sunni mosques. A Zanzibari Muslim would enter without hesitation into any mosque near the place where he found himself at the time of the call for prayers.

Zanzibar is Muslim in terms of norms and values, a society that emerged through its key teachings and culture. Islam, being the religion of the majority of the population (about 95 per cent), constitutes the backdrop and the major reference of the whole process of cultural enlightenment. Starting right from birth, the process of socialisation is conducted through the observation of different rites of passage as well as religious and moral teachings. This is particularly so since parents have an absolute moral obligation towards God of assuring the religious education of their children up to the age of puberty. It is only after this age that parents cease to be accountable for all the deeds of their children, if the latter were brought up in conformity with religious obligations. Parents who do not properly assume their religious duty towards their children share the responsibility of all the sins the latter might commit during the rest of their lives (Saleh 2004).

Socialisation Process and Acquisition of Religious Knowledge

Traditionally, the Qur'an schools constitute the basis for the acquisition of Islamic religious knowledge. It is in these informal institutions (*vyuo*), most of the time established in individual people's houses, where Zanzibari children start their learning process very early before they start their secular and formal schooling. The two education systems are not incompatible but rather complementary. The children attend secular schools in the morning and Qur'anic classes in the afternoon.[1] The Islamic education system does not vary much and is transmitted from one generation to another through the teachings of the Qur'an, the traditions of the Prophet, *hadith*, as well as Islamic jurisprudence *(fiqh)*, Qur'an exegesis, and Islamic mysticism *(tasawuf)*. The Islamic mysticism *Sufism* played an important role in the spread of Islam and in bringing the believers close to their God through the ritual *dhikr*. The latter consists of recitations and recollection of God through repeated invocation of His name in order to attain spiritual union with Him. In Zanzibar, the prominent Sufi orders include: Qadiriyya, Shadhiliyya, Rifaiyya, Askariyya, Ahmadiyya Dandarawiyya, Naqshbandiyya and Alawiyya.[2]

The Islamic education focuses on the transmission of religious knowledge but also and particularly on moulding each and every individual Muslim to fit into a particular model of life that leads to obedience to Almighty God and one's parents, who come second in the hierarchical order, to abide by Divine laws and conduct one's life in conformity with the Islamic religious teachings. The Islamic learning process usually revolves around five major cycles:

1. Basic teaching of Arabic alphabet and learning of some basic Qur'an *suras* (chapters), such as *Al-Fatiha* and *Kulhuwallah*, which everybody is expected to know by heart, before attaining the age of seven.

2. The second cycle consists of learning the whole Qur'an *(msahafu)*, the completion of which is called *kuhitimu*. At this stage one is expected to be able to read or recite all the *suras*, from the beginning to the end.

3. The third cycle is dedicated to the translation and analysis/commentary of the Qur'an. At the end of this cycle, a learner is expected to understand the Qur'an and its significance.

---

1. Secular schooling took place from 7.30 in the morning to 13.00 (Monday to Thursday), and from 7.30 to 12.30 (Friday). Qur'anic classes took place in the afternoon from 14.30 to 16.30 (Monday to Wednesday and Friday). The children would have a break on Thursday when all the Qur'anic Schools were closed. At the week-end Qur'anic classes used to take place on Saturday morning from 08.00 to 12.00 and resumed after two hours break, from 14.00 to 16.00; and on Sunday Qur'anic classes were held from 08.00 to 12.00. However, during the last decade the problem of overcrowded classes in secular schools led to the introduction of a two shift system: morning and afternoon. This move also had an impact on the organisation of Qur'anic classes in the *madrasas*: Qur'anic schools.
2. For more details especially on Qadiriyya, see Issa 2006.

4.   The fourth cycle consists of studying Arabic and Islamic literature and other disciplines such as Islamic law, economy, sociology, history and even interpretation and translation.

5.   Some pursue their studies abroad in the major Islamic centres, such as Hadhramawt (Yemen), Al-Azhar (Egypt), Mecca and Medina (Saudi Arabia).

Most of the *darsas*, i.e., teachings of religious sciences are conducted in the mosques in the evenings, between *salat maghrib*[1] and *salat isha*[2] or after *salat isha*. The mosques are the principal pillars of learning, and each one of them has its own particular reputation, concentrating on a particular science, such as inheritance, matrimonial law, and so on. Like in many Muslim countries, mosques in Zanzibar not only serve as places of cults and schools of learning, but they also serve as libraries, cultural centres and meeting points between different people attending the same studies or who have the same interests. Msikiti Baraza and Gofu are among the most famous mosques and learning centres of Zanzibar. Through the religious teachings other elements of good citizenship are also emphasised. *Heshima* (respect), *uaminifu* (honesty), *uadilifu* (ethics) and *ari* (honour) are among the ideals, which each and every Zanzibari family would wish to inculcate in their descendants. As an essential source of recognition in the society, these norms and values are not only the abstract concepts of the Swahili language, but are the basis of day-to-day life in the society (Saleh 2004). They are the criteria that are used to evaluate one's attitude and create an opinion on one's reputation.

As we have seen earlier, religious and secular studies have always been complementary and developed in parallel. By the time a young Zanzibari reaches the age of puberty and becomes responsible for his/her own sins he/she is intellectually well equipped with all the necessary tools to objectively become an enlightened member of the society and able to expand his/her knowledge and world outlook on his/her own. Seyyid Omar Abdalla, commonly known as Mwinyi Baraka, was a pure product of this part of the world where a number of scholars of his calibre emerged through this very subtle system of teaching, which put particular emphasis on the balance between secular and religious studies. A Doctor of Philosophy from the School of Oriental and African Studies, London University, Mwinyi Baraka accomplished simultaneously his religious and secular learning.[3] He was one of the

1. The fourth ritual of the day.
2. The fifth and the last ritual of the day.
3. For more biographical details on him see: Bakari 2006, Soilhaboud, 2001.

products of Makerere University of East Africa. Sheikh Abdulla Saleh Farsy, former Chief Kadhi of Zanzibar, who later on occupied the same function in Kenya, was another eloquent example of a Zanzibari scholar produced through the same system of education. This factor is clearly pointed out by a prominent Zanzibari Sociologist, Dr. Ahmed Gurnah (1997): "Before engaging with English literature in secondary schools, Zanzibaris would have learnt Kiswahili sayings, Arabic and Qur'an", hence "Our appreciation of Islamic literature, theology and culture was organic."

Tradition versus Culture

It is in this context that the concept of *dini wal duniya* should be understood. It is digested in a society, which has a strong base of *mila* (traditions) and *utamaduni* (culture) of openness and tolerance. Mohamed Said Abdalla, a well-known Zanzibari writer who published a number of Swahili novels,[1] used to like to distinguish between these two words, *mila* (traditions) and *utamaduni* (culture). According to him the former is an accepted term for traditions and hence is not charged with any particular bad connotation, while the latter is common terminology, which connotes culture, but needs to be used with delicacy. It could subtly transmit a negative message if it is not employed properly. For instance, the word *utamaduni*, although it means culture, but if it is used as an adjective to qualify a Zanzibari Swahili person as *mtamadun*, it could be misunderstood, as it becomes derogatory and hence could hurt one's feelings. The notion *mtamadun* is almost synonymous with *mstaarabu*. The latter could also have both positive and negative connotations, depending on how it is said and/or presented. In the Zanzibar context, *Mstaarabu,* a cultured and hence civilised person is quite often related to urban, i.e., being urban and mundane. It is in contrast with *Mshamba*, from the countryside. In the general locution of the Zanzibari urban dwellers *mshamba* is synonymous with un-cultured, hence un-civilised or un-sophisticated person.

The major differentiation of the two above mentioned concepts could equally be looked at in terms of general exposure to the socio-cultural and political aspects of the global world, which reflected more into the situation of the urban dwellers than the inhabitants of the countryside.[2] Indeed, the urban dwellers were more in tune with what was going on in almost all the

---

1. Among them: *Duniani Kuna Watu; Siri ya Sifuri, Mke Mmoja Waume Watatu.*
2. The situation is progressively changing now with the massive development of tourism and the mushrooming of hotel complexes in every corner of the countryside.

spheres of the international community through the channel of networks, linking the Islands with the outside world. Quite naturally, the historical developments and the geographical position of the Islands allowed the Zanzibari urban dwellers to have a World outlook, which went beyond their insularity. The sociological analysis of the Zanzibari urban youth brought forth by Dr. Ahmed Gurnah in his article 'Elvis in Zanzibar' highlights some of these fundamental aspects:

> As a community we were sophisticated and our culture wide-ranging and complex. Most young people I knew were worldly and capable of holding on their own. A lot of this was as a result of our parents being involved in international commerce with the Middle East, India, the Far East and further north and south on the African coast. Many of us travelled to these countries or had relatives who came from them to stay with us. Exchange of information and know-how was routine, frequent and considerable. Equally we had easy access to other metropolitan cities in Europe, America, North Africa, India and so on (Gurnah 1997:5).

Commercial activities, secular and religious educational exchange programmes with different learning institutions abroad, and working on ships as seamen, were some of the major factors of the mobility of Zanzibaris. This is why it was very common to find Zanzibari *maskani* in a number of port cities worldwide. The most famous Zanzibari *maskani* were found in Dar Es Salaam (the then Tanganyika), Mombasa (Kenya), Aden (Yemen), Bombay (India), Liverpool and Portsmouth (England). It is important to distinguish here between the *maskani* introduced by the President of the third phase government of Zanzibar, Dr. Salmin Amour in the 1990s from the initial *maskani* established by Zanzibaris in different port cities. While the former were created as a pure strategy of political manipulation, with the view of replacing the ruling party CCM[1] branches in the advent of the multiparty system in the country, the authentic *maskani* never had any political function. They were the places – houses or apartments – where Zanzibari seamen used to live together while waiting to find a job on a ship or at a dockyard. The term *maskani* was also used in a general sense, connoting a group sharing accommodation. An important number of the first generation of the members of the Zanzibari Diaspora were seamen, some of whom have since retired but are still continuing to live in major city ports, such as Amsterdam, Liverpool and Portsmouth.

---

1. *Chama Cha Mapinduzi*" Revolutionary Party."

The slow pace of life on the islands did not incapacitate Zanzibaris from adjusting to a fast western life style while abroad. Nevertheless, in the archipelago the tranquil life created favourable conditions for them to enjoy the simple pleasures of the islands, including fishing, watching bull and cock fights as well as playing football, hockey, tennis and cricket. The then economic, social and political conditions equally allowed Zanzibaris to spend time talking and engaging in debates on different issues. In different *barazas* Zanzibaris would discuss politics freely, prior to the 1964 revolution,[1] and argue about films, especially westerns and Egyptian ones. Some of them would read an enormous amount and devoured worlds out there that they have never seen. These rational discussions, arguments, or dogmatic conflicts were laced all the time, as Dr. Gurnah (1997) put it, with humour and mutual taunting, while everyone was consuming numerous cups of strong black coffee without sugar.[2]

In the 1950s the major movement among the Zanzibari urban dwellers could not be circumscribed within the limits of *mila* (traditions), as a particular emphasis was put on the aspects of *utamaduni* (culture), through cultural interaction with the outside world. This was the time when Zanzibar was still an important centre of gravity, i.e., a political, economic and cultural centre with its own elite who could influence ideas and give an orientation to the society. During this period the Zanzibaris were always in tune with what was going on in the rest of the world, and as the metropolis of the region Zanzibaris had their social and cultural destiny in their own hands. It is important to remember here that Zanzibar was one of the important centres of learning in East Africa in religious sciences as well as secular studies. Up to the early 1960s Zanzibar was in the forefront of intellectual achievement in the region. This was in terms of the production of religious as well as secular learning material.

This prevailing situation seemed to have played an important role in reassuring those Zanzibaris who were in search of new ideas and intellectual enrichment, in the process of which an important number of them even

---

1 Under the dictatorship of Abeid Amani Karume, it was not allowed for more than two people to sit and talk on *baraza*. They were forbidden for fear that this would provide a framework for people to talk politics like in the past.

2 It was rare for Zanzibari families to prepare coffee at home. Zanzibaris generally drink tea. This is why *"chai"*, which means tea, was synonymous with breakfast in Zanzibar. Coffee was usually bought from mobile street coffee vendors, knocking on their small coffee cups to announce their presence in the neighbourhood. Each and every person/family had their own specific vendor from whom they bought their coffee. They recognized and differentiated between them by their cups beats.

rebelled against the preconceived ideas and moral teachings. To quote the words of Dr. Gurnah (1997):

> On the whole, Zanzibaris were not intimidated by European racist attitudes towards Africans: perhaps in a way such racism might have impacted on brothers and sisters in Tanganyika or Kenya. We did not see any reason to imitate European ways or assume their attitudes or culture in order to hold on to our own dignity. When rock and roll arrived, many of us in the urban areas hungrily embraced it. Fused with our nationalist views, our enthusiasm was probably in part to piss off our European teachers and elderly parents and not because we thought that dressing up like Elvis or the Beatles made us acceptable to Europeans. We might have even thought that the European establishment was limited in its taste in clothes and that its style was rather dour. We laughed at the immodesty that prompted English people to claim modesty and having the finest sense of humour. Europeans we encountered were our secondary school teachers, whom we liked but also enjoyed winding up, particularly, regarding things that mattered to them.

This statement corroborates what Maulid M. Haj (2001) had to say in his autobiographical novel, in which he explored life and politics on the spice islands of Zanzibar and Pemba before the revolution of 1964. As a central character, young and passionate, like the young Zanzibaris of his generation he did not have any complexes *vis à vis* the Europeans. In confrontation with his European boss who was determined to use his position to manipulate him for political purposes, Maulid M. Haj sent him packing, reminding him of the terms of reference of the contract of his employment. He stood firm and refused to compromise his principles for whatever favour. Following a strong disagreement with Sullivan, who was the Senior Commissioner, Head of Public Administration, as a punishment Maulid M. Haj was transferred to Pemba where his life took another turn. He took the challenge and refused to bow down and went to Pemba to start a new life.

The mid-1950s to the beginning of the 1960s was also a period famously known as *zama za siasa*, 'political epoch'. It was during this period that the anti-colonial movement was taking shape in Zanzibar and East Africa. The political environment at the time encouraged a number of young Zanzibaris to participate in politics against colonialism and imperialism. In the process they were exposed to radical anti-colonial and imperialist political literature and to refine their opinions they read authors like Kwame Nkrumah, Frantz Fanon, Che Guevara, Mao Tse Tung and Peter Abrahams. Zanzibaris morally supported independence and anti-imperialist struggles in Ghana,

Tanganyika, Egypt, South Africa, Kenya, Vietnam and so on. Being young Zanzibaris, according to Gurnah (1997), amounted to being progressive and metropolitan in outlook. He further emphasised:

> Our reading of key Third World revolutionaries and thinkers increased the sense of humanity that was ingrained in our way of living. The new language of freedom and struggle of the oppressed people integrated comfortably with the deep-seated human values current in our language and outlook.

It is not surprising to see that of all the four countries of East Africa (Tanganyika, Kenya, Uganda and Zanzibar) it was only in Zanzibar where the independence struggle went in parallel with the development of ideological diversity. In this island-country of East Africa, there emerged more than two Marxist parties, one Populist Party, two nationalist parties and a Human Rights Party. In fact, the first and only Communist Party in East Africa, was formed in Zanzibar. The political movements in the other three East African countries, Tanganyika, Kenya and Uganda, were all based on the ideology of African Nationalism. The political thinking in Zanzibar was not insular in its outlook but rather internationalist. Global world politics were part and parcel of the anti-colonial struggle and the socio-political context of the epoch was favourable to the development of ideological diversity but also and especially radical politics. The Korean War in 1950[1] and the 1956 Suez Canal crisis captured the minds of a great number of Zanzibaris.

In the last ten years of colonial power the political environment was becoming more and more favourable to the African nationalists' cause. They could agitate for self-government and independence, often with support of important members of parliament in London. African nationalist leaders were at times arrested and even imprisoned. However, on the whole, there was a level of openness and frank agitation in the last decade of colonial rule which stood out in marked contrast to previous decades and certainly in marked contrast to more recent times in independent Africa (Mazrui, Ali A. and Mazrui Alamin M. (1999:22)).

The Zanzibaris whom I observed for this particular study are those from this generation. They were at their prime age, during the anti-colonial struggle, when a lot of traditional values were also put into question. Most of

---

1. The Korean War, occurring between June 25, 1950 and a ceasefire on 27 July, 1953, was a civil war between the states of North Korea and South Korea that were created out of the post-World War II Soviet and American occupation zones in Korea, with large-scale participation by other countries.

them were enjoying their lives to the fullest with deviations from their religious and moral up bringing. Some of them were not performing at all
their 5 daily prayers and/or drinking alcohol on a daily basis and behaving
in manners that are in total contradiction to the precepts of Islam. Today,
most of them have repented and are becoming more and more religious. For
instance, people who were famously known to have been heavy drinkers (al-
coholics), hashish and marijuana smokers, womanisers or women-swingers,
have become very religious. Some became Imams leading prayers in different mosques or are involved in religious lecturing and teachings. Some have
even became radical religious preachers convincing those who are not in line
with the religious teachings and behaviour that they should be prepared to
go to hell *motoni* or to be subjected to hard and burning clubs in the grave
kupigwa marungu ya moto. Those I happened to ask as to why they have
changed and transformed their attitude and behaviour towards religion and
moral thinking would answer *dini wal duniya*. The question is not welcome
to most of them. It is embarrassing. This is why the answer *dini wal duniya*
is a good pretext to avoid answering the question. This is a general trend of
the majority of Zanzibaris. It is easier to mention the examples of those who
do not follow the trend – as there are just a handful of them – than the contrary. However, it is important to note here that the deviance from religious
obligations committed by Zanzibaris was most of the time committed in
privacy. Zanzibaris were enjoying their lives while at the same time respect-
ing their intimacy, i.e., without any kind of showing off.

The spirit of *dini wal duniya* and the changing religious attitude of
Zanzibaris are very well depicted and reflected in the character of Mkadam
in Adam Shafi's (2003) novel *"Haini"*. The novel narrates the conditions
of life in the two wings of the Zanzibar prison *Kumbakumba* and *Kwa
Bamkwe*. While in the former, some political prisoners could find themselves together with common criminals, in the latter they were exclusively
detained by themselves under the conditions of an abattoir, and tortured.
The novel describes in details the conditions in the torture chambers during the 1972 treason trial in Zanzibar, where a substantial number of young
Zanzibaris among whom former members of the Umma Party "Comrades"
accused of treason were detained. Confronted with the death sentence for
alleged participation in the assassination of the *Kigogo,* Big Shot, the first
President of an African country in 1972, Mkadam who was living an extravagant life before his arrest, all of a sudden became very religious. He was
spending most of his time in the prison cell praying and trying to recover
all the past prayers that he had not observed before he was arrested. He was

also trying to recover the fasting days that he had not observed for all those years before he was detained.

The example of Mkadam is one among many others. One could write a whole book without being able to exhaust the subject. One case in point is that of a famous Zanzibari journalist who was known for harassing the early morning callers to prayers when he was drunk: asking them to stop making a noise and disturbing people in their sleep. This is an illustrative example especially as today this same person has not only stopped drinking but also become a very pious Muslim religious observer. Like many Zanzibaris of his generation who lived their lives to the fullest, he does not like to be reminded of his past deeds as that could tarnish his present *"born again"* image.

Being a maritime civilization, nurtured by contacts Swahilis have always been exposed to different aspects of modernity throughout their history. They are known to have been a dynamic people, adapting to new social, economic and political realities of the time. Islam as a core of their culture remains intact and could always be brought back when needed as we have seen in the case under study: Zanzibar.

References

Al Barwani, Ali Muhsin, 1997, *Conflict and Harmony in Zanzibar,* (Memoirs), Dubai.

Bakari, Mohamed, 2006, "Sayyid Omar Abdalla (1918–1988): The Forgotten Muslim Humanist and Public Intellectual", in Loimeier, Roman, and Seesemann Rudiger (eds), *The Global Worlds of the Swahili, Interfaces of Islam, Identity and Space in 19th and 20th-Century East Africa*. Lit Verlag, Berlin.

Gurnah, Ahmed Salim, 1997, "Elvis in Zanzibar", in Alain Scott (ed.) *Limits to Globalisation*, Routledge, London.

Gurnah, Ahmed Salim, "Death of a Zanzibari", in Gurnah, Ahmed Salim, and Saleh, Mohamed Ahmed, (eds), *Nostalgic Zanzibar* (forthcoming).

Haj, Maulid M., 2001, *Sowing the Wind: Zanzibar and Pemba before the revolution*, The Gallery Publications, Zanzibar.

Issa, Amina Ameir, 2006, "The legacy of Qadiri Scholars in Zanzibar", in Loimeier, Roman and Seesemann (eds), *The Global Worlds of the Swahili. Interfaces of Islam, Identity and Space in 19th and 20th Century East Africa.* Lit Verlag, Berlin.

Mazrui, Alamin and Shariff, Ibrahim Noor, 1994, *The Swahili: Idiom and Identity of an African People*, Africa World Press, Inc, Trenton, New Jersey.

Mazrui, Ali A. and Mazrui Alamin M., 1999, *Political Culture of Language: Swahili, Society and the State*, Institute of Global Culture Studies (IGCS), Binghampton University, New York.

Middleton, John, 1992, *The World of the Swahili: An African Mercantile Civilization*, Yale University Press, New Haven and London.

Saleh, Mohamed Ahmed, 1996, 'Zanzibar et le monde Swahili', *Afrique contemporaine*, Paris, Trimestriel N° 177, janvier–mars, La documentation Française, pp. 17–29.

Saleh, Mohamed Ahmed, 1997, 'Zanzibari Diaspora: Identity and Nationalism', *Western Indian Ocean: A Cultural Corridor*, Stockholm, Department of Social Anthropology of Stockholm University.

Saleh, Mohamed Ahmed, 2002, 'Tolerance: The Principal Foundation of the Cosmopolitan Society of Zanzibar', *Cultures of the World Journal*, March, Barcelona.

Saleh, Mohamed Ahmed, 2004, 'Going with the Times: Conflicting Swahili Norms and Values Today' in Caplan, Pat and Topan, Farouk (eds), *Swahili Modernities*, Africa World Press, Trenton, p. 145–155.

Shafi, Adam, 2003, *Haini*, Longhorn Publishers, Nairobi, Kampala.

Soilhaboud, Hamza, 2001, *Omar-La-Baraka*. Biographie-Roman, Editions Encres du Sud

CHAPTER II

Understanding Modernity/ies

The Idea of a Moral Community on Mafia Island, Tanzania

Pat Caplan

Introduction

In the introduction to their book *Millenial Capitalism and the Culture of Neoliberalism* (2001), Jean and John Comaroff identify a number of important characteristics of modern capitalism, but for them the heart of the matter is 'the ontological conditions-of-being under millenial capitalism' (2001:3). This is an issue which I want to explore with reference to Mafia Island, Tanzania. What concerns me is what people at the local level make of developments at the global level which affect their lives: what knowledge of such developments do they have? Where do they get it from? What do they do with it? I propose here to explore local knowledge and experience of local modernities through utilising the concept of risk. This is because risk, as Mary Douglas suggests, is a *forensic* tool (Douglas 1992). It is also because using ideas about risk and danger, trust and blame, leads inevitably to ideas about morality.

Mafia Island, Tanzania

I have been carrying out research on Mafia Island off the southern coast of Tanzania since 1965. From the time when I first encountered it, Mafia has been considered one of the poorest parts of Tanzania. In the 1960s and 1970s, people made a living by subsistence agriculture and the sale of coconuts, a situation which had pertained since German rule at the beginning of the 20th century. Mafia has been a food deficit area since at least that time and probably earlier, when coconut plantations were set up by Arab colonists in the south of the island in the 19th century. In the north, where most of my work has been conducted, people supplemented the food they grew by the sale of coconuts.

By the 1980s, life was getting harder in many respects, and in the last decade or so, it has become more difficult still. During my 1994 visit, it was clear that change was accelerating, and that even in this relatively remote area of Tanzania, global processes were impinging at an increasing rate. People talked constantly about *maisha magumu* – a hard or difficult life. Letters I received from villagers between 1994 and 2002 made it clear that for most, economic problems were increasing and that food insecurity, long problematic on Mafia, was worsening (Caplan 2004).[1]

When I visited the island in 2002[2] and again in 2004 I was interested in finding out how people interpreted this situation. Where did they place responsibility for it? How did such issues link to political processes, especially the relatively new multi-party democracy? What strategies did people adopt to cope, and what view did they have of the future? How much trust did they place in 'experts' such as government officers? How much room for manoeuvre did people consider they had? Did they see themselves as agents or victims – or both? What were their conceptualisations of processes beyond the local with the acceleration of so-called globalisation? I wanted to know not only how they made sense of this situation, but also to whom they attributed responsibility and blame for it. I also wanted to know what they did about it. Inevitably, I found that in carrying out such research, I actually had to move far beyond the level of the village, where most of my previous research had been carried out, and cover other parts of the island, including government offices in the District Capital. I also had to take account not only of government ministries and NGO offices in Dar es Salaam, but also of investors and donors hailing from a variety of foreign countries.

1. Local Views of Modernity

First of all, however, let us consider some local, village-level views of modernity, often referred to as *mambo ya kisasa* (new developments):

a) Kwenda na wakati: changes in values – these include lack of trust, and corruption *(rushwa)*, as well as the perceived bad behaviour of young people.

b) Vyama vingi (multipartyism) – a topic which I will not have space to consider in this chapter[3]

---

1. There is a significant disjuncture between many of the macro-economics indicators (GNP, GDP, growth rates etc.) and the reality of lives of many people.
2. I am grateful to the Nuffield Foundation for financial support for this work.
3. Cameron considers this topic with reference to Zanzibar in his chapter in this book.

c) Soko huru: the free market, or liberalisation of the economy. This encompasses the arrival of outside investors *(wawekezaji)* who, on Mafia, include the owners and managers of tourist hotels (Italian, South African, French), a fish processing factory and a planned large-scale prawn farm (Kenyan Asian); most recently, they also include multinational oil companies.

d) Wafadhili (donors): while Tanzania has long been a recipient of both multilateral and bi-lateral aid, increasingly it receives the attention of large numbers of foreign-based multilateral agencies like UNICEF and CARE, some of which operate on Mafia. There are also growing numbers of new Christian mission stations (American, Swiss, Polish), mainly from the newer Pentecostal churches, which have been set up on the predominantly Muslim island. While their major aim is conversion, they have also organised projects such as a nursery school. In addition, there are several aid projects around health, including an anaemia eradication project on Chole Island lying off the southern coast of the main island (Harvard Medical School) which is in turn linked to a filariasis eradication programme (Michigan State University).

Civil society and local NGOs: Mafia now has a number of locally based NGOS,[1] but they are small and resource-poor, constantly seeking outside funding from larger international agencies in order to be able to carry out their aims (see for example Caplan 1998).

How do people feel about these forms of modernity? On the whole they are viewed either equivocally or negatively:

- These things (tourist hotels, prawn farms) are not for people like us and will not benefit us. They will not employ us because we lack sufficient education.

- Such developments mean that we have lost our existing rights, especially our land rights.

Although some of the younger men spoke positively of new forms of income from fishing, especially for crustaceans, they too expressed frustration about lack of educational and employment opportunities.

How are such views translated into practice? One way is through *resistance*, as Cameron also discusses in his chapter: people may resist develop-

---

1. These include *Changia cha Maendeleo Mafia (Chamama)* – Society for the Development of Mafia; MICAS – *Mafia against AIDS and Sexually Transmitted Diseases; Kimama,* a women's organisation; and Tasisi ya Dini – a committee of religious leaders from all faiths concerned with HIV/AIDS.

ments through refusal to sell land for tourist development[1] or by objecting to proposed developments,[2] even taking their objections to the national press or national NGOs to seek redress. Another is through *adaptation* and seeking to use whatever opportunities arise, for example, taking advantage of the increasing demand for fish both in Dar es Salaam and abroad.

How then do people make sense of all of this? And how does the ethnographer interpret the knowledge they construct to do so? One way to discuss local perceptions of modernity is by considering first risk and danger, and then trust and blame.

2. Risk and Danger: Local Perceptions

What do people see as the main risks (*hatari* – danger) in their lives? In this section I consider four issues which were referred to repeatedly in my most recent fieldwork: increasing poverty and lack of food security; illness, including HIV/AIDS; perceived exclusion from development; and loss of existing rights.

Food Security

The major perceived risk is food security. Most people in the village argued that they had less security now than previously. This was because food prices had risen, while ability to earn money through the sale of cash crops had fallen considerably. Although people grow their own food, they cannot produce enough to feed themselves, partly because of the low level of technology, but also because of the vagaries of the weather and the high incidence of pests. Rice remains the most favoured food, and, if people cannot grow enough, they will buy it. While this area is not usually famine-prone, people often do not have enough to eat. At the same time, because of numerous nutritional campaigns, both local[3] and national, people are more aware than ever before of the importance of eating well and of giving their children healthy food.

Yet food here, as elsewhere, is never 'just food', it is about other matters too.

---

1. As happened in the northern village in which I have mainly worked.
2. As has happened in the neighbouring village which is the site of the prawn farm.
3. Campaigns have been waged by UNICEF, and, on Chole Island, by the Anaemia Project funded by Harvard Medical School.

Extract 1: Interview with a middle-aged man

> People today don't have enough strength because they don't eat as well [as they used to do]. The food they eat comes from all over the place, some of it's alright, but some of it isn't....
> Q. So is the food which is grown here better [than that which is imported]?
> A. Yes, first of all it's heavy (kizito), the other [kind of food] is very light (kinyepe-si). A person has to fill their stomach, but these days people don't feel satisfied!

Extract 2: Interview with another middle-aged man

> Q. What about the food people eat nowadays?
> A. The [imported] food has its problems – it's been around for years before it gets sold. It's like medicine – you shouldn't use it after its due date [has expired]. So can it be real food?

Food grown locally is valued and considered satisfying, being described as 'heavy' and 'filling your stomach', but it is insufficient in quantity and it has to be supplemented by food bought in local shops and markets. Because cash incomes have decreased so dramatically in the last decade, most people have little choice but to purchase the cheapest food. Since economic liberalisation in Tanzania this increasingly includes rice imported from countries like Thailand and Pakistan, which is bought because it is cheaper than locally-produced rice, whether grown on the island or elsewhere in Tanzania. This is seen as unhealthy and unsatisfying, not least because it has travelled far and 'sat around for too long' before being sold. In short, then, there is little enthusiasm at the village level for the effects of free-market policies on food supply.

Illness as a Risk

In Kanga village, they are proud of their new clinic and their own part in its construction; they speak highly of their clinic paramedic and his hard work; they are very pleased that their children are now vaccinated and that women can give birth in the clinic. At the same time, people are concerned about illness not just for themselves or their children, but about its implications: how will they manage if they get sick? How will they find the necessary cash to make the long journey to the district hospital, and once there, to pay for consultations and medicines?[1]

---

1. Medical treatment is supposed to be free at the primary health care level, but, since economic liberalisation and structural adjustment, has to be paid for at District level or higher. This is a major disincentive to seeking treatment.

There is growing concern about AIDS, especially on the part of women, who feel that they are vulnerable to infection from husbands who are likely to have liaisons when travelling to Dar es Salaam on trading trips. Some have begun to be active in the clinic and women's groups and are discussing such matters more openly than before. Yet people recognise that many of their health problems come from poverty, particularly the inability of many to obtain not only a healthy and balanced diet, but even sufficient food to fill the stomach; it also comes from over-work, especially that of women.

Exclusion from Development

A further danger mentioned by many people at the village level concerned the feeling that they were being left further and further behind, not only in terms of global, but even national comparisons. They bemoaned what they saw as the backward state of Mafia. When asked what development or progress (*maendeleo*) there had been since my last visit, most said that there had been very little, if any at all and some people even said 'we are going backwards'.

There is widespread recognition that for things to change for the better, education is vital. Mafians are excluded from the few existing job opportunities by their low levels of education, and this also means that it is more difficult for most villagers to participate in decision-making processes. Yet for people at the village level, education is a major problem. Although virtually all children now attend primary school, which means that most are now literate, very few go on to secondary school, and even among those who do, there is a high drop-out rate. So far none of the children of the island's sole secondary school has gone beyond Form IV.[1] Some young people have managed to take courses which have qualified them in a variety of professions, such as health workers, primary school teachers or village-level government officials but these are a small minority. Furthermore, training courses which a few years ago admitted primary school leavers now demand at least a certificate for Form IV if not Form VI, which at present is beyond the reach of most villagers.

Loss of existing rights, loss of 'our culture'

Finally, another perceived risk comes from some of the new developments themselves. People talked about the building of tourist hotels or the set-

---

1. Equivalent to GCSE, taken at age 16 after 11 years of schooling in the British system.

ting up of prawn farms more in terms of loss than gain. Such developments might involve the loss of access to land, whether it be a path over a salt flat, or the use of a beach for fishing-related activities, or even the loss of land altogether through the sale of trees which confer land ownership rights. At the same time, many people complained that their rights were being trampled upon by people higher up: they feel that they are disregarded and if they go to complain, they do not receive justice.

But concern was not only with material factors, it was also, particularly on the part of the older generation, a concern about their way of life[1]. For example, many had seen tourist hotels in the south of the island, or on the mainland, or in Zanzibar, and they worried about what the influence of foreign tourists – improperly dressed, consuming alcohol, turning them into objects by photographing without permission – might be on their young people.

So whom do they blame for their current situation? Who is deemed responsible? Who can help? And who can be trusted?

3. Local Perceptions of Trust and Blame

Discussions about trust and blame revolved around people's ideas about the government (at several levels); NGOs and cooperative groups; households, families and kin networks; neighbours and fellow villagers; 'we Swahili'; God and the individual him or herself. In this section, I consider each of these in turn.

Trusting and blaming the government

The majority of people at the village level felt that the government had a major responsibility for ensuring their well-being and that the present government was not fulfilling its function.

Extract 3 from interview with a woman in her thirties

> *You see the state of things here. There is no one who has even a couple of lakhs[2] in their house. Poverty has really entered.*
> *Q. So how do you manage?*
> *We live, we pray.*
> *Q. And whose responsibility is that?*

1. Cameron too in this book refers to the growth of a nostalgia for the past alongside globalisation.
2. One lakh of Tanzanian shillings is worth U$100.

The main responsibility is that of the government.
Q. So how do you think your taxes are spent?
We are told it is spent on the villages! But we only get bits and pieces!
Q. Do leaders come here to Kanga?
Yes, they do and they see what's going on but they don't actually DO anything.

Extract 4 from interview with a middle-aged woman

Q. And how does the government come in?
The government has to come in. For example people were having to pay T.Sh. 2,000
fees p.a. for primary school, now they've stopped the payment of fees (as a result of
protests and the drop in numbers of children in school).

Extract 5 from interview 2 with another middle-aged woman

Q. What drives development? (maendeleo)
The government has to be involved. For instance, if people don't cultivate [they have
to make them] – previously the Agricultural Officer used to come and tell people to
plant crops [now he does not].

Extract 6 from Interview 7 with older woman

Everyone has to want to improve their own lives, but the government has to
come in as well. You need help, a foundation, something to start with...

I asked many informants what they thought of free market policies. Few
were in favour, but the following reply also indicates a particular view of the
appropriate role of government:

Extract 7 from interview with middle-aged man

Q. What do you think of free market policies?
The government should be like a kind of father who has to feel pity for his children
[and look after them]. *If you just leave it to others, they'll do whatever they like.*
So I don't like the current policies.

Several points emerge from such interviews. One is that major responsibility is attributed to 'the government'. This however is seen to operate differently at different levels. Whereas some people thought that the village government tries to be helpful and is approachable, there is a recognition that
important matters are decided elsewhere. Hence there is criticism of local
leaders for apparent failure to 'do something', and particularly to communicate local problems to leaders higher up. But there is also criticism of the

people at the top for selling off national assets, for not using taxes to the benefit of the villagers, and for implementing policies which negatively affect local people. These include allowing imports which lessen the market for local products, taking away controlled pricing for food and imposing charges for medical treatment [at the District level and beyond]. In short, they see the government as 'irresponsible', to use the felicitous term of the Tanzanian scholar Chachage.

Most importantly, the main discourse for talking about state-local relations is one of corruption, the perception of which colours most dealings between village people and officialdom. Some of the many stories are probably true, but the point is that people believe all of them to be true, they hear everything said by officials in this light: 'we are being consumed' (*tunaliwa*)[1] was a frequent phrase. As a result, government officials, who are almost invariably from the mainland and therefore 'strangers', find it very difficult to motivate people because the premise is that officials are acting in their own interests, and that they, the 'small people', cannot get anything they want unless they can pay bribes. Here is a sample of statements from villagers:

Extract 8 from interview with middle-aged man

> *Our leaders are all strangers here. They haven't come to raise the place up, but to get their own profit... They treat the place like a field – they harvest and leave... They get their millions, we get ripped off. We weep, we can't do anything, while they get their income.*
>
> *There is a major problem here – all the big people are outsiders (to the island) and they 'eat'. Occasionally they have local friends who benefit a bit (wanarambaramba – literally 'lick'). The people here [on Mafia] are not educated, they are backward, so the others do as they like.*
>
> *Q. What about the members of the District Council?*
> *A. They try, but they are not educated, so they are not equal [to the appointed officials], the educated and the uneducated are quite different (hawalingana)... [For example] Most of the money for the road was 'eaten' – you see its state now.[2] Similarly with the airport. The big and the little people conspire to defraud. They use our money as they like, they build their big houses...*

At the official level, the rhetoric was, of course, quite different. It was frequently argued that policies had to change – the government could not possibly pro-

---

1. "Being eaten" means both being the victim of corruption, and also being bewitched. Compare Bayart 1993.
2. See Caplan 2004.

vide everything that people needed, they had to do a lot more for themselves. Furthermore, in theory planning was now supposed to come from below, not from above, as a senior government official on the island stated:

> People have to realise they can't depend on the government any more – they have to help themselves. So we don't give government loans any more – that just didn't work... We can request the [national] government to give us extra assistance. For example, take a local school... The people build it themselves, but they ask for government help with materials and the District Council may also give something.

This view is echoed at a village meeting:

> Let me finish by saying that these days we have to start things ourselves, then the government will come in and help. For the government of today, we have to show our own efforts (juhudi zetu wenyewe) first.

Such views are clearly in conflict with one in which the government is seen as being 'like a father who cares for his children'.

One way of thinking about trust is through a consideration of exchange. Exchange is a moral issue, and previously accepted moral values are being vitiated at all levels, from that of the household to the state and beyond. Things are different today not only because exchange has been commodified but because it is totally distorted and unequal – economically and politically. For example, Mafians feel that they work hard to produce a cash crop, but that not only do they fail to get a fair price for it, but the free market policies have allowed competition from imported cooking oil to the detriment of coconut prices. They are required to render respect to the government, but in return, it not only fails to help them but inflicts on them rent-seeking behaviour. Hence the discourse about state-local relations is essentially one of 'corruption'.

Trust and blame – 'civil society'

One of the tenets of neo-liberal thinking which has captured development experts and been widely exported is that it is important to encourage the growth of 'civil society', a point also discussed by Cameron in this volume. Formerly socialist regimes, in particular, are thought to suffer from a dearth of civil society institutions, which are viewed as necessary to mitigate the power of the state, and harness the energies of the people (see Putnam 2000). Indeed, the rise in the number of NGOs in Tanzania, both local and international, has been dramatic. To some extent, this has been encouraged by government policies which have sought assistance wherever it might be forthcoming as can be demonstrated in the case of health care on Mafia, where a plethora of international aid agencies operates.[1] Foreign aid agencies and NGOs see themselves as working in partnership with governments and their agencies. As a result, there may be little local awareness of the role of multilateral agencies, since much of the funding provided is directed through government channels. According to a UNICEF officer:

UNICEF works alongside NGOs at the District level. In Mafia infant feeding activities are being supported by UNICEF through the District Planning Officer, the District Executive Director and the District Medical Officer.

Here we see what Gupta and Freguson (2002) have called 'the privatisation of the state' and the serving of non-state organisations as 'horizontal contemporaries of the organs of the state'. Hardt and Negri (2000) even argue that such international institutions constitute a new form of governmentality or 'sovereignty' as they term it.

Local NGOs such as Chamama and MICAS (see footnote 3) have also been established, but they are constantly seeking links with and funding from the international NGOs since it is very difficult for them to raise funds locally. The same UNICEF officer continued:

On Mafia, CARE, whose office is in the Coast Region capital Kihaba, is also beginning to work with local NGOs. They have done surveys of all NGOs and checked them out to ensure they are not just 'brief-case', that is, people who are setting up NGOs just to tap money.

Current government policy is also to encourage self-help through the formation of cooperative groups (*vikundi*) set up to work on particular projects, particularly income-generation. For example, in one village where I have carried out research, there are a number of income-generating women's groups and men's fishing groups. The latter are somewhat more successful than the former because they have a ready market for their produce, both locally and in Dar es Salaam. The leader of one such group commented:

We've been in existence for some years. There are six of us, and some of us are related. We fish with nets from an outrigger canoe. We divide the money from the catch into two: one part is kept in reserve to do repairs, buy nets, rope, etc. and the rest is divided equally. Currently we plan to buy a sail in DSM – that will cost T.Sh. 10, 000 [approx. U$10].
Q. Where do you sell your fish?
A. At the ferry in DSM.

---

1. CARE, UNICEF, DANIDA, World Wildlife Fund, DFID (Department for International Development UK), NORAD for example.

Even in this context, however, profits remain fairly small. Women's groups tend to be even less successful, as the following conversation with a member of a group of ten women which came together in 2000 reveals:

Extract from interview with Women's Group 1

> *Q. Why did you start this group* (kikundi)*?*
> *To improve our lives a bit* (kuendesha maisha kidogo)…
> *Q. So what are your needs?*
> *We want a sewing machine and then we could learn to sew and make some money, but we have no capital - we also need money to buy things like pots and khangas from DSM to sell here. We have discussed these things with [the NGO] CARE and sent our request but we haven't had a reply yet…*
> *Q. There didn't used to be such groups, did there?*
> *No, but now life has become harder*
> *Q. In what ways?*
> *No food, no clothes, no money!*

Another group had been in existence since my previous visit in 1994, when they had been involved in digging a well in their neighbourhood. I asked the Secretary about their current activities of making mats:

Extract from interview with women's Group 2

> *Q. Where do you sell your products?*
> *Ah, that's the problem. We get only T. Sh. 2,000* [approx. U$2] *for each mat sold here [in the village]. If we ask someone to sell them for us, he'll want his profit.[1] There is no market here* (soko hakuna)*!*
> *Q. Isn't there any way that you could improve your market?*
> *We were told that we should get together with all the groups in our village and the neighbouring one and send a request to the government.*

In short, then, for the most part, forming co-operative groups was not seen as the answer to women's economic problems. Women's groups are limited by their lack of capital, lack of spare time, and lack of market for their finished goods. They are forced to use male middlemen to take their goods to sell in Dar es Salaam for three or four times the price they receive.

---

1. Mats sold in Dar es Salaam for between T.Sh 6–8,000, i.e. 3 to 4 times as much.

Trust and blame in households, families and kin networks

To what extent do kin relations remain a major area of support for individuals, or has this situation changed over the last few years? There is certainly a perception that increasing poverty has obliged people to restrict their assistance, especially financial, to close kin only. Even within households, many women find that they have to depend increasingly upon themselves in order to buy clothes, considered to be the responsibility of the husband under Islamic law, because the poverty of many men makes it very difficult for them to support their wives. And, as I discussed recently (Caplan 2000), the rate of marriage has actually fallen and, after a first divorce, many women remain unmarried, either by choice or from necessity.

In 2002, I asked a friend in the village to give me his annual budget, as I have done on each of my visits over several decades. He has two wives, and several children and grandchildren live with him. At one time, he would have expected to provide new clothes for each of them at least once, preferably twice a year. This time he didn't even know the price of a dress:

A. *I haven't bought one for ages.*
Q. *Don't you still have to buy new clothes for everyone each year?*
A. *[These days] you might go a whole year and not buy anything.*

Most women do not blame men for this situation. As one said: 'Life is hard these days – we have to help each other'. But in addition to complaints about poverty and lack of ability to give assistance, there were many complaints that people's ideas about sharing and cooperation had also changed as the man quote above noted:

In the old days people helped each other more. They'd get together in cultivation groups of 10–15 – now they want money or they don't help. And these days they don't get on with each other (hawasikilizani). *And in marriage too – everything is a mess* (mambo yote yamepaparikapaparika). *The times have changed – it is the end of the world. Everything has changed. Only your close family helps you these days.*

His views were shared by a male Islamic religious leader:

Q. *What are the differences between today and when you were young?*
Everything then was good. There were good relations with the elders, when you cultivated, you got a good harvest, when you fished, you caught something, when you prayed, you received [what you asked for]. The world has changed because people don't respect each other, they are drunkards, adulterers etc. so God has taken his blessing (baraka) *away from them.*

He went on to complain about relations between the generations:

> The young people think we know nothing. They call us older people madinge (dinghies) – we are just small boats pulled along by big ones!

Another older male informant also criticised the younger generation:

> I am worried: the customs of this village will break down (desturi za mji zitavunjika). For example, did you see the pictures[1] my son put up on the wall (of their tea-shop)? I don't like them at all, or the kind of videos[2] they show here, or the drinking...
> Q. What about the future for your children?
> It will be worse – the things they want are not good.
> Q. What do you think they want?
> To go with the times (mwendo ya kisasa), that's what they want. They scorn our customs (desturi), they might not even greet you respectfully (kukuamkia). And if you do want your children to do something, you have to ask them quietly, and if they refuse, it's between them and you [i.e. you can't order them about like you used to do].

Part of this gulf between the generations is not only to do with wider social changes, but is also connected to earning capacity. Until a few years ago, men gradually accumulated capital in the form of coconut trees by planting, inheriting and buying. In this way, they were able to earn cash and support their households. Control of cash gave fathers and husbands considerable authority in the household. Today, they can no longer do so while young men can earn more from fishing, especially diving for lobsters. But young men do not want to spend their income supporting their natal households – they want consumer goods such as radios, watches, bicycles and smart clothes, and to spend their evenings watching videos.

Blaming Swahili culture

Earlier in this paper, I cited the view that local culture should be protected from undesirable foreign influences. Yet sometimes in the course of a discussion about why things were not going well, people would blame Swahili culture. 'You know what we Swahili are like' is a self-deprecating phrase I

---

1. They were cut-outs from newspapers and magazines – sports stars, female models, cars.
2. In his village two enterprising youths had purchased a TV monitor, a video player, and a generator. They regularly screened videos, which they obtained from the district capital, in a large purpose-built hut, and charged admission to the youths who came. The videos ranged from kung-fu, through comedies, to Islamic sermons.

have heard many times over the years. What did people mean by this? That people would seek to take advantage of a situation, put their own interests first. As one man put it: "Here there's a lot of back-biting (*fitina*), that's our character, we Swahili people". It is widely thought that people would suffer from the jealousy (*wivu*) of others if the latter did better than they did. For this reason, secrecy is highly cultivated – gifts are given in private, with promises of not telling anyone, lest they too come and demand.

Yet such negative views of Swahili values are outweighed by ideals[1] which state that people should help each other, respect each other, speak the truth, as indeed many do.

Trusting God, blaming oneself

It was not uncommon to hear, when someone died, that the death was 'God's work' (*kazi ya Mungu*'. Similarly, people might attribute the 'state of the times' (*wakati*) to God's will: 'the times have changed – it's God's work only'. Some saw AIDS as a punishment or test from God, who is said, as in the quote above, to have withdrawn his blessing because of people's bad behaviour. Such attitudes are not simply examples of fatalism, which deny agency to human beings. People do recognise that they have agency, even as they attribute power to God. This gives them the right to complain about those whom they consider have let them down. But it also means they have the responsibility to take action themselves, especially in terms of work and self-control. A number of men, in particular, criticised others for not working hard enough. While conceding that times were hard, they argued that those who cultivated as much land as possible or engaged in fishing could make a living, albeit with difficulty:

> Q. *Why do you think people keep saying that life is hard?*
> Because they don't work hard enough. Once they've reached a certain age, they rest on the verandah.
> Q. *But surely that's only men, not women?*
> That's true.

The second area in which the individual was thought to carry responsibility was in terms of sexual mores. Many people who were asked about HIV/AIDS said that the only solution was the control of sexual urges and restricting relations to a single partner. Here is part of a conversation with a young woman:

---

1. For a discussion of Swahili ideals and their breakdown, see Saleh, 2004.

Q. Do you think life will be harder or easier in future?
Harder because of AIDS. People may die before their children are grown.
Q. What can you do to stop this?
You have to depend on yourself, control yourself.

Summary and discussion: Responsibility trust and blame

In all of the areas mentioned above, people bemoaned what they saw as a diminution in trust. Government policies have changed, and so have the methods of implementing them. Government officials were blamed for being corrupt, for caring only about their own welfare, for misusing public resources. Many thought that the Village Government, even the District Government, was ineffectual, since decisions were made at the top, in spite of the rhetoric which said otherwise.

Civil society such as NGOs and cooperative groups were not seen as the complete answer – they need government or some other forms of outside assistance to be able to achieve their goals. Even people who previously could have been counted on – kin, neighbours, fellow villagers – no longer gave support or showed sympathy for troubles. Kin were seen to be overwhelmed with their own problems and unlikely to help, which means that people are forced back on to trying to help themselves. So whom do they blame for their current state of increasing poverty, for the *maisha magumu* that most of them have to put up with? While, as shown above, there is frequent blaming of the government and its policies, especially in terms of a discourse of corruption, blame is also laid closer to home. "We Swahili" is a phrase frequently used in the context of a negative evaluation of Swahiliness which suggests that some of 'our problems' are also 'our fault'. Further, while people often say that everything which happens is God's work, they also suggest that God's ways cannot be fathomed – they are beyond human knowledge. But there is a category of people who can be blamed – witches (see Caplan 2003).

4. Managing Risk: Modernities and Occult Economies

When a team of witch-finders[1] arrived on Mafia in the summer of 2002, they were welcomed in many villages. In one northern village, at the end of a funeral, a group of men attending put forward a resolution that the vil-

---

1. Historically, witch-finding movements have arisen regularly in East Africa in the 20th century, usually during times of rapid change. See Richards 1935, Schoenman 1975.

lage should invite the witch-finders and pay for their services. I discussed this with a village official:

> *Yes, 80 people said they wanted them. There are witches* (wachawi)[1] *who frighten people and make them ill – we want to stop this.*
>
> *Q. Have they come before?*
>
> *A. No not these people but some others called Matoroka came when I was young, a long time ago.*
>
> *Q. What do they do?*
>
> *A. They take out the things which make people suffer* (kutesa). *They take out stuff like bottles and charms from houses.*
>
> *Q. What happens then?*
>
> *A. Nothing, we are not like the people in some parts of the mainland where they kill witches* (see Mesaki 1994). *They [witch-finders] just remove things and go away.*
>
> *Q. So will everyone agree to their coming?*
>
> *A. It looks like it, judging by the meeting yesterday. Some illnesses … can't be recognised by the hospital but they can play their rattles and find out what the problems are.*
>
> *Q. Where are they from?*
>
> *A. I think they are from the Rufiji. They will have to come via the village office to be given permission. They have been to Jibondo Island and other parts of the south, now they are in the north of Mafia.*
>
> *Q. I have heard many people say that there isn't the same trust as before and that people don't agree between themselves like they did – what do you think?*
>
> *A. It's not about the administration* (utawala), *it's about people persecuting each other* (kutesana), *things have really got worse in terms of witchcraft and people's wickedness* (mambo yamezidi, uchawi, ubaya wa watu).

Discourses of corruption and witchcraft have much in common, they are even talked of with a common vocabulary – that of 'being eaten'. But there are also differences: in the first, blame is laid externally, on the government and its officials, while in the second, it is laid internally, on the community itself.

The classic anthropological literature on witch-finding suggests that historically, such movements tend to arise at times of acute social upheaval and change. They were a notable feature of colonial Africa, interpreted as being the result of new institutions and socio-economic breakdown. Thus they

---

1. In this conversation, the term *mchawi* (usually translated as 'witch') was used, but others, as is seen below, used the term *mwanga*, which is often translated as 'sorcerer'. In the conversations around the topic of the witch-finders, people used either term.

need to be studied over the *longue durée*, and via continuities as well as discontinuities, as Niehaus (2001) has done for the Lowveld of South Africa.

The recent global proliferation of what has come to be termed 'occult economies' includes discussion of a wide variety of beliefs and practices such as witchcraft, zombie conjuring, the sale of body parts, and other satanic practices. Such occult economies have also been analysed by Ashforth (2002) for South Africa, as well as Geschiere (1997) for West Africa. The Comaroffs note: 'Magic has become as much an aspect of mundane survival strategies as it is indispensable to the ambitions of the powerful' (2001:21) while other commentators such as Fisiy and Geschiere (1996 and 2001) and Geschiere (1997) suggest that the rise of such 'occult economies' is often linked to the inability of the state to look after its citizens either economically or politically. In other words, *it has a material basis.*

This was clearly recognised by some of the village people with whom I discussed the current perceived lack of trust between kin and neighbours:

> Q. *Why do you think there is a lack of trust?*
> It comes from problems and lack of basic needs (shida na dhiki). *People can't support themselves, let alone others.*
> Q. *Do you think poverty has increased?*
> Yes, definitely. We can't depend on anything now.
> Q. *So you can't depend on coconuts any more?*
> No, that's when trust disappeared.

'Occult economies' are not, of course, unique to Mafia Island, but are found in other parts of Tanzania, as the work of Sanders on ideas of human skin trafficking (2002), or White on vampires (2000) demonstrates. Sanders argues that many Tanzanians have experienced their recent involvement in the 'free market' with great ambivalence since some have greatly enriched themselves while the vast majority have instead been excluded from novel forms of wealth. This has led to increased speculation – in some areas expressed in idioms of occult-related trafficking in human skins – about new relations of production, accumulation and consumption, and people's differential access to these processes through occult means. Sanders concludes: "These are not simply a mis-recognition of capitalism or the workings of the economy, but metaphysical speculations about the origins of value" (ibid:16). He shows that ordinary Tanzanians reject the claims of 'efficiency' promulgated in structural adjustment programmes, and their amoral stance. 'They argue that recent changes raise a host of moral and moralizing questions that demand attention: at whose expense do market reforms come? Who wins? Who loses? Is this desirable? Is it acceptable?' (ibid:162).

Green suggests that it is the very 'normativity' of witchcraft which has negative consequences, deflecting attention from the political causes of misfortune (2004: 2): 'it contributes to a culture of suspicion and mistrust of kin and neighbours' (ibid:11). Her argument raises important issues around distinctions between 'real' and imagined causes of misfortune:

> If witchcraft as an institution complements a politics which denies responsibility for social outcome in the south, and which deflects blame for misfortune back onto the local communities who suffer, [then] witchcraft suppression institutions must be re-evaluated as contributing to the entrenchment of witchcraft, not so much as a public good, but as a public bad (ibid:12).

Green argues that, by their insistence on cultural relativity, anthropologists have colluded in a double standard, in which it is legitimate to criticise the negative effects of imported practices and institutions, but unacceptable to subject indigenous institutions to the same critical scrutiny (ibid:13). Yet my research makes it clear that people *do* recognise the imperfections of their government and the machinations of the powerful, and they *do* understand the material basis for their present misfortunes. So why then turn to witchcraft as an explanation? One reason may be concerned with agency. It is actually very difficult for people at the bottom of the socio-economic hierarchy to do very much about the workings of the local or national state, to counter corruption or to challenge policies. Even the much-vaunted multipartyism has left the same ruling group in power. But using witch-finders does allow for a modicum of agency – it allows blame to be allocated and dealt with, in short it is an apparently effective form of risk management.

It is also a way of talking about the moral community, including about how kin and neighbours *should* behave towards one another, but today do so more rarely, largely because they do not have the means to do so. In his study of *sorcellerie* in the Cameroons, Geschiere notes:

> Witchcraft and sorcery remain very important in modern contexts in Africa. Its discourse bridges the gap between the domestic community and the large scale processes of change with possibilities for enrichment but also new forms of dependency that are all the more frightening because they appear to be impersonal (ibid:24–5).

He quotes the French priest, anthropologist and initiated *nganga* Eric de Roisny, who argues that witchcraft discourse does not express an opposition to modern developments as such, rather it is a concerted attempt to make life in modern circumstances 'more liveable' (ibid: 221). Moore and Sanders likewise argue that it represents 'thoroughly modern manifestations of uncertainties, moral disquiet and unequal rewards and aspirations in the contemporary moment' (2001:3). They conclude that 'Witchcraft and the occult in Africa are a set of discourses on morality, sociality and humanity: on human frailty. Far from being a set of irrational beliefs, they are a form of historical consciousness, a sort of social diagnostics' (20). In this respect, they are following the earlier ideas of Mary Douglas that witchcraft, like risk, is a 'forensic' concept.

Conclusion

In most societies, there is a harking back to a past 'golden age' when people's lives were better. This is as true on Mafia as elsewhere, and I have heard elements of the discourse I discussed above on previous visits. On this occasion, however, there were differences. One was in the prevailing view of government and politicians as corrupt, the other was in the levels of pessimism people expressed. Most people look to the future with fear. 'We will eat grass' is how one man (actually a civil servant) put it, after lamenting the sale of national assets to foreigners. I asked many people what they thought the lives of their grandchildren would be like: 'Perhaps good, but more likely harder. They will have to scrabble for a living' and 'We are finished, we will die' (*Tumekwisha, mama, tutakufa*) were typical replies. In short, the past was better, the present is worse, and the future will be worse still.[1] Given such cataclysmic views of the future, it is not surprising that ways need to be found of conceptualising it. Some of the discourses such as witchcraft practices are readily to hand even as they are used in new ways. But, like earlier times, such discussions are essentially ways of talking about morality.

This is the issue that emerges from many of my discussions with people on Mafia about what is happening to them and why. So what is a moral community? Whether at the level of the nation-state, the village or the household, it is one in which trust resides, and people take responsibility both for other people and for their own behaviour. For Mafians, a government which is 'selling the country', or a relative or neighbour who does not

---

1. This is similar to what Ferguson (1999/2004), writing of the Zambian Copperbelt, calls 'abjection': 'a sense that the promises of modernization had been betrayed and that they were being thrown out of the circle of full humanity' (2004:140).

fulfil their obligations, is not behaving morally. While they recognize their responsibilities to 'respect the government', they argue that the government no longer looks after them, as is evidenced by policies around education and health, and by the practice of corruption. And fellow villagers and neighbours who do not fulfil their obligations may be considered as witches. What all this suggests is that ideas about witchcraft and other occult economies are an intrinsic part of modernity, indeed, Moore and Sanders (2001) have argued that such beliefs and practices are actually *constitutive* of modernity.

So where has this discussion taken us? I have sought to listen to local voices, and allow them to speak, but have done so in a framework of anthropological theory on risk, particularly that which acknowledges that all risk (or perception of it) is socially constructed, and is thus a result of human agency. The voices tell us of the risks and dangers in their lives, but they also tell us whom they trust, and whom they blame, and why. In talking about trust and blame, they invoke notions of morality, moral behaviour, the moral community. Their own village community is subject to the policies and politics of the wider community, ranging from the District to the nation-state and beyond.

The processes which are described here involve a diminution of trust at many levels. This is expressed in two parallel discourses: corruption, in relation primarily to external agencies, especially the 'irresponsible state' and witchcraft, which relates to those which are internal. Both, as Douglas has suggested, are forensic tools, both bespeak views of morality. However, when one is at the bottom of the socio-economic hierarchy, corruption is difficult to counter, and although resistance can be and is offered, it is rarely successful. Witchcraft, on the other hand, like other occult economies, offers a modicum of agency, and through cleansing rituals, the promise of a renewal of the moral community.

Acknowledgements

Earlier versions of this paper were presented at the Department of Anthropology, University of Oslo; Centre of African Studies, University of Cape Town; Institute of Social and Cultural Studies, University of Oxford. I am grateful to all of the participants, as well as those attending the 2005 Swahili Workshop, for their useful comments and especially want to thank Lionel Caplan, Owen Sichone and Greg Cameron. I am also grateful to the Nuffield Foundation for financing my research and the Tanzania Council for Science and Technology (COSTECH) for granting me permission to carry out fieldwork.

References

Abrams, Ray, 1994, "Introduction" to his edited book *Witchcraft in Contemporary Tanzania*. Cambridge: Department of Social Anthropology

Arce, Alberto and Norman Long, (eds), 2000, *Anthropology, development and modernities: Exploring discourses, counter-tendencies and violence*. London and New York: Routledge.

Ashford, Adam, 2002, "An Epidemic of Witchcraft? The Implications of AIDS for the Post-Apartheid State", *African Studies* 61; 1, pp. 121–142.

Bayart, Jean-Francois, 1993, *The State in Africa; the politics of the belly*. London: Longman.

Caplan, Pat, 1998, "La vie politique en mutation d'un village cotier de la Tanzanie" in F. le Guennec-Coppens and David Parkin (eds), *Autorite et Pouvoir chez les Swahili*. Paris: Karthala, IPRA, Nairobi. pp. 77–97.

Caplan, Pat, 2000, "Monogamy, polygyny or the single state? Changes in marriage patterns in a Tanzanian coastal village, 1965–94" in C. Creighton and C.K., Omari *Gender, Family and Work in Tanzania*. Aldershot: Ashgate cop.

Caplan, Pat, 2002, "Anthropology as a moral discipline: Social justice, ethics and human rights" keynote lecture given at the Canadian Anthropology Society Conference, *Social justice, culture and power*, University of Windsor, Canada (available on http://homepages.gold.ac.uk/pat-caplan)

Caplan, Pat, 2003, "Witchcraft, terrorism and risk", unpublished paper presented at the University of Stellenbosch.

Caplan, Pat, 2004, "Struggling to be modern: Recent letters from Mafia Island" in P. Caplan and F. Topan (eds), *Swahili Modernities*. Lawrenceville, NJ: Africa World Press.

Comaroff, Jean and John Comaroff, 2001, "Millenial capitalism: first thoughts on a second coming" in their edited book *Millenial capitalism: The culture of neoliberalism*. Durham and London: Duke University Press.

Dahl, Gudrun, 1999, "On consuming and being consumed" in Fardon et al. (q.v.)

Douglas, M., 1992, *Risk and Blame: Essays in cultural theory*. London and New York: Routledge.

Fardon, Richard, Wim van Bimsbergen and Rijk van Djik, (eds), 1999, *Modernity on a shoestring: Dimensions of globalization, consumption and development in Africa and beyond*. Leiden and London: EIDOS.

Ferguson, James, 2004, "Global disconnect: abjection and the aftermath of modernism" in J.Z. India and R. Rosaldo (eds), *The Anthropology of Globalization: a Reader*. Oxford: Blackwell (extract from his 1999 book *Expectations of Modernity*. Berkeley: University of California Press).

Fisiy, Cyprian. F. and Peter Geschiere, 1996, "Witchcraft, violence and identity: Different trajectories in post colonial Cameroon" in R. Werbner and T. Ranger (eds), *Postcolonial Identities in Africa*. London: Zed Books.

Fisiy, Cyprian. F. and Peter Geschiere, 2001, "Witchcraft, development and paranoia in Cameroon" in Moore and Sanders 2001.

Geschiere, Peter, 1997, *The Modernity of Witchcraft*. Charlottesville and London: University Press of Virginia.

Green, Maia, 2004, "Discourses on Inequality: Witchcraft, Poverty and Public Bads in Post-Adjustment Tanzania", unpublished paper presented at the ASA-USA, New Orleans, November.

Gupta, A.K. and James Ferguson, 2002, "Beyond 'culture': space, identity and the politics of difference" in Jonathan X. India and R. Rosaldo, *The Anthropology of Globalization: a Reader* Oxford: Blackwell (extract from Guypa and Ferguson (eds), *Culture, Power, Place: Explorations in Critical Anthropology* Durham, NC: Duke University Press, 1997).

Hardt, Michael and Antonio Negri, 2000, *Empire*, Harvard: Harvard University Press.

Mesaki, Simeon, 1994, "Witch-killing in Sukumaland" in R. Abrahams (ed.) *Witchcraft in contemporary Tanzania*. Cambridge African Monographs. Cambridge: African Studies Centre.

Moore, Henrietta and Todd Sanders (eds), 2001, *Magical Interpretations, Material Realities: Modernity, Witchcraft and the Occult in Postcolonial Africa*. New York and London: Routledge.

Niehaus, Isak, 2001, *Witchcraft, Power and Politics: Exploring the Occult in the South African Lowveld*. London and Sterling, Virginia: Pluto Press; Cape Town: David Philips.

Putnam, David, 2000, *Bowling Alone: The Collapse and Revival of American Community*. New York: Touchstone, Simon and Schuster.

Saleh, Mohamed Ahmed, 2004, "'Going with the Times': Conflicting Swahili Norms and Values Today" in Pat Caplan, and Topan, Farouk (eds), *Swahili Modernities*. Trenton: Africa World Press, p. 145-155.

Sanders, Todd, 2001, "Save our skins: structural adjustment, morality and the occult in Tanzania" in Moore and Sanders 2001.

Sardan, J-P. O. de Sardan, 1999, "African corruption in the context of globalization" in Fardon et al. 1999.

White, Luise, 2000, *Speaking with Vampires: Rumor and History in Colonial Africa*. Berkeley and Los Angeles: University of California Press.

CHAPTER 12

The Role of Islam in the Political and Social Perceptions of the *Waswahili* of Lamu

Assibi A. Amidu

Introduction

The present study is built around the *Kimondo* verses gathered in 1975 in Lamu and the views of Mr. Omar Maka of Lamu.[1] The verses were published in Amidu (1990). Since then thematic aspects have been published in Amidu (1993, 2003, 2004). The present study looks at the influence of Islam on the political and social perceptions of Lamuans in the past and present. We will begin by giving a brief introduction to *mashindano* poetry and the *Kimondo* among the Waswahili. After that, we shall examine the theocratic nature of Islam and its influence on the political and social perceptions that Lamuans have about Lamu and their relations with non-Lamuans. We shall also take a look at the relationship between Lamuans and business opportunities, wealth, poverty and Islam. The study will conclude that the Waswahili of Lamu, whether or not they regard themselves as Lamuans, are keenly aware of their rights and heritage and wish to be involved in decisions about what is good for themselves as well as for Lamu generally.[2]

---

1. Bwana Omar Maka, a Lamuan, is a carpenter by profession. He used to work at Lamu Secondary School. I had asked him to comment on reports on the internet to the effect that there was severe hunger along the Kiswahili coast of Kenya and that people had died as a result of it. I also wanted to know the current state of life in Lamu and what Lamuans thought of events in Iraq and Palestine. His letter to me is dated 27th November 2004. I thank Bwana Omar Maka sincerely for finding time to respond to my questions and for the meticulous answers he sent to me. I thank the organizers, participants and discussants of the 6th Swahili Workshop 2005 in Oslo for their invaluable comments on my presentation. I am extremely grateful to Alena Rettova of Charles University in Prague for reading through the draft and offering me very useful comments. Finally, I thank Kjersti Larsen for final comments on the revised draft. Except where indicated, all translations in this paper are my work. All shortcomings are, however, my own.
2. In this study, a Lamuan is a person who is by definition Mgunya or Gunya or Mbajuni or Bajuni. He or she also claims close historical affinity with the Mijikenda,

Mashindano poetry and the Kimondo among the Waswahili

The Waswahili have a long tradition of written literature dating back to the 17th century. We can imagine that before the rise of the written literature, much of the literature of the people was oral. Poetry occupies a central place in the literary culture of the Waswahili. Both in the old days and to this day, it was and is recited and performed in public, especially at the *ngoma* "dance" sesssions or on important occasions and at ceremonies. In modern times, the poets make use of both live performances and electronic recordings to get their messages across.

The Kiswahili poetic tradition has a special sub-component known as the *mashindano* "competitive" verse contest (Amidu 2004). A key characteristic of the competitive verse form is the dialogue that takes place between competing poet-singers. The poet is also a spokesperson for the section or the community or the society in which he lives. The contest usually takes the form of one poet or group of poets challenging other poets or members of the society to a duel of public poetic performance in song or intonation. The opposition accepts the challenge, willingly or unwillingly, and responds in poetic song or intonation too. The goal in all cases is to draw attention to matters of principle that the poet-singer or the society holds dear and which require some discussion amd debate.

The participants in the *mashindano* need not perform at the same venue or at the same time. But once the audience hears the initial poem in song or intonation, they wait eagerly for a response from the person or persons affected by it. When a response does come, it signals that a competitive dialogue has been set in motion and will end with one party as victor of the duel. Thus on these occasions of *mashindano* song-intonation and/or dance competitions, orality says something about the Waswahili, their society and their way of life, both positively and negatively.

Among the Waswahili generally, poetry, whether written or not is intended to be performed orally. Because of this, Kiswahili oral literature has continued to flourish within the East African homeland of its speakers and, hence, it is one of the pillars on which Kiswahili culture and values rest.

---

irrespective of other affinities that may exist. The term Mbajuni or Bajuni is more widely used today. A distinction is made between the two terms Mgunya or Gunya and Mbajuni or Bajuni on Lamu Island and this has been referred to in Amidu (1990:64–65). Parkin (1989:165) also refers to the Lamuan as Gunya. The Gunya or Wagunya and the Bajuni or Wabajuni are, therefore, the Waswahili indigenous or native inhabitants of Lamu, at least so they claim themselves. They spread northwards to Rasini island and to the mainland (see also Parkin 1989:165–166, Amidu 1990:64–65).

Paradoxically, therefore, native written Kiswahili poetry is founded on an oral performance premise. It is the only premise that guarantees that the Waswahili will accept the performance as good literary art and appreciate its message.

Oral performance has several attractions. One of these is that it allows its practitioners to bring their art live to an audience in addition to saying something meaningful or debatable about themselves and their surroundings. In my view, orality includes the electronic media as a substitute for face-to-face performances. Following Hagège (1985), Ricard makes the following point about orality:

> In the first place, orality involves the phonic reality – breathing, panting, cries – of the human voice that becomes incantations, imploration, invocation and abuse. Each of these forms corresponds to a rhythm and a particular intonation that is recognized in every language and culture (Ricard 2004:30–31).

Ricard names other features of orality, which we will not go into here. Among the Waswahili, orality in verse can be divided into two parts: a) rigid metrical verse and b) free "metrical" verse. The former type is definitely inspired by oriental traditions of verse composition, while the latter is more properly "native" and was/is probably indistinguishable from dance verse-songs used at initiations, weddings, childbirths, wakes, and so on (Harries 1962, Knappert 1979, Amidu 1990).

This study is primarily interested in a particular sub-component of the *mashindano* verse-song tradition, which is called the *Kimwondo* or *Kimondo* verse tradition (Amidu 1990). The *Kimondo* verse tradition is a tradition of satirical verse-songs or verse-intonations, but its scope extends over a wider area and embraces all forms of satire in the Kiswahili language. The development of satire in Kiswahili and in Lamu is discusssed *in extenso* in Amidu (1990:25-39, 43–48). In this introduction, we wish to mention particularly that it was in Lamu, specifically the Lamu East constituency as it was in 1974–75, that the name *Kimondo* was used to refer to the body of Kiswhaili literature, both oral and written, that is known as "satire". Mahmoud Ahmed Abdul-kadir, also known popularly as Mau, of Lamu is the poet who "outdoored" the word and made it "acceptable" as a literary term. Researchers who visit Lamu Island in Kenya can still find him at his bakery. Amidu (1990) brought the adapted use of the term *Kimwondo* or *Kimondo* to the attention of the rest of the world. In short, the basic meaning of the term *Kimondo* is a "shooting star" or a "falling star'. It has added semantic extensions to its meaning, among which is the concept of satire (Amidu 1990:43–45).

One of the areas where one is likely to find the *Kimondo* in active use among the Waswahili, particularly in Lamu, is in the political theatre and in matters of topical social and religious interest, such as corruption, problems of leadership, and inappropriate or even scandalous social and religious behaviour by individuals and groups of individuals, whether they are Waswahili people, government officials, or just residents among the Waswahili. The place of Islam in modern Kiswahili culture figures prominently in *Kimondo* verses. The use of the *Kimondo* is a favourite tool of poets in Lamu, but various versions can be found in all the Waswahili enclaves of the East African coast. With regard to politics, consider the following:

> The *Kimondo* verses are aggressive verses in the satirical genre. The term *kimondo* itself means a shooting star with a blinding flash. Its aim is to blind the enemy, and expose his or her weaknesses, lay bare failings to public scrutiny so as to allow an electorate to make an informed choice (Amidu 2004:160).

The best *Kimondo* genre is, therefore, essentially satirical-dialogue poetry that goes beyond just political discourse. It may be used for social, communal or interpersonal goals too. One of its earliest recorded practitioners was Fumo Liyongo of Pate. *Fumo* means "chief" and this means he belonged to royalty. Noone knows for certain when Fumo Liyongo lived. Some place him as early as the 11th century, others the 12th century or the 13th century and others even place him at the time of the arrival of the Portuguese, hence between the 15th and 16th centuries A.D. (Harries 1962, Knappert 1979). With reference to the *Kimondo* and Fumo Liyongo, consider also the following:

> Throughout the long history of Swahili literature and in many of the literary works whether written or oral, the satirical genre formed an important aspect of the Swahili social, political, and religious development. ... The "Utendi wa Liyongo" gives the reader a fascinating insight into Swahili social and political life of the time of Liyongo. But the saga is made even more interesting by Liyongo's deliberate taunts of his half-brother Mringwari who despite ascending the throne lives in fear of the redoutable Liyongo and plots to put him to sleep for good. The whole epic revolves around this saga and the tragic end of the hero, Liyongo, killed by his own son in return for a wife promised him by Sultan Mringwari. Not only does the Sultan renege on his promises, but the son is viciously taunted until he runs away to his mother's hometown in Galla country. What is intriguing then is the power of the satire: firstly it is used by Liyongo himself to put fear in his half-brother's breast. For, as one attempt af-

ter another is foiled, so the songs of Liyongo have biting sarcasm, and secondly the satire is used by Liyongo's admirers against his murderous son until he goes into a self-imposed exile (Amidu 1990:6).

The *Kimondo* satirical dialogue verse feeds on controversy and debate about political, social and religious propriety and events, which fire the poet's indignation or praise. A *Kimondo* debate ignited in this fashion does not die down until one party to the dialogue throws in the towel. A *Kimondo* event therefore allows the Waswahili to discuss their shared values in the open and arrive at a consensus that will guide future behaviour and conduct by the members of its community. It is a healthy outlet for pent up feelings and a medium for praising good conduct, public or private, condemning bad ones, and suggesting a better alternative that fits Kiswahili values and culture. Reasoned argumentation in satirical form that has a satisfactory outcome for all members of a society or community is better than needless violence, destruction, endless acrimony and recrimination. This is the basic rationale behind *mashindano* competitions in the *Kimondo* satirical-dialogue tradition. The failure of African discourses in Sierra Leone, Liberia, Côte d'Ivoire and even Ghana and Nigeria, Somalia, Uganda, Darfur in Sudan, the Democratic Republic of the Congo and Zimbabwe, to name a few, reveals just how fortunate the Waswahili are in having an artistic and literary mechanism for engaging in peaceful discourse about almost every aspect of their lives.

The Theocratic Nautre of Islam among the Waswahili

For the Waswahili generally, everything and everyday begins with Islam and ends with it. No aspect of life is useful or meritorious unless it is centred on Islam. In short, for the Waswahili, Islam is knowledge and knowledge is encapsulated in Islam. The verses below illustrate how important religion, specifically the Islamic religion, is in the life of the Waswahili.

1.	*Watu wote na majini*	All human beings and Jinnees
	hangewaumba Manani	would not have been created by God
	illa sababu ya dini	but for the sake of religion.
	ya fahamu sana haya.	This much you must understand.
2.	*Shikamana na ibada*	Adhere to the rites of worship.
	uifanye ndio ada	Make them your daily ritual
	utaepuka na shida	and you will escape misfortune
	na kheri kukujalia.	and be blessed with happiness.

3.   *Hangekuumba Khallaki*   The Creator only created you
       illa ufuate haki   to follow the path of righteousness.
       aloumba Khalaiki   It is he who created mankind
       na kulla lilo na ndia.   and everything that moves about.

(Knappert (1967:14, verses 1–2, 4)

The message of the verses above is quite clear. All created beings are on earth for just three reasons: to follow Islam, to praise and worship their maker, the Almighty God, and to be righteous Muslims. In addition, it is the duty of every Mswahili to uphold and defend Islam when it is threatened from within or without. It is the duty of every Muslim to defend his or her right to worship God. It is also the duty of every Muslim to defend his or her right to live a just and religious life. These duties, obligations and rights form collectively the *jihad* concept of Islam.[1] The *jihad* concept also implies that committing injustice against others in the name of Islam is forbidden. In like manner, it is not legitimate or proper to deprive any Muslim of his or her natural rights, lands and properties, and so on. If the individual transgresses the laws of the land or goes against the dictates and the will of God and his beloved prophet, Mohammed, then he or she may be punished for his/her crimes.

The Mecca Perception in Lamu

Muslims everywhere have their holy sites or towns or cities. The principal one in Islam is Mecca, followed by Medina and then Jerusalem. In all these places, one finds the most important and holy mosques of Islam. In addi-

---

1. The Islamic Foundation (1975:5) tells us about *jihad* in Islam as follows:

> *Jihadi n'kujipinda kwa uweza ulonao ili kuyashika mafundisho ya Kiislamu na kujitahidi kuyatekeleza katika jamii. Kwa namna Jihadi ilivyoelezwa ndani ya Qurani na Suna, n'jambo lililofuatana na nguzo za Imani. Kuishika ndia ya Mwenyezi Mngu n'kuutumia wakati wako na nguvu zako na mali yako ili kuipeleka mbele Dini ya Haki. Hwenda ikambidi Islamu kuifilia dini yake awe Shahidi, bora aihifadhi Haki. Jihadi ndio nia ya kukitoa ulichonacho, hata maisha yako, kwa ajili ya Mwenyezi Mngu.*

> 'Jihad consists in doing everything in one's power to follow the Islamic teachings and to try to carry them out within the society. According to the interpretations given in the Qur'an and the Traditions, *Jihad* is something that goes hand in hand with the articles of Faith. To follow the way of the Almighty God means using one's time, energies and wealth to advance the cause of the Righteous Religion. The Muslim might be called upon to die for his/her religion and be a Martyr; in that case it is better for him/her to defend Righteousness. *Jihad* also implies the concept of giving all you have, even your life, for the sake of Almighty God.'

tion, sites on which mosques stand are deemed hallowed and sacred by the followers of Islam. When we look at the Kiswahili coast, we learn from the *Kimondo* no. 2 that Lamuans and other Mulsim inhabitants of Lamu regard it as a holy town. They believe strongly that Lamu town is the holiest site of Islam in Kenya and Eastern Africa. Lamuans further believe that their town was and is one of the holiest Muslim towns in the Islamic world (Amidu 1990:103–104, 2003:259). Indeed, Lamu is also a centre for the celebration of important Muslim feasts and holidays. Every year, Lamu town celebrates the *Maulidi* and the *Miiraji* with grace, dignity and fervour. Lamu is a centre of Muslim devotion, teaching and activities for Lamuans and Eastern African Muslims. The poet Mahmoud Ahmed Abdul-Kadir, alias Mau, describes Lamu in glowing terms in his *Kimondo* no. 2 as follows:

4.	*Kwani sote twafahamu*	For we all know
	mji wetu hunu Lamu	this Lamu town of ours
	ni muyi ulo muhimu	is a very important town
	kwenye Kenya yote pia.	known throughout the whole of Kenya.
5.	*Lamu yetu maarufu.*	Our Lamu is very famous.
	Ni muyi wa uongofu.	It is a town of righteousness.
	Watu wengi wausifu	It is greatly praised by many people
	katika yote dunia.	throughout the world.
6.	*Jinale limetangaa*	Its fame has spread so far
	Hata umeitwa taa.	that it is called a beacon.
	Nuru yake huzagaa	Its rays shine forth brightly,
	muangawe huenea.	and its luminous light reaches afar.
7.	*Ndio kituo cha dini*	It is the citadel of the religion
	kwenye mkoa wa pwani.	on the whole of the East Coast.
	Hata nchi za jirani	Even the neighbouring countries
	Lamu waizingatia.	think and talk about Lamu.
8.	*Jumla ya kusifika*	To crown its praises,
	hata imeitwa Makka.	it is even called Mecca.
	Wageni wengi hufika	Many pilgrims come here
	Maulidini wakaya.	to attend the *Maulidi* celebrations.[1]

(Amidu 1990:103–104, verses 233–237)

We see that Lamuans perceive their town as a Mecca of Islam.[2] In this situation, citizens, religious and political leaders of the town are expected to

---

1. On celebrations of the *Maulidi* in East Africa, see Knappert (1971:41–48).
2. In a conversation with Abdulaziz Yusuf Lodhi of Uppsala University in Sweden during his recent visit to Trondheim, in October 2004, he disclosed that as far as he could remember, members of his family and people from Zanzibar used to travel to Lamu for the *Maulidi* celebrations. He says up to this day, people from

exhibit a very high standard of social and political morality in their daily lives and in their public and social functions. In short, political and religious leaders are expected to be paragons of virtue in the holy town of Lamu and to guide the faithful through the dark maze of worldly illusions, follies and vanities called *ghururi* (Middleton 1992:164, 168–170). A successful Lamuan must, therefore, be imbued with the *Mecca perception* of Lamu. It is the leader's ability to live up to the Mecca perception that endears him or her to Lamu's Muslim inhabitants.

The Paradox of the Mecca of East Africa

The Waswahili of Lamu expect that visitors to Lamu will embrace and respect its "Mecca" status, its Mecca perception of life and its Kiswahili hospitality. The expectation is particularly strong among inhabitants who regard themselves as Lamuans. And yet, at the same time, Lamu is a key and central tourist destination in Kenya. Every year, the tourist industry brings to Lamu people who are not concerned with matters of religion, and do not care about the so-called Mecca status and perception that Lamu's native Muslim inhabitants have about their own town and Islands. Because of this, tourists tend to violate the Islamic holiness of Lamu and infuriate its inhabitants. The Waswahili of Lamu and Lamuans in particular, therefore, frequently lament the steady rise in sinful activities in the town and on its Islands. We find this lamentation echoed in Lamu's *Kimondo* verses of 1975 (Amidu 1990). In 1975, the MP Abubakar Madhubuti who was facing re-election was blamed for the decline in morality because of his liberal and tolerant views and attitude towards the industry (Amidu 2003). His opponent, Mr. Mzamil Omar Mzamil, was regarded as an example of a good Muslim. Today, Mr. Abubakar Madhubuti is a retired old man who is not a major actor on Lamu's political and economic landscape. Nevertheless, the decline in moral values ushered in by the tourist industry continues. Mr. Omar Maka, my friend in Lamu, has written to inform me about the following:

Upande wa utalii. Utalii ni mzuri. Wale Wazungu wa kuingia na kutoka wa-
naleta faida fulani lakini hawa wa kununua majumba wengi wao ni waharibifu.
Wengine wanataka kufanya Lamu ni Head uuarter ya Mashoga katika ulim-

all over Eastern Africa, including Zanzibar, still troop to Lamu for the festivities because they believe that Lamu is a sort of Mecca. Hence a pilgrimage to Lamu is as good as a pilgrimage to Mecca. This account confirms the sentiments expressed by Lamuans about the holy status of their town in the Muslim world.

*wengu. Mfano Mzungu mmoja amenunua jumba kubwa Mkomani kazi yake ni
ushoga na anaitwa Bw. Malik. Hili jina amejibandika hapa hapa Lamu. Yeye ni
Muamerika Mweusi* (pers. communication).

About tourism. Tourism is good. Those white people who come and go bring
us some benefits, but many of those who come to buy mansions are wreckers.
Many of them want to turn Lamu into the Head Quarters of Homosexuality
in the world. For example, a certain "Whiteman" has bought a huge mansion
at Mkomani, his only occupation is homosexuality and he is called Mr. Malik.
He took this name, right here in Lamu. He is an African American.[1]

Leadership and Riches in Lamu

To be a rich person, an investor, a pragmatic businessperson, a devout
Muslim and son or daughter of Lamu at the same time is very difficult. We
have seen that the MP of the Lamu East constituency during the by-election of 1975 was Mr. Abubakar Madhubuti. He was narrowly defeated in
the parliamentary elections of 1974 by Mr. Mzamil Omar Mzamil. Mr.
Abubakar Madhubuti's sub-party within the then sole ruling party KANU
(Kenya African National Union) was called NDEGE "aeroplane', while his
opponent's sub-party within the same party was called SAA "clock'.

Mr. Madhubuti was, by Lamu standards, a very rich man. It was agreed
by all that his wealth was God given. Mr. Madhubuti was however accused,
by a section of the Lamu electorate, during the run up to the by-election
of 1975, of using his vast wealth in a manner that went against Islamic
teachings. For example, he opened a beer bar called *Baada ya Kazi* "After
Work" right on the sea front of Lamu, close to the pier, the landing site for
pilgrims to the Mecca of Eastern Africa (Amidu 2003:261–266). This was
viewed as a very serious and grievous sin and a major defect in a Muslim
son of Lamu.

The paradox of Lamu's status is that the same landing pier was and is
the gateway through which hundreds of non-Muslim tourists enter Lamu.
Their goals and interests are mundane. They come to Lamu to have a bit of
fun and relaxation. Catering for the interests of tourists was and is, how-

---

1. My attention has been drawn to the fact that the term *mzungu* has several sub-
senses. It could mean "a foreigner, a stranger, a Westerner, a tourist, etc." who is
not necessarily a white person or European. Indeed, it could also mean an educated
African with a certain social status. The translation "whiteman" is designed to capture these nuances of meaning without losing the primary or original sense of the
word. Furthermore, Mr. Maka's expression *Muamerika Mweusi* refers to a specific
individual who is an African or Black American. It will not be appropriate to infer
any other meaning from his expression in this study.

ever, not an excuse for a Lamu Muslim to open a public house of sin and debauchery in the holy town, at least in the view of Lamuans.

Mr. Madhubuti also built a cinema, which he named *Zinj*, quite close to a mosque (Amidu 2003:259–261). We know from § 2 and footnote 3 above that every Muslim, whether devout or not, knows or is supposed to know that a central purpose of existence on earth is *ibada* "worship" (see Topan, this volume). Not surprisingly, therefore, Lamuans and other Muslims, especially the devout ones, complained that the cinema was a distraction to the faithful. In addition, among Mr. Madhubuti's perceived transgressions against Islam, he was accused of flaunting his wealth and sharing it with crooks and unscrupulous people. According to his opponents, his wealth had gone completely to his head and he had become vain and fallen into the trap of folly and illusion. For all these reasons, Mr. Madhubuti was not praised for his business acumen or for trying to gain a foothold in the tourist industry or for his attempts to create jobs for Lamu people. He was rather rebuked. For example, *Kimondo* no. 2 accuses Mr. Abubakar Madhubuti of the following:

9. *Alisema mara nyingi*   He has said often enough that
    dini na mila hachungi.   religion and tradition he cares not for.
    Zimemghuri shilingi,   Money has corrupted him,
    zimempotea ndia.   and led him off the straight path.
    (Amidu 1990:89, verse 73)

A true Muslim cannot be an atheist or dispense with his or her religion, namely *dini*. When the Muslim is from Lamu, devotion to Islam is no longer a matter of choice but an obligation. Thus, if the accusations above are correct, then at the height of his success and opulence, Mr. Madhubuti, it is suggested, forgot the basic and common exhortation to the faithful that is embodied in (1) above and repeated below as (10).

10. *Watu wote na majini*   All human beings and Jinnee
    hangewaumba Manani   Would not have been created by God
    illa sababu ya dini   but for the sake of religion.
    ya fahamu sana haya   This much you must understand.

In the Eastern African Mecca, devotion to prayer and worship of God ranks higher than satisfying the mundane needs of fellow human beings, especially the needs of non-Muslims for cinemas, public houses and brothels. Liberal interpretations of the commandments of Islam are also not favoured by some Lamuans. Thus the poet of the *Kimondo* no. 2 tries to warn Mr. Madhubuti about the consequences of his actions as follows:

11. *Amesahau kabisa*   He has completely forgotten
    kuwa ajali ikisa,   that when this life is done,
    aloyachuma mapesa,   whosoever has amassed wealth,
    hapa hapa utalia.   there and then he/she will begin to weep.

12. *Huko hakuna wakili*   Yonder there will be no defence counsel
    Mbele ya Mola Jalali.   before God, the exalted one.
    Ni zile zako amali   It is only your deeds on earth
    ndizo zitakutetea.   which will be your defence.

13. *Mambo huwa ni mazuri*   Your ordeal will in fact be pleasant
    ikiwa walitenda kheri.   if you did good things in your life.
    Kiwa walifanya shari,   If you were engaged in villainous acts,
    motoni utaingia!   you will be thrown into Hell fire.

14. *Wala hatujisifu*   We are by no means bragging here
    ya kuwa ni watukufu.   that we are men of great dignity,
    Hatutendi lilo chafu   or that we do not do baneful things
    kabisa hata moya.   at all under every circumstance.

15. *Lakini kitendo chake*   But he has the unfortunate habit
    husaidi wenzi wake   of assisting his fellow men
    kumuasi Mola wake,   to disobey their God,
    na kuhalifu sharia.   and break the Sharia laws.[1]

(Amidu 1990;91, verses 96–100)

---

1. The religious conduct and actions of Mr. Madhubuti are condemned even though the poet acknowledges that he is a capable and astute leader, as the following verses in *Kimondo* no. 2 show:

    141. *Na wala hatuizi*   And we do not deny that
         kuwa aziweza kazi.   he is competent in his work.
         Lakini hazitimizi,   But he never gets them done,
         ndilo hilo twatukia.   and that is what we resent.

    142. *Uwezo unao kweli*   He certainly has the power
         sumu kufanya asali.   to turn poison into honey.
         Lakini ni watu mbali   But it is always to other people
         ndio huwasaidia.   that he does these favours.

    143. *Watu wa wilaya hini*   But as for the people of this district,
         huwaona hayawani.   he regards them as mere brutes.
         Wengine awathamani   But he values outsiders a great deal
         mno kuwatumikia.   and renders invaluable services to them.

    Ironically, verses 141–143 above seem to suggest that if only Madhubuti had made Lamuans and Muslims his close associates and partners, they would have looked upon his so-called religious transgressions favourably or at least with less resentment.

From (11–15), it appears that the Mecca perception makes it difficult for Lamu's rich men and women to exploit investment opportunities offered by the tourist industry, the only major industry on the Islands. It also prevents Lamuans, in particular, from seeking jobs in significant numbers in the industry. This attitude inhibits the development of Lamu district by Lamuans. The Mecca perception allows non-Muslims, both Kenyans and non-Kenyans, to dominate the only viable industry on the Islands of Lamu thus compounding the poverty of many Lamuans and Muslims. At the same time, investors and workers who are not native to Lamu get richer and richer. Thus, the religious convictions of a good number of Lamuans keep them out of the lucrative aspects of the tourist trade. Has the situation changed since 1975? Mr. Omar Maka provides the assessment below.

> *Kuhusu kufungua hotel kwa watu wa Lamu hata mmoja hakuna alie miliki hotel yoyote isipokuwa hizi ndogo ndogo kama zile za kawaida tu. Bali Wazungu wenyewe! Kuna Mjerumani mmoja ana hotel kubwa inayoitwa Palace Hotel, iko ndani ya mji, pwani kabisa, na inauzwa beer, whisky na wenyeji wanatumia mkoma kama kawaida* (personal communication).

With reference to ownership of hotels by Lamu people, there is not a single one who owns any hotel, except these rather small ones, just like the common types (of lodging houses). It is rather the White people alone (who own hotels)! There is a German here. He has a huge hotel called Palace Hotel. It is in town, right on the sea front, and beer, whisky are sold there, while the natives drink palm wine as usual.[1]

The passage above reveals that many years after the *Kimondo* verses appeared, the ownership of large hotels is still in the hands of foreigners and new ones have sprung up. The hotel industry seems to exacerbate and worsen the plight of Lamuans and the Waswahili of Lamu generally by creating a big contrast between the life of affluence and wealth of tourists and the ordinary and humble life of the Waswahili generally. In addition, the imposing hotels with their non-Muslim lifestyles within and also without their

---

1. In many countries in Africa, it is believed that only the wealthy and elite with good incomes can afford the cost of whisky and non-native beers. Native alcoholic drinks, such as palm wine, are associated with the poor and low income earners. Mr. Omar Maka is suggesting that those who can afford to patronize foreign owned hotels, whether they are Muslims or not, are the well-off in Lamu. The poor or less endowed are the natives of Lamu who depend on native alcoholic drinks. Mr. Omar Maka skifully illustrates, by his example, the gap between the rich and poor in Lamu, whether or not they are Muslims defying Muslim reservations about the use of alcohol.

walls depreciate the status of Lamu as a holy town in addition to depriving the holy town of its valuable lands.

The government of Kenya or investors, or both, could explore new types of investment opportunities, but they seem uninterested in alternative ventures. Their interests centre on ventures that yield quick high profit margins. At the same time, it is the quick high profit yielding ventures forbidden by Islam or operated along unIslamic lines, in the view of devout Muslims, which often offend the sensitivities of Lamu's Muslims. It seems fairly clear that the kinds of investments that Lamuans and the Waswahili of Lamu could partake in attract little capital support. On the one hand, therefore, Lamu's native inhabitants feel increasingly marginalized in their own holy town and squeezed out of the economic competition in their district. This subject has been discussed *in extenso* in Amidu (2003:267–268). On the other hand, the doctrines of the Islamic religion and especially the perception of Lamu as a holy town make it difficult for Lamu's native inhabitants to renew themselves and take advantage of investment opportunities on their Islands. The resultant inequality of life and resources only worsens their personal wellbeing. And yet paradoxically, religion is the only thing that brings Lamuans hope and comfort in their daily lives.

Poverty, Religion and Renewal in Lamu

One of the common complaints of the electorate during the Lamu by-election campaign of 1975 was the lack of job opportunities in the town and on the Islands. The electorate wanted jobs, better schools, good health posts, good drinking water, regular and reliable electricity supplies, access to land for agricultural activities and the availability of cheaper goods and services. These demands were repeated during the run up to the elections of 2002 (see also Amidu 2003:266–268). KANU has since lost power to NARC (National Rainbow Coalition) led by President Mwai Kibaki. So the question is whether the situation and conditions under which Lamu people live will change for the better now that a new government has been installed in Nairobi. Mr. Omar Maka provides us his personal assessment of the situation below:

> *Kuhusu Raisi wetu Bw. Kibaki ana uzuri wake, ana ubaya wake. Mwai Kibaki anajitahidi kurejesha mali yaliyoibiwa na serikali iliyopita kwani serikali iliyopita, wabunge na mawaziri waliyo kuwako wamenyakuwa mashamba na mali mengi, hata katika Lamu Barani na Visiwani wana siasa wamefaulu kupata mali mengi wakitumia vyeo vyao. Kwa mfano ukija Lamu ukitembea upande wa Fisheries uk-*

ielekea Shela kumejengwa majumba na mahoteli ya Wazungu ambapo wameuz-
iwa na wana siasa, hizo ni kazi kubwa sana kuzirejesha kwa serikali ama kwa
wananchi kuzipata tena. Kwa hivyo maskini anaendelea kubaki masikini (personal communication).

With reference to our President Mr. Kibaki, he has his merits and demerits.
Mwai Kibaki is trying to return properties stolen by the previous government,
because in the past government, members of parliament and government ministers stole farms and lots of property, especially on Lamu Mainland and on the
Islands: politicians have succeeded in acquiring a lot of wealth by using their
office. For example, if you come to Lamu and walk towards Fisheries and towards Shela, mansions and hotels belonging to White people have been built.
Politicians sold them to them. So, it is a very huge task to revert ownership to
the State or for the citizens to recover them again. For this reason, the poor
man continues to remain poor.

We learn from Mr. Maka that the standard of living of the average Lamuan
has gone down and deteriorated dramatically. The downturn started under
the former regime of KANU led by ex-President Arap Moi and has continued under the present regime of NARC. The significant part of Omar
Maka's assessment is that "maskini anaendelea kubaki masikini" namely
"the poor man continues to remain poor." Mr. Maka continues his analysis
of the state of Lamu by observing that,

Kuhusu maendeleo, Raisi Kibaki hajafanya kitu chochote. Maji na stima ndivyo
vitu vinavyosumbua sana watu wa Lamu, hata wewe ukija utatembea gizani,
hakuna viwanda vyovyote kisiwani isipokuwa vile vya kutengenzea mafuta ya nazi
na uvuvi wa watu binafsi kama wale wanaovua kwa madau yao. Kazi inayoende-
lea sana ni ya Carpentry kwani kumewekwa viwanda vingi zaidi na watoto wengi
wamejiunga nazo. Hayo ndio maendeleo yalioko Lamu pamoja na punda nao ni
wengi katika kisiwa cha Lamu. Na isitoshe upande wa elimu nao umeendelea ku-
wekewa shule za msingi bure, isipokuwa tunalipa elimu za upili. Juu (ya) malipo
ushuru pia umeongezeka. Lamu haiwezekani kufanya biashara kama huna gari au
boti; gharama ya kuvuka ni Shs. (50) kwa mtu! Mbali mizigo, pia kuna gharama
ya K.P.A. ambayo ina miliki bahari. Kwa hiyo Kibaki atashindwa kuendesha
(personal communication).

When it comes to progress, President Kibaki has not done anything yet. Water
and electricity are the things that are plaguing the people of Lamu a great deal.
For example, if you come to Lamu today you will walk in darkness, and there
is not a single industry on the Island, except those for pressing coconut oil, and
individual fishing enterprises, such as those who use their own native fishing
boats. The enterprise that seems to be thriving is carpentry because very many
workshops have been opened and many young people have registered with

them. These are the developments in Lamu together with donkeys, and there are many of them on the Island of Lamu. In addition, with regard to education, they continue to expand free primary education, but we have to pay for secondary education. On top of these expenses, come taxes, which have also gone up. It is not possible to do business in Lamu if you have no vehicle or boat; the fare of a ferry is now Shs. 50 per person! This does not include his/her load and then we have the levy to the K.P.A., which controls the sea routes. Because of this, Kibaki will fail to steer the State.

Note the grim prediction to the effect that "Kibaki atashindwa kuendesha", namely "Kibaki will fail to steer the State." It is clear from the above accounts that Lamuans and the Waswahili of Lamu in general feel not only left out of the sharing of the national cake but helpless and impoverished too. The complaints raised in the *Kimondo* verses of 1975 with regard to jobs, affordable living conditions, water, electricity, affordable transportation and industrial development have still not been addressed. At the same time, at every step of the way, the entrepreneur must stop to reflect on the fate of his or her soul and the approval of religious leaders.

Squeezed by the government's development policies which go against the Mecca status of Lamu and by religious conservatives who see the new kind of knowledge and development flowing into Lamu as threats to Kiswahili and Islamic forms of life, Lamu's entrepreneurs and business persons have become handicapped and paralysed. Lamuans, and indeed other Muslim inhabitants, wish to make progress in all aspects of life and enjoy the same quality of life that is found in larger cities like Nairobi, Dar es Salaam, Mombasa and Kampala. However, the more they perceive certain forms of tourist oriented development in Lamu as threats to their Islamic values, the more they tend to seek refuge and solace in religious commandments and practices. Their Mecca perceptions appear to provide them salvation from their plight vis-à-vis the harsh realities of modernisation and modern times.

Religious Knowledge, Local Politics and Palestine

Religion for Lamuans and the Waswahili of Lamu does not stop in East Africa. Lamu people see themselves as part of the Islamic community of the world. Whatever happens to any member of this community is a matter of grave concern to them. Any disaster or tragedy in one part of the Muslim world sends shock waves throughout the Waswahili communities of Eastern Africa. Sometimes, they even live in fear that a fate that has befallen Muslims in one part of the world might also befall them. Consider, for example, Lamu's by-election of 1975. The Lamu East constituency by-election was essentially a local matter. But, somehow, the survival of Lamu within the Muslim world was dragged into the election campaign. In short, it was argued that Lamu's status as the Mecca of Eastern Africa necessarily means that voters need a leader who is a strong and reliable defender of the faith of Islam against its enemies.

In the *Kimondo* no. 2, the poet Mr. Abdul-Kadir, who supported Mr. Mzamil, saw a threat hanging over Lamu. The alleged threat came from Israel and the local MP, Mr. Madhubuti. He linked the predicament of Lamu under Mr. Madhubuti with the predicament of Palestine under Israel's occupation and rule. It was during Mr. Madhubuti's period of stewardship that Kikuyu people were brought into the Lamu enclave, specifically into the area in and around Mpeketoni in the Tana River basin, to farm in the river basin. The Lamu MP, Mr. Madhubuti, supported the settlement policies of the government. But most Lamu citizens saw this as a threat to their way of life and an encroachment on their lands. In addition, the migrants were not even Muslims. It is during Israel's occupation of Palestine that Jewish settlements have mushroomed in the Palestinian territories in defiance of international public opinion. Consequently, Mr Madhubuti metamorphoses into the agent of doom of Lamu. That is, it is alleged that he has been sent by Jews to destroy Lamu and Islam (see (24–27) below). The poet begins by arguing his case in the *Kimondo* no. 2 as follows:

16.	*Na mambo haya mazuri*	And for all these beautiful accolades[1]
	kuna viumbe mashari	there are evil beings,
	kabisa hawakukiri.	who have not accepted this situation.
	Wataka kutufutia!	They are bent on wiping us out!
17.	*Wamefanya ghadhabu,*	They are in great temper,
	wataka kuyaharibu.	and want to destroy all we have.
	Hutafuta kisababu	They are looking for an opportunity or excuse
	ya dini kutuvundia.	to break up our religion.

(Amidu 1990:104, verses 238–239)

In the verses above, Lamu has attracted the attention of the enemies of Islam. Their goal is the destruction of Islam, and with it all the holy places including Lamu. The poet singles out the Jews of Israel as the enemies of

---

1. The accolades that the verse refers to are the qualities and virtues that make Lamu attractive to Muslims. They are listed in (4–8) above. Alternatively, see *Kimondo* no. 2, verses 233–237.

Islam and of the Lamu people by tracing Lamu's plight back to the plight
of the Palestinians as illustrated in the verses below.

18.	*Na mipango kama hini* *yalifanyika zamani.* *Na huko Palastini* *ndiko ilikoanzia.*	And such a plan was drawn up long ago. And it was over there in Palestine that it all began.
19.	*Mayahudi waliona* *nchi hiyo imefana.* *Mitukufu lake jina* *sifaze zimeenea.*	The Jews saw that this land was prosperous. Its name was time honoured, and its fame a household word.
20.	*Wakaanza taratibu* *kwa kuwaghuri Warabu.* *Pesa nyingi za ajabu* *wakawa huzitumia.*	They began gently by beguiling the Arabs. Staggering amounts of money were poured into the area.
21.	*Wakanunua piloti,* *kwa malukuki ya noti.* *Wakazimwaya senti* *aridhi kununulia.*	They bought plots of land, with bundles of notes. They poured in millions of cents to buy land for themselves.

(Amidu 1990:104, verses 240–243)

According to the account in *Kimondo* no. 2, Jews hoodwinked the
Palestinians with lots of money and bought up much of their lands. As
the Waswahili say, "*Mlevi wa mvinyo hulevuka, mlevi wa mali halevuki*"
(Sacleux 1939: 571). The saying means "A person drunk on wine sobers up,
but one intoxicated by wealth never does'. Thus, the Palestinians, intoxicated by the massive wealth that the Jews in Israel were allegedly doling
out to them in exchange for their lands did not sober up in good time. And
when they did, they discovered that their lands were gone. In this manner,
the Jews in Israel gained control over most parts of Palestine. The *Kimondo*
no. 2 tells us what happened next.

22.	*Wakisa kufanikiwa,* *ziwanda kuvinunuwa,* *wenyewe waliwatowa,* *wao wakajikalia!*	As soon as they succeeded in this venture, and had bought up all the factories, they then drove all the inhabitants away, and settled there themselves.
23.	*Na tokea siku hizo,* *kumekuwa ni mzozo,* *na mingi mno mikazo* *ya kuwadhili raia.*	And from that day onwards, there has raged a conflict, resulting in several oppressive acts aimed at subjugating the Palestinian people.

(Amidu 1990:104, verses 244–245)

The poet's message is unambiguous. Lamu town has attracted the attention of the Jews in Israel. For this reason, the fate that befell the Palestinians is almost upon Lamu, the Mecca of Eastern Africa. The *Kimondo* no. 2 links Madhubuti with Jewish interests in the following manner:

24.	*Na sisi sasa twaona*	And now we can see
	ametumwa huyo bwana,	that this man has been sent,
	kiswa niliokinena	as the events I have described show,
	kwetu kuja tufanyia.	to come among us and do us likewise.
25.	*Twawajua Mayahudi*	We know that Jews
	ni wakubwa mahasidi	are great enemies
	wa dini ya Muhammadi.	of Mohammed's religion.
	Hawapendi kusikia.	They never want to hear about it.
26.	*Ni wao walomtuma,*	It is they, who have sent him (Madhubuti),
	wakamwambia simama,	and have urged him to contest the seat,
	nao wasimame nyuma,	while they stand in the background
	kwa pesa husaidia.	and help him out with money.
27.	*Jamani na tufahamu,*	Countrymen, let us understand this,
	kuna hatari adhimu	there is an impending grave disaster
	atakalo likitimu	which he wants to bring to fruition
	naye bunge akingia.	once he manages to get back to the *Bunge.*

(Amidu 1990:104–105, verses 246–252)

We have seen that Mr. Madhubuti supported the settlement of Kikuyu farmers and their families in and around Mpeketoni, the fertile forested swathe of land on the Lamu mainland in the Tana River basin. The goal was to speed up food production in order to minimise the seasonal effects of drought and hunger that often plague the Kiswahili coast of Kenya (Amidu 2003:249–256, for discussions). The settlement policy was badly received by Lamuans. It was seen as a threat to Lamu's survival as a holy town. The majority of Lamuans soon began to picture in their minds a stream of "foreign migrants" from abroad and inland arriving on the Island and in the holy town with large purses. They are poised to buy up lucrative plots of land that belong to ordinary Lamuans of Lamu district. This picture of things to come was enough to sow panic among the electorate.

The comparison between the settlement policies in Lamu and those in Palestine worked wonders. And the suggestion that Jewish interest groups had a hand in it was very persuasive. In matters of religion and politics, knowledge, truth and fact are not what matter but belief, fear of the unknown, and conviction.[1] To put an end to the perceived threat against Lamu and allay their own fears, all that Lamuans and their supporters needed to do was to prevent Mr. Abubakar Madhubuti from winning the Lamu East seat by denying him their votes. The *Kimondo* no. 2 puts it this way.

28. *Hawezi kupata kitu*   He cannot get anything
     kiwa tutafanya utu   if we act with manly courage
     zote hizi kura zetu   and all these votes of ours
     Saani tukizitia.   we cast into the box for Saa.

     (Amidu 1990:106, verse 258)

And so, Mr. Madhubuti lost the by-election (Amidu 1990, 1993, 2004). Mr. Madhubuti's activities and interests in free trade, investment and free movement of labour were interpreted by a section of Lamu as little more than a policy for selling out Lamu to foreigners, whether they were Kenyans or non-Kenyans.

The conflict between the Palestinians and the Jews of Israel is no doubt oversimplified in the *Kimondo* account.[2] But it was enough to persuade many Lamuans and their Muslim and non-Muslim supporters, among other things, to vote for Mr. Mzamil Omar Mzamil, the opponent of Mr. Madhubuti (Amidu 2003). Did Lamu people succeed in preventing the anticipated take over of their lands by Kikuyu settlers? Here is Mr. Omar Maka's update on the status of Lamu lands today.

Jambo lingine, ukabila umeingia. Serikali imekuwa ya Wakikuyu. Wao sasa wananyakuwa ardhi, hata kuiba pia. Serikali, mawaziri ni wale wale kwa hivyo sina mengi.

Kuhusu hawa Wakikuyu walioletwa wana faida na pia hasara lakini hasara ni kubwa kuliko faida. Hapo mwaka (1975) Wakikuyu waliletwa (17,000). Sasa wamekuwa 50,000. Wametukaribisha kupita idadi ya wenyeji na pia wamekuwa matajiri kushinda wenyeji kwa upande wa ardhi ambayo ndio mali katika Africa. Na wakati wa Moi aliweza kuwazuia wasiingie zaidi lakini sasa wanaingia kwa

---

1. The argument for the removal of Mr. Madhubuti from the Lamu East Constituency seat on the grounds that he is an agent of Jews is clearly not founded on any shred of truth. It is dictated simply by political expedience. The use of political expediency is found all over the world. For example, the argument for the invasion of Iraq in 2003 and the toppling of its regime by the United States and its allies was based on expediency. It was founded, with hindsight, on belief, fear of the unknown and conviction without the backing of truth and facts.
2   If the Kimondo verses had come to light today, the SAA sub-party of KANU, its supporters and poet would be the objects of accusations and innuendoes. This is on account of their support for the Palestinians and their claim that Jews in general are enemies of Islam who are out to destroy it and Lamu too.

nguvu hadi Manda pia tunapokonywa polepole - watu WaAmu hawalimi (personal communication).

Another thing, tribalism has become endemic. The government is now a government of the Kikuyu. Today, it is they who are taking over our lands, and even steal portions too. The government and the ministers are the very same people, for this reason, I have nothing more to add.

And concerning the Kikuyu people who were brought here, they have their advantages and also their disadvantages, but their disadvantages outweigh all their advantages. Originally (in 1975) the Kikuyu who were brought numbered 17,000. Today, they are about 50,000 strong. They have almost overtaken the total number of indigenous people and in addition they have become richer than the indigenes, particularly from their ownership of land, which is a symbol of wealth in Africa. During President Moi's stewardship, he was able to restrain them from encroaching further (onto Lamu lands) but now they are encroaching with impunity, even as far as Manda; we are being dispossessed slowly – the people of Lamu/Lamuans no longer engage in farming.

The figures of 17,000 and 50,000 Kikuyu people cited by Mr. Omar Maka are exaggerated.[1] The population of Lamu town, now called a municipality, has not been updated since the census of 24th August, 1999 when it stood at 17,076. Thus the Kikuyu population was probably 1,700 or much less in 1975 and may have grown to about 5,000 today. Omar Maka has magnified the figures ten times in the Kiswahili tradition of exaggeration, namely *kutia chumvi*, "to add salt". Let us overlook the exaggerated figures, and focus on the sentence, "Wametukaribisha kupita idadi ya wenyeji na pia wamekuwa matajiri kushinda wenyeji kwa upande wa ardhi ambayo ndio mali katika Africa." Recall that it means, "They have almost overtaken the total number of indigenous people and in addition they have become richer than the indigenes particularly from their ownership of land, which is a symbol of wealth in Africa." This is a genuine expression of a Lamuan's fear of being overwhelmed by migrants. This fear played a major role in the by-election campaign of 1975, as verses 16–28 above illustrate, and culminated in the defeat of the sitting MP. Thus the typical Lamuan sees around him or her ten times more Kikuyu people than are actually in the area, a very common characteristic feature of people who live in fear of being swamped by foreign migrants. Indeed, even in Western Europe, Australia and the USA,

---

1. I wish to sincerely thank the anonymous assessors of this paper, one of whom drew my attention to the exaggerated figures of Omar Maka. I agree with their comments entirely, but I leave the figures unchanged since they highlight the impact that fear and exaggerated belief have on the kinds of assessments and judgements that people make about others living in their midst.

the increased arrivals of refugees and job seekers from Africa, the Middle East, Asia, the former Eastern Europe and Latin America, have added fuel to a fierce debate about immigration. The debate is even driving many a government policy on the subject, and right-wing parties find it particularly rewarding to magnify and exploit the fears and concerns of the electorate during national elections. All over the world now, people tend to see more aliens than there are, particularly when they feel insecure about their jobs, the stability of their society and the future of their traditional way of life.

Evaluating Lamu's Situation Today

Many years have passed since the *Kimondo* verses played a role in Lamu and Kenya's political system. The *Kimondo* no. 2 tells us that the sub-party of KANU, namely SAA, favoured a strategy of progressive Islamization of politics, the market economy and development projects in Lamu. This has failed to bring economic prosperity to the majority in Lamu. Apart from a growth in tourism, in terms of new hotels and video houses, not a great deal has changed in Lamu on the social front (Amidu 2003). Children who have finished school have no jobs. Corruption among politicians has not diminished and accusations and counter-accusations between politicians and the electorate continue. To make a bad situation worse, Lamuans are losing their lands to foreign investors from abroad and to local capitalists, such as the majority Kikuyu who also now hold power in the country under NARC.[1] The majority of Lamu's voters, both Lamuans and non-Lamuans, voted for KANU at the general elections in 2002 and lost power. Loyalty to KANU, perhaps out of fear of Kikuyu dominance, is good, but in African politics, being on the losing side is also very costly. Mr. Omar Maka sums up the dilemma facing Lamuans and their supporters today as follows:

1. A contributor to the 6th Swahili Workshop in Oslo 2005 observed that many of the Lamu people who have sold their lands, homes and properties to foreign interests and up-country capitalists have become richer and better off and have been able to resettle elsewhere or in the countryside. The significant issue here is whether it is right, in principle, to encourage people in a historical area like Lamu to sell off their heritage in return for extra income. There is no evidence to show that the extra income makes those who sell lands and properties better off in the long run. Mr. Omar Maka, a native of Lamu, believes his fellow Lamuans are not becoming well off. The sales, however, have one lasting impact. They lead to the conversion of historical sites into tourist spots and the loss of Lamu's Kiswahili identity and status as a major Islamic Island and an important link in the history of the Indian Ocean trade. Would the same foreign investors and up-country capitalists allow the historical heritage of their homelands or hometowns to be destroyed and erased in this way?

Kwa hiyo Wazungu wameijenga Shela mpaka ikabadilika sura mpya. Wamenunua Shela yote mpaka wenyeji wamesukuma mashambani. Hakuna Mshela ndani ya mji. Pia wamebadilisha utamaduni wa watu wa Shela. Hawana utamaduni wa Kiswahili tena, pia wameanza kununua majumba Amu Mkomani. Wako karibu kumaliza Mkomani. Wanamaliza utamaduni wa Kiswahili. Na pia ukija Lamu ni adimu sana kupata mtu anae juwa Kiswahili cha kisawasawa. Wengi wame-kufa, wamebaki kidogo sana (personal communication).

And so, White people have built up Shela to the extent that it has a new look. They have bought up the whole of Shela to the extent that the inhabitants have moved into the countryside. There is not a single Shela person in town. Furthermore, they have transformed the culture of the people of Shela. They no longer have a Kiswahili culture, and now they have started buying mansions in Lamu at Mkomani. They are close to swallowing up Mkomani. They have destroyed Kiswahili culture. And in addition, if you come to Lamu, it is very difficult to find a person who knows proper Kiswahili. Many (of the experts) have died and those left are very few.

Renewal and the infusion of new knowledge into Lamu by or for Lamuans in the midst of poverty and despair are difficult to achieve at the present time. The scenario is rather suitable for the growth of religious conserva-tism. Knowledge and renewal are useful if they enhance the quality of life but not if they demean it and marginalize it in favour of others.

An Assessment of the Study

The study reveals contrasting landscapes of Lamu and of Kiswahili society. We see Lamu from the perspective of its indigenous inhabitants. We also see Lamu from the perspective of investors, tourists, migrants from inland and the Kenya government. Lamuans appear to be engaged in an attempt at creating new discourses with non-Lamu people. They want to negotiate space between themselves and agents of change in Lamu. The negotiations do not, however, appear to be leading anywhere at present. The picture we gather of Lamu as a political and social entity with Islam as the religion of its native inhabitants is therefore one in which there are a number of con-flicts and contrasts.

There is, for example, a clash between tradition and modernity. On the one hand, the Waswahili are Muslims. They see their town as a holy town, a Mecca, with a rich cultural and historical heritage linking it with the Indian Ocean, specifically with Arabia, Egypt, India, the Far East, as well as Europe and America and the general Islamic community world wide.

Lamuans would like to keep most of these features and aspects of their lives, culture and civilisation unchanged both for themselves and for posterity. At the same time, Lamuans welcome the modernisation of Lamu, but wish to see it done on their own terms and premises. On the other hand, the rise in tourism is changing the face of Lamu radically. It is bringing to Lamu new actors and investors and new ways of life associated with the tourist industry and a new type of wealth not associated with Islamic religious piety and the grace of God. These paradoxes raise questions about what is the acceptable norm and what is the profane norm in Kiswahili society. For example, the majority of native Lamu inhabitants do not accept the introduction of drinking bars, thinly clad women, homosexuality, the sale of Lamu's historical sites which end up as tourist spots like hotels and brothels. Lamuans are also strongly opposed to the taking over of their arable lands by Kikuyu farmers as well as investors from abroad and from within Kenya.

My study has revealed that Lamu's native inhabitants are not happy about the changing face of their Islamic and Kiswahili culture and the gradual replacement of Kiswahili civilisation with a Western capitalist life style and civilisation. Lamuans, therefore, see change in Lamu as something that is being dictated not by themselves but by others, i.e. by non-Waswahili actors and agents, such as the central government, indigenous and foreign entrepreneurs, such as the Kikuyu, Americans, Germans, Israelis, and so on. Within this scenario, we discover that there is a contrast between progress and alienation in Lamu. There is a contrast between wealth and poverty in Lamu and this has divided the people into two camps: the possessors of wealth and the dispossessed. Lastly, Lamuans wonder whether, at the rate at which change is taking place, there will still be a Kiswahili town of Lamu, a Mecca of Eastern Africa, on the Kenya coast by the end of the present century or the next.

These then are the problems and dilemmas that face Lamu in a changing world. Naturally, given the Lamuans' sense of marginalization, it is not surprising that many of them are increasingly stressing the virtues of Islamic religious purity and condemning lewdness and profanity. Islam, after all, offers hope of quietude of mind and soul both in the present world and the next. Modernity, with its profane baggage, brings disquiet, a feeling of hopelessness to Lamuans, and a fear that the Kiswahili light that has burned for so long on the East African coast and beyond will be extinguished altogether.

Conclusion

Planners, investors, etc. ought to factor the Mecca perception of Lamu into their investment and development programmes for Lamu to stem the alienation of Lamuans and the Waswahili in this part of the Kiswahili coast. Lamuans and the Waswahili of Lamu are eager to participate in the development of tourism in Lamu. They do not, however, approve of the emphasis on investments and developments in the tourist trade that shock their sense of propriety and decency. They also do not approve of investments and developments that transfer their lands and properties to others leaving them dispossessed. There is, in fact, no conflict between Islam and democracy or new ideas. There is also no unwillingness on the part of Lamuans or the Waswahili of Lamu generally for compromise and renewal in a changing world. There is only a conflict between Islam and uncontrolled liberalism and non-Muslim interference in Muslim affairs. Knowledge is in-built into Islam and the Mecca perception of Lamuans keeps this alive.

In the verses and reports in this study, we observe that Lamuans and other Waswahili Muslims of Lamu are keenly aware of their rights, what is happening in their country and beyond and everything that is going on around them. For the people of Lamu, therefore, renewal of knowledge can only take place within the religious diathesis *dini*, i.e. religion encoded in the Mecca perception of Lamu, and *haki*, i.e. natural justice for Lamuans.

References

Amidu, Assibi A., 1990, *Kimwondo: A Kiswahili Electoral Contest*. Vienna: Afro-Pub.

Amidu, Assibi A., 1993, "Lessons from Kimwondo: An Aspect of Kiswahili Culture", *Nordic Journal of African Studies*, vol. 2, no. 1, pp. 34–56.

Amidu, Assibi A., 2003, "Conflict between Tradition and Social Change: A Case Study in Kenya", in, Chandan Kr. Sharma (ed.), *Culture Studies: Themes and Perspectives: Essays in Culture, Folklore, Linguistics, Aesthetics, and Literary Criticism*. Tezpur: NEACTAF, Tezpur University, pp. 242–269.

Amidu, Assibi A., 2004, "Political Poetry among the Swahili: The Kimondo Verses from Lamu", in, Pat Caplan and Farouk Topan (eds), *Swahili Modernities. Culture, Politics, and Identity on the East Coast of Africa*. Trenton, N.J.: Africa World Press Inc., pp. 157–174.

Hagège, Claude, 1985, *L'Homme de Paroles*. Paris: Fayard.

Harries, Lyndon, 1962, *Swahili Poetry*. London: Oxford University Press.

Knappert, Jan, 1967, *Traditional Swahili Poetry*. Leiden: Brill, E. J.

Knappert, Jan, 1971, *Swahili Islamic Literature, vol. I*. Leiden: Brill, E. J.

Knappert, Jan, 1979, *Four Centuries of Swahili Verse*. London: Heinemann Books Ltd.

Middleton, John, 1992, *The World of the Swahili. An African Mercantile Civilization*. New Haven and London: Yale University Press.

Parkin, David, 1989, "Swahili Mijikenda: Facing Both Ways in Kenya", *Africa,* vol. 59, no. 2, pp. 161–175.

Ricard, Alain, 2004, *The Languages and Literatures of Africa*. Oxford: James Currey Ltd.

Sacleux, Le Père Charles, 1939, *Dictionnaire Swahili–Français*. Paris: Institut D'Ethnologie, Place du Trocadero 16e.

The Islamic Foundation, 1975, *Uislamu. Masharuti Yake*. Nairobi: The Islamic Foundation.

– CHAPTER 13 –

"In the Olden Days We Kept Slaves"
Layers of Memory and Present Practices

Ulla Vuorela

On 20 November 2004, I received the following text message, as I was pre-
paring myself for chairing a panel on Postcolonial Feminisms and Situated
Knowledge that was part of the annual conference of women's studies in
Finland.

Uncle. It's me. Chale. Msoga. Your Mama Perpetua. Passed Away.[1]

Soon came another one:

*UULA VUOLELA PLEASE CALL ME SO THAT I CAN TELL YOU
NEWS FROM MSOGA. THINGS ARE VERY BAD THERE. THANK
YOU. IT'S ME JOHN.[2]*

The first message that announced the death of Perpetua Furaha, my friend
and closest associate in the village of Msoga, where I conducted research
in the latter half of the 1980s, came from her son. The second one came
from her husband who had after their divorce moved to Chalinze, a nearby
crossroads village. During the previous August I had briefly visited the village and we had exchanged mobile phone numbers. This might sound a bit
surprising, since up to now the village does not have electricity and to my
knowledge, none of its inhabitants ever owned a car. The traffic to nearby
villages and to larger centres had improved a lot since the 1990s; a number
of private *dala dalas*, small buses and luxurious express buses travel the main
Dar es Salaam Chalinze Arusha Tanga road at frequent intervals. The villagers travelled to Chalinze or Lugoba (both at 7 km distance from the village) to charge their mobiles that were sparingly used for text messages and
occasional phone calls. I was told there was a net café available in Lugoba.

This paper, written in memory of Perpetua Furaha, who died on 18
November 2004, in her early fiftiess, looks at the ways in which history is
preserved in story telling and how a locality that looks like a wayward vil-

---

1. Mimi.Mjomba. Chale. Msoga.Mama yako.Perpetua.Amefariki
2. UULA VUOLELA TAFAZALI NIPIGIE SIMU NIKUJULISHE HABARI ZA
MSOGA HUKU NI KUBAYA SANA ASANTE NI MIMI JOHN.

lage to the present eye has been historically a crossroads of local and global streams of events and influences. In Msoga village of the 1980s (and probably even now) stick cultivation was practised alongside the use of the hoe. This is a village where the use of the tractor was successfully demonstrated in the 1970s, but became a tool that at present exists mainly in the dreams of the people. This is a village where the people live in mud houses that may also have cement walls on which the most important mobile phone numbers have been scribbled in paint, charcoal or lime.

In the village life of the 1980s, a number of elements from various modes of life were intertwined. Hunting and gathering featured not only in oral stories but were practised and contributed supplementary items to the diet. Some of the village people hunted small game such as *dik dik* and birds and many of them relied almost daily on gathering wild greens (*mchunga*) and various types of nuts and roots. Pottery was still practised by some women, even though it was a rapidly disappearing skill. Efforts to revive it for commercial purposes tended to fail with no obvious marketing outlets. A project for making charcoal stoves from clay was again partly successful.

In the 19th century the village was situated along the major caravan routes that took people from inland to the coast, into slavery on the plantations or overseas. The village oral history cites the Nyamwezi as both the agents in this traffic, but also as significant contributors to the village history. The village history mentions cultural influences from the Nyamwezi, such as a certain type of a hoe, seeds for the cultivation of maize and other things. Looking at the pots made by village women, their shapes are greatly reminiscent of the types of pottery that the Nyamwezi women also continue to make now. Various moments of history were embedded both in the objects and in social relations that could provide points of entry for delving deeper into history.

My presence in the village as an anthropologist in the 1980s was related to a Finnish–Tanzanian cultural research project (Jipemoyo) and coincided with an increasing interest towards the village from several aid organisations, starting from the local UNICEF and international NGOs, such as CUSO-Canada in addition to the interventions and guidance from the national government. The presence of all these agents is part of a long chain of interventions; at the height of the slave trade the village was situated on one of the main routes for caravans; in the colonial times a government rest house was constructed there – a small building that became the seat of the ruling party in postcolonial Tanzania. The party office was transformed into my dwelling place while I was doing my research there. The village has not only received people, visitors and administrators; the villagers have never been just "stuck on the spot"; but they have moved in different directions; they have commuted from one locality to another as well as commuting between town and country both in search of a livelihood or out of reverence for the ancient spirits, identified with certain localities. During my latest visit, both my friends and the village authorities told me about their diminishing chances of survival as an economically viable village. They hoped for practical advice with regard to livelihoods in the midst of scarcity. They had also noticed that the village was attracting a lot of new people, and I gathered that these were people from Dar es Salaam, looking for new farming land.

Time and Place

It is paradoxical that Western imagination has for so long put the African traditions in a timeless, or, remote past, while the same imagination does not easily agree to seeing early history and human agency as part of the African past. The tendency to identify Africa (and other places, too) with tradition and the Western countries with modernity has been a point of critical debate for a couple of decades by now. At the beginning of 1980s, Johannes Fabian provided a poignant critique of Western approaches to the rest of the world, when he argued that there is a tendency among European scholars to see other continents in *allochronic* terms. With this he referred to the tendency to mentally locate the "Other" as an object of study into a past that is then read as a testimony of the beholder's history. He warns us about seeing the past as an anachronism, outdated and mainly geared to satisfying an outsider's exotic curiosity. Fabian's argument in 1983 was to say that the anthropologist and his interlocutors only "know" when they meet each other in one and the same *co-temporality*. What Fabian thus called for is an understanding of *coevalness*: the "Other" must be met on the same ground, in the same time (Fabian 1983:165).

One of the arguments presented here is that oral stories as well as material practices and artefacts can be seen as symptoms of, or carry clues that refer to, larger fields of knowledge. Likewise, it highlights how different layers of memory and history are articulated in the minds of people and how they inform their present practices. In terms of time and place, in anthropology and development studies, one still confronts moments where people either see tradition and modernity as opposites in either temporal terms or in terms of societies and place. My paper will make an emphatic point that history is not a total movement from things past to things present: there is no pure present nor is there a pure past, but objects live on and memories reach different layers of events. The past lingers in surprising ways and coexists obstinately with things modern. Therefore, I think that a scholar who is interested in the unwritten history of places like the village of Msoga in the Bagamoyo District in coastal Tanzania may sometimes benefit from following some tiny clues that refer to a historical past. Different layers of memory exist in our daily lives and we could not survive without access to things past in our personal histories. It is amazing, how this obviously trivial point has to be repeated to Western audiences time and again.

I take the text message as a point of departure to discuss how an articulation of past and present can be observed in the village of Msoga. The point becomes a methodological one also, since coevalness also means that what we see now also carries layers of memory from the past. While we live *coevally*, it does not mean that all things observable do have the same history or same age in any one location. Any anthropological research is an encounter that is framed by the stories of those who meet. While the historian and the archaeologist are able to anchor their knowledge in dated documents, the anthropologist and the student of folklore can only observe the simultaneity of things past and present in a number of things. Anchoring some events and the historicity of things into precise time, place or agents, is much more difficult, if not impossible.

This framing also sets the conditions for the ways in which we can know. In this paper I focus on the ways in which the history of slavery and the importance of a major social division between freeborn and slaves was revealed to me in roundabout ways. In addition I make use of the stories to comment on different kinds of feminisms and the limits of an outsider's knowledge. Putting my observations of the first visits to the village together with the ways in which I read the stories 20 years later may give an example of the ways in which anthropological knowledge is produced, and the kind of pathways one single insight may have to wander.

The Text Message

To go back to the text message from Chale, one of the things in the message that might sound surprising is the fact that the word uncle, *mjomba* referred to me, a *mzungu*, a Western woman who had landed in the village from afar. During my latest visit, Chale, the eldest son of Perpetua whom I had know since the end of the 1970s, had already started calling me uncle. In our discussions, I consequently called him my sister's son. The first time he called me "uncle" was when he came to ask for my advice on what he should do to improve his life chances; all of his small scale businesses such as running a tea shop never took off to give him enough money to support a family. It turned out that this nice young man had already been married and divorced twice. The divorces happened because his mothers-in-law came and collected their daughters and took them away, saying that their husband was not good enough for them. This was a gentle young man who, I believe, never maltreated his wives, but was just considered too poor.

However, the text message does not call Perpetua my sister, but as my mama, mother. I had always talked about Perpetua as my *shoga*, which is a Swahili word referring to a woman's best and intimate woman friend; *shoga* for a woman is the other woman with whom you share your deepest secrets. To call her mama surely referred to our mutual history and reminds me of the fact that in real life we also accumulate kinship positions and words to name them. On my visits when I had stayed in the village for my research, it was Perpetua who received me, hosted me and nourished me. Even if I mostly took my own food there, such as rice, cabbage, beans and fruits, it was Perpetua who prepared the food for me, or else saw to it that I was given enough and properly prepared food. On my later visits, she prepared the bath for me as well as sharing her bed with me. Incidentally, it was also in the evenings spent on the *baraza* in front of her house that I first started recording stories, told by neighbours and children. This became an activity that provided a major form of entertainment during my stay in the village in the 1980s.

During the last two years Perpetua's health had not been good and she was often in pain. When she died, she died a shadow of her previous self, looking like a very old fragile woman, even if she was ten years my junior. I think that it was she who had masterminded the idea that I should become the uncle for her children.

That a female *mzungu* (a non-African) was addressed as a maternal uncle through a text message can certainly be read in many ways. Becoming a maternal uncle in a matrilineal society is to have a position of authority, power and responsibility. Uncles are the ones who have to be informed about all major events and decisions in one's life. It is the uncle who has the decisive say about whom to marry, when to be taken to a doctor or when to move house. Uncles are also the ones who are supposed to help you when you are in trouble. By "relativising" me as a maternal uncle, they in fact, made me into a patriarch. Becoming a patriarch as a woman is not surprising as such, because being one is not necessarily tied to female gender, a point also indicated by many African scholars, who have argued that age is more important than sex with regard to positions of authority and power. Discussing "male sisters and female husbands" Ifi Amadiume drew our attention to the flexibility of gender categories in Igbo society. A dual-sex principle in social organisation meant that biological sex did not always correspond to ideological gender: women could play roles usually monopolised by men or be classified as 'males' in terms of power and authority over others. Positions of authority were not rigidly masculinised or feminised and no stigma was attached to breaking gender rules (Amadiume 1987; 1997:140). Likewise, in Yoruba society, the seniority principle is dynamic and fluid, and the fundamental organizing principle within the family is seniority based on relative age, not gender (Oyewumi 2000:1097). Naming me uncle should not be surprising from my own background, considering that the term *eno* in the Finnish language for maternal uncle could also refer to males and females (Vuorela 2002). But thinking of the implications of giving me a patriarchal status as an uncle, I also knew that naming me uncle by Chale also entailed expectations that I could only guess at to start with. What crossed my mind initially was that the expectation might be (no suggestion to that effect had been made so far) that I contribute to the education of the youngest son, who seemed to be the first one in the family to gain entry into a secondary school. In many ways, this sounded fair, considering that Perpetua and her fellow villagers actually "educated" me in many ways. Becoming an uncle then is also about responsibility and care.

Uncles, Nephews and Slaves: On the Importance of Kinship

Had I been called to uncle-hood, say about a hundred years ago, I would have also been given the powers of selling my nephews and nieces or other kinsfolk into slavery or, more mildly, of pawning them to do away with my debts. The maternal uncle was also the holder of the marriage contract that could not be dissolved without consulting him. The contract itself, symbolised by the *mbera ubaka,* a string of white beads or even just a feather that was given to the maternal uncle of the bride at the wedding held the important message that "this is a wife, not a slave" – a fact I duly recorded in my youthful study (Vuorela 1987). This was another early hint of the importance of the distinction made between freeborn and slaves in the local discourse. I could have understood that the history of the slave trade and the history of Bagamoyo as an entrepot for the slave trade, has contributed to the making of the place in many ways.

Even if people did not speak directly about slavery in my encounters with them, small clues can also be read from the stories that I recorded in the village. To what extent the villagers pawned their people or practised slavery is difficult to know. However, the memory of slave relations can be heard in their stories, another symptom of history that links the local and the global together.

Below I will discuss some of the ways in which the issue of slavery and the intergenerational relations between parents and children appear in a collection of about 100 stories that were told to me in evening sessions in the village of Msoga during the period 1984–95. Even though stories are not historical records in the same way as a historian looks at documents, from the point of view of narrative and discourse studies one can argue that stories can be seen as constructing their fields of knowledge. Above all, they are indicants of the kind of social relations that a storytelling community easily receives and the kind of rhetoric that makes sense to the same community. As is now commonly accepted in scholarship of narratives, there is also truth in fantasy. Moreover, even if the truth of a story lacks precise dates, its very telling is context-bound in the sense that it makes sense to the listeners. The reader, though, has to be careful in his/her appreciation of the ways in which fact and fiction are intertwined in the stories and the ways in which the metaphorical aspects of a story are to be understood.

"In the Olden Days We Kept Slaves" – Two Stories

The following stories told to me by Ali Mrisho and Amina Salum[1] deal with the importance of not confusing the freeborn and the slave children, even though the two presentations of the same story differ somewhat. While Ali Mrisho emphasizes the importance of knowing one's kin as a safety measure for the child in avoiding being mistaken for a slave and hence becoming maltreated, Amina Salum puts the story into a different moral order when she underscores that all children need to be equally treated, because you might never know who, after all, is a slave and who is a free child. While Ali Mrisho tells the story without names, Amina Salum links the story to the

---

1. Ali Mrisho 29.11.1984, "Msoga. Story of the child and the slave". U.V. Cassette VI. Translation from Swahili to English U.V. Amina Salum 5.9.1985, "Msoga. Mgoli na Chilwa". U.V. Cassette XIII,

characters of Mgoli and Chilwa. Ali Mrisho introduced the story by saying, "Let me tell the story of the uncle who lived in a far away place…".

Story of the Child and the Slave

Once upon the time there were two old people. Luckily they had one child and they also had a slave. For in the olden days, in whatever way they got them, people kept slaves. (Walikuwa wamefuga watumwa)

Unluckily the father died and the child was left with (his) mother. The parents had only taken the child to see the uncle, when it was still very small, (when it was) an infant who could not understand yet who was who, so the child did not know what kind of a person the uncle was. The uncle did not care very much about the child either, that is, he did not see it as his own child. This is how they lived, and then unluckily, the child's mother (mama ya mtu) *also died, and the child and the slave were left alone.*

The child said that because they were both still quite young, they had better go to the uncle. So they agreed upon this and set out to go to the uncle. The child put on (his) best clothes and decorated (himself) with his beads. Now the slave did not have such clothes, nor did (he) have any beads to wear. So they left.

On their way they bumped into a very big tree, which cut across their way. So the slave said, "Let us lift this tree so that we can go on". The boy said, "But I can't". The slave told him, "If you can't lift the tree, you have to take off your beads and give them to me to wear, and I will lift you over the tree". The child agreed; he took off his beads and gave them to the slave. The slave put on the beads and helped the boy over the tree. They went on. When they were coming close to the uncle's place, they came across a broad river, which was filled with water. The slave told the boy, "Let us jump over the river so we can continue our trip". The boy said, "But I cannot jump over the river". "Now, if you want me to give you a helping hand, I want you to change clothes with me!" The boy agreed and gave his clothes to the slave and so they went on.

When they arrived, the slave told the boy, "Now, this is your uncle's house!" They were told to come in, and once they came in the slave said, "Uncle, we have come to you because father and mother died, and apart from you, we have nowhere else to go". So they were welcomed and the uncle said, "You are welcome, both you and your slave (mtwana) *can stay here with no problem." Then he told the slave that there was some work to be do ne: he should go to chase away birds from the field. He agreed. But it was the nephew whom the uncle told to go to the field because he was wearing the slave's clothes.*

Early in the morning, the uncle woke him up and told him to go to the field. He said, "Eh, my uncle, you want me to go there at this early hour, before six o' clock!" He told him to hurry up. So the child got up and left early in the cold and damp morning mist and went to the field. On his way to go and chase the birds, he started thinking hard about what to do and said to himself, you just wait!

One day he climbed up on the roof of the ringo [the roof of the shelter that had been erected near the field to protect the people watching the fields from too much sun] and started singing:

"Uncle, God is bad, let us chase the birds from the field! You took the slave and keep him in the house while your nephew you send out to work..."

Now the people, who were passing by, were astonished to hear the song. They said, "Jamani! Why on this field where they chase birds, is somebody singing? How come, he sings such a song? What does it mean?"

When the child saw people coming, he hid himself, and was quiet, and only chased the birds, haya, haya, haya!

The people were wondering what the child wanted to say with such a song. When he saw them leaving, he started singing again, "Uncle, God is bad...."

So those people thought that they had better go and tell him.

When the child returned in the evening, he came back even if it was raining. He came back, sat quietly and ate his food. He was given husks of maize to eat, and this was what they pounded for him, while the other one was having chickens, goats slaughtered for him! Yes, that is what they made for him while the other one was given bad, poor food to eat. He thought, "Well, what can I do?"

So in the morning he was again told to go to the field, even if it was raining. He went there, climbed on the shelter and started singing again, "Uncle, God is bad...." People passed by, and they said, "No, we have to go and tell him again!" So they went and told him, "Bwana, there is this child on your field who keeps singing this song. If you hear it, this song makes you feel sorry." He said, "You people, what are you talking about". They told him "But it is true, if you just heard this song, you yourself will be unhappy, let us go!" So he came with them and they went. As they came closer, the song could be heard, "Uncle, God is bad...

They told him, "Did you hear these things?" When the uncle came nearer, the boy came down, sat down and kept quiet. So there and then the uncle told him that he should come home, but the child said, "I am chasing birds". Uncle said, "No, let us go!"

So he took him, they came home and he told him to explain himself. He told him, "It is true, we were living together at home. Father died and mother died and then we had to come to you, uncle. But uncle, I did not know where you lived, and the one who knew where you lived was this slave of ours; he was my ayah and took care of me. It was he who was taken by my parents here to see you, but I was not. So when we were coming here, there was a big tree on the way and I could not jump over it, so my friend asked me to give him my beads and only then did he agree to help me climb over the tree. When we came further, there was this river, and I could not jump over it, so he wanted my clothes in order to help me, so I gave him my clothes and that is why I came here without [decent] clothes and I was ashamed of myself in front of you, even if it is me who is your nephew, the child of your sis-

ter. I am grateful to God. So the uncle said, "Oh, true?" So then, the uncle of the human [mtu] started crying. He told the slave, "You, after having done all this, I cannot punish you or do anything to you; you [can] stay on. But give all your clothes back to whom they belong, and wear your own clothes!" So the slave who had pre-tended to be human [mtu], from then on, he had to go on doing all the work and the nephew of the (human) stayed behind and lived in the house in the position that rightly belonged to him.

The meaning is that if you get a child; don't forget to introduce the child to your relatives so that if you die, they have no problem in knowing who should take care of them.

Constructing Differencies

There are many things about the difference between freeborn and slaves that one can read from this one story alone. The freeborn child wears nice clothes, eats good food and does not do much work compared with the slave child. On the other hand, the slave child is much more skilful in many ways, while the free child is shown as helpless and ignorant of the ways of the world. The slave child has not only been exposed to more mobility and even knows the place where the uncle lives, but he also knows how to move about in a skilful way. The nephew admits this as he tells his uncle: he was our slave and he was my yaya, he took care of me. In other words, the slave boy did domestic chores and tended to the child. "It was he who was taken by my parents here to see you, but I was not." The free child had the liberty to sleep late in the mornings and had barely gone out from the homestead; at the same time he was "liberated" from mastering his milieu and his ability to act as a knowing subject. He was not stupid, though, because even if the slave child was able to outsmart him in many ways, the free child knew the traditions well enough to be able to resort to singing, a role usually played by the truth-telling birds of oral stories, the constantly available helpers in the narrative tradition.

The uncle is shown in the story as a friendly man, who admits the good deeds of the slave boy; nevertheless, order and hierarchy have to prevail: while the slave boy is allowed to stay on, he is returned to his "rightful po-sition". The "rightful" position of the slave is shown in the story as that of someone who is "not human". He is not a "human child" or a child of a human and that makes a crucial difference. The story names the uncle the "uncle of the human" and the slave who had pretended to be human was returned to his rightful position as a "domestic". Order prevails when the distinction between those who labour and those who don't is reconstructed.

The question arises, when did this distinction disappear, or did it ever? Did it just give way to another way of thinking, another discourse, alongside this one? It also calls for reflections on the perseverance of social hierarchies across historical changes and politics, which compel one to study the role of memory. In an oral communication, I was told in 2002 that in Bagamoyo town, descendants of former slave owners and descendants of former slaves do not pray in the same mosque. Likewise, they do not intermarry (oral communication from Dr. Msemwa 2002).

Perseverance of Memory

Pondering on the perseverance of the memories of slavery, I would like now to cite a short story told by a little girl in our story telling sessions of 1984. Tukae Ramadhani, then nine years of age had the following story to tell.

Here is a story! Story come! Hadithi, hadithi! Hadithi njoo!
   Once upon the time there was a woman. This woman wanted to have a child. She went to the neighbour and called Hodi! (May I come in?)
– "Come in!"
– "I want to have a child."
– "There is no child. Go to the next house!"
So she went to the next house.
– "Hodi! Hodi!"
– Come in!"
– "I want to have a child".
– "There is no child. Go to the third house!"
So she went to the third house.
– "Hodi! Hodi!"
– "Karibu! "
– "I want to have a child."
–"Yes there is a child. But you have to spend the night here."
–"Very well."
So she slept the night there and when she opened her eyes in the morning, there was a child for her. So she went home with her.
The first day, this woman told the child,
– "Go to the shop and buy me some cigarettes!"
The child went.
   On the second day the child was told to go and fetch water from the well. So she went.
   On the third day the woman told her: wash the dishes. Then the child refused. She did not want to wash the dishes. The child started singing a song:

– "*Mother called me slave* (Mtwana). *Farewell mother, Mother called me slave. Farewell mother, you treated me like a slave.*"
So she went back where she came from and this is where my story ends.

When I asked about the meaning of the story, a village elder that partici-pated in the session explained that the child went away because she did not want to be treated like a slave. The story told by the little 9-year-old girl was, as you can hear, a fragmentary little piece, but its message was clear; par-ents should not treat children as if they were slaves. Or, if you want to have your own child, you will have to treat the child as truly your own. Current concerns about how to treat children were enhanced by reference to the dis-tinction between freeborn and slaves. This was an aspect of social division, a hint of the persistence of slave relations and the existence of social divisions that I was not "tuned" to hearing when doing my research.

Comparing the clues with other literature (Douglas 1964, Wright 1983 and 1993, Strobel 1979 and 1983) it certainly appears that some people did have rights over other people as persons, while others could not consider even their own person as their property.

In her study on coastal slavery in Mombasa, Margaret Strobel observed how the slave system was supported by an ideology that demanded defer-ence from the slaves as it considered them inferior to the freeborn. Slaves were considered inherently inferior, incapable of learning and unable to achieve religious purity. In this ideology they belonged to the sphere of *na-ture, disorder and impurity*, which contrasted with *culture, order and purity* (Strobel 1979:45). Paradoxically, as in the story told by Ali Mrisho about the relationship between the slave and the child, the domestic slaves had more freedom than their female mistresses. While slave women took part in the weddings of the freeborn women, the reverse was not always the case. Often it was the slave women who explained about menstruation and sexuality to the daughters. They thus sometimes mediated between moth-ers and daughters in matters they were not supposed to speak freely about with each other (p. 12–13). The slave women were skilful assistants of their mistresses in many domestic chores, be it massaging and giving them oint-ments or other more mundane household chores. Certainly the Mombasa domestic slaves were part of a sophisticated urban culture, but they were also mediators that brought a number of cultural elements of their ethnic groups to the coast.

The distinction between freeborn people and slaves was one of the im-portant social divisions in the inland societies too. Ownership of slaves was a means with which male elders; chiefs or kings could gain prestige. In

Douglas's reading, pawnship in matrilineal societies was also a means to manipulate and go beyond the enclosures otherwise restricted to kinship based social thinking.

Zaulole! Come and See Us!

This was the name of a women's dance group in the village of Msoga I first met in 1977. They were the ones who received visitors to the village and also had an air of self-confidence and authority. However, my feminism of the 1980s did not grasp what was so "radical" about these women whom I otherwise saw as meekly subordinated to their husbands. Only in the context of writing this paper and rereading the story told by Amina Salum, i.e. Mama Rukia, did I realise that "Zaulole!", the Kwere call for "Come and See!" was one of the key lines of the song attached to the story of Mgoli and Chilwa. The song about the unfair uncle thus gave the name to the women's dance group who could be interpreted as saying, "Come and see us! We are free-born and not slaves", hence reminding of a social divide between freeborn and slaves that people still remembered. The "freedom" of women expressed in the name of the dance-group was to emphasise that, people should not think otherwise, they were free women, free from slavery. I must say that the distinction between freeborn and slaves and humans and animals has been brought to my notice only with hindsight.

Coevality and the Mobile Phone

The way in which I was appointed an "uncle" makes visible the continuing significance of maternal uncles and matrilineal relations in Msoga village. That my uncle-hood is mediated by the mobile phone makes the medium a nodal point that momentarily puts us in the same time, same discourse, as well as it seems to delete the significance of time, place and distance from between us. This possibility needs to be qualified a little, though. To what extent does the easiness of speaking on the phone or sending each other text messages put us "on the same ground"? The issue of coevality is more complex than simple erasure of distance and time for an improved "rapport" that was the methodological and political point made by Fabian. While we confront each other on the same ground in terms of time and place, the medium does not take away our different positions in the political economy of the world, now heavily restructured by global processes. The difference between Kisemvule and me is not about "difference" in terms of "developmental stages" or temporality, but about "difference" in terms of "access" and relative affluence, poverty and riches. Having access to a mobile phone gives some help in providing access to information about people living at a distance. Yet, simply connecting us through the phone certainly does not make us equal. This applies to our readings of history as well as our understandings of the present. The problem addressed by Fabian covers only one dimension, time, and thus provides only a good starting point for considering the significant social relations in their other dimensions.

That globalisation is uneven and leaves many people in its shadow, or as James Ferguson puts it, "hops over", means that networks of political and economic connections may "span the globe", but they do not cover it (Ferguson 2006:14). Such gaps can be only partially and haphazardly patched up as in the case of Chale, through personal relations, through relativising old acquaintances or else, for instance, through the activities of non-governmental organisations. Money does not move by itself, but presupposes a social relationship and needs to be put in motion by consent. Moreover, as Cindi Katz has alerted us to observe: while scholars on globalisation have celebrated the time-space compression, it does not apply to everybody in the same way. Apart from the compression of time and space, there is a need to speak of the time-space expansion, too. The time–space expansion refers to the ways in which people who wish to stay put have to seek livelihoods within areas that are exponentially larger than previously. Her study on the livelihoods of villagers in Howa, Sudan, indicates that people can stay put but the geography of sustenance and labour covers a hugely expanded field of work, manifest in men's travels and the spatial strategies needed for agriculture, animal husbandry and forestry. Katz suggests that time-space expansion is one of the key means through which people in Howa made their lives workable (Katz 2004:228). Clearly, one of the reasons that made the prospects for a better livelihood so dim for Kisemvule and others living in the same village is the impossibility of making money and resources productive within the scope of a small locality. One of the problems of the tea-shop that he once started with such great zeal and devotion, rested on the impossibility of getting any customers from within the village whose inhabitants are few (about 1,000) and all of whom are more or less poor. No wonder that, whoever can make an effort, does like Chale did, and tries to extend the relations of care transnationally. Sooner or later this requires transnational mobility and seeking work over long distances. The need to extend relations of care transnationally is one of the strategies needed for expanding the earning potential for those staying put and bespeaks of the dearth in the local earning prospects for those who wish to stay put. Secondly, time and place represent only limited dimensions in our encounters. Katz's argument is also valid for Msoga people: global economic restructuring transforms the scale of uneven economic development producing common effects in disparate local settings. Globalisation that "hops over" also displaces young people from secure employment, along with their reconstitution as "deskilled", and leads to a recalibration of the relationship between production and social reproduction (Ibid: 228).

A couple of months later I received another text message that informed me of the fact that Perpetua's daughter had been hospitalised with cancer and needed help. Money travelled in the nick of time via Western Union to enable an operation. It was too late, though, since after her return to the village after the operation I was informed later that the daughter had passed away at the age of 35. Some weeks later, I was duly informed about the passing away of Chale's stepfather, Perpetua's divorced husband. This was a death that made Chale the main provider for his younger siblings and a number of grandchildren, step-siblings and step-grandchildren. An adopted uncle does not mean much in this equation and we are painfully aware of the precariousness of this connection.

The points that the story of the communications between a Tanzanian village and Finland should bring home to me are at least twofold. Anywhere, at any point in time, one can observe the simultaneity of traditions, things past and present. One of the challenges of studying cultural change and social relations is the need to address the distinctions between things old and new and their life. Lastly, the "consumer choice" of Msoga villagers in procuring mobile phones even if there is no electricity in the village cannot be seen as a mere parallel or an imitation of "consumerism" in advanced capitalist societies. The technical innovation has turned out to be very important in its ability to serve such social relations and processes that have been vital for survival and have been carried on and retold in the form of stories, too. Innovation here enhances tradition, even if the case of the remote uncle remains an incident in the story of Perpetua and her children.

To make the circle of the argumentation full, the use of the mobile phone in the village is another example of the ways in which things old and new appear intertwined, contemporarily.

References

Amadiume, Ifi, 1987, *Male Daughters, Female Husbands: Gender and Sex in an African Society.* London: Zed Books.

Amadiume, Ifi, 1997, *Reinventing Africa. Matriarchy, Religion & Culture.* London and New York: Zed Books.

Douglas, Mary, 1964, "Matriliny and Pawnship in Central Africa", *AFRICA* 34:301–313.

Fabian, Johannes, 1983, *Time and the Other. How Anthropology Makes Its Object.* New York: University of Columbia Press.

Ferguson, James, 2006, *Global Shadows. Africa in the Neoliberal World Order.* Durham and London: Duke Uiversity Press.

Geiger, Susan, 1997, *TANU Women. Gender and Culture in the Making of Tanganyika Nationalism 1955–1965.* Heinemann, James Currey, E.A.P. Mkuki na Nyota.

Katz, Cindi, 2004, *Growing Up Global. Economic Restructuring and Children's Everyday Lives.* Minneapolis, London: University of Minnesota Press.

Oyewumi, Oyeronke, 1997, *The Invention of Women: Making an African Sense of Western Gender Discourses.* University of Minnesota Press.

Oyewumi, Oyeronke, 2000, "Family Bonds/Conceptual Binds: African Notes on Feminist Epistemologies", *Signs: Journal of Women in Culture and Society,* Vol. 25, no 4.

Robertson, Claire C. and Martin A. Klein (eds), 1983, *Women and Slavery in Africa.* Madison: The University of Wisconsin Press.

Strobel, Margaret, 1979, *Muslim Women in Mombasa 1890–1975.* New Haven and Londond: Yale University Press.

Strobel, Margaret, 1983, "Slavery and Reproductive Labour in Mombasa," in C.C. Robertson and Martin A. Klein (eds), *Women and Slavery in Africa,* Madison: University of Wisconsin Press.

Sudarkasa, Niara, 1996, *The Strength of Our Mothers: African and African American Women and Families: Essays and Speeches.* Trenton and Asmara: Africa World Press.

Vuorela, Ulla, 1987, *The Women's Question and the Modes of Human Reproduction. An analysis of a Tanzanian Village.* Uppsala: Scandinavian Institute of African Studies.

Vuorela, Ulla, 2004, "Motherhood in the Naming: Mothers and Wives in the Finnish/ Karelian Cultural Region". *JENdA. A Journal of Culture and African Women Studies.* Issue 4. www.jendajournal.com

Wright, Marcia, 1983, "Bwanikwa: Consciousness and Protest among Slave Women in Central Africa, 1886–1911", *Women and Slavery,* 246–270.

Wright, Marcia, 1993, *Strategies of Slaves and Women's Life Stories from East and Central Africa.* New York: Lillian Barber Press. London: James Currey.

Appendix

The story told by Ali Mrisho in Swahili

Mimi Ali Mrisho, natoa hadithi yangu moja. Kutokeani!

Hapo zamani za kale kulikuwa na wazee wawili. Kwa bahati nzuri walizaa mtoto wao moja. Kwa bahati pia walikuwa na mtumwa, yaani pale zamani walipokuwa wa-nachukua watumwa, wanawafuga. Kwa bahati mbaya, baba ya mtu akafa, na baada ya kufa yule mtoto akabaki na mama yao. Yule mtoto wakaja wakamtembeza kwa mjomba wake wakati akiwa bado mtoto mdogo kabisa, hajui kama mjomba yuko namna gani na yule mjomba wa mtu hakumjali sana yule mtoto kama ni mtoto wangu. Wakakaa hivyo na mama ya mtu, kwa bahati mbaya, mama mtu naye pia akafa, ikawa wamebaki yule mtoto tu na mtumwa wake. Yule mtoto akasema kwa vile sisi bado ni watoto wa-dogo, inafaa sisi twende kwa mjomba, akakubali wakaenda. Yule mtoto akaanza kuvaa ushanga, nguo akaanza kujipamba vizuri sana.

Yule mtumwa sasa hana zile nguo na wala ule ushanga anaovaa. Sasa akaona tuondo-ke, twende, wakaenda. Walipofika njiani wakuta jiti limelala chini, ndipo yule mtumwa akasema, ”Bwana, tuvuke hili jiti, twende”. Yule kijana akasema ”Mimi si-wezi”. Yule mtumwa akasema, ”Kama huwezi, basi, uvue ushanga wote ulio nao, ni-vae mimi, ndipo nikuvushe”. Yule mtoto akakubali, akapambua ule ushanga, kampa yulá”áe mtumwa, akavaa, akamvusha pale kwenye jiti. Wakaenda. karibu ya kufi-ka kwa mjomba wao sasa pana mto umejaa maji,mtumwa akamwambia, ”Sasa tu-vuke hapa, twende!” Yule mtoto akasema, ”Mimi siwezi”. akamwambia, ”Ukitaka, unishike mkono, ndipo naweza kuvuka”. Yule mtumwa akamwambia, ”Kama uki-taka nikushike mkono, ni lazima uvue nguo zako zote,nivaae mimi na wewe uchukue hiki cha kwangu, uvaae”. Yule mtoto akakubali. Akachukua zile nguo zake, akampa yule mtumwa, wakaenda. Walipofika, akamwambia ”Sasa nyumba hiyo ya mjomba wako!” Sawa! Wakapiga hodi, pale wakakaribishwa. Sasa kufika tu akasema, ”Sisi mjomba sasa tumekuja”. Aansema yule mtumwa kwa sababu yeye ndiye aliyetangulia, kwa sababau yule mpwa wake, hata kusema anaona haya kutokana na hali aliyo nayo, maana yule mtumwa alikuwa amevaa vizuri. Akamwambi, ”Sisi, mjomba tumekuja sasa nyumbani kama vile baba na mama wote wameishakufa, ndipo tukaona, hakuna mahali pengine popote pa kwenda, isipokuwa ni kwako”. Akakubali, ”Basi, ni sawa, mtakaa na wewe bwana utakaa sawa. ”Sasa kuna kazi moja wewe bwana”, anamwam-bia yule mtumwa, ”hapa kuna kazi moja, kuna shamba, nataka uwe unakwenda ku-hamia ndege”. Akamwambia, ”Sawa, nimekubali”. Yaani ni yule mpwa wake ambaye yule mtumwa alimpa nguo zake, ndiyo, anaambiwa hivyo. (Wakakaa) Kufika asub-uhi akamwamsha, ”Nenda bwana!” Akasema, ”Hee, mjomba hivi, natoka mimi saa hizi nakwenda huko? Kabla ya saa kuminambili!” Akamwambia, ”Aa, bwana, uwahi bwana!”. Yule mtoto akatoka na umande umande anakwenda kule shambani. Kwenda kule akahamia ndege zake, sasa akafikiriii, akaona, ngoja! Siku moja akapanda juu, akakaa, sasa anaimba:

Mjomba Mulungu kwa mbaya, we chihamile ndege kungunda

Kusola mtumwa kuwika hakaye

Kusola iwako kundunnsa....

Maana yake: Mjomba Mungu ni mbaya, we tuhamie ndege shambani (x2)

Umemchukuwa mtumwa unamweka nyumbani

Ukamchukuwa wako (mpwa wako) unmtumikisha...Sasa wale watu wanaopita wanasema, jamani, mbona hapa kwenye shamba hii, wanaohamia hizi ndege, mbona kuna mtu hapa anaimba? Sasa huyu anaimbaje wimbo huu? Nao una maana gani? Na yule mtoto akiona watu kule wanakuja, anajificha, ananyamaza kimya, ahamia ndege tu, haya, haya, haya, haya! Watu wanajiuliza huyu mtoto ana maana gani, mpaka anaimba wimbo huu? Akiwaona wameondoka, yeyeanarudia wimbo wake:

Mjomba Mulungu...

Wale watu wakaona, "Hata, inavyofaa, tuwende tukamwambie! Yule mtoto anaporudi usiku, hata kama amerudi, mvua inanyesha, lakini yeye anarudi, ananyamaza kimya, chakula chake anakula maganda ya mahindi, ndiyo anatwangiwa. Yule anakula na yulemtumwa, anachinjiwa kuku, mbuzi, wanamchinjia, wanakula, lakiniSasa yeye wanampa chakula kibaya, kibaya, ndicho anachokula.Akasema, "Ha, sawa, nitafanyaje?" Mpaka kumekucha, hata kamakuna mvua, anaambiwa "Nenda tu!", anasema "Haya, mimi nakwenda, anatoka, anakwenda mpaka kule. Anakaa, anapanda juu, anaanza kuimba tena:Mjomba Mungu Wale watu wanapita, wanasikia ule wimbo tena, wakaona, "Hapana, tumrudie mwenyewe!" Wakaenda,wakamwambia, "Bwana we, shambani kwako yule mtoto uliyemuweka anavyoimba, ukiusikia, ule wimbo unasikitisha". Akasema, "Aah, na ninyi, nanyi, namna gani?" Wakasema, "Kweli, ukiyasikia na mambo yanayotoka huko, wewe mwenyewe utafurahi, twende!" Akatoka yule akaenda. Kwenda, kufika karibu ya shamba, kweli anasikia wimbo ule tena,

Mjomba Mungu....

Wakamwambia, "Umesikia hayo mambo?" Alipokuja kumwona tu akateremka juu ya ulingo, akakaa kimya. Akamwambia mjomba, mjomba, hapo hapo, "Twende nyumbani!" Yeye akasema, "Mimi nahamia". Akasema, "Hata, twende!" Akamchukua yule, wakaja nyumbani, akamwambia, "Hebu, nieleze vizuri!" Akamwambia, "Kweli sisi tumekaa nyumbani, baba akafa na mama akafa. Sasa ikatubidi kwamba tuje huku kwako mjomba sasa. Mimi kwako sijakujua, aliyekujua ni huyu mwenzangu, na huyu ndiyo mtumwa wetu tuliokuwa naye, na huyu ndiye aliyekuwa yaya au mlezi wangu mimi. Huyu ndiye aliyetembezwa na wazee mpaka anamjuani ninyi, sasa mimi sikuwajua. Sasa wakati tunakuja huku, njiani kulikuwa na jiti kubwa, mimi kuvuka nilishindwa, sasa mwenzangu akanipambua ushanga wangu woote, akachukua ndipo akakkubali kunivusha katika mti ule. Tukaja tena, kufika hapo, kwenye mto huu hapo chini, mimi nilikuwa siwezi kuvuka, akaniambia, ukitaka nikuvushe, unipe nguo zako na mimi nikampa nguo zangu na ndiyo maana nikafika hapa bila ya nguo, hata nikaona aibu kufika karibu yako, lakini huyo ndiyo mtumwa, mimi ndiye hasa niliyekuwa mpwa wako, mtoto wa dada yako. Sasa baada ya kufika mimi nikawa mtumwa, huyu mwenzangu akawa mtoto wa dada yako, mpwao. Mimi nimeshukuru kwa Mungu". Akasema, "Oh kweli?" Basi, yule mjomba mtu akaanza kulia. Akamwambia yule mtumwa, "Wewe pamoja na kufanya haya yote, mimi sitaweza kukuadhibu au kukufanya nini, ila wewe utakaa. Lakini hizo nguo ulizo nazo, umrudishie mwenyewe na wewe chukua zile za kwako, uvaae". Yule mtume aliyeufanya mtu, yeye sasa akawa ndiye anayefanya kazi ile, na yule mpwa wa mtu akarudi kukaa nyumbani na kurudia hadhi yake kama invyomstahili.

Maana yake, ukizaa mtoto usiache kumtambulisha kwa ndugu zako, ili ukifa asipate taabu ya kuyatambua ndugu zako ambao ndio watakaomtunza.

Hadithi yangu ndipo ilipoishia.

The Story told by Tukaye Ramadhani in Swahili

Hapo zamani za kale palikuwa mama mmoja. Mama mmoja huyo alikuwa anataka mtoto. Akaenda chumba cha kwanza: Hodi!
– Karibu!
– Nataka mtoto.
Mtoto hakuna. Nenda chumba cha pili.
Akaenda chumba cha pili:
– Hodi! Hodi!
– Karibu!
– Nataka mtoto.
mtoto hakuna, nenda chumba cha tatu!
Akaenda chumba cha tatu.
– Hodi! Hodi! Nataka mtoto. Yupo, lakini ulale hapa hapa!
– Haya!
Akalala. Alipoamka asubuhi, alipofunua akakuta mtoto. Akaenda naye nyumbani.
Siku ya kwanza, mama yule akamtuma:
– Nenda dukani ukaninunulie sigara!
Yule mtoto akaenda.
Siku ya pili kamtuma, nenda kisimani ukateke maji, akaenda.
Siku ya tatu, akamtuma: Osha vyombo. Yule mtoto akakataa. Osha vyombo hataki.
Yule mtoto akaanza kuimba wimbo wake:
Mama kaniambia mtwana
Mama kwa heri mtwana.
Mama kaniambia mtwana, mama kwa heri mtwana
Akaenda pale alipofika, na hadithi yangu ndio ilipomalizia.
Maana yake: Hakutaka kutumwa mfululizo kwa sababu siyo mtumwa (said Nambari Kivunja, mzee)

– CHAPTER 14 –

Wonders of the Exotic
Chinese Formula Medicines on the East African Coast

Elisabeth Hsu

Medicines in East Africa

In contemporary East Africa, medicines exert a strange attraction, foreign and exotic medicines, in particular.[1] Susan Reynolds Whyte (1988) who works among the Nyole of Uganda, stresses this in her article on "The Power of Medicines in East Africa": "One of the most striking characteristics of the Nyole medicine men was that they so frequently had foreign experience and used exotic techniques ... The use of exotic substances and techniques was not only recognized, but emphasized" (Ibid:225). One wonders why.

In the above article Whyte takes a broad approach to this question. She asks what the choices are that people have for managing misfortune and illness, and she finds that they basically have two. They can take recourse, on the one hand, to 'medicines' - African herbal remedies, talismans, Qur'anic spells and/or the ingestion of water that has been spilled over the holy script, as well as Western pharmaceuticals – or, on the other hand, to 'the healing powers of elder kin, ancestors, and spirits'. Whyte observes that there currently is "a general trend towards treating suffering by the application of substances", i.e. medicines, "rather than the ritual manipulation of relationships" which involves kin, ancestors, and spirits (Ibid:217).

A comparison of the two choices highlights that a 'medicine', in contrast to other forms of transforming an individual's condition of life, 'is a sub-

---

1 This article synthesizes a paper presented at the European Symposium on Material Culture, 16th-17th November 2001, at the Museum of Mankind, Department of Ethnography, The British Museum, called: 'Wonders of the Exotic: Chinese Medicines in the African Context of Dar es Salaam', which shortly thereafter in slightly modified form was presented at the Anthropology Seminar of the School of Social Sciences and Cultural Studies, University of Sussex, on the one hand, and as a paper presented at the Medical Anthropology Seminar, University College London, in November 2004, called: 'Chinese Formula Drugs on the East African Coast', on the other. Ideas came also from informal conversations during the 6th Swahili workshop on 'Knowledge, Renewal and Religion', at the Museum of Cultural History, University of Oslo, on 31st March–2nd April 2005.

stance that transforms something – for better or worse' (Ibid:218). A medicine achieves this through powers that are inherent to it, and it achieves this 'without reference to morality, relationships or intention' (Ibid: 218). In this way medicines differ from curing 'through prayer, ritual and sacrifice' or 'harming through cursing or the power of spirits' (Ibid:218). The fact that 'the power to transform lies within the substance' makes it possible to apply medicines in private, and often also secretly (Ibid:219).

Whyte (Ibid:219) states that "misfortune caused by senior relatives or spiritual agents requires negotiation, gift giving and sacrifice in a public ritual", "while the response to sickness caused by medicine was more medicine". In the first case, "words had to be spoken so that all, including the agent and the victim, were conscious of the nature of suffering, the relationship involved and the transformation desired". In the second case, "open confrontations between presumed sorcerers and their victims were extremely rare". Whyte (Ibid:220) furthermore notes that "medicines and ritual were actual alternative choices which Nyole faced in daily life", and that therefore: "Choosing medicines ... might be a way of avoiding ritual obligations and inconveniences."

As an example, Whyte (Ibid:222) mentions a man, Samwiri, who had a strained relationship with his father-in-law and whose wife thought that therefore his children – one after the other – were falling ill. Samwiri was considered a bad son-in-law because he had not visited his wife's father in prison, and although he had a steady income, he had not offered any gifts, and, moreover, he had not even paid off the last cow for his wife's bride wealth. As the first child fell ill, he intended to take it to hospital. However, since an injection given at the dispensary was seen to have no effect on the child's improvement, his wife considered the case to be caused by her father's curse and she pleaded that he go and see her father to remove the curse. Medicines – in this case Western pharmaceuticals - would only treat the symptoms while a ritual was necessary to remove the cause. Samwiri openly expressed his dislike of her father, accused him of greediness and a drinking problem, and refused to give him the satisfaction of receiving a goat for withdrawing the curse. The child was brought to hospital but then the second child fell ill. Whyte remarks: "In this case, Samwiri's motives for seeking Western medicines were surely not simply that they were effective. In fact, the opposite had been demonstrated; an injection had failed to cure the one child, and even after his hospitalization and recovery, sickness still threatened the lives of Samwiri's other children. Samwiri insisted on Western medicine because he wanted to avoid what Nyole custom required

– that he go humbly to his father-in-law." Whyte also points out that the view of the 'pragmatic patient', as constructed by some anthropologists, is a bit simplistic. In order to understand the choice of taking medicines, she says, one has to account for both the "push as well as the pull factors". The push factors are that medicines allow one to obviate ritual inconveniences.

Notably, the power of medicines comes from outside the domain of human relationships that are morally regulated - the public, social and moral domain. In East Africa, medicine men, herbalists, and more recently also Western biomedics typically come from another group than one's own. The advantage of these medicine men and their medicines is that they are from outside one's own social and moral order. However, Whyte (Ibid:226) warns about drawing too crass a contrast: "All medicines, in a sense, come from outside, so that it may be misleading to make too strong a contrast between Nyole medicine and foreign medicine, or between African medicine and hospital medicine" or, in the context of this article, Chinese medicines.

Whyte (Ibid:226) furthermore points out that the stereotype of "the African medicine man as a local resident, embedded in his own tribal culture, serving the needs of his neighbours by manipulating the symbols with which they are familiar" may apply to some but perhaps not even to the majority of situations. Ole Bjorn Rekdal (1999:459), who argues along the same lines, observes with regard to the Iraqw of Tanzania: "Many of these healers did not speak any Iraqw, they often had a very limited knowledge of Iraqw culture, and in their divination and healing procedures most applied techniques and employed paraphernalia from their respective home areas." Whyte and Rekdal (who curiously seems to be unaware of Whyte's article) both emphasize that cultural distance imbues medicine men and their medicines with power.

In this context, David Parkin's (1968:428–9) earlier observation comes to mind, which is that people in possession of medicines often challenge traditional authority: "The point should not be missed ... that it is people living and working outside the society or having major external contacts who import medicines; and it is often these same people who challenge established authority within the society." The external and exotic is not only considered powerful but also potentially dangerous due to its difference. The exotic, by definition, is unusual, and therefore, it cannot be treated as equal and typically has an ambiguous status: while it is imbued with great potential and power (good or bad), it is also potentially dangerous. Rekdal (1999) reports on a much respected healer among the Iraqw whose ethnicity was Maanda Uwa. On the one hand, the Maanda Uwa were disdained because they were considered unclean; they married their cross-cousins, which the Iraqw found incestuous, and they ate donkey meat. On the other hand, the Maanda Uwa had provided the apical ancestor of the Iraqw clan, which possessed the greatest ritual expertise and power. Such ambiguity between the unclean and the powerful is often inherent to the external, culturally distant and exotic, and perhaps it is precisely this ambiguity that enhances the power of exotic medicines.[1]

Which medicines then belong among the culturally distant and exotic? Whyte points to the parallel of the medicines from the bush that is culturally distant in that it is wild and to the medicines of far away places that are culturally distant in a spatial sense. There is yet a third sense in which medicine men and their medicines may represent the culturally distant. This is that they are 'traditional' only in Eric Hobsbawm's (1983) sense: while they may well manipulate people's traditional values at times, they are in fact often cosmopolitan and innovative, and their medicines are accordingly often newly concocted substances. These medicine men and their medicines are exponents of 'invented traditions', inventors of new traditions tailored to the requirements of 'modern' times, the 'modernity' one encounters in urban places.

Many medicine men have travelled far, and combine diverse techniques. This mobility likens them in yet another way, metonymically, to their medicines: in the East African context, medicines, unlike rituals, are rarely tied to particular relationships and they can be anonymously transferred. As these "physical commodities subject to transaction" (Parkin 1968:428), medicines are eminently suited to entrepreneurial experimentation and to activities that are not kin-specific (Whyte 1988:226). Medicine men as merchants and medicines as commodities fit perfectly into modern ways of life. The impersonal aspect of the transfer of medicines and their individualistic application makes some perceive them as liberating, as part of the 'modern' and 'global'. While the concept of medicines may be ancient in Africa (Ibid:229), medicines today often are considered powerful because of their affinity with what is considered 'scientific' and 'modern'.

---

1. The above ideas were formulated before *Borders and Healers* was published, which further elaborates on the theme. West and Luedke (2006:3–4) point to a wide range of authors from Evans-Pritchard and Richards to the Comaroffs and Vaughan who all noted that the movement of healers and of their materials across geographical and social boundaries enhanced the power of their medicine.

Anti-Imperialist Feelings
and the Magical Powers of Distant Colonisers

How do Chinese medicines fit into the pattern sketched out above? Since 1996, over twenty Chinese medical practices have mushroomed in Dar es Salaam, and many more in the Tanzanian hinterland. Chinese practitioners are even more culturally distant than the powerful healers of Pemba who live off the East African coast on an island of the Indian Ocean. One would thus expect that Chinese medicines work wonders solely through being culturally distant and exotic.

There are two further reasons that heighten the powers attributed to Chinese medicines. One is that there is a general anti-imperialist tenor against anything Western: it is often said that white tourists brought AIDS to Africa, that the humanitarian donations of clothes brought skin diseases, and that in a similar vein the expensive Western biomedical drugs are but another facet of the imperialist underdevelopment of Africa (fieldwork in Dar, March 2001). In Tanzania, there is apart from this pan-African anti-imperialist feeling, which explains the principally favourable attitude towards the Chinese, also a rather specific neo-colonialist experience that imbues them with magical powers.

Much like the Germans who were the first colonial rulers of what they called Tanganyika, and who variously were said to have magical powers (fieldwork in Dar, March 2001), I have heard people say that the Chinese understand how to do magic (fieldwork in Dar, March 2002). For one, the Chinese when engaged in construction work typically worked at night, and these are the times when witches are at work (fieldwork in Malindi, January 2006). Apart from that, there is also one specific episode that is often told to prove that the Chinese are knowledgeable about magic. Once during the construction of the Tazara railway from Dar es Salaam to Lusaka, which went through an difficult mountainous region, it was simply impossible to make a tunnel through a mountain that was infested with spirits. Thereupon the Chinese boiled vast amounts of herbal medicines and with their cooking pots in their hands, walked all over the mountain to sprinkle it with these medicines: as a result, the spirits retreated and the tunnel was built (fieldwork in Dar, December 2002). The construction of the Tazara railway line in itself was an operation that came close to doing magic: the Chinese came, made it, and went again, and this all happened in less than five years (see also Monson 2008).

Two Sensitive Areas of Tanzanian Health Policies

When I started fieldwork in 2001, Chinese practitioners, and in particular, their medicines were a media item. The matter involved delicate issues of health care policies and 'big money' as much as questions of cultural difference, attitudes of ostensibly declared friendship and undercurrent suspicion. Chinese practitioners rely mostly on formula medicines, which puts them in competition with biomedical physicians and pharmacists on the one hand and local 'traditional medicine' practitioners on the other. The rapid emergence of the entrepreneurial Chinese medical clinics touches thus on two sensitive areas of Tanzanian health care policies: one concerns the private practice of medicine, the other attitudes to traditional medicines. As becomes apparent from reading John Iliffe's (1998:200–19) chapter on Tanzanian doctors, these two sensitive issues date back to socialist oriented health policies in the 1970s and 80s.

The private practice of medicine is commonplace in neighbouring Kenya, but not in Tanzania. Tanzanian salaries for medical professionals were not only notoriously low, prominent politicians launched several attacks on doctors having private practices. However, as Iliffe (Ibid:218) points out, it was impossible to implement the bills to close down private practices, and many were covertly reopened after temporarily being shut. After Julius Nyerere renounced his presidency in 1985, there was a liberalisation of the mainland economy, but the ban on private practices remained in place until 1992. Iliffe (Ibid:219) remarks that liberalisation brought a new degree of privileges and power to medical practitioners, while some foreign observers I spoke to mentioned the World Bank had put considerable pressure on the Ministry of Health to liberalise the health market (fieldwork in Dar, March 2001), and they thereby pointed out the creation of new dependencies. Whatever the motives for the changes of the legality of private health care were, it led to the installation of several privately owned hospitals and innumerable smaller clinics and dispensaries in the mid-nineties. The "take-off" had taken place in 1996–97 and apparently there were over five hundred privately owned facilities of biomedical health care in Dar es Salaam in March 2001 (J.P. Pichet, personal communication). The owners were often of Indian descent and/or had strong Muslim connections, so I was told by a whole variety of different people (Tanzanian, Indian, Swiss, Canadian, etc.).

The first Chinese medical practice was opened in the period of the "take-off", and Chinese practitioners have ever since been in competition with biomedical doctors not only because they provide private health care but because they sell biomedical drugs. The sensitive issue of practising medicine in the private sector, in the case of the Chinese medical doctors, has been exacerbated by the competitive prices and the observed effectiveness of Chinese drugs, which in some Tanzanian health professionals' viewpoint were in the main Chinese manufactured Western biomedical drugs. Since these Chinese biomedical drugs are produced in the People's Republic of China, they are significantly less expensive than those manufactured in the Americas, Europe, and Africa. However, for selling Western pharmaceuticals, one needs to obtain licenses that can only be obtained if one has a certificate of having undergone medical training in Tanzania, or an equivalent (no Chinese or Western medical training of whatever prestigious institution and level is considered equivalent). Western medical pharmacists and doctors, and Tanzanian intellectuals to whom I spoke about this issue, were under the impression that Chinese medical doctors were successful in particular because they unlawfully sold Western drugs.

Chinese medical practitioners, secondly, have stirred up Tanzanian health care professionals because their practice impinges on the sensitive issue of 'traditional medicine': biomedical doctors, whether of German, English, Indian or Tanzanian descent, have always treated indigenous medicines with reserve (Langwick 2006). They are sometimes prepared to accept that some indigenous plants may have pharmaceutically active substances with an identifiable chemical structure. Thus, indigenous knowledge is stripped of its 'superstitious' elements and reduced to pharmaceutical efficacy, and, with the exception of some anthropologists, the odd psychiatrist, and some NGO-activists, lip service may be paid to indigenous medical knowledge without, however, according it much relevance.

The biomedical profession has encouraged traditional midwives and healers to organise themselves into associations (Last & Chavunduka 1986). In this way they can be governed more easily through institutions of a modern nation-state while being granted at most para-medical status. In both cases, biomedical hegemony is not called into question. On the contrary, biomedical influence expands as substances of herbal remedies are turned into biomedical drugs, and midwives and healers into medical para-professionals. The history of traditional medical associations in Tanzania, which is yet to be written, involves interesting initiatives, strong personalities, rivalry and discord, but Chinese medical practitioners who are competitors over a clientele that seeks 'traditional' medical treatment, are not part of it. Hence, they are doubly suspect to the health professionals in Tanzania, as their private practice stirs up sensitive areas of health policy over private care and also traditional medicine. They rival the biomedical and do not fit into the traditional medical organizations.

The Drugs on Display in Chinese Medical Clinics

In March 2001, Chinese practitioners who were concerned about the future of their commerce, complained that without a previous personal warning, some of their formula drugs had been confiscated by Tanzanian officials, to be examined and repackaged in Dar es Salaam. The problem was that the labels were written in Chinese. However, patients tended to consider the packages with illegible Chinese characters more exotic and powerful than if labelled in Swahili. Like other businessmen, Chinese practitioners emphasized that the packaging really matters: one shipment brought a formula medicine in one form, the next one in another, with the result that clients refused to buy the medicine in the new packaging. Every merchant knows that the appearance of the packaging plays a role, its colour, size, the material of which it is made, its form and shape, and also the pictures and script on the package. During my fieldwork, which consisted of eight about one-month long visits between 2001 and 2006, Chinese doctors (ca. twenty in Kenya, and about the same number in Tanzania, and five on Zanzibar) were therefore wary about letting me record the drugs they used.

Nevertheless, two doctors in Nairobi, one in Mombasa, one in Stonetown on Unguja, one in Chake Chake on Pemba and one in Dar es Salaam allowed me to record all the drugs that were exhibited for sale on their shelves, often in the waiting room. One doctor in Dar es Salaam allowed me to assist on a daily basis his consultations during a period of three weeks (December 2002), one doctor in Mombasa permitted me to do the same during a fortnight (December 2005), as did two doctors on Zanzibar during periods of ten days each (December 2003, July 2004). They allowed me to tape record the consultation, if the patient agreed, to take notes of the consultation and copy, word for word by hand, their case records which were always written in Chinese. Furthermore, Tanzanian young men in Tanga who sold the drugs of a doctor located in Dodoma let me photocopy the list of the more than a hundred drugs they had on sale in a community centre, each presented on a piece of paper that contained a brief description in Swahili (January 2003). In some clinics, the drugs in the show cabinets numbered less than forty, and the doctor in charge had drugs in stock in other cabinets all over his clinic which he used but did not exhibit. In many other practices, however, the drugs on the shelves were fairly representative of the entire stock of different kinds of drugs used in medical practice. One doctor allowed me to record by hand in my notebook all the drugs he had on display (but he did not allow me to take any leaflets nor make photocopies). It took me seven days of copying the information given on the packages of in total about seventy-five formula drugs (April 2003). This doctor also had over two hundred deep-frozen powdered drugs on display, many of which by that time were out of stock, but one year later he had found means of renewing the most important ones. He then let me photocopy the list of those.

No attempt is made here to list all the drugs I recorded in his practice. Suffice it to say that only a few of the drugs recorded were Western medical ones, about five. He stocked vitamin C, Viagra, and two different kinds of two antibiotics, but with this enumeration the list of Western medical drugs he stocked was pretty much exhausted. I never saw him dispense a Chinese-manufactured Western medical drug as the sole item. He advertised himself as providing Chinese 'herbal' medicine and his clientele was largely from the middle to upper middle classes. He mostly used 'Chinese medical drugs' and 'Chinese formula drugs' (discussed below).

Another doctor in a better-off district of Dar es Salaam also allowed me to record all the medicines she had on display. She also had about a hundred different kinds of medicines on the shelves. The Chinese medical ones were displayed in their original packaging, while the Western medical ones were in glass bottles without a label. She had about eighteen such glass bottles, and explained that she preferred me not to record what she stored in them. Comparatively, she had more Western medical drugs in reserve than her colleague mentioned above, but still, they were few compared to the number of different kinds of Chinese formula drugs on display (December 2003).

Another practitioner whose practice was in a popular neighbourhood of Nairobi also allowed me to copy and even photograph her stock. She displayed a greater percentage of Western medical drugs than the two above-mentioned doctors. In this doctor's practice, almost all the drugs were offered in local white plastic bottles, with simple typescript labels, giving the name, condition for which the drug was indicated, dosage, and expiry date. She had repackaged the medicines, as she explained, because it would enable her to sell medicines in smaller amounts, which were affordable to her clientele (April 2003). The appearance of the Chinese formula drugs she sold was thus very similar to the ones available elsewhere at bus stations and markets (e.g. Van der Geest 1991).

The medicines were stored on the shelves according to the categorization of this Chinese doctor in the following order: medicines for treating diabetes, for enhancing [male] *yang* potency, asthma, stomach ulcers, obesity, skin problems, rheumatism, cough, women's problems, tooth ache, athlete's foot, liver inflammations, heart problems, colds, high blood pressure, epilepsy, malaria, 'supplementing medicines' (*buyao*), such as ginseng, immune-system boosters for treating HIV/AIDS, drugs for urinary tract infections, and anti-inflammatory drugs. Several medicines were Chinese formula drugs, others were Western medicines. Some were Western alternative medicines, such as a bottle of evening primrose and a cream of Aloe Vera.

Furthermore, this doctor sold vitamin C, aspirin, no-flu, ceez cold, various anti-malarials, herbal soaps, Viagra and venegra (sildenafil citrate, which also treats erectile dysfunction). The evening primrose, ceez cold and venegra she sold on behalf of an 'Indian woman', she explained, who worked at a herbal health care centre nearby. From studying the photos that she allowed me to take, one can guess that she displayed about a hundred different medicines. I did not record them all. Of the thirty-three medicines I recorded, she commented on about half that they were Western. This is a very high percentage of Western medical drugs in a Chinese medical practice. It is the only practice of the around forty practices that I visited in Kenya and Tanzania that had as many Western medical drugs on display. This practitioner was also the only doctor I visited who sold drugs in local plastic bottles, and she was among the few who catered to a low-income clientele. She was the youngest of several university-trained Traditional Chinese Medical (TCM) doctors. She appeared, within limits, to do her low-income community a valuable service in primary care, but her practice is not representative of Chinese medical clinics in East Africa.

Having said this, the range of medicines on display gives no reliable indication of the quantity of medicines actually sold. In some Chinese medical clinics more than 50% of over the counter purchases were strictly speaking of a biomedical drug substance, Artemisinin (Hsu 2002), which is a very effective anti-malarial (e.g. Hien & White 1993). The Chinese brands of this purified substance available in Tanzania and Kenya were Cotexin, Artesunate, Artemether, and possibly also Artecom, which contains Dihydro-artemisinin in combination with Piperaquine and Trimethoprim. Between 2001–2004, a course of treatment was sold for about 4,500 TS and 500 KS in Tanzania and Kenya respectively. Indian pharmacists sold some Belgian and French brands, in the summer of 2002 for about 6,500 TS. A Tanzanian brand started to be used on Zanzibar, so-called Malather, sold for about 3,500 TS in the summer of 2003, and Thaitanzunate, a brand of Artesunate that was produced from plant materials grown on plantations near Arusha, became available in the summer of 2004 at about the same price. These drugs contained the purified anti-malarial compound Artemisinin that is extracted from the plant Artemisia annua L. (*qinghao*).

Strictly speaking, drugs containing Artemisinin and its derivatives are biomedical drugs. However, Chinese scientists had 'discovered' the anti-malarial efficacy of a Chinese medical drug *qinghao* in the early seventies (Hsu 2006), from which they isolated, purified, tested and prepared Artemisinin for the market between the late seventies and mid-eighties (interview with Prof. Tu Youyou in Beijing, September 2005). Chinese doctors therefore claimed this drug was a Chinese one and, playing the ethnic card, aired their anguish over being prohibited from selling an intrinsically Chinese product while Indian pharmacists were allowed to do so. The simple reason was that Indian pharmacists had Western medical training and a license. But a Traditional Chinese Medicine practitioner who has received higher education as a regular university student would have attended in the 1980s about 1,948 hours of Traditional Chinese Medicine classes and 835 hours Western medicine classes, apart from general education, during four years of classroom training (the fifth being spent in practical training at various clinics, Hsu 1999:157). Chinese medical practitioners hence can claim to have sufficient knowledge to dispense Artemisinin. They furthermore complained that the regulations of the Tanzanian authorities were arbitrary, as they put chloroquine into a class of anti-malarials that could be sold over the counter but not Artemisinin-based drugs and other anti-malarials, like Fansidar.

Finally, neither the display on a shelf nor over the counter transactions alone can give a conclusive answer on the medical practice Chinese practitioners engage in. A detailed analysis of the case material I recorded could throw light on the degree to which Western drugs and purified chemical substances are actually utilized, but would an anthropologist want to undertake such a study, considering the complexities involved and the outright suspicion and hostility among biomedical professionals in the Ministry of Health? At this stage, it is possible to say that very occasionally a Western medical drug was prescribed together with Chinese medications. More frequently, Chinese formula drugs contained purified chemical substances (see below).

Evidently, the accusation that Chinese medical doctors primarily engage in selling Western medical drugs is not justified and in some cases, as in the case of Artemisinin, there is reason for contesting existing regulations. The Western medical polemic against Chinese medical practitioners selling Western medical drugs clearly takes place in a field within which the Western medical profession strives to maintain hegemony. On the other hand, Chinese medical doctors do little to inform their clients over possible misunderstandings. Interviews with patients showed that they buy *dawa ya Kichina* either because they do not make the distinction between Western and Chinese medical rationale or because they believe they are buying exotic Chinese natural herbs (fieldwork in Dar, January and July 2003). From the few cases studied, it seems that the wealthier the clientele, the richer a practitioner's Chinese medical arsenal.

Zhongyao versus Zhongchengyao
– 'Chinese Medical Drugs' versus 'Chinese Formula Drugs'

As already noted above, Chinese medical doctors make ample use of Chinese formula medicines, and these can contain purified chemical substances. Furthermore, they do, very occasionally, prescribe one of the few Western medical drugs they have on display together with a Chinese medication. This is because the rationale of their medicine relies on so-called 'integrated Chinese and Western medicine' (*zhongxiyi jiehe*). This rationale not only provides the conceptual framework for the developing of 'Chinese formula drugs' (*zhongchengyao*), but also recommends the combination of Western and Chinese medical practice, even if 'Chinese medical drugs' (*zhongyao*) and Chinese medical 'formulae' (*fangji*), rather than formula drugs, are used in medical practice.

In this context, it is necessary to elucidate in an excursus the difference between 'Chinese medical drugs', *zhongyao*, and 'Chinese formula drugs', *zhongchengyao*. If a patient is treated with 'Chinese medical drugs', *zhongyao*, he or she is never prescribed one single Chinese medical drug alone but always a variety of drugs in a formula, *fangji*, that takes account of his or her particular constitution. *Zhongyao* treats persons and not diseases. Representatives of health policies insist one should speak of 'natural herbs' and not of 'drugs' since *zhongyao* do not contain purified chemical substances with structures that have been identified, as do Western medical drugs. However, the term 'herbs' is misleading for at least two reasons. First, it suggests that Chinese medical drugs are parts of herbs or trees, whereas they can also be made of minerals or animal parts. Moreover, Chinese medical drugs are not raw materials, although they may appear so to a Western-trained doctor.

'Chinese medical drugs' (*zhongyao*) need to be seen as an aspect of Chinese material culture, i.e. as highly culture-specific objects that have been subject to sophisticated procedures of production. Often they are harvested in a particular season, sometimes at a particular time of the day, some are consumed fresh but most are dried, in the shade, the sun, over the fire, and in other ways. Some are additionally treated, for example, roasted or fried, and some are treated further such as being ground into powder or simmered into a paste and made into pellets. Needless to say the quality of these drugs varies, depending not only on the geographical region they come from, the soil in which they were grown (people always consider the wild plants and animals more potent than the cultivated ones) but also on the mode of preparation. Finally, just as there are different brands of biomedical drugs, so are there of Chinese medical drug companies, and the quality of the Chinese medical drug is known to vary accordingly.

Most people in East Africa do not know what 'Chinese medical drugs' look like and how they used to be (and in some places still are) dispensed in China. There were two clinics in Kenya, which had imported Chinese medical drugs in deep-frozen and powdered form. Both clinics kept these powdered Chinese medical drugs in plastic containers, both stocked over two hundred different kinds of them. This made it possible for these two doctors to write prescriptions (*fangji*) of powdered Chinese medical drugs (*zhongyao*) for their patients as one does in the much valued, 'precious' (*zhengui*) way of Chinese medicine. The powder was wrapped in paper in small portions that could easily be dissolved in water. Doctors usually prescribed one to three portions a day, for treatment cycles of three to seven days. Some other doctors in Nairobi also had a small stock of such powdered drugs. Other practitioners said that deep-freezing and powdering affected their potency; for this reason, they said, they preferred formula drugs. However, it was certainly not the only reason.

'Chinese formula drugs', *zhongchengyao*, consist of powdered, but generally not deep-frozen, *zhongyao*, usually a mixture of several different kinds; some come as tablets, some as capsules, some as tiny seeds, some as pellets. While a patient who takes *zhongyao* needs to simmer them over a small fire, for about twenty minutes twice a day, formula drugs (*zhongchengyao*) are easy to consume. Some are swallowed in seconds like Western medical drugs, others are dissolved in water and drunk. Formula drugs are designed to treat 'complaints' – pain in the joints, irregular menses – not distinguishing patterns particular to a person. In general, the dispensing of 'Chinese formula drugs', *zhongchengyao*, requires significantly less sophistication than the prescription of 'Chinese medical drugs', *zhongyao*, and 'formulae', *fangji*. This may be an important reason why Chinese medical practitioners in East Africa make use of them, although no one was explicit about it.

'Chinese formula medicines/drugs' (*zhongchengyao*) are of concern to Western medical professionals because they sometimes contain stimulants, vitamins, or aspirin that have been added to their main ingredients, namely powdered herbal, animal or mineral Chinese *materia medica*. In particular, they can contain purified substances obtained through Western scientific procedures that usually are not available over the counter. Indeed, Chinese formula drugs do sometimes contain such purified substances but by no means all. Again, a careful analysis is warranted and still in progress.

To give an example, one clinic displayed slimming capsules which contained lactoalbumine, one or two skin creams that contained steroids, a Chinese formula drug for treating stomach ulcers that contained bismuth potassium citrate, another one against high blood pressure that contained dihydralazine sulphate and hydrochlorothiazine, and others of the same kind, constituting no more than merely a very small percentage of all the drugs that were on display. In this clinic, one 'Chinese formula drug', namely the slimming tea that contained the purified substance lactoalbumin, rather than the 'purely herbal' *zhongyao* slimming tea, was the most popular medicine sold over the counter.

'Guo's slimming capsules' (*Guoshi jianfei jiaonang*) contained according to the packaging: 1. '*linzhi* seed substance', which is a Western medical description for the Chinese medical drug *linzhi cao* (Ganoderma Sinense or Ganoderma lucidum), as known from the famous *materia medica* from Yunnan (*Diannan bencao*) but not recorded as such in the textbooks on *TCM formulae* (*Fangjixue* 1985) and *TCM drugs* (*Zhongyaoxue* 1984), 2. lactoalbumin, 3. oligosaccharides, 4. the Chinese medical drug *danshen* (Salvia miltiorrhiza) and 5. the leaves of Gingko biloba, *yinxingye*, rather than its fruits (the leaf extracts are a modern German phytotherapeutic item, the fruits a Chinese medical drug). It is unlikely that the leaflet listed all the ingredients, as formula medicines are primarily mercantile goods, and rather than efficacy and safety, market rules apply to them, such as protecting the 'secrets of one's commerce' (*shangye mimi*).

With the information at hand it is obvious that the above formula drug consisted of a mixture of different components: local Chinese medical ones (1.), scholarly Chinese medical ones (4.), German phytotherapeutic ones

(5.), nutritive additives (3.), and a purified substance (2.). Clearly, this is not a Western medical drug, and but an item of Chinese material culture developed in an era of globalization that deserves to be studied and understood in more detail. It is presumably best framed as an object of an 'alternative modernity' (Hsu in press). In this context, we are reminded that another slimming tea was on offer, 'Pellets for moistening the bowels' (*Runchangwan*), which consisted according to the accompanying leaflet only of Chinese medical herbs.

Potancy-Enchancing Drugs

Among the most attractive Chinese formula drugs belong male potency-enhancing drugs. This was the view of all clienteles in Dar es Salaam, Mombasa, and rural Pemba (I interviewed thirty patients in each place between 2002–2004). Often, the male Chinese doctors who dispensed these drugs would explain to me, the female anthropologist, that a patient was suffering from asthma or stomach problems – so-called *gesi* (gas) was a frequent complaint – but when I saw them pack the medicines, more often than not, a package of potency-enhancing drugs was included. Many patients were found to have high blood pressure and accordingly, were prescribed antihypertensives, when they had hoped to get a potency-enhancing drug. Memorable is the over seventy year old *mzee*, who I visited for an interview in his modest dwelling on the other side of Pemba island, surrounded by two wives and many children and the children's children. He had managed to assemble the 7,000 TS that two capsules of such a drug cost, but then spent all that money on getting an expensive version of a Chinese-produced Western medical drug against hypertension, when he could have obtained an equivalent for free from the nearby dispensary. Other patients who also had suffered from high blood pressure recounted that the Chinese doctor had treated their 'pressure' in consecutive sessions often over several weeks, and only after it had been brought under control would the doctor allow them to buy the potency-enhancing drug, which then apparently 'worked'. This shows that Chinese doctors were not merely pharmacists who sold potency-enhancing drugs but diagnosed the patient's condition and treated it before selling the sought after drugs, thereby enhancing these drugs' potency.

As already said, some Chinese doctors sold Viagra, one also sold the Indian brand venegra, which looked much the same - a blue tablet, in rhomboid form - and some sold Chinese patent drugs with that appearance, as for instance *weigewang* (power-elder brother-king), but these were not the most popular potency-enhancing drugs. Many patients remembered the red-capsule formula drug best, some showed me the bright red carton package with golden script across it. The drug in question was called *Nanbao*, which means the 'treasure of men/manlihood'. Since none of the patients had been told the meaning of its name, the 'meaning response' that enhances a drug's efficacy (Moerman 2002) was on the East African coast reduced to primarily its appearance in colour and capsule form. In one of the most successful clinics I visited, many men upon entering it would not bother to have a consultation with the doctor but steered directly towards the counter and purchased *Nanbao*. Probably, they had had experience with it previously or been told by someone else of its potency.

The potency-enhancing *Nanbao* was one of the many formula drugs that according to educated Chinese medical doctors was based on a 'folk recipe' (*minjian fang*), and not on the scholarly medical rationale of 'Chinese medicine' (*zhongyi*). Its ingredients were generally not indicated on its packaging but I came across one package that named thirty-one ingredients and a more recent one with five of these thirty-one. The five ingredients were 'donkey's penis' (*lüshen*), 'dog's penis' (*goushen*) 'sea-horse' (*haima*), 'donkey hide' (*ejiao*), and 'ginseng' (*renshen*). There were also other formula drugs that built on the sympathetic principle of using a donkey's and dog's penis for strengthening a man's penis, one of them was called *huarong weixiong* (label given in *pinyin* only, not in Chinese characters). Furthermore, the penis of the water buffalo, the goat, the horse, deer, and of two different kinds of dogs (the *haigou* and the *guanggou*) were used in another formula drug (namely, *weigewang*).

Another animal associated with male potency was the wolf. A brand produced in the Autonomous Region of Tibet depicted several howling wolves on packaging that was extravagant as it consisted of a metal box that contained on a deep red satin base one tablet only. The packaging showed Tibetan and Chinese script, and its wording in Chinese played on the homophony of *xing* 性 meaning 'sex' and *xing* 興 meaning 'joy'. In this particular case, Tibet was probably exploited as a topos for Chinese clientele, Tibet being associated with the wild and in this case, evidently, the virile.

The USA is another place that Chinese tend to associate with the powerful, and one of the formula drugs on sale, called 'Kiss me', which came in tablets with a light blue colour in rhomboid form that connoted the efficacy of the American Viagra, had been "studied and supervised" by the "Wisdom Development Co. Ltd." in the USA and was "produced" by the

Pharon Group Co. Ltd. in Hong Kong, Shenyang Pharmaceutical Co. The Chinese doctor who had it on display commented that it worked too slowly, in contrast to *Nanbao* and others that apparently were effective if taken one to two hours before a sexual encounter. In general, however, when Chinese doctors prescribed potency-enhancing medicines, like *Nanbao*, they advised their clients not to have intercourse before finishing the prescribed treatment course of often several days of medication, which would suggest that the Chinese formula medicines were not expected to be effective in the same way as Viagra.

Their ingredients need not exclusively be based on animal substances, as in the case of the Heroic Wind capsules from the place called Qingyang in Henan province (*Xiongfeng Qingyang jiaonang*), which contained according to the accompanying leaflet as their four main ingredients: the herbs Epimedium grandiflorum (*yinyanghuo*) and Astragalus complanatus (*shayuanzi*), the velvet on the antlers of the deer Cervus Nippon or Cervus elaphus (*lujiaoshuang*), and moth droppings (*xiongcan'e*). Their efficacy was probably enhanced by the meaning response to their appearance: red capsules similar to those of *Nanbao*.

A Chinese medical doctor explained that there were several kinds of male dysfunction, as for instance, premature ejaculation, insufficient erection, and the inability to have an erection. In terms of Chinese medicine, the patient could suffer from kidney *yang* depletion or kidney *yin* depletion or a lack of kidney *qi* (fieldwork in Zanzibar, July 2004). His explanations consisted of a simplified rendering of Traditional Chinese Medicine teachings, which emphasized dysfunctions between the liver, kidney and *yang* brightness, whereby *yang* brightness generally refers to the stomach, and sometimes also the heart (*Zhongyi neikexue* 1985). Moreover, as already said, patients often presented with other symptoms, such as high blood pressure, asthma, stomach problems, back pain, and those had to be treated first. Furthermore, some Chinese doctors commented that their African clients had performance expectations of frequency and duration of intercourse that in their opinion were 'exaggerated' (*guodu*). They explained that according to Chinese medical theory, frequency of intercourse was age-related. Above forty years of age a man should not make love more than once week. One Chinese doctor was very explicit on this: "Africans have sex every day but it is actually bad for their health." When I asked this doctor whether he told his clients that they should not have sex too often, he said, only when he prescribed medication, otherwise not. "That is their life style and custom. I do not interfere with that. As I told you previously, this is what I call the 'soft touch'. The whites always interfere with what Africans are used to doing" (diary, 15.4.03).

In addition to tablets and capsules, there were sprays. The ones I encountered came in a lipstick-like packaging, a gold tube with a red top for women and a blue top one for men. They were called 'Royal oil for women' (*nüwangyou*) and 'Royal oil for men' (*nanwangyou*). All potency-enhancing drugs, regardless of colours, shapes and packaging, were exceedingly expensive, one single pill could cost 3,500 to 10,000 TS (approx.1.214 TS to 1 US Dollar), and it happened more than once that clients would purchase potency-enhancing medicines that amounted to several 10,000 TS. In interviews with patients, my local male translator and I were once asked completely out of context whether we knew how these medicines worked (fieldwork on Pemba, January 2004). Did they cause virility instantly, and if they did so, was it that once one had taken them, one was hooked forever and dependent on taking them thereafter every time one wanted to make love.

In general, however, people were not forthcoming on this issue. As one would expect, anything to do with sexuality was very much a private matter, and a visit to the Chinese clinic was, unlike one to government clinics, valued for the privacy it ensured.[1] It was unlikely that one was going to bump into one's neighbour or relative there. Moreover, Chinese people were known to keep to themselves, some Tanzanians considered them even secretive, others were uncertain as to whether they had magic powers. The Chinese medical doctors who were among the most successful had their consultations with their patients in separate parts of the practice, behind closed doors, often in cosy and very small spaces, reminiscent of those of diviners on the East African coast (see Whyte 1997 and also Hsu 2005).

Outlook

If one applies Susan Whyte's insights on the power of medicines in East Africa to the new phenomenon of *dawa ya Kichina* on the East African coast, one would expect that regardless of whether they are Western drugs or Chinese medical prescriptions, all are indiscriminately considered exotic, and therefore potent and effective, because they come from far away China. Among the medications dispensed, it would appear, however, that the Chinese formula medicines are those, which most ostensibly fall into the category of being popular, primarily, because of the wonders ascribed

---

1   Not surprisingly, my presence as a female anthropologist was several times met with discomfort and I had to leave the consultation room.

to the exotic. They are packaged like modern Western scientific drugs, but have the looks of the exotic. They are easy to prescribe and easy to consume. Provided in the privacy of a consultation, the exotic male potency-enhancing drugs and formula drugs are considered particularly powerful.

Sexual practice, as are food ways, is a well-known marker of cultural difference. It is important not to draw caricatures. The above has shown how cultural distance and personal proximity, perceived exoticism and assured secrecy play together. It highlights how important the notion of the 'other' is for enhancing the potency of the self. One wonders who can extract capital and of what kind from this cultural encounter on the East African coast. Certainly, the issue cannot be reduced merely to economies of commerce, nor exclusively to those of manhood and reproduction.

References

Hien, T. T. and N. White, 1993, "Qinghaosu", *Lancet* 341: 603–608.

Hobsbawm, Eric, 1983, "Introduction: Inventing Traditions", in E. Hobsbawm and T. Ranger (eds), *The Invention of Tradition*. Cambridge: Cambridge University Press, pp. 1–14.

Hsu, Elisabeth, 1999, *The Transmission of Chinese Medicine*. Cambridge: Cambridge University Press.

Hsu, Elisabeth, 2002, "The medicine from China has rapid effects: Patients of Traditional Chinese Medicine in Tanzania", in E. Hsu and E. Høg (eds), *Anthropology and Medicine,* Special Issue: Countervailing Creativity: Patient Agency in the Globalisation of Asian Medicines, 9 (3), pp. 291–314.

Hsu, Elisabeth, 2005, "Time Inscribed in Space, and the Process of Diagnosis in African and Chinese Medical Practices", in W. James & D. Mills (eds), *The Qualities of Time: Anthropological Approaches*. Oxford: Berg, 155–170.

Hsu, Elisabeth, 2006, "Reflections on the 'Discovery' of the Anti-Malarial Qinghao". *British Journal of Clinical Pharmacology,* Special Issue on Future Developments in Clinical Pharmacology 61 (6): 666–70.

Hsu, Elisabeth, 2007, "La Médecine Chinoise Traditionnelle en République populaire de Chine: d'une 'tradition inventée' à une 'modernité alternative'", in A. Cheng (ed.), *La pensée en Chine aujourd'hui*. Paris: Gallimard, 214–238.

Hsu, Elisabeth, (in press)"Chinese formula drugs (zhongchengyao) – an alternative modernity? The case of the anti-malarial substance Artemisinin (qinghaosu) in East Africa", in E. Hsu & G Stollberg (eds), *Medical Anthropology,* Special Issue, Globalising Chinese medicine.

Iliffe, John, 1998, *East African Doctors*. Cambridge: Cambridge University Press.

Langwick, Stacy, 2006, "Geographies of Medicine: Interrogating the Boundary between "Traditional" and "Modern" Medicine in Colonial Tanganyika", in T.J. Luedke and H.G. West (eds), *Borders and Healers: Brokering Therapeutic Resources in Southeast Africa*. Bloomington: Indiana University Press, 143–165.

Last, Murray and G.L. Chavunduka (eds), 1986, *The Professionalisation of African Medicine*. Manchester: Manchester University Press.

Moerman, Daniel, 2002, *Meaning, Medicine and the 'Placebo Effect'*. Cambridge: Cambridge University Press.

Monson, Jamie, 2008, "Liberating Labor? Constructing Anti-Hegemony on the TAZARA Railway in Tanzania, 1965–76", in D. Large et al. (eds) *China returns to Africa: A Superpower and a Continent Embrace*. London: Hurst.

Parkin, David. J., 1968, "Medicines and Men of Influence", *Man* 3 : 424–39.

Rekdal, Ole Bjørn, 1999, "Cross-Cultural Healing in East African Ethnography" *Medical Anthropology Quarterly* 13 (4):458–82.

Van der Geest, S., 1991, "Marketplace Conversations in Cameroon: How and Why Popular Medical Knowledge Comes into Being", *Culture, Medicine and Psychiatry* 15 (1):69–90.

West, Harry, G., and Tracy J. Luedke, 2006, "Introduction: Healing Divides: Therapeutic Borderwork in Southeast Africa", in T.J. Luedke and H.G. West (eds), *Borders and Healers: Brokering Therapeutic Resources in Southeast Africa*. Bloomington: Indiania University Press, 1–20.

Whyte, Susan Reynolds, 1988, "The Power of Medicines in East Africa", in S. van der Geest and S.R. Whyte (eds), *The Context of Medicines in Developing Countries*. Dordrecht: Kluwer Academic Publishers, 217–233.

Whyte, Susan Reynolds, 1997, *Questioning Misfortune: The Pragmatics of Uncertainty in Eastern Uganda*. Cambridge: Cambridge University Press.

TCM textbooks

Fangjixue (*The Study of Formulae*), 1985, Xu Jiqun (ed.). Shanghai: Shanghai kexue jishu chubanshe.

Zhongyaoxue (*The Study of TCM Drugs*), 1984, Ling Yigui (ed.). Shanghai: Shanghai kexue jishu chubanshe.

Zhongyi neikexue (*The Study of TCM Inner Medicine*), 1985, Zhang Boyu (ed.). Shanghai Shanghai kexue jishu chubanshe.

Authors

Assibi A. Amidu taught Swahili language, literature and culture at the University of Ghana before becoming Associate Professor in Swahili at the Department of Language and Communication Studies, formerly Linguistics Department, of the Norwegian University of Science and Technology. He has published widely on Lamu and on the Swahili language.

Marie Pierre Ballarin is an historian and an anthropologist working at IRD (Research Institute for Development, Paris, France). She has conducted field work on the west coast of Madagascar and on the East African coast. Ballarin focuses her research on the relationship between religion and power in the ancient kingdoms of this area from the nineteenth century until today. Currently she explores the social and political implications of traditional cults on people's lives today.

Gerard C. van de Bruinhorst gained a PhD in social anthropology from Utrecht University. The subject of his thesis was the interface between (authoritative) texts and ritual practice as seen in Islamic sacrificial rituals in Tanga, Tanzania. He is currently working as a librarian at the African Studies Centre in Leiden.

Greg Cameron lived, worked and researched on Zanzibar for the best part of a decade from 1988 to 1998, first as a trainer and organizer with the Tanzanian co-operative movement and later as a researcher. His doctoral thesis from SOAS, University of London, examines Zanzibar's Co-operative Movement. Cameron has been Assistant Professor of Political Science at the University of Asmara in Eritrea, and is at present Assistant Professor of Political Science and Rural Studies at Nova Scotia Agricultural College, Canada.

Pat Caplan is Emeritus Professor of Anthropology at Goldsmiths College, University of London. She has carried out fieldwork in Tanzania, Nepal, Madras India, and West Wales UK, and has published a number of monographs on her Tanzanian and Indian research and edited collections on sexuality, Swahili culture, dispute settlement, food, risk, ethics and Swahili identity. She also served as Chair of the Association of Social Anthropologists from 1997–2001. She is currently working on local understandings of modernity on Mafia Island, Tanzania.

Felix A. Chami is an archaeologist from University of Dar es Salaam and Uppala. Since 1968 he has been employed by the University of Dar-es-Salaam since 1986 with promotions ranging from Tutorial Assistant to Full Professor in 2003. Between 1994 and 1997, he was Head of Department of Archaeology. Since 2001 Chami is General Coordinator for the Society of African Archaeology Network. His research focuses on the Swahili Coast and on the Lake Victoria Region. His writing includes a wide range of publications and he is also the Chief Editor of the book series entitled *Studies in the African Past*.

Francesca Declich is a social anthropologist and received her PhD at the Istituto Universitario Orientale di Napoli and at the University of London. She is currently a researcher and teaches at the University of Urbino in Italy. Her major fieldworks have been carried out in southern Somalia and Tanzania, and her research focuses on ritual, sufism and gender as well as conflict and forced migration.

Linda L. Giles is an independent scholar with a PhD in Socio-Cultural Anthropology from the University of Texas, Austin. Her main area of research has been spirit possession on the Swahili coast. Recently she has also been involved in an ongoing joint research project on the illicit trade in *Mijikenda* ancestor statues.

Elisabeth Hsu is a lecturer at the Institute of Social and Cultural Anthropology, University of Oxford. She has published widely on the anthropology and history of Chinese medicine. She has conducted ethnographic fieldwork on Chinese medicine in East Africa since 2001.

Kjersti Larsen holds a PhD in Social Anthropology from the University of Oslo, Norway. She is Associate Professor at the Department of Ethnography at the Museum of Cultural History, University of Oslo where she was Head of Department in 2003–06. Larsen has also been Adjunct Professor at the Department of Development Studies, University of Life Science, Norway in 2001–2008. She has conducted field work in Zanzibar and northern Sudan, and explored issues related to modernity, ritual and gender, identity and mobility as well as migration.

Roman Loimeier has been a research fellow at the University of Bayreuth and at the Centre for Modern Oriental Studies, Berlin. Currently, Loimeier holds a position as assistant professor at the Department of Religion and Centre for African Studies, University of Florida, and from 2009 he will be at Zentrum Moderner Orient, Berlin. He has conducted research in Senegal, Northern Nigeria and Tanzania which has resulted in extensive publication on Muslim societies in Sub-Saharan Africa.

Mohamed Ahmed Saleh, is a doctoral candidate in social anthropology working on "The Zanzibari Diaspora: Identity and Nationalism". He conducts fieldwork in fishing communities in Zanzibar and in Swahili Communities in East Africa, the Comoros and Europe and focuses on identity, marriage, and community development. Saleh has worked for France 3 Television, in the conception and production of a documentary film on Zanzibar (*Escale à Zanzibar*).

Farouk Topan is a senior lecturer at the School of Oriental & African Studies (SOAS), University of London. He has taught at universities in East Africa where he introduced the study of Swahili literature in Dar es Salaam and Nairobi. He was a founding member of the Department of Kiswahili at the University of Dar es Salaam in 1970. Apart from his academic publishing, he has also published three plays in Swahili.

Ulla Vuorela has a PhD from Helsinki University. She is professor of social anthropology at the University of Tampere with a special interest in transnational anthropology. Her research interests focus on gender, development, postcolonial feminism and Muslim societies as well as on marginalisation and ethnic relations in Finland. Vuroula is currently directing projects on multisited lives in transnational Russia and Eastern Europe with particular focus on intergenerational relations of care and issues of identity.

Index

ompliance